May all your travels be wonderful!
Barb Whitaker and Ginger

Have Dog Will Travel
Northwest Edition

Oregon—Washington—Idaho

Hassle-Free Guide to
Traveling With Your Dog

Barbara Whitaker

Ginger & Spike

Printed in the United States of America.

Fourth printing

Publisher's Cataloging-in-Publication
(Provided by Quality Books, Inc.)

Whitaker, Barbara.
    Have dog will travel : Oregon, Washington, Idaho :
hassle-free guide to traveling with your dog / Barbara
Whitaker. – Northwest ed.
    p. cm.
    Includes index.
    ISBN 0-9660544-8-2

    1. Hotels–Pet accommodations–Northwest, Pacific–
Directories. 2. Dogs–Housing–Northwest, Pacific–
Directories. 3. Pets and travel–Northwest, Pacific.
I. Title.

TX907.3.N96W45 2002   647.94795'01
                  QBI02-200561

Cover and interior illustrations by Bob Sleeper

Ginger & Spike Publications
PO Box 937
Wilsonville, OR 97070-0937
Phone 503-625-3001, Fax 503-625-3076
Email barbw@havedogwilltravel.com

Acknowledgments

I want to thank all the wonderful people who helped to bring this fourth book in the *Have Dog Will Travel* series to completion.

Every creative work has an "angel" and for this book, that's my husband Linn. Many, many thanks for your ongoing encouragement and support.

Kudos to Randi Goodrich and Jacquie Jones for your incisive critiques of the content and layout, and for keeping me focused (and sane!) throughout the long research stage. Thanks also to Susan Foster and Carol Beck for your help during the research and verification stages.

And of course, I want to acknowledge my four-footed buddies Ginger and Spike, whose companionable presence, as I sat at my computer day after day, motivated me to finish this updated and expanded *Northwest Edition*.

I couldn't have done it without you—many thanks, one and all!

In loving memory of
Brujo, Jack, Kala, Jeremiah,
Kaka, Irish, and Almond—
faithful companions, all.

Table of Contents

4: The Well-Behaved Traveler On the Road

5: First Aid for Your Traveling Dog

6: Emergency Clinics

7: If Your Dog Gets Lost

8: Dog-Friendly Lodgings in Idaho—Oregon—Washington

A: Business Name Index

B: Topics Index

1: Touring With Your Well-behaved Traveler

So you plan to travel around the Pacific Northwest by car, and you want to take your dog along? Well, you're in good company—lots of dogs travel with their owners. Ginger, my German Shepherd/Norwegian Elkhound, certainly does. After all, she's part of the family, and a vacation just wouldn't be the same without her.

Traveling with a well-behaved dog can be great fun and a minimum of fuss. But it does involve some advance planning and effort on your part. It also requires extra consideration for your fellow travelers and for the friendly people who provide your accommodations.

Chapters 1–7 in this book are packed with common-sense information you can use to transform your dog into a well-behaved traveler—making your trips more fun for both of you. There's even a common-sense first aid guide, with a list of 24-hour emergency veterinary clinics in each state, for your pet's safety and your own peace of mind.

In Chapter 8 you'll find detailed listings for more than 2,100 hotels, motels, and bed & breakfast inns throughout Idaho, Oregon and Washington where you and your well-behaved dog are welcome guests.

At the back of the book you'll find two separate indexes:

🐾 A: Business Name Index—alphabetical list of all the business names, cross-referenced to their detailed listings in Chapter 8

🐾 B: Topics Index—alphabetical list of the pet travel topics that are discussed in Chapters 1 through 7

How to have fun and get invited back

The numbers of hotels, motels, and bed & breakfast inns that accept pets have dwindled in recent years, due largely to a few dog owners who allow their dogs to damage furnishings and landscaping, or behave aggressively toward other guests and their pets.

As responsible dog owners, we can all help to reverse this trend. Preparing in advance and taking appropriate equipment along not only ensures more enjoyable trips for ourselves and our dogs—it also provides positive examples of well-behaved traveling dogs, to help encourage more establishments to accept pets.

This book will help you prepare for a great trip with your dog, including the following important steps:

🐕 Attend obedience training classes with your dog *before* you travel. When you are both familiar with the basic commands for good behavior, you'll be ready when the unexpected happens. (And believe me, it *does* eventually happen!)

🐕 Prepare a canine first aid kit and learn (in advance) how to handle a medical emergency

🐕 Pack the appropriate pet travel supplies

🐕 Call ahead to reserve a dog-friendly room—be aware that most of the hotels, motels and bed-and-breakfast inns included in this book allow dogs in some, but not all, of their rooms

🐕 Always pay attention to your dog's impact on other guests and on the facilities, both indoor and outdoor, where you're staying—in short, be well-behaved travelers!

When to bring your dog—and when NOT to

Obviously you want your dog to travel with you, or you wouldn't be reading this book. But also ask yourself whether or not he *wants* to come along.

Your dog will probably enjoy the trip if:

🐾 You're traveling by car

🐾 Driving time will be fairly short, so he won't be in the car for hours

🐾 You've planned lots of activities that your dog can share, like hiking or walking on the beach

But consider traveling *without* your dog when:

🐾 Adverse weather conditions would make him miserably hot or cold

🐾 You're traveling by plane or train—these are more of an ordeal for your pet than a vacation

🐾 Most of your time will be spent in activities that your dog cannot share—after all, would *you* want to spend your entire vacation locked in an empty car or motel room?

And now, a word from Spike

The feline member of our family ("He Who Must Be Obeyed") wants to point out that he definitely prefers to stay home while Ginger goes traveling. Call him a homebody if you like, but Spike insists that most cats would much rather stay at home in their own familiar places. On Spike's advice, then, this book addresses the issues related to traveling with dogs, but not cats.

Obviously you'll be making arrangements for your cats to be properly cared for in your absence. So, you can rest assured that they will be just fine while you're gone. Though it may hurt to admit it, they probably won't even miss you.

As Spike puts it, "I'm staying here. And as long as I'm properly fed and admired, my servants *[that's us mere humans]* can go wherever they like!"

2: Puppy, Pack Your Bags

It has been said that every successful vacation begins with careful packing. This is just as true for your dog as for yourself—you need to bring along the proper supplies. Use the handy checklist on page 21 to be sure nothing important gets left behind.

Many of these supplies are as close as your local pet store. You can also check in dog magazines at your library or newsstand for the names of mail order pet supply houses and write or call for their catalogs. You'll be amazed at the variety of new gadgets available to make traveling with your pet easy and fun.

Collar and leash

Every dog should wear a sturdy leather or woven collar at all times, with the appropriate license, identification and rabies tags attached.

Don't use a choke collar as a permanent collar! Properly used, it can be helpful during training sessions, but if left on your dog all the time, the choke collar could snag on a low branch or other obstruction. Don't let your beloved pet become one of the many sad stories of dogs who choked to death when their owners were not there to rescue them.

If your dog is really hard to control, check with a reputable trainer about using a *prong collar* during your training sessions. This type of collar has blunt metal prongs that momentarily pinch the dog's neck when he pulls against the leash or when you administer a *correction*. Again, this is for use during training sessions only; don't leave it on your dog all the time!

You'll need a 1-ft to 6-ft long leash for walking with your dog close to your side. Woven nylon or leather works better than metal chain, which is noisy and harder to hold onto. Also check out the new retractable leashes that extend to 16 feet or more so your pet can investigate his surroundings without dragging you every which way, and retract fully for close walking.

🐕 Attending a basic obedience class with your dog is one of the very best ways to help him master the fine art of walking on leash.

All the proper ID tags

As important as your dog's license and ID tags are at home, they're even more vital when you travel. If you and your pet lose track of each other, those ID tags will enable his finders to contact you. In addition to the permanent ID tag with your home address and phone number, I also recommend that you add a travel tag to your dog's collar, showing how you can be reached *during* your trip if at all possible.

Dog license tag—Among the many other good reasons for licensing your dog, the license number and phone number of your county dog control department that appear on this tag represent another way to trace a lost dog's owner.

Permanent identification tag—This should list your name, home address and phone number, and perhaps your dog's name. (Ginger's tag even has her veterinarian's phone number.) Ideally, this information should be permanently engraved or stamped onto a metal tag. The rectangular style of tag that fastens flat to the collar will stay cleaner and doesn't add to the jingling of the other tags.

Any number of companies can create permanent ID tags for you. Veterinary offices often have ordering information from several of them. Dog magazines are full of ads for this service—check your library or newsstand. Some mail order catalogs also offer them.

Rabies tag—Provided by your veterinarian. This tag bears a serial number that can be traced back to the veterinarian and then to the dog's owner. There could be dire consequences if your dog were to get picked up as a stray and not have proof of current rabies vaccination.

Travel tag—Very important! This tag shows where you can be reached *during your vacation*. Check your pet store for a two-part tag consisting of a paper liner you can write on, that fits inside a clear plastic case. You can also get a barrel-type tag that unscrews to hold a rolled-up slip of paper—just be sure to tighten the two halves together *very securely* to keep them from accidentally separating.

Write or type the name, address, city and phone number where you're staying. If your trip includes several destinations, either list them all or prepare a separate tag for each destination. As an alternative, list the name and phone number of someone who can receive messages for you. Also write "Reward Offered" (no specific dollar amount) and "Please call collect" on the tag.

Microchip ID system

Microchipping is one of the newest and most promising ways to identify a lost pet. While tags or collars can fall off or be removed, a microchip stays with your pet forever. Each chip is programmed with a unique code that can be detected by a hand-held scanning device, similar to the ones used in retail stores.

Your veterinarian can implant the microchip, no bigger than a grain of rice, beneath your pet's skin in a safe, quick office procedure. Then all you have to do is register your pet's unique code and your contact information with the national database agency to receive coverage anywhere you travel in the USA.

Microchip scanners are now used at thousands of animal control agencies, shelters and veterinary clinics across the country. Once the chip's code has been retrieved, the staff simply calls it in to the national database agency, which is accessible 24 hours a day, 365 days a year through a toll-free number. The database agency then notifies you that your dog has been found.

The cost of implanting the microchip and the onetime fee to register your pet in the database add up to about $50—pretty inexpensive insurance for your dog's safe return if he should ever get lost.

Health certificate and Vaccinations

Get this certificate from your veterinarian not more than 10 days before beginning your trip. Effective for 30 days, it states that your pet is in good health and includes a list of his current vaccinations. While not strictly required when traveling by car, you'll *definitely* need this if you plan to travel by air (even just within your state) or to enter Canada. Before traveling to any other countries, check with their embassies for specific vaccinations and other requirements.

If your pet takes medication or has other problems, get a copy of his medical records along with the health certificate. Make sure the paperwork includes your veterinarian's name, address and phone number, in case follow-up information is needed.

The most well known canine vaccination is for rabies. In fact, you can't get a dog license without proof of a current rabies vaccination. And as a caring, responsible pet owner, *of course* you license your dog, right?

In addition, your pet should be immunized against distemper, hepatitis, parainfluenza, leptospirosis and possibly parvo. Depending on where you'll be traveling, your veterinarian may also recommend a preventive for heartworm or Lyme disease.

Also ask about annual booster shots for corona and bordetella. These safeguard your pet against kennel cough and other infectious diseases he might be exposed to from contact with other dogs, and are often required before your dog can attend obedience classes or stay in a boarding kennel.

Bottom line on vaccinations: Your traveling dog is exposed to many new health hazards at rest stops, parks and other public areas. Along with the stress of drinking unfamiliar water and meeting new dogs, these factors add up to very real dangers for the non-vaccinated dog. So be safe—vaccinate!

🐕 Some vaccines can take up to 30 days to develop their full protective strength, so check with your veterinarian and *plan ahead!*

First aid kit

A basic first aid kit is easy to put together and enables you to deal with emergencies until you can get to a local veterinarian. You'll find a list of the items that belong in your first aid kit on pages 38–39.

Of course you'll also bring along any special medication your veterinarian may have prescribed. If fleas are a problem in the area you're visiting, you may want to include flea-and-tick spray or powder— just be sure to apply it to your dog only when outdoors, never in your motel room.

Travel crate

Many trainers, breeders and veterinarians recommend using a dog carrier, or *crate,* when your dog travels in the car. Obviously, this is more practical with small dogs than with larger ones—it is much easier to fit a Beagle-sized crate into the back seat than one for a Rottweiler.

Several types of crate are available, from collapsible wire mesh panels to heavy molded plastic. A wire crate works especially well in the flat back of a van or station wagon, while the plastic carriers often fit better into the back seat of a sedan. Of course, when traveling by plane, your dog *must* be in an airline-approved travel crate.

The crate should be large enough for your dog to turn around, lie down, and stand or sit up without hitting his head. If he's still a puppy, get a crate that will be large enough for his full adult size. Think of this as his den—*cozy* and *secure*—so don't get anything larger than your adult pet will need.

To cushion and provide traction underfoot, place a folded blanket on the bottom of the crate. Better yet, cut a thick piece of carpet to fit snugly without slipping—ask your local carpet dealer for a remnant or sample square.

Restraints and safety barriers

If a travel crate isn't the answer for your situation, not to worry—there are a number of other safety options you can use instead for a car-traveling dog.

Seat belts—Available for dogs of all sizes, these consist of a chest harness and a strap that fastens to the car seat or to the regular seat belt. These allow your dog to either sit up or lie down in the passenger seat, yet prevent him from being thrown forward in the event of a sudden stop. Various sizes and types are available.

Metal barriers—These allow you to close off the back seat or the back of a station wagon, and can be ordered for specific makes of cars. Your dog can see and hear you through the barrier, but is securely restrained from jumping or being thrown into the front seat. Metal barriers may be either temporarily or permanently installed.

Mesh barriers—These nets create a temporary barrier between the front and back seats. Stretch nets are available in generic sizes and shapes to fit most car models, with elastic bands that fasten to special hardware installed on the interior of the car.

Collapsible window screens—Made of strong plastic struts that expand like a child's safety gate, these fit securely into a partially opened car window. With screens in place on both sides of the car, there is plenty of air circulation but no danger of your dog jumping out—or of someone reaching into the parked car. When removed, the screens take up almost no space and fit easily under a car seat.

Food

First and foremost, you'll need to bring along dog food and a bowl to serve it in. Unless you are absolutely certain that your dog's preferred brand of food is available wherever you plan to travel, pack enough dog food for the entire trip.

If your dog typically nibbles at his food without finishing it all right away, bring a bowl with a snap-on lid that can go back into your dog's tote bag without spilling kibble everywhere. The shallow containers used for whipped toppings or margarine work very well.

You may also want to bring along a vinyl placemat for catching spills under the food and water bowls. This is an item you can pick up for pennies at garage sales. Or you can buy really fancy mats and bowls in pet stores or mail order catalogs.

Remember to pack a can opener for canned food, along with a serving spoon and a snap-on lid for covering any portion to be saved for the next meal. If your dog is accustomed to frequent dog treats or snacks, pack those too. And a small cooler may be helpful in hot weather, for keeping drinking water or leftover canned food cool.

Water

Pack a plastic gallon jug of water and an unbreakable bowl where they'll be accessible during your travels, since your dog will need a drink of water every few hours. Don't let him drink from streams or puddles—drinking unfamiliar or polluted water can lead to stomach upsets and diarrhea.

Also, *never* allow your dog to drink from the toilet in your motel room—some establishments put chemical cleaning solutions into the toilet tank, which could make him very sick.

Many veterinarians recommend bringing enough water from home to last at least halfway through your trip. By gradually mixing your own water with the local tap water, you can prevent an unpleasant reaction. You can also buy distilled water for about a dollar a gallon at most grocery stores.

Bedding & towels

You should always travel with your dog's own bedding and cleanup towels. Your dog will thank you—and so will the hotel and motel managers, for sparing their furnishings. If your dog is accustomed to sleeping on the bed with you, or on other furniture, bring a sheet from home to protect the bedspread or upholstery. And do consider training your dog to stay off the furniture, at home *and* when traveling.

A travel crate, so useful in the car, also makes the perfect bed. It is reassuringly cozy and safe. If you're not using a crate, then bring along a *familiar* washable blanket or other bedding. Ginger travels with the same trusty sleeping bag that she sleeps on at home. Zipped up and folded in half, it makes a thick, soft bed. Opened out full length, it protects the back seat of the car from dirt, mud and beach sand.

An absolute must is a pair of towels especially for your dog. Use these to rub down a wet coat or wipe muddy or sandy paws. Spread one out under the water bowl if your dog is an enthusiastic drinker.

The sheet, dog towels, and bedding can all be found very inexpensively at garage sales, rummage sales, or second hand stores. Ginger's sleeping bag cost a dollar, and her towels were a quarter apiece. The

tote bag which holds her travel supplies was another garage sale find—
all for less than three dollars.

Grooming aids

Pack your dog's brush or comb, since you'll probably be going to fun
places that will result in a dirty or sandy dog. A quick brushing *before*
going indoors will keep your motel room clean, and will endear you to
the housekeeping staff—not to mention how much your pet probably
enjoys being groomed. Ginger jumps up and down with delight at the
mere sight of her brush.

Take care of major grooming chores *before* your trip—trim those too-
long toenails and brush the loose hair out of his coat. And pack a bottle
of pet shampoo if he has a tendency to roll in smelly things. I'll never
forget the day that Jeremiah, my husband's 100-pound Great Pyrenees,
found a dead seal on the beach—enough said!

Cleaning up

Even seasoned canine travelers occasionally have car sickness
accidents, so it's a good idea to pack supplies in the car for quick
cleanups. Paper towels, pre-moistened towelettes, or just a wet
washcloth in a plastic bag are all good. Stash them in an easy-to-reach
spot in the car, such as under the front seat.

Many hotels and motels lay out free amenities such as shampoo and
hand lotion. Wouldn't it be great if they offered guests with dogs the
choice of a few disposable pooper scoopers instead! In the meantime,
however, it is up to us as dog owners to take full responsibility for
cleaning up after our dogs.

Please, please be considerate of others by cleaning up after your dog's
rest stops—whether in a park, on the motel grounds, or at a highway
rest stop. You can use either disposable pooper scoopers, or a reusable
scooper with disposable bags—plus another bag for storing the scooper
between uses.

For a low cost, low tech method, use a plastic produce bag saved from
a trip to the grocery store. Place your hand inside the bag and use this
"glove" to pick up the doggy doo. With your other hand, turn the bag

inside out, then twist the top shut and secure it with a knot. Properly dispose of the bag in a trash can.

Keep several clean, folded bags in your car, ready for the next rest stop. And *always* tuck one in your pocket when taking your dog out for a walk. Zip-top plastic bags also work well.

Last but not least, a flashlight

Keep one in your dog's tote bag so it will be handy when you leave the motel room for those just-before-bedtime walks.

Tote bag checklist

- First aid kit, health certificate/medical records

- Dog bed (sleeping bag or blanket) and towels

- Dog food, bowl, serving spoon, can opener
  and snap-on lid, vinyl placemat

- Jug of water, drinking bowl

- Dog brush or comb, shampoo

- Pooper scoopers (reusable or disposable)
  or a supply of plastic bags

- Paper towels, pre-moistened towelettes,
  or wet washcloth in a plastic bag

- Flashlight

- A favorite chew toy!

3: Good Behavior is a TEAM Effort

Which sort of pet would you rather vacation with: a barky, uncontrollable bundle of energy, or a well-behaved traveler? The answer is obvious, and basic obedience training is the key.

"Obedience" simply means that your dog is reliably under your control, both on and off the leash. Mastering just a few useful commands—and reviewing them often with your pet— can make all the difference in his behavior.

What commands are necessary?

According to noted dog trainer Bruce Sessions, only two commands are truly required for the traveling dog: *come* and *no*. Check your local library for his excellent article "Training the RV Dog" in the September 1985 issue of *Trailer Life* magazine—he explains how to teach these vital commands in just 15 minutes a day for one week. The practice sessions can be a lot of fun, and they help to strengthen the bond between you and your dog.

Ginger and I have also learned a few more commands in obedience class that come in very handy: *sit, down, stay* and *heel.* Does your dog absolutely have to know all these commands before he can travel with you? No, but they will definitely make your trips more relaxed. Compare the following two scenarios…

Before obedience training

It was early morning at the motel, and I had just let Ginger off her leash (my first mistake) in a far corner of the motel grounds for a relief stop.

Another guest and her dog suddenly appeared and Ginger ran to investigate the newcomer, ignoring my call to *"Come back here right now!"* I had to chase Ginger and grab her by the collar. The other guest glared as our two dogs bristled and snarled at each other in the traditional "I'm a tougher dog than you are" dance. On the leash again, Ginger lunged along the path at full speed, dragging me behind her.

In the motel room, Ginger ran back and forth between the window and the closed door, barking at the sounds of people and cars outside—in spite of my repeated scolding to *"Stop that barking and lie down."* Loaded down with luggage, I opened the door and she ran out ahead of me, nearly tripping another guest in her excitement.

And after

Let's try this again now that Ginger and I have completed our obedience classes: I take her outside *on the leash* for her morning rest stop. If she moves toward an approaching dog, I tell her *"Heel"* and we walk in the opposite direction. If she makes any aggressive move or sound, I say *"No!"* sharply and we keep walking—without her pulling on the leash.

Back in the motel room, if Ginger barks at a sound outside, I say *"No!"* followed by *"Down."* She lies down quietly on her own bed. When checking out of the room, I put her on the leash *before* opening the door, tell her *"Heel"* and she walks politely beside me to the car. Once she's safely inside, I retrieve the luggage and finish loading the car.

What a difference!

Feel the difference in stress levels between these two scenarios? And that's just the beginning of the day—imagine an entire weekend trip with an uncontrollable dog versus a well-behaved traveler.

Obedience 101

You *can* learn about obedience training from books, and there are some excellent ones available. However, I definitely recommend that you and your dog attend at least a beginners' obedience class. A trained instructor can get you off to a great start and help to avoid behavior problems before they begin.

Professional dog trainers usually offer both group and one-on-one sessions—check the Yellow Pages under "Dog Training." Beginning, intermediate and advanced levels of obedience classes may also be available through your local school district or community college. Call the school office and ask about their Continuing Education or Community Education programs. Class schedules may also be available at the Post Office or your local bank.

Train BEFORE you travel

The time to begin obedience training is *before* your trip—so that your dog can learn the basic commands in a controlled area without distractions. Once he understands the commands, start practicing with him in a public area like a park, surrounded by people and other dogs. He'll soon learn that you expect the same good behavior wherever he goes with you.

Relax and have fun with this training time. Your dog will love the extra attention and he'll try to please you. Be patient and upbeat even if he gets confused at first. If you reach a stumbling block, go back to an earlier command that he knows well to get his confidence level back up. Then try the more difficult command again.

Keep your training sessions short so that they don't turn into torture for either one of you. And always end with a few minutes of plain old playing—toss a ball for your dog to fetch, or lead him on a run around the yard to release any leftover tension. After all, good behavior is supposed to make your time together more fun, right?

Basic commands

The following discussion is based on the collective expertise of a number of well-known trainers and authors. For more detailed information on obedience training, check your local bookstore or library.

Come—This is an easy command that most dogs pick up very quickly. You want to get your dog's attention in such an inviting way that there's nothing else he'd rather do than come running to you. While your dog is on a leash or long cord, call his name followed by the command *"Come."* As soon as he starts toward you, praise him lavishly. Giving a small food treat at first for every positive response helps to reinforce the idea that coming when called is a wonderful idea.

No—There is no specific routine for teaching this command. Just belt it out in a very firm tone of voice, whenever your dog is doing something you *really* don't want him to do. Don't overuse it though—save it for when he does something you absolutely will not tolerate; otherwise you risk losing its impact. The sudden loud command should startle him out of whatever he's doing. Then as soon as he begins to pay attention to you, praise him. You may even want to call him over to you for a pat on the head or a good ear-scratching.

Sit—With your dog on the leash, say his name and then *"Sit."* At the same time, pull up gently on the leash and push down on his hindquarters to guide him into the sit position. Praise him *("Good sit")* and then release him from this position with *"Okay"* or *"Release."* Only after you give the release command is he allowed to stand up again. Then give lots of praise, both verbal and hands-on. Most dogs will be so delighted with themselves by this time that they'll happily repeat the exercise over and over as long as you keep telling them how wonderful they are.

Down—With your dog on the leash, say his name and the command *"Down"* while you pull downward on his leash. At first, you may also need to push down on his hindquarters or shoulders until he is lying down. Again, give lots of praise to reassure him that he's doing well. Use patience and lots of repetition here.

Stay—With your dog in the Sit or Down position, hold your hand in front of his face, palm toward him, while saying *"Stay."* Praise lavishly for even the shortest compliance, then release. Gradually increase the time your dog is expected to hold this position, then practice staying while you step further and further away. Always remember to release him from this position before going on to another command or ending the practice session, so he doesn't get the idea that *he* can decide when this command is over!

Heel (walking on leash)—Start with your dog sitting at your left side, leash in your left hand. Say his name, then give the command *"Heel"* just before you step out with your left foot. Take just a few steps the first time, then say *"Sit"* as you stop walking. You want him to learn to stay right beside you, and to immediately sit down when you stop.

Say *"Heel"* and start walking again, and so on. He'll soon learn to follow your steps. In fact, he'll probably anticipate your takeoff and start too soon at first, so be patient. Once he catches on to the routine, stop giving the Sit command every time, so that he learns to do it automatically.

Try carrying a small food treat right in front of his nose to keep him at your side rather than rushing ahead. Give him the treat after you walk a few steps and then stop. And of course, give lots of praise. (If you think this is starting to sound like the secret to obedience training—you're absolutely right!)

Controlling aggression

If you intend to take your well-behaved traveler out in public, he must be reliably *not* aggressive toward people or dogs. Some dogs don't start out being comfortable with other dogs. Their reactions range from defensive postures like raised fur along the back of the neck and fierce stares, to outright barking or growling.

The best way to overcome defensive or aggressive tendencies is to begin at an early age to get your dog accustomed to the presence of other dogs. Simply attending obedience classes will go a long way toward helping him relax around dogs and people. Your instructor can also offer specialized help for problem dogs.

The most important step in preventing aggression is to *always* have your dog under your control—this means on the leash—whenever you venture outside your car or motel room. Dog behaviorists say that once you establish yourself as the "pack leader," your dog will follow your lead on whether to charge ahead or hold back.

If your dog is a barker

Simply put, barking is *not* to be tolerated. A barking dog makes everyone around you miserable. You should train your dog to stop barking as soon as you give the all-purpose command *"No!"*

A really insistent barker may need more at first than a spoken command to break through his mental barriers. I've had good luck with plain water in a plastic squirt bottle. One good squirt in the face (aim for the forehead) doesn't hurt your dog, but it certainly interrupts his train of thought, especially when accompanied by a loud *"No!"* and followed with praise the minute he stops barking.

Of course, a dog left behind in a motel room, barking incessantly, is absolutely out. This kind of barking is a sign of stress, as in "They left me here all alone and I'm scared/bored/frustrated." It isn't fair to your dog or to the unfortunate neighbors who have to endure the noise.

Never leave your dog alone in the motel room. He should be going with you—isn't that why you brought him on the trip in the first place? If you must leave him for a short time, while you're in a restaurant for example, let him wait in your car, not in the room.

If you already use a travel crate, your dog should be accustomed to sitting or lying down quietly when he's inside it. Put him in the crate for a few minutes to calm down when he becomes upset and barky. Be sure to practice this "time-out in the crate" exercise at home before you travel, so that your dog knows exactly what is expected of him when he is put into his little den.

Learning to love car rides

Many dogs just naturally love going anywhere in the car with you, but others have difficulty getting used to the sound and motion. Pacing back and forth, drooling, panting excessively or throwing up are all signs that your dog is nervous about being in the car. Some advance preparations will help to ensure a comfortable trip for all concerned.

Getting used to the car—A few practice rides can help to reassure him that riding in the car can be fun rather than intimidating. In extreme cases, you may need to start by sitting quietly with him in the car, not even starting the engine. Ignore him for a few minutes—perhaps read a magazine article—then let him out of the car with a simple word of praise and a pat on the head.

Repeat this exercise until he can enter the car, sit quietly, and exit without any problems. Then try starting the car but not going anywhere. Next, try driving just around the block, and so on. By the time you've progressed to taking him with you on short errands, such as to the grocery store and back, he'll probably just take a nap while you drive.

Arrange some of your practice trips to include a fun destination or activity, like a brisk walk in the park. For example, Ginger loves traveling to the drive-up bank window with me, because the teller always has a bowl of doggy treats handy!

Avoiding a "nervous stomach"—Stress can trigger car sickness, so don't give food or water for at least an hour before a practice ride. Allow time for a few minutes of exercise and a chance to relieve himself just before you leave. If he still gets carsick, see page 50 for some simple remedies.

Riding politely—Train your dog to sit or lie down quietly—no jumping around, and no barking in your ear or out the window. Consider using one of the safety restraints described on pages 17–18. Reassure him by remaining calm yourself. Don't keep asking anxiously if he's all right—that will just make him more nervous. Praise him for sitting politely in his assigned spot, then ignore him as long as he behaves himself.

Loading and unloading—For his own safety, your dog *must* learn to wait for your command before getting into or out of the car. Never open the door without checking that the leash is attached to his collar, and that you have a firm grasp on the other end of the leash. Losing control of an excited dog in unfamiliar territory can be disastrous—so use the Stay command to keep him safely in the car until you are ready for him to get out.

Reviewing what your dog already knows

A brief practice session makes a great exercise break during your trip. It also helps to reinforce the idea that obedience is expected even when surrounded by unfamiliar distractions. Start by walking your dog on the leash. Pause periodically to practice the Sit or Down command, then release him and continue your walk. Or tell him to Sit and Stay while you walk ahead a few steps—still holding the leash, of course. Then call him to you once more, with lots of praise.

A few minutes of this activity at each rest stop will leave you with a happy dog who settles down comfortably as soon as you start driving again.

4: The Well-Behaved Traveler On the Road

Okay, you've faithfully completed your dog's obedience training, assembled his first aid kit (see page 38) and packed his food, water, and other traveling supplies. You've made your advance room reservations, you're ready to go, and your ecstatic pet is running in circles around the car. This is the payoff for all your preparations—it's time to hit the road!

Tips for traveling in the car

The safest way for a smaller dog to ride in the car is in a travel crate. This protects him in case of a sudden stop and keeps him from jumping around in the car or getting underfoot while you're trying to drive. If your pet is too large for a travel crate, consider using a doggy seat belt that offers similar protection but still allows him to sit or stand up. Whatever form of restraint you decide on, make sure your pet knows that he must stay in his assigned location in the car until you release him. Ginger's travel spot is on her sleeping bag, which has been spread out across the back seat to protect the upholstery.

Don't leave your dog's leash attached to his collar while the car is in motion. If you have to stop suddenly, the leash could snag on something and strangle him. Take the leash off once he's safely inside the car, and remember to put it on again *before* you let him out.

If you feel you must open the car window, roll it down just enough for your dog to put his nose into the fresh air, not his whole face. Never let him hang his head out the window of a moving car—not only could he squeeze his whole body out if he decided to chase something, but airborne objects such as insects or flying gravel could injure his ears and eyes. Or the force of the wind could actually give him an earache.

It goes without saying that your pet belongs *inside* the vehicle. A dog riding in the back of an open pickup truck is an accident just waiting to happen. He is exposed to wind-borne hazards and harsh weather, and could be thrown out of the vehicle if you swerve or brake suddenly.

If you need to leave your dog in the parked car—while you stop for lunch, for example—take steps to be sure that he won't suffer from heat buildup in the car, which can lead to heatstroke or even death. Park under cover if you can, or at least in the shade. For cross-ventilation, open a window on each side of the car and insert the collapsible screens described on page 18. Check frequently to be sure the temperature in the car is still comfortable.

Rest stop pointers

When traveling a long distance, stop every few hours to give both you and your pet a chance to stretch and relax. Keep him on the leash the whole time you're at the rest stop, and stay in the designated pet areas.

If you've been traveling for quite awhile or the weather is warm, he'll appreciate a drink of water. Then give him a few minutes to relieve himself and walk around a bit. Be considerate of others by *always* cleaning up after your dog—use plastic bags or pooper scoopers, and properly dispose of the waste in a garbage can.

This is a great time for a short exercise break, especially if you combine it with a review of obedience commands. Try walking a short distance and have him sit or lie down, then walk for another minute and practice a different command, and so on. A few minutes of activity will have you both feeling refreshed and ready to continue your trip.

Room etiquette

When you arrive at your overnight destination, be sure to remind the staff that your dog is traveling with you. Of course, you should already have stated this when making your advance reservation, but tell them again now that you have arrived. That way, they can be sure not to put you in a "no-pets" room by mistake—many establishments reserve certain rooms for guests who suffer from allergies. Sneaking a dog into a no-pets room hurts all dog owners by jeopardizing the management's willingness to accept dogs in the future.

Ask where on the grounds you can exercise your dog, whether or not they have disposable pooper scoopers available, and if there are designated trash cans you should use for disposal.

Place your pet's bed in an out-of-the-way spot in the room and show him where it is, then make sure that he uses his own bed and not the furniture. If you allow your pet to sleep on your bed or other furniture at home, bring along one of your own sheets or blankets to cover the motel furnishings—and resolve to begin breaking that habit as soon as your trip is over. Place your dog's bed on the floor beside you so he's still close, but don't let him sleep on your bed.

If your dog gets bored or rambunctious in the room, offer him a favorite chew toy to play with. Watch that he doesn't damage the furnishings—remember, you are legally and financially responsible for any damage your dog does, both indoors and out.

While it's natural for dogs to bark at unfamiliar sounds, don't tolerate any barking in the room, no matter what's going on outside. Incessant barking is the single most common reason given by managers for not allowing dogs to stay. *Never* leave your pet alone in the room when you go out, for example, to dinner. Take him along and let him wait for you in the car rather than in the room. He'll feel safer in that familiar place and should settle right down for a nap while you're gone.

Mealtime arrangements

Put the food and water bowls on your dog towel or vinyl placemat in the bathroom—its smooth floor is much easier to clean than the bedroom carpet. If your pet is a messy eater, the mat is easy to rinse off and drip-dry in the bathtub. Don't let him drink out of the toilet—cleaning chemicals that may have been added to the water could make him sick.

On checkout day, it's a good idea to withhold food and water at least an hour before starting a long drive. If your pet tends to suffer from car sickness, you may need to do this as much as six hours before departure, meaning the night before if you plan to leave early in the morning.

Walking on the grounds

Shortly after eating or drinking, your dog will need a walk outside, in the designated pet relief area. This is also true after he has been waiting in the car while you were out having your own dinner. And of course, just before bedtime is another important walking time. Be sure to always take along the pooper scooper or plastic bag for cleaning up after him.

Before you and your dog leave the room, make him sit down by the door while you put his leash on. He should remain sitting while you open the door and step outside, then he can follow you out. Don't let him charge through the door ahead of you.

Always keep your dog leashed while on the premises, of course. And be courteous when taking him for a "relief walk"— use the designated pet area or at least go to the far end of the grounds, away from buildings, major footpaths and children's play areas, and clean up after him. Don't let him romp in landscaped areas like flower beds, decorative ponds or streams. Basically, just be aware of your pet's energy level and potential for destruction, and seek out areas where he can play harmlessly.

When you and your pet return to the room, check him over before stepping inside. Use the dog towel you brought from home to wipe off any mud or sand on his feet. This small courtesy only takes a second, helps to keep the carpet clean, and has a definite effect on the manager's willingness to continue accepting pets as guests.

On the trail

When you go out for the day's activities, remember to bring along the doggy water jug and drinking bowl, just as you would pack your own water bottle for a hike. And of course, the first aid kit should be in your car, not left behind in the room.

Be aware of your pet's effect on other people and animals when you're out in public. You are responsible for making sure that he doesn't cause anyone else discomfort. If you're walking along a trail, for example, rein him in to walk closely beside you when you encounter other hikers. Don't let him monopolize the whole walkway or run up to greet them— or worse yet, to challenge their own pet.

Remember that although your dog is the apple of your eye, not everyone shares your enchantment. In fact, some people are very fearful of even the smallest, meekest dog. So keep your pet on the leash unless you're absolutely sure that no one else is around and that there is no local leash law prohibiting dogs running free. Even then, put the leash back on as soon as you encounter another person or animal. Many towns have ordinances that require dogs to be on leash *at all times,* as do most city, state and national parks.

Watch out for potential hazards underfoot: broken glass, nails or other sharp objects, burning hot pavement, melted road tar, chemical sprays or wet paint could all injure his feet or poison him when he licks his fur. Also remember to clean his feet after walking on snow or ice that may have been treated with salt or other de-icing chemicals.

At the beach

Many dogs love playing in the ocean, and few scenes are more enjoyable to watch than a happy dog chasing waves up and down the beach. However, a naturalist friend has asked me to remind dog owners not to let their pets chase the shore birds, which can cause the birds to suffer severe or even fatal stress.

Keep a close eye on your pet while he's in the water—don't let him wade or swim out too far, as dangerous currents can arise suddenly and carry him away from shore.

Also watch that he doesn't drink a lot of salt water, or else he may be throwing up later in the car. A little bit won't hurt him, and he'll soon learn that he doesn't like the taste after all. Offer him a drink of fresh water when he gets back to your parked car, and then wait a few minutes before bundling him inside—he may still need to throw up any salt water already in his stomach.

After walking your dog on the beach, brush off any sand clinging to his feet or coat. Salt water that dries on his skin can cause lasting irritation, so if he's been in the surf, rinse the salt away as soon as possible— definitely *before* returning to your room. This is where those dog towels you packed in his tote bag come in handy. And of course, the motel's towels should *never* be used for dogs!

5: First Aid for Your Traveling Dog

Whether your pet sustains a minor scratch or a life-threatening injury, you need to know what first aid measures to take. Then, for all but the most minor problems, your immediate next step is to get him to the nearest veterinary clinic. If you're not sure just how serious the problem is, call them—most clinics are happy to answer questions over the phone, and can give you exact directions for getting there if it becomes necessary.

Before first aid is needed

Put together your dog's own first aid kit in advance (see page 38) and *always* bring it (and this book) along when he travels with you. Keep it in your car when you're out and about, not in the motel room with the luggage.

Read through this chapter *now* to get a basic idea of what to do in an emergency, and how to use the supplies in the first aid kit.

Knowing your dog's healthy state will help you to recognize when something is wrong. Sit down on the floor with your dog—he'll love the attention!—and listen to his breathing. Place your palm on his chest just behind the "elbow" and feel his heartbeat. Check the size and color of his pupils, the color of his gums and tongue, and how warm his body feels normally.

In an emergency, refer to specific sections in this chapter for the proper first aid steps to take. Or better yet, have another person read the steps aloud to you while you perform them on your pet. As soon as you complete the emergency procedures, take him to a veterinary clinic, or at least call the clinic for further instructions.

🐕 It's a good idea to identify nearby veterinary clinics at your vacation destination *before* the need arises. See the list of 24 hour emergency clinics starting on page 55, or check the local Yellow Pages.

Your dog's first aid kit

This list includes the emergency supplies you'll need until you can get to the clinic. All items are available from your veterinarian or local pharmacy. The dosage of some medicines varies according to body weight, so write your pet's correct dose on a piece of masking tape attached to each medicine container. Pack everything into a sturdy container, such as a fishing tackle box or cosmetics travel case.

Travel papers—copies of your dog's license, health certificate, veterinary records if he has special medical problems, and a master lost-and-found poster with extra photos of your dog as described on page 63; store all this paperwork in a zip-top plastic bag

Any medication your dog is taking—and a copy of the written prescription

Packets of **honey**—available in restaurants, or **hard candies** *(no chocolate!)*

Antibacterial ointment—such as *Panalog* from your veterinarian, or *Neosporin* from any pharmacy

Tranquilizers—but *only* if prescribed by your veterinarian *and* you have tested the dosage on your pet before the trip. The ASPCA discourages the use of tranquilizers because the effects can be unpredictable

Plastic dosage spoon—to measure liquid medicines (available at any pharmacy, often for free)

Paper or **flexible plastic cup**—that you can squeeze into the shape of a pouring spout to administer liquid medicines

Slip-on muzzle—the quick-release kind that fastens with hook-and-loop tape is especially easy to use.

Emergency stretcher—flat piece of wood or cardboard stored in your car's trunk (see page 47)

Kaopectate

Hydrogen peroxide, 3% solution

Activated charcoal

Olive oil

Petroleum jelly

Sterile eye drops

Zip-top plastic bags

Sterile gauze pads

Adhesive tape and **elastic bandages**

Cotton-tipped swabs

Rectal thermometer

Ice pack

Tweezers

Pliers

Blunt-tipped scissors

Taking your dog's temperature

Have another person restrain your dog while you take his temperature, unless he's too weak to put up a fuss. Coat the rectal thermometer with a bit of petroleum jelly or hand lotion to make insertion easier.

Firmly grasp your dog's tail and very gently insert the thermometer about one inch while rotating it back and forth slightly. After one minute, remove it to read the temperature. Wash the thermometer with soap and *cool* water before returning it to its protective case. Normal body temperature is 100° to 101°—anything over 102.5° deserves a phone call to the veterinary clinic.

What to do in a life-threatening emergency

You have to give your pet the first aid he needs to survive until you reach a veterinarian. Remain calm and focused on what you need to do. Speak to him reassuringly while you work.

Each step listed here is described in greater detail in the sections that follow—exact page numbers are indicated for each step.

1. *Do not move your dog* until you have checked his injuries. The only exception is when it's unsafe to leave him where he is, such as in the middle of a busy street.

2. Check for a heartbeat—if there is none, start cardiac massage *immediately* (page 42).

3. Check whether he is breathing—if not, begin artificial respiration *immediately* (page 42).

4. Muzzle and restrain him if he's in obvious pain, seems dazed or starts to struggle (page 43).

5. Check for obvious injuries and control severe bleeding (page 43).

6. Check for symptoms of internal bleeding (page 44).

7. Check for signs of poisoning—depending on the type of poison, induce vomiting or make him swallow an antidote (page 45).

8. Move him to your vehicle using a board, stiff cardboard or a blanket as a stretcher (page 47).

9. Treat for shock by keeping him warm (page 47).

10. Rush him to the nearest veterinary clinic. If possible, have another person call ahead so they can prepare for your pet's arrival.

If your dog is choking

The traveling dog may encounter chicken bones at picnic areas, fishing line at the river's edge—even more dangerous if a fishhook is still attached—or any number of other choking hazards that can be potentially fatal unless you act quickly.

Signs of choking include violent pawing at his mouth or throat and loud gasping or gagging sounds. In his panic, he may even bite your hand when you try to help.

If possible, have another person hold your pet while you open his mouth wide and pull his tongue out straight with your fingers or a cloth.

If you can see the entire object, pull it out. But *never* pull on a fishline that extends out of sight down his throat—there could be a hook at the other end. Instead, take him to a veterinary clinic for an x-ray.

If you can't see what he's choking on, place your hands on each side of his chest and squeeze in a sudden, forceful movement. The air expelled from his lungs may dislodge the object in his throat.

If he is still choking, head straight for the emergency clinic. Keep him as immobile as possible during the trip, and speak reassuringly to calm him.

If your dog is drowning

If your pet is in the water and can't make it back to shore, *do not* swim out to him. First, try to help him from shore by extending out a board, rope or any floating thing that he can hold or climb onto. If you still can't reach him, wade part of the way out and try again. If you absolutely must swim out to him, bring something he can cling to—otherwise you could be seriously clawed or even pulled under in his panic to get out of the water.

After you get him onto the shore, clear any debris out of his mouth and lift his hind legs as high as possible to help drain his airway.

If his heart has stopped, start cardiac massage *immediately* (see page 42).

If he has a heartbeat but is not breathing, give artificial respiration *immediately* (see page 42).

Once he begins breathing on his own, dry him off and keep him warm. If he's willing to drink, give him warm liquids. If his body temperature doesn't quickly return to normal, check with a veterinarian for follow-up treatment.

Cardiac massage

Place your palm on your dog's chest just behind the elbow. (Practice this at home until you can easily detect his normal heartbeat.) If his heart has stopped beating, you have to restart it *right now!* Gently lay your dog on his side with head extended—don't move him suddenly, as that can further deepen his shock. Pull his tongue out straight to clear the airway.

Place your hands on each side of his chest just behind the elbow. Squeeze firmly and quickly to compress the chest, then release. Repeat once every second for one minute, then check for heartbeat again. If there still is none, repeat the steps above. As soon as his heart starts beating, give artificial respiration to restore his breathing.

Artificial respiration

Check your pet's heartbeat before beginning this procedure. If his heart has stopped, you must perform cardiac massage (see above) before giving artificial respiration.

If your dog has swallowed water while drowning, or choked on vomit or other liquids, lift his back legs as high above his head as possible for fifteen seconds and give three or four downward shakes to drain his airway. Gently pull his tongue out straight and clear any debris from his mouth with your hand or a cloth.

Place your hands on both sides of his chest just behind the elbow. Squeeze hard, then release. Repeat once every five seconds for one minute. If the movement of air in and out of the lungs seems blocked, open his mouth wide to see if an object is lodged in his throat, and remove it.

If he doesn't start breathing within one minute, grasp his muzzle firmly to hold his mouth shut. Take a deep breath, place your mouth over his nose forming an airtight seal, and blow gently. His chest should rise as the lungs expand.

Listen for air leaving the lungs, then repeat every five seconds for one minute (ten to fifteen breaths). Check to see if he's breathing on his own, then repeat for another ten to fifteen breaths, and so on.

Have someone drive you and your dog to the veterinary clinic while you continue helping him to breathe. Don't give up even if there is no immediate response—dogs have been successfully revived after extended periods of artificial resuscitation, as long as the heart keeps beating.

Restraining an injured dog

An injured dog is also frightened, dazed, and in pain. He may not even recognize you, and may bite when you try to help him. Unless he's unconscious, you'll need to muzzle him before you can check his injuries.

Use the slip-on muzzle in your first aid kit or improvise one from a handkerchief, scarf, or his own leash—whatever is handy. Since a muzzle doesn't work well on a short-nosed dog, loosely place a coat or blanket over his head instead. Whatever you use, be sure not to restrict your dog's breathing. And be ready to remove the muzzle *immediately* if your dog starts to vomit or has trouble breathing.

Broken bones

If your dog is unable to move his leg or holds it at an odd angle, the bone may be fractured. Muzzle and restrain him before checking for broken bones, and handle the injured leg as little as possible. If the bone is protruding from an open wound, cover with a clean cloth and control the bleeding with direct pressure.

If you can find a rigid stretcher (see page 47) for moving your dog, don't waste time applying a splint. But if you have to jostle him in a blanket stretcher or carry him in your arms, you've got to immobilize the broken ends of the bone before moving him.

To apply a temporary splint, wrap a clean cloth around the leg for padding. Fold a newspaper, magazine or piece of cardboard in a U-shape around the leg or lay a strip of wood alongside it. Hold it all in place with adhesive tape or strips of cloth. The splint should extend beyond the joints above and below the fracture in order to hold the broken bones still.

External bleeding

Your first concern is to stop any major bleeding. Minor wounds that are losing only a small amount of blood can wait for the veterinarian. But if blood is either spurting out or flowing steadily, you must act *now*.

Cover the wound with a sterile gauze pad or clean cloth if possible, or just place your hand directly over the source of the blood flow. Apply firm, steady pressure until the bleeding stops.

If the wound is on the leg (or tail) and you cannot slow down the blood loss after a few minutes of direct pressure, you must apply a tourniquet. This may result in having to amputate the limb, so use this method only as a last resort—always try direct pressure first. And *never* place the tourniquet over a joint or a fractured bone.

Wrap a handkerchief or other strip of cloth in a loose loop around the leg about one inch above the wound. Tie it with a double knot, then place a strong, short stick in the loop. Twist the stick to tighten the loop until the blood flow stops.

Now take him to the emergency clinic, *fast*. On the way to the clinic, you *must* loosen the tourniquet every ten minutes to allow some blood to flow through the limb. Apply direct pressure to the wound to prevent further bleeding, and tighten the tourniquet again only if absolutely necessary.

If you suspect internal bleeding

Hidden bleeding inside your dog's body can result from a traumatic blow or from certain kinds of poison. Even if he has no visible wounds, his internal organs may be seriously damaged. He may go into fatal shock without immediate veterinary care.

Signs of internal bleeding include: pale skin, gums and tongue; bleeding from ears, mouth or anus; bloody vomit or stool; difficulty breathing; or extreme sleepiness. Symptoms may appear either right after the accident or hours later, even if he seemed fine initially.

Use a rigid stretcher (see page 47) if at all possible to move your dog to and from your car on the way to the emergency clinic. Keep him warm and don't jostle him any more than you absolutely have to.

Poisoning

Your dog can be poisoned by eating or drinking a toxic substance, by inhaling it, by licking it off his coat or paws or by absorbing it through his skin. Poisons that your pet might encounter when traveling include spilled antifreeze, toxic bait intended for insects or rodents (or their dead bodies), garbage that contains poisonous substances, or chemical sprays that have been applied to plants that your dog chews or rolls in. Even your own prescription medicine can poison your pet if he discovers it in your luggage and accidentally swallows some while playing with this new "toy."

Symptoms of poisoning include: drooling or difficulty swallowing; trembling; cringing; abdominal pain or vomiting; rapid, shallow breathing; twitching; or coma.

Contact poisoning

Rinse his coat immediately with lots of water—fresh water, sea water, mud puddle by the side of the road, whatever it takes to dilute the chemical and wash it away. Wear rubber gloves, if available, to avoid getting the toxic chemicals on your skin. Then wash him with mild hand soap or dog shampoo and rinse thoroughly with clean water. Repeat until all traces of the chemicals are removed.

Watch your pet closely over the next few hours. If his skin appears irritated or he shows any symptoms of internal poisoning, see or call a veterinarian.

Swallowed poisons

Your first step is to determine what kind of poison your pet has swallowed. If the product container is available, it may identify the ingredients, the antidote and whether or not to induce vomiting.

Depending on the type of poison, you must choose between two very different first aid treatments—see **Method A** and **Method B** on the next page. If you can't identify the type of poison, check inside your dog's mouth and throat. If the tissues look burned or raw, use Method A, otherwise use Method B.

Try to collect a sample of the poison in one of the zip-top plastic bags included in your first aid kit, or bring the poison container itself if at all possible. Also collect some of the material your dog vomits up. These samples can help the veterinarian identify the exact antidote that your dog needs.

Method A. When the poison is CORROSIVE, such as an acid, alkali, or petroleum product: NEUTRALIZE THE POISON BUT DO NOT INDUCE VOMITING!

These extremely corrosive poisons will injure your dog's throat and mouth even more if he throws up. Rinse his mouth with water to wash away any remaining chemicals.

Make him swallow two to three tablespoons of olive oil or up to one cup of milk. Keep him warm with a blanket or coat while you rush him to the nearest veterinary clinic.

Method B. When the poison is NOT corrosive: INDUCE VOMITING IMMEDIATELY!

Mix equal parts of hydrogen peroxide and water. Make him swallow $1\frac{1}{2}$ tablespoonfuls of this mixture for each ten pounds of body weight.

Example: the dose for a 60-lb dog would be $6 \times 1\frac{1}{2} = 9$ tablespoons.

If he doesn't vomit within ten minutes, repeat this dosage, but not more than three doses altogether.

After he vomits, make him swallow a mixture of three to four tablespoonfuls of activated charcoal in a cup of warm water. Wrap him in a blanket or coat while you rush him to the nearest veterinary clinic.

A special warning about antifreeze

Every year, dogs die from drinking antifreeze that had dripped onto the ground from leaking car radiators, or was spilled by careless people. This coolant has a sweet smell and taste that attracts many pets to drink it—but even a tiny spoonful can be deadly.

If your dog has swallowed even the tiniest amount of antifreeze, induce vomiting *immediately* and rush him to a veterinarian for an antidote injection—but you must work *fast*. Minutes can make the difference between losing him or saving his life.

🐾 Pet-safe antifreeze is now available at auto supply stores and some service centers—ask for it the next time you have the radiator fluid in your car changed.

Moving an injured dog

The safest way to move your pet is on a *stretcher,* a flat rigid surface that won't flex under his weight. A piece of wood or heavy cardboard will do, or even an air mattress blown up as firm as you can make it. If that's unavailable, use a blanket, tarp or piece of clothing that you can carry by its corners to make as flat a surface as possible.

Slide your dog onto the stretcher without twisting or shaking him. If possible, have a helper lift his hindquarters and abdomen at exactly the same moment that you lift his head and shoulders.

If you are alone and can't find a rigid stretcher, you'll have to carry him in your arms. Place one arm around his hindquarters and the other around his front legs at the shoulder, supporting his head on your arm. Keep his spine as straight as possible.

Treating for shock

Shock is a sudden collapse of your dog's circulatory system, brought on by sudden injury or other trauma. Be very careful not to jostle or quickly move him—any rapid movement can bring on the *fatal* stages of shock.

Symptoms of shock include: extreme muscle weakness; loss of bladder and bowel control; shallow, rapid breathing and pulse; pale or whitish gums and mouth; he feels cold to the touch; he appears asleep or semiconscious.

Pull his tongue out straight to clear the airway—but be very cautious, as even the most gentle dog may bite when dazed from great pain or fear. Try to get his head lower than his body to encourage circulation. However, if he has a head injury, keep his head level with his body.

Cover him with a warm blanket or coat, unless the shock is caused by heatstroke and his temperature is already too high. Now take him to a veterinarian for follow-up care. Have someone call ahead so the clinic can prepare for the emergency procedures he'll need as soon as he gets there.

Treating burns

Watch for hazards that can lead to your dog being accidentally burned—sparks from a beach bonfire, boiling hot liquids spilled from a tiny kitchen unit, licking meat juices from a hot barbecue grill or brushing against a space heater. Chewing on an electrical cord can lead to burns in the mouth as well as unconsciousness, shock, and even death—be sure to *unplug the cord* before touching your dog.

If the burned skin is red but not broken, run cold water over it, or cover with an ice pack or a cold wet towel. If the burned area is heavily blistered, raw, weeping or bleeding, blackened or whitish, *do not apply ice or water*—just cover with a sterile gauze pad or clean cloth. Treat for shock (see page 47) and get your dog to the nearest veterinarian *immediately.*

Minor cuts and scrapes

When Ginger is on the trail of a squirrel (though she never catches one) she'll gleefully charge into the thickest blackberry patch. She returns covered with thorns and scratches—grinning like a fool and enormously pleased with herself. So I've gotten plenty of practice at removing stickers and cleaning up her scrapes and scratches.

Rinse away any dirt in your pet's wound with clean water, then swab with hydrogen peroxide. If it's still bleeding, cover with a gauze pad and apply pressure until the bleeding stops. Then lightly apply an antibiotic ointment such as *Panalog* or *Neosporin*.

If the wound is large or your dog just won't leave it alone, cover with a gauze pad held in place with adhesive tape or an elastic bandage. And of course, for anything more than a minor scratch or scrape, you should have a veterinarian take a look at it.

Removing foreign objects

Use common sense on whether or not to try removing an embedded object such as a burr or porcupine quill. In some cases, incorrect removal can do more harm than if you just keep your dog as motionless as possible while taking him straight to the nearest clinic to let the veterinarian do the job.

From the ears—Use tweezers to gently remove seeds or burrs from the *outer* ear canal. If your dog still shakes his head or scratches repeatedly at his ear, seeds may also be deeper inside the ear canal and must be removed by a veterinarian.

From the eyes—If your pet paws at his eye or rubs his face along the ground, gently hold the eyelid open and check for seeds or debris. To wash away a loose object, apply sterile eye drops. Don't try to remove an object that is embedded into the surface of the eye. Instead, take him to the nearest veterinary clinic *right away.*

From everywhere else—You're already familiar with this routine if your dog loves to crash through the underbrush like Ginger does. Run your hands gently over his face, body and feet to check for thorns. If he's limping or holding up his paw, he has already zeroed in on the problem for you.

Use tweezers to pull out embedded stickers. If there's any bleeding or tearing of the skin, swab with hydrogen peroxide. When a foreign object is buried too deeply to find, either soak the affected body part in salt water (one teaspoon salt per cup of lukewarm water) several times a day until the object works its way up to the surface where you can remove it, or else have a veterinarian remove it to begin with.

Remove sharp objects—such as porcupine quills or a fishhook—with pliers. Begin by using the wire cutter notches at the center of the pliers to clip off each porcupine quill tip, or the barbed point of the fishhook *if it is exposed.* When finished, rinse all wounds with hydrogen peroxide. But if the fishhook point is hidden below the skin surface, or your dog won't submit to having the quills pulled out, take him straight to a veterinarian.

Watch out for ticks—Examine your dog closely after outdoor activities, especially his head, shoulders and feet. Forget the old wives' tales about using a match to burn the tick off, applying gasoline or petroleum jelly to make it let go, and so on. However, dousing the tick with alcohol or nail polish remover *may* make it easier to remove.

Use tweezers to grab the tick by its head, very close to the dog's skin, and firmly pull it out. Don't squeeze its fat abdomen—doing so might force disease-carrying blood back into the bite wound.

Above all, *don't use your fingers.* Ticks can carry Lyme disease and Rocky Mountain spotted fever, both of which are dangerous to humans. Swab the bite area with hydrogen peroxide. If the skin becomes red or irritated, see a veterinarian for follow-up treatment.

Treating an upset stomach

Car sickness is one of the most common complaints for the traveling dog—whether it's because he's fearful of the car, or just overly excited about coming along. Try reducing his stress level with practice rides as described on page 28. Don't give him food or water for at least an hour before traveling. And always allow him a few minutes of exercise and a last-minute chance to relieve himself.

If your dog still gets carsick, try giving him a small spoonful of honey, a piece of hard candy or a spoonful of plain vanilla ice cream to calm his stomach. *However, you should never give your dog any food containing chocolate, as it can be toxic!*

If these simple remedies don't help, ask your veterinarian about stronger medicines for motion sickness.

An upset stomach can also be caused by eating unfamiliar or spoiled food, or drinking unfamiliar water—contaminants in the water or a different mineral content can throw your pet's system for a loop. Give him two teaspoons of Kaopectate for each ten pounds of body weight, once every four hours.

If the problem doesn't clear up within 24 hours, this may be a symptom of a more serious illness—see a veterinarian.

Treating diarrhea

This may be a temporary upset caused by the stress of unfamiliar surroundings, food or water, or a symptom of a more serious illness. Give two teaspoons of Kaopectate for each ten pounds of body weight, once every four hours.

See a veterinarian if the diarrhea doesn't clear up within 24 hours or if other symptoms appear, such as labored breathing, bloody stool, either a rise or a drop in body temperature, listlessness or loss of appetite.

Dealing with heat problems

Summer can mean added hazards for your pet. Short haired dogs can become sunburned just as easily as people can. Older or overweight pets are more prone to heat problems, as are short-nosed breeds and dogs who are taking certain medications. Heat problems are even more likely if the humidity is also high.

When walking your dog, pay special attention to the surface underfoot— if it's too hot for your bare feet, then it's too hot for your dog's paws as well.

Heatstroke can be caused by too much exercise in the hot sun, not drinking enough water, or simply from sitting in a hot car. On a sunny 80° day, the temperature inside your parked car (even with the windows partly rolled down) will climb well above 100° in just minutes, putting your pet in danger of permanent damage to the brain and internal organs, and even death.

Recognizing the danger signs

Symptoms of heatstroke may include some or all of the following: frenzied barking; a vacant expression or wild-eyed stare; rapid or heavy panting; rapid pulse; dizziness or weakness; vomiting or diarrhea; deep red or purple tongue and gums (the normal color is light pink, except in breeds where the gums and tongue are naturally black); twitching, convulsions or coma.

Use a rectal thermometer to check your dog's body temperature. Normal body temperature is 100° to 101°—but it can rise to 106° or more with heatstroke.

First aid for heatstroke

First, get your dog out of the sun. Then cover him with towels soaked in cool water, or pour cool water over him every few minutes. *Do not* immerse him in ice water or apply ice directly to his skin, but an ice pack is okay if wrapped in a towel.

Give him a small amount of cool water to drink, or let him lick ice cubes or a bit of plain vanilla ice cream. (Remember—no chocolate!) As soon as his body temperature begins to come down, take him to the nearest veterinarian for follow-up care.

Keeping your pet safe in cold weather

Many dogs, Ginger included, love outdoor activities in the snow. But don't assume that your dog is as safe and comfortable as you are in your insulated boots and down-filled clothing. Wintertime hazards include hypothermia, frostbite, and irritation from road salt and other de-icing chemicals.

After playing outside, wash off any remaining ice or road salt and towel him dry. Then give him a well-deserved rest in a warm place—but not too close to a fireplace or space heater. If he's really chilled, he could burn himself before even realizing it.

Watch out for hypothermia

Smaller or older dogs are most likely to suffer from hypothermia. However, exposure to the cold *when he's wet* can be extremely hazardous for any dog, especially if immersed in icy water for even a few minutes. When your pet starts to lag behind you instead of bounding ahead, that's the signal to get him back indoors and warmed up. If he becomes listless, ignores your calls or just wants to lie down in the snow, you've definitely stayed out too long—you need to warm him up right away.

Dry him off and boost his circulation by rubbing vigorously with a towel. Wrap him in a warm blanket, and offer warm (not hot) water if he's willing to drink it. If his body temperature has dropped below 98.5° take him to a veterinarian *immediately.*

Treating for frostbite

When the weather turns windy, check frequently to see if your dog's feet, ears, and tail are getting pale or numb. If so, bring him indoors right away.

Massage the affected areas *very gently* to encourage circulation—rough handling can bruise damaged tissues. Soak frostbitten paws or tail in lukewarm (90°) water to gradually restore circulation. Keep him warm and check with a veterinarian for follow-up care.

6: Emergency Clinics

Time is a critical factor when your pet needs emergency medical care. Your best bet for quickly finding a veterinary clinic is the local phone book. Always call ahead, even during their posted office hours. That gives their staff a chance to prepare so that any lifesaving procedures that the doctor may deem necessary will be ready the minute your pet arrives. They can also give directions so that you don't waste time or get lost along the way.

It is also a good idea to glance through the local Yellow Pages when you first arrive at your vacation destination, to see what veterinary clinics are located near you. And remember that even though the nearest clinic in your area may not be open at the moment, many do offer 24-hour "on call" emergency service. When you phone them after normal business hours, their answering service takes down your name, the nature of the emergency, and the phone number you're calling from. That information is immediately relayed to the doctor who is "on call" at the time. He or she then calls you back with either instructions for handling the situation yourself or directions for meeting the doctor at the clinic.

Some of the emergency clinics listed on the following pages are open 24 hours/day, every day of the year. Several more are "after-hours" clinics, meaning that they are open all night on weeknights, and around the clock on weekends and holidays.

Idaho's Emergency Veterinary Clinics

Boise (westside)
Pet ER: 24-Hour Emergency & Critical Care
3435 N Cole Road (at Mountain View Animal Hospital)
208-375-0251
> 24 hours/day, 365 days

Garden City
Animal Emergency & Referral Center
5019 Sawyer Ave
208-376-4510
> 24 hours/day, 365 days/year
> Veterinarian on site at all times

Oregon's Emergency Veterinary Clinics

Bend
Cascade Animal Emergency Center
425 NE Windy Knoll (at Eastside Animal Hospital)
541-318-5829
> Monday–Thursday 6 PM–8 AM
> Friday 5 PM–Monday 8 AM
> Holidays 24 hours/day

Corvallis
Animal Emergency & Critical Care Center
650 SW Third St (at Willamette Veterinary Clinic)
541-753-5750
> 24 hours/day, 365 days/year
> Veterinarian on site at all times

Portland–Northwest
Dove Lewis Emergency Animal Hospital-Downtown
1984 NW Pettygrove St
503-228-7281
> 24 hours/day, 365 days/year
> Veterinarian on premises at all times

Portland–Southeast
Dove Lewis Emergency Animal Hospital-Eastside
10564 SE Washington
503-262-7194

Monday–Thursday 6 PM–8 AM
Friday 6 PM–Monday 8 AM
Holidays 24 hours/day

Portland–Southeast
Southeast Portland Animal Hospital
13830 SE Stark St
503-255-8139

24 hours/day, 365 days/year
Veterinarian on premises at all times

Salem
Salem Veterinary Emergency Clinic
3215 Market St NE
503-588-8082

Monday–Thursday 5 PM–8 AM
Friday 5 PM–Monday 8 AM
Holidays 24 hours/day

Springfield
Emergency Veterinary Hospital
103 "Q" St
541-746-0112

Monday–Thursday 6 PM–8 AM
Friday 6 PM–Monday 8 AM
Holidays 24 hours/day

Tualatin
Emergency Veterinary Clinic of Tualatin
19314 SW Mohave Ct (10 miles southwest of Portland)
503-691-7922

Weeknights 6 PM–8 AM
Weekends & Holidays 24 hours/day

Washington's Emergency Veterinary Clinics

Auburn

After Hours Animal Emergency Clinic
718 Auburn Way N (at Auburn Veterinary Hospital)
253–939–6272

> Monday–Friday 6 PM–8 AM
> Saturday Noon–Monday 8 AM
> Holidays 24 hours/day

Bellevue

After Hours Animal Emergency Service
2975 156th Ave SE (at Aerowood Animal Hospital)
425–641–8414

> Monday–Friday 6 PM–8 AM
> Saturday Noon–Monday 8 AM
> Holidays 24 hours/day
> Veterinarian on site during all hours of operation

Bellingham

Animal Emergency Care
317 Telegraph Rd
360-758-2200

> Monday–Friday 5:30 PM–8 AM
> Saturday Noon–Monday 8 AM
> Holidays 24 hours/day
> Veterinarian on site during all hours of operation

Bellingham

Animal Medical Center of Bellingham
720 Virginia St
360-734-0720

> www.amcbel.com
> 24 hours/day, 365 days/year

Everett

Animal Emergency Clinic of Everett
3625 Rucker Ave (at Diamond Veterinary Hospital)
425–258–4466

> Monday–Friday 6 PM–8 AM
> Saturday 1 PM–Monday 8 AM
> Holidays 24 hours/day

Issaquah
Alpine Animal Hospital
888 NW Sammamish Rd
425–392–8888
>24 hours/day, 365 days/year

Kennewick
Mid–Columbia Pet Emergency Service
8802 W Gage Blvd (at Meadow Hills Veterinary Center)
509–783–7391
>Monday–Thursday 5:30 PM–8 AM
>Friday 5:30 PM–Monday 8 AM
>Holidays 24 hours/day

Kirkland
Animal Emergency Service East
636 7th Ave
425-827-8727
>Monday–Friday 6 PM–8 AM
>Saturday Noon–Monday 8 AM
>Holidays 24 hours/day
>Please call ahead

Lacey
Olympia Pet Emergency Clinic
4242 Pacific Ave
360-455-5155
>Monday–Friday 6 PM–7:30 AM
>Saturday Noon–Monday 7:30 AM
>Holidays 24 hours/day
>Please call ahead

Lynnwood
Agape Pet Emergency Service
16418 7th Pl W (at Seattle Veterinary Hospital)
425-741-2688
>Monday–Friday 6 PM–8 AM
>Saturday Noon–Monday 8 AM
>Holidays 24 hours/day

Washington's Emergency Veterinary Clinics (continued)

Lynnwood
Animal Emergency and Referral Center
19511 24th Ave W
425–697-6106
>   24 hours/day, 365 days/year

Poulsbo
Animal Emergency & Trauma Center
19689 7th Ave NE #325 (Poulsbo Village Shopping Center)
206–842–6684, additional local numbers: 360-895–8050, 360-697–7771
>   Monday–Friday 5 PM–8:30 AM
>   Saturday Noon–Monday 8:30 AM
>   Holidays 24 hours/day

Poulsbo
Animal Hospital of Central Kitsap
10310 Central Valley Rd NE (near Silverdale and Bremerton)
360–692–6162
>   24 hours/day, 365 days/year
>   Veterinarian on premises at all times

Seattle
Emerald City Emergency Clinic
4102 Stone Way North (at Animal Surgical Clinic of Seattle)
206–634–9000
>   Monday–Friday 6 PM–8 AM
>   Saturday Noon–Monday 8 AM
>   Holidays 24 hours/day

Snohomish
Small Animal Emergency Clinic of PSCVM
11308 92nd SE (at Pilchuck Veterinary Hospital)
360–563–5300
>   Monday–Friday 6 PM–8 AM
>   Saturday Noon–Monday 8 AM
>   Holidays 24 hours/day

Spokane
Pet Emergency Clinic
21 East Mission Ave (at Veterinary Referral Service)
509–326–6670

Monday–Friday 5 PM–8 AM
Friday 5 PM–Monday 8 AM
Holidays 24 hours/day

Tacoma
Pierce County Animal Emergency Clinic
5608 S Durango
253–474–0791

24 hours/day, 365 days/year
Veterinarian on site at all times

Tacoma
Puget Sound Pet Pavilion
2505 S 80th St
253–983–1000

www.petpavilion.com
24 hours/day, 365 days/year

Vancouver
Clark County Emergency Veterinary Service, Inc.
6818 E 4th Plain Blvd Ste C
360–694–3007

Monday–Thursday 5:30 PM–8 AM
Friday 5:30 PM–Monday 8 AM
Holiays 24 hours/day

Vancouver
St. Francis 24 Hour Animal Hospital
12010 NE 65th St
360–253-5446

24 hours/day, 365 days/year

7: If Your Dog Gets Lost

You've heard the saying "carry an umbrella and you'll never get rained on." Hopefully, being prepared in case your dog gets lost will work the same way for you. And it will remind you of how important—and easy— it is to *prevent* losing him.

The basic prevention measures (you've seen all these before) include:

- Make sure your dog is *always* wearing his collar with ID tags attached. (See page 14 for information on proper travel tags.)

- Put his leash on *before* letting him out of your car or motel room— and hold onto the other end!

- *Never* leave him alone and unrestrained—he should be in his travel crate or at least inside your car, with adequate ventilation and shade.

That said, if by some chance you and your dog do get separated, don't panic. Your cool-headed actions now, plus a few advance preparations that you wisely made before leaving home, will maximize your chances of finding him as quickly as possible.

Preparing a Lost Dog poster

Your first advance effort should be in creating a master lost-and-found poster, complete with your dog's photo and detailed description. Feel free to copy the fill-in-the-blanks poster on the following page and use it to create your own poster.

First, write a brief description of your pet. Include his name, age, breed, sex (and if neutered or spayed), coat and eye color, height (at top of head or ears when standing), weight, and any special characteristics, such as a crooked ear or a limp.

LOST DOG

Name:

Breed:

Age:

Sex:

Ht: Wt:

Eye color:

Coat color & length:

Collar & ID tags:

Distinctive markings or behaviors:

Last seen at:

Owners:

Home address:

Home Phone (call COLLECT!):

Staying locally at:

Dates at this location:

Local phone:

(Call collect or leave message and we will reimburse you.)

REWARD!

Attach photo here

Second, dig out a close-up photo of your pet, or take a new one right now. It should clearly show his color, any distinctive markings and his relative size. Photograph your dog standing beside a person or a car, for example. Have copies made of this photo that you can attach to multiple copies of your completed lost-and-found poster when needed.

List your home phone number—for leaving a message—and if possible, include another number that will be answered by a live person who can receive and relay messages for you. Of course, if you have a mobile phone that works in the area you're visiting, list that number as well. Leave blank spaces for the name, address and phone number of your motel. You'll add that information if and when you actually use the poster.

Store the master poster and photos with your dog's other travel papers, which I recommend keeping in a plastic bag inside his first aid kit. Also tuck in a broad tipped marking pen.

Searching for your lost dog

As soon as you realize your pet is missing, begin searching the immediate area in an ever-widening spiral pattern. Keep calling your dog's name—if he's within the sound of your voice, *he'll* find *you.* Try to enlist the aid of other people in your search, and offer them a reward.

It's important to search *on foot,* not in your car, for several reasons. First, if you're walking, your dog is more likely to catch your scent and come back to you. Second, if you're cruising along in the car, your pet may hear you call him, but by the time he runs to that location, you could be a block—or a mile—away, missing him altogether.

When to call for reinforcements

If you've already searched for an hour or two without finding your dog, it's time to move on to public announcements. Phone the police or county sheriff's office, the dog pound or humane society, and the local veterinary clinics to see if anyone has already found your pet. Remember to tell everyone if your dog has been implanted with an identification microchip (see page 15 for more information).

Leave your local phone number with everyone you speak to, and check with them periodically. Also ask if any local radio or TV station broadcasts lost pet announcements as a public service. (Then after you find your dog, be sure to let everyone know, so they don't continue to put out the alert!)

Putting up Lost Dog posters

If you've already checked with local authorities and still haven't found your dog, you'll need to start posting "Lost Dog" notices around the area. That way, when someone does find him, they'll know how to contact you.

Get out your master poster and fill in the name, address, and phone number of the place where you're staying. Then take it to the local quick print shop, or any other store with a copy machine available, and run off multiple copies for posting around town. Use white or light-colored background sheets—neon yellow is especially eye-catching from a distance and still light enough to be readable.

Attach a photo of your pet to each poster copy. If you only have one original photo, you could attach it to your master poster and then make multiple *color copies* at the quick print shop.

Beginning at the location where your dog was last seen and spiraling outward again, start putting up your posters wherever people congregate:

- On bulletin boards in parks, shopping malls, or in front of convenience stores

- In store windows—be sure to ask for permission first!

- At bus stops or parking lot entrances

- On street signs or light posts, especially where cars are likely to be stopping or moving slowly

- Near schools or churches

Since the motel's phone number appears on each poster, notify them of your situation right away. If you can, have a family member stay by the phone in your room in case that all-important "Found Dog" call comes in while you're out searching. If not, see if the folks at the front desk can take messages for you.

Continue to check back periodically at the place where your dog disappeared, in case he returns there. By the end of the day, he will be increasingly hungry, thirsty, and anxious about being separated from you. Leave a handful of his food there, along with something that has your scent on it, such as a dirty sock. Finding this sign of you during the night may encourage him to stay there until you come back in the morning.

Stay in the local area as long as possible. Even if you don't find your pet right away, he may turn up after another day or two. A local person may take him in overnight, then deliver him to the dog pound or animal shelter the next day.

When you do have to leave town, be sure to leave your home phone number with everyone—motel management, police, dog pound, local veterinarians—along with instructions to call you "COLLECT."

And of course, check your home phone often for messages. If your dog is picked up and traced by his license number, rabies tag number or microchip ID, you'll be contacted at your *permanent* address and phone number, so keep that line of communication open as well.

May your dog never be lost

Your pet is a beloved member of your family, and I sincerely hope you never lose him. Please, spend just a minute or two reviewing the simple steps at the beginning of this chapter to prevent losing him in the first place.

Happy travels to you and your dog from Ginger—and Spike too!

8: Dog-Friendly Lodgings in Idaho—Oregon—Washington

This directory chapter is alphabetized by state, then city, then business name. If you know the business name but not the city, you can look it up in the cross-referenced Business Name Index, beginning on page 349. All the hotels, motels, B & Bs and vacation rentals listed here have reported that they allow dogs in some—but not necessarily all—of their facilities. Always call ahead to specifically reserve a dog-friendly unit. Also, please be aware that some of these establishments accept dogs "by manager's approval only," meaning they reserve the right to refuse overly dirty, large or out-of-control pets.

The room rates shown represent a range from off-season lows to peak-season highs. In many cases, these are "before tax" prices; all are accurate as of the time each location was contacted prior to the publication of this book. However, as in most industries, prices shown are subject to change without notice, so be sure to ask about the current rates when you call for reservations.

If you don't see one of your favorite establishments listed here, don't despair. Some managers said that although they do accept dogs, they didn't wish to "go public" with that information, and therefore requested not to be included in this directory. However, most of them also said that they will continue to accept customers who've stayed there with their well-behaved dogs in the past.

Abbreviations used in this directory

In order to include as much useful information as possible in each listing, some abbreviations became necessary. A shaded "legend" appears at the top of each even-numbered page to explain all the abbreviations.

C = coffee
CB = continental
  breakfast
F = refrigerator
FB = full breakfast
	IP = indoor pool
	K = full kitchen
	(k) = kitchenette
	L = lounge
	M = microwave
		OP = outdoor pool
		R = restaurant
		S = sauna or
		  steamroom
		T = spa or hot tub

	(# of units) & rates	food & drink	pool, sauna & hot tub

Idaho's Dog-Friendly Lodgings

Albion, Idaho

Mountain Manor B & B 208-673-6642 249 W North St (Hwy 77) nonsmoking rooms, laundry, lawns, short drive to "City of Rocks" national monument and hiking trails	(3) $40– $130	FB K

American Falls, Idaho

American Motel 208-226-7271 2814 Pocatello Ave nonsmoking rooms, laundry, designated dogwalking area, close to marina with beach and picnic area	(10) $32– $45	(k)
Hillview Motel 208-226-5151, 800-538-5112 2799 Lakeview Rd $25 refundable pet deposit nonsmoking rooms, laundry, lawn for walking dogs	(34) $25– $59	C M/F

Arco, Idaho

Arco Inn 208-527-3100 540 W Grand Ave $10 refundable pet deposit nonsmoking rooms, public park and fairgrounds across street	(12) $38– $50	M
D-K Motel 208-527-8282, 800-231-0134 316 S Front St www.atcnet.net/~dkmotel laundry, lawn and open walking area	(25) $30– $65	C M/F
Grand Avenue Motel 208-527-3468 101 W Grand Ave area behind building for walking dogs, ½ block to small park, 4 blocks to larger park	(16) $30– $50	M/F
Lazy A Motel 208-527-8263 318 W Grand Ave nonsmoking rooms, lawn, ¼ mile to public park	(20) $25– $50	C K M/F

Lost River Motel 405 Hiway Dr nonsmoking rooms, public park across street	208-527-3600 pets $5/day	(14) $26– $65	C K

Ashton, Idaho

Log Cabin Motel 1001 Main St RV sites, cabins, yard for walking dogs	208-652-3956	(11) $37– $60	
Rankin Motel 120 S Hwy 20 limited area for walking dogs, last town before the mountains, 65 miles to Yellowstone Park	208-652-3570 www.rankinmotel.com	(6) $37– $60	
Super 8 Motel 1370 Hwy 20 nonsmoking rooms, laundry, open area, 2 blocks to public park with swimming pool	208-652-3699 $20 refundable pet deposit	(38) $54– $73	CB M
White Pines Travel Plaza 1370 N Hwy 20 nonsmoking rooms, laundry, open field for walking dogs, 4 blocks to public park	208-652-3699	(38) $42– $68	CB

Athol, Idaho

Athol Motel 5950 E Hwy 54 nonsmoking rooms, large lawn, 3 blocks to park	208-683-3476 pets $5/stay	(9) $30– $62	M/F
Kelso Lake Resort 1450 Kelso Lake Rd www.kelsolakeresort.com nonsmoking rooms, cabins and travel trailers with fully equipped kitchens and half-baths, all linens provided, RV sites, beach, lakefront lawn, state park	208-683-2297	(5) $45– $75	K

Avery, Idaho

Swiftwater Motel & RV Park 645 Old River Rd RV sites, forested riverfront area to walk dogs	208-245-2845 pets $10/day	(5) $30– $60	C (k) M/F

C = coffee IP = indoor pool OP = outdoor pool CB = continental K = full kitchen R = restaurant breakfast (k) = kitchenette S = sauna or F = refrigerator L = lounge steamroom FB = full breakfast M = microwave T = spa or hot tub	(# of units) & rates	food & drink	pool, sauna & hot tub

Bayview, Idaho

MacDonald's Hudson Bay Resort 208-683-2211 17425 E Hudson Bay Rd pets $15/stay laundry, RV sites, lake swimming, lots of area for walking dogs	(10) $75– $115	K	
Scenic Bay Marina, Motel & RV Park 208-683-2243 102 Scenic Bay Dr pets $25/stay nonsmoking rooms, grassy dogwalking area, next to Farragut Park, ½ mile to sandy beach	(4) $74	K R	

Bellevue, Idaho

High Country Motel & Cabins 208-788-2050 765 S Main St pets $10/stay, 800-692-2050 nonsmoking motel rooms and cabins, open fields for walking dogs, greenbelt paved path	(20) $55– $85	C (k) M/F	

Blackfoot, Idaho

Best Western Inn 208-785-4144 750 Jensen Grove Dr 800-937-8376 www.bestwestern.com, nonsmoking rooms, exercise room, "beach" and walking paths across street	(60) $40– $85	CB M/F	IP T
Sunset Motel 208-785-0161 1019 W Bridge St pets $5/day nonsmoking rooms, 1 to 2 pets only, grassy area for walking dogs, 2 blocks to public park	(10) $35– $45	(k)	
Y Motel 208-785-1550 1375 S Broadway St lawn, short drive to public park	(20) $39– $50	K	

Bliss, Idaho

Amber Inn 208-352-4441 17286 Hwy 30 (Exit 141) pets $4/day nonsmoking rooms, lawn and open walking area	(30) $29– $47	C	

Y-Inn Motel 208-352-4451 260 W US Hwy 30 pets $3/day nonsmoking rooms, lawn, 1 block to public park	(19) $28– $42			

Boise, Idaho

Ameri Suites Hotel 208-375-1200 925 N Milwaukee St 800-833-1516 www.amerisuites.com, 1 dog under 25 lbs only, nonsmoking rooms, landscaped walking area	(128) $99– $109	CB M/F	IP
Best Western Safari Motor Inn 208-344-6556 1070 Grove St www.bwsafari.com, 800-541-6556 dogs allowed in smoking rooms only, fitness room, landscaped walking area, 2 blocks to trails and park	(103) $59– $135	CB F	OP S T
Bestrest Inn 208-322-4404, 800-733-1418 8002 Overland Rd pets $10/stay nonsmoking rooms, laundry, open field	(87) $39– $59	CB	OP T
Boise Centre Guestlodge 208-342-9351 1314 Grove St nonsmoking rooms, 3 blocks to greenbelt walking trail	(48) $45– $60	CB M/F	OP
Bond Street Motel 208-322-4407, 800-545-5345 1680 N Phillippi St # 126 pets $5/day www.bondmotel.com, nonsmoking rooms, studios and 1-bdrm apartments, laundry, lawn, ½ mile to paved greenway walking path	(57) $44– $50	C K	
Cabana Inn 208-343-6000 1600 Main St $25 refundable pet deposit nonsmoking rooms, grassy area behind building, near several public parks and riverside walking path	(50) $39– $90	CB K M/F	
Chinden Motor Inn 208-322-8668 4678 Chinden Blvd $50 refundable pet deposit dogs allowed with manager's approval only, weekly rates available, grassy area	(16) $38	(k)	
Doubletree Riverside Hotel 208-343-1871 2900 Chinden Blvd pets $15/stay www.doubletree.com, dogs under 50 lbs only, nonsmoking rooms, laundry, fitness center, 48-mile paved greenbelt walking path along river	(304) $69– $395	C F R/L	OP S T

C = coffee
CB = continental
    breakfast
F = refrigerator
FB = full breakfast
	IP = indoor pool
	K = full kitchen
	(k) = kitchenette
	L = lounge
	M = microwave
		OP = outdoor pool
		R = restaurant
		S = sauna or
		    steamroom
		T = spa or hot tub
			(# of units)
			& rates
				food
				& drink
					pool, sauna
					& hot tub

Boise, Idaho (continued)

Econo Lodge 208-344-4030, 800-553-2666 4060 Fairview Ave each pet $10/day www.econolodge.com, nonsmoking rooms, lawn, 1 block to greenbelt walking trail	(52) $40– $60	CB M/F	
Hampton Inn 208-331-5600, 800-426-7866 3270 Shoshone St www.hamptoninn-suites.com nonsmoking rooms, open field, 2 blocks to park	(64) $69– $89	CB M/F	IP T
Holiday Inn-Boise Airport 208-344-8365 3300 Vista Ave pets $10/day, 800-465-4329 www.holiday-inn.com, nonsmoking rooms, laundry, workout room, grassy area, 3 miles to greenbelt path	(265) $65– $95	C M/F R/L	IP T
Holiday Motel 208-376-4631 5416 Fairview Ave pets $3/day open lawn area for walking dogs	(18) $27– $45	M/F	
Motel 6 208-344-3506, 800-466-8356 2323 Airport Way www.motel6.com, nonsmoking rooms, laundry, open field for walking dogs	(90) $40– $52	C M/F	OP
Owyhee Plaza Hotel 208-343-4611, 800-233-4611 1109 Main St $25 refundable pet deposit www.owyheeplaza.com, 10 blocks to public park and greenbelt trail, nonsmoking rooms	(100) $61– $132	C F R/L	OP
Pioneer Condominiums at Bogus Basin Ski Resort 1770 W State St #394 208-332-5200, 800-367-4397 www.pioneercondos.com, dogs allowed by advance reservation and in summer only, nonsmoking rooms, laundry, linens provided, game room, walking trails	(39) $100– $130	K	S T
Residence Inn 208-344-1200, 800-331-3131 1401 S Lusk Pl pets $10/day www.residenceinn.com, nonsmoking units, laundry, workout room, small grassy area, large public park	(104) $59– $165	FB K	OP T

Robin's Nest B & B 208-336-9551 2389 W Boise Ave www.robinsnestinn.com completely nonsmoking, discounts on midweek stays, laundry, 2 blocks to greenbelt walking trail	(4) $65– $95	FB	
Rodeway Inn 208-376-2700, 800-727-5002 1115 N Curtis Rd pets $10/stay nonsmoking rooms, designated pet walking area, ¾ mile to greenbelt trail	(98) $60– $90	CB R/L	IP T
Sawtooth Lodge 208-344-2437 130 N Haines St 208-259-3331 www.sawtoothlodge.com pets $25/stay 100 miles north of Boise near Sawtooth Wilderness Area, cabins have fully equipped kitchens, bed linens provided, hot springs pool at lodge, handicap access, walking trails	(11) $45– $90	K R	
Seven K Motel 208-343-7723 3633 Chinden Blvd pets $5/day nonsmoking rooms, fitness center, dogwalking area behind bldg, 1½ miles to fairgrounds, 2 miles to park	(23) $35– $65	CB K	OP
Shilo Inn-Boise Airport 208-343-7662, 800-222-2244 4111 Broadway Ave each pet $10/day www.shiloinns.com, nonsmoking rooms, laundry, pet beds and treats, lawn, open field, 2 miles to public park and riverside greenbelt walking trail	(125) $60– $106	CB M/F	OP S T
Shilo Inn-Boise Riverside 208-344-3521 3031 Main St 800-222-2244 www.shiloinns.com each pet $10/day nonsmoking rooms, laundry, fitness center, pet beds and treats, close to greenbelt walking trail	(112) $59– $89	CB M/F	IP S T
Sulphur Creek Ranch 208-377-1188 7151 Emerald St scranch@mindspring.com nonsmoking rooms, fishing excursions, horseback riding, hunting, dogs can play off-leash, walking trails	(10) $65– $135	R	
Super 8 Motel 208-344-8871, 800-800-8000 2773 Elder St $25 refundable pet deposit www.super8.com, nonsmoking rooms, laundry, open field for walking dogs, short drive to public parks	(108) $40– $80	CB M/F	IP

		# of units) & rates	food & drink	pool, sauna & hot tub
C = coffee CB = continental breakfast F = refrigerator FB = full breakfast	IP = indoor pool K = full kitchen (k) = kitchenette L = lounge M = microwave	OP = outdoor pool R = restaurant S = sauna or steamroom T = spa or hot tub		

Boise, Idaho (continued)

WestCoast Parkcenter Suites 208-342-1044 424 E Parkcenter Blvd 800-325-4000 www.westcoasthotels.com/parkcenter, nonsmoking, laundry, ¼ mile to waterfront park and walking trails		(238) $59–$129	CB M/F	OP T
West River Inn 208-338-1155 3525 Chinden Blvd dogs allowed at manager's discretion only, nonsmoking rooms, open walking area, close to fairgrounds and public park		(21) $28–$55	(k)	
WestCoast Downtown 208-344-7691 1800 Fairview Ave pets $15/stay nonsmoking rooms, small lawn, ¾ mile to greenbelt paved walking path		(182) $95–$144	F R/L	OP T

Bonners Ferry, Idaho

Bear Creek Lodge 208-267-7268 5952 Main St pets $6/day, refundable deposit nonsmoking rooms, grassy walking area		(12) $49–$85	C M/F R/L	T
Best Western Kootenai River Inn 208-267-8511 7160 Plaza St 800-346-5668 nonsmoking rooms, dogs under 15 lbs only, casino, workout room, riverside lawn area for walking dogs		(65) $73–$110	R	OP T
Bonners Ferry Resort 208-267-2422 6438 Main St RV sites, open field and walking trails		(24) $25–$55	K R/L	OP T
Feast Creek Lodge 208-267-8649 195 County Rd 34 advance reservations highly recommended, laundry, completely nonsmoking, meadow and woods for walking dogs		(14) $65	C R/L	
Kootenai Valley Motel 208-267-7567, 888-292-0490 6409 S Main St pets $10/day nonsmoking rooms, large grassy field to walk dogs		(22) $35–$105	C	T

Town & Country Motel & RV Park 208-267-7915 Hwy 95 S pets $5/day nonsmoking rooms, RV sites, lawn and open areas, 5 miles to hiking trails	(12) $35– $75	CB K	IP T

Buhl, Idaho

Oregon Trail Motel 208-543-8814 510 Broadway Ave S small dogs only, nonsmoking rooms, grassy area and quiet street for walking dogs 6 blocks to park, 7 miles to Miracle Hot Springs	(17) $34– $49		

Burley, Idaho

Best Western Burley Inn 208-678-3501 800 N Overland Ave 800-599-1849 www.bestwestern.com $20 refundable pet deposit nonsmoking rooms, laundry, dogs up to 30 lbs only, lawn and open areas for walking dogs	(126) $58– $75	C R/L	OP T
Budget Motel 208-678-2200, 800-635-4952 900 Overland Ave nonsmoking rooms, laundry, open grassy area for walking dogs	(139) $39– $69	C R/L	OP T
East Park Motel 208-678-2241 507 E Main St open field for walking dogs, next to public park	(12) $23– $46	F	
Lampliter Motel 208-678-0031 304 E Main St pets $5/stay nonsmoking rooms, laundry, 1 block to public park	(17) $25– $55	C M/F	
Starlite Motel 208-878-7766 500 Overland Ave nonsmoking rooms, vacant lot for walking dogs	(9) $25– $45	C M/F	

Calder, Idaho

St Joe Lodge & Resort 208-245-3462 St Joe Rd pets $5/day RV sites, riverfront location, great flyfishing, walking trails	(6) $45– $65	(k) R/L	

C = coffee IP = indoor pool OP = outdoor pool CB = continental K = full kitchen R = restaurant breakfast (k) = kitchenette S = sauna or F = refrigerator L = lounge steamroom FB = full breakfast M = microwave T = spa or hot tub	# of units) & rates	food & drink	pool, sauna & hot tub

Caldwell, Idaho

Best Western Inn 208-454-7225 908 Specht Ave 888-454-3522 www.bestwestern.com $50 refundable pet deposit nonsmoking rooms, laundry, 24 hour pool and spa, large vacant lot to walk dogs, short drive to parks	(69) $69– $139	CB M/F R	IP T
I-84 Motor Inn 208-459-1536 505 Hannibal St nonsmoking rooms, lawn, 2 blocks to public park	(26) $36– $43	(k)	
La Quinta Inn & Suites 208-454-2222 901 Specht Ave 800-531-5900 www.laquinta.com $20 refundable pet deposit nonsmoking rooms, in-room spa, 24 hour pool, laundry, lawn area for walking dogs	(65) $49– $120	CB K	IP T
Sundowner Motel 208-459-1585, 800-454-9487 1002 Arthur St each pet $10/day nonsmoking rooms, open walking area, close to public park	(66) $43– $53	CB M/F	OP

Cambridge, Idaho

Frontier Motel & RV Park 208-257-3851 Hwy 95 nonsmoking rooms, laundry, RV sites, lawn, walking trail along old railroad line	(16) $32– $36	C M/F	
Hunter's Inn B & B 208-257-3325 10 S Superior St completely nonsmoking, fields for walking dogs, ½ block to 83-mile walking trail on old railroad line	(13) $35– $65	FB (k)	

Carey, Idaho

Carey Motel 208-823-4312 20487 N Main St RV sites, lawn, 2 blocks to public park	(5) $35– $55		

Cascade, Idaho

Bears Knight Inn 208-382-4370 403 N Main St pets $5/day www.bearsknightinn.com, nonsmoking rooms, grassy area, 2 blocks to lakefront parks	(7) $45– $65	C F	
Cougar Mountain Lodge 208-382-4464 9738 Hwy 55 pets $5/day lodge rooms sleep up to 4, completely nonsmoking, small field and riverside walking area	(7) $55	R	
Mountain View Motel 208-382-4238, 800-265-7666 762 S Main each pet $5/day nonsmoking rooms, workout room, large yard, patio and BBQ, near public park, 1 mile to Lake Cascade	(26) $40– $65	C (k) M/F	
Pinewood Lodge Motel & RV Park 208-382-4948 900 S Main St 866-382-4941 www.thepinewoodlodge.com each pet $5/day nonsmoking rooms, laundry, dogs allowed at owner's discretion only, RV sites, open area for walking dogs, ball parks and paved riverside walking path	(10) $45– $65	C M/F	

Challis, Idaho

Benjamin's at Garden Creek Inn . 208-879-5021 842 North Ave www.gonorthwest.com/Idaho/ central/Challis/benjamins-garden.htm, nonsmoking homes, linens and breakfast supplies provided, laundry, fenced yards, grills, close to public park	(5) $75– $180	C	
Challis Motor Lodge 208-879-2251 State Hwy 93 & Main St each pet $3/day nonsmoking rooms, lawn, 3 blocks to public park	(19) $36– $54	R/L	
Darling Creek B & B 208-879-5222 Darling Creek Rd dogs allowed by owner approval and advance reservation only, nonsmoking rooms, laundry, 40 acres and BLM land for walking dogs	(4) $39– $65	FB K	
Holiday Lodge Motel 208-879-2259, 866-879-2259 Hwy 93 North mtlinda@custertel.net, nonsmoking rooms, laundry, open field and city park for walking dogs, horse corrals, French and Dutch spoken	(10) $39– $55	C M/F	

C = coffee IP = indoor pool OP = outdoor pool CB = continental K = full kitchen R = restaurant breakfast (k) = kitchenette S = sauna or F = refrigerator L = lounge steamroom FB = full breakfast M = microwave T = spa or hot tub	(# of units) & rates	food & drink	pool, sauna & hot tub

Challis, Idaho (continued)

Northgate Inn 208-879-2490 Box 1665 Hwy 93 each pet $4/day nonsmoking rooms, guest kitchen, horse corral, open field and lawn for walking dogs, close to Salmon River, 7 miles to Challis Hot Springs	(57) $37– $55	C K	
Rainbow's End B & B 208-879-5999 7 Mile Hwy 93 N www.rainbowsendbb.com completely nonsmoking, laundry, kennel facility, on 12½ riverside acres, 7 miles to Challis Hot Springs	(4) $138– $375	FB	
Village Inn 208-879-2239 Hwy 93 each pet $3/day nonsmoking rooms, vacant lot for walking dogs, 6 blocks to public park	(54) $38– $64	(k) R	T

Clark Fork, Idaho

Clark Fork Lodge 208-266-1716 421 E 4th Ave pets $10/stay nonsmoking rooms, laundry, designated pet area	(15) $45– $79	C (k)	T
Diamond T Guest Ranch 208-266-0490 5361 River Rd Cabin #7 pets $10/day tvwagoner@juno.com, cabins sleep up to 5, linens provided, working horse ranch so dogs must be on leash, lots of walking area	(7) $55– $70	(k)	
River Delta Resort 208-266-1335 60190 Hwy 200 cabins with kitchens, linens provided, laundry, RV sites, lots of walking area	(6) $50– $80	K	

Coeur d'Alene, Idaho

| Bates Motel   208-667-1411
2018 E Sherman Ave   pets $5/day
large yard, ¼ mile to lakefront | (12)
$30–
$45 | M/F | |

Lodging	Phone / Pets	Rooms / Price		
Bennett Bay Inn 7904 E Coeur d'Alene Lake Dr in-room spa, 3½ miles out of town, Centennial trail	208-664-6168, 800-368-8609 pets $5/day	(20) $55– $150	C K	T
Best Western Coeur d'Alene Inn 414 W Appleway Ave pets $10/stay, 800-251-7829 www.cdainn.com, nonsmoking rooms, laundry, small grassy area for walking dogs, bike trail	208-765-3200	(122) $59– $139	C M/F R/L	IP T
Budget Saver Motel 1519 E Sherman Ave each pet $5/day nonsmoking rooms, laundry, open lot for walking, 2 blocks to Centennial trail, 4 blocks to public beach	208-667-9505	(45) $22– $60	C	
Coeur d'Alene KOA Resort 10588 E Wolf Lodge Bay Rd www.koa.com, sleeping cabins with outdoor cooking grill and picnic table, close to public bathhouses, laundry, RV sites, designated pet rest area	208-664-4471 800-562-2609	(19) $45– $63	R	OP T
Coeur d'Alene Resort 115 S 2nd St each pet $50/day www.cdaresort.com	208-765-4000, 800-688-5253	(337) $90– $429		
Cricket-on-the-Hearth B & B 1521 E Lakeside Ave dogs allowed by advance reservation only, completely nonsmoking, grassy area, 1 mile to Centennial trail and lakeside trail	208-664-6926	(5) $55– $85	FB F	T
Days Inn 2200 Northwest Blvd www.daysinn.com $25 refundable pet deposit nonsmoking rooms, exercise room, 24 hour hot tub and spa, small lawn, Centennial trail across street	208-667-8668 800-329-7466	(62) $47– $107	CB F	S T
El Rancho Motel 1915 E Sherman Ave www.geocities.com/elranchomotelcda pets $5/day nonsmoking rooms, lawn, 2 blocks to Centennial walking trail	208-664-8794 800-359-9791	(14) $35– $60	C (k)	
Garden Motel 1808 Northwest Blvd nonsmoking rooms, laundry, open walking area, ¼ mile to Centennial trail, ¾ mile to public park	208-664-2743	(23) $45– $100	K	IP T

C = coffee IP = indoor pool OP = outdoor pool CB = continental K = full kitchen R = restaurant breakfast (k) = kitchenette S = sauna or F = refrigerator L = lounge steamroom FB = full breakfast M = microwave T = spa or hot tub	(# of units) & rates	food & drink	pool, sauna & hot tub

Coeur d'Alene, Idaho (continued)

Holiday Motel 208-765-6760, 866-880-6760 219 Coeur d'Alene Lake Dr pets $15/stay small dogs only, recreation area, Centennial trail	(9) $30– $75	K M/F	
La Quinta Inn & Suites 208-765-5500, 800-531-5900 280 W Appleway Ave www.hotels-west.com nonsmoking rooms, laundry, exercise room, lawn, 2 miles to lakefront public park	(51) $50– $150	CB K	IP S
La Quinta Inn & Suites 208-667-6777, 800-531-5900 2209 E Sherman Ave www.laquinta.com, laundry, nonsmoking rooms, lawn, near lakefront public park	(62) $59– $159	CB K	IP T
Motel 6 208-664-6600, 800-466-8356 416 W Appleway Ave nonsmoking rooms, laundry, lawn, 1 mile to Centennial trail and lakefront parks	(109) $35– $71	C M/F	OP
Resort Property Management 208-667-7402 1801 Lincoln Way #7 $100 refundable pet deposit www.resortpropertiesidaho.com, laundry, weekly rentals only, lake cabins to executive homes	(40) $850– $3000	K	T
Rodeway Inn Pines Resort 208-664-8244 1422 Northwest Blvd 800-651-2510 www.rodewayinncda.com, nonsmoking rooms, laundry, large lawn, ½ mile to lakefront public park	(65) $49– $89	CB	IP T
Roosevelt Inn B & B 208-765-5200, 800-290-3358 105 E Wallace Ave pets $25/stay www.therooseveltinn.com, rooms and 2-bdrm suites, 24 hour sauna, completely nonsmoking, open field for walking dogs, chocolate bonbons and dog treats	(15) $79– $249	FB	S T
Shilo Inn 208-664-2300, 800-222-2244 702 W Appleway Ave each pet $10/stay www.shiloinns.com, nonsmoking rooms, laundry, pet beds and treats, fitness center, lawn, 1 block to walking trail, 2 blocks to Centennial trail	(139) $92– $129	CB K M/F	IP S T

Super 8 Motel 208-765-8880, 800-800-8000 505 W Appleway Ave $20 refundable pet deposit nonsmoking rooms, grassy area, 1 mile to park	(95) $33– $100	C M/F	

Coolin, Idaho

Cavanaugh Bay Marina 208-443-2095 4024 Cavanaugh Bay pets $10/stay www.cavanaughbayresort.com, lakefront swimming area, boat rentals, air strip, grassy area, walking trails	(3) $79– $150	(k) R/L	
Inn at Priest Lake Resort 208-443-4066 5310 Dickensheet Rd pets $10/stay www.innatpriestlake.com, nonsmoking rooms, RV sites, 10 acres in national forest, 1½ blocks to lake	(24) $69– $150	K R/L	OP T

Cottonwood, Idaho

Dog Bark Park 208-962-DOGS Hwy 95-"At The Dog" pets $12/day nonsmoking cottage sleeps 4 INSIDE 3-story beagle sculpture created by a chainsaw carving studio that specializes in "canine art," 4 blocks to public park	(1) $75– $95	CB M/F	
Mariel's B & B 208-962-5161 3½ miles east of Ferdinand on Meadowcreek Rd nonsmoking, private baths, country walking area	(7) $45– $55	FB	

Council, Idaho

Starlite Motel 208-253-4868 102 N Dartmouth St 5 blocks to public park, ¼ mile to walking path on old railroad bed	(12) $35– $52		

Dixie, Idaho

Silver Spur Outfitters & Lodge B & B 208-842-2417 10 Main St www.silverspurlodge.com well-behaved dogs only, completely nonsmoking, shared bath, forest service land for walking dogs	(6) $60	FB	
Southern Star Inn 208-842-2730 Forest Road 222-D www.southernstarinn.com completely nonsmoking, woods and trails for walking dogs, tent spaces and equipment available	(4) $45– $110	C K R	T

C = coffee IP = indoor pool OP = outdoor pool CB = continental K = full kitchen R = restaurant breakfast (k) = kitchenette S = sauna or F = refrigerator L = lounge steamroom FB = full breakfast M = microwave T = spa or hot tub	# of units) & rates	food & drink	pool, sauna & hot tub

Donnelly, Idaho

| Long Valley Motel   208-325-8545
161 S Main
nonsmoking rooms, 1 block to public park | (8)
$38–
$50 | K | |

Driggs, Idaho

Best Western Teton West 208-354-2363 476 N Main Driggs www.bestwestern.com nonsmoking rooms, next to walking trail	(36) $50– $90	CB M/F	IP T
Grand Valley Lodging 208-354-8890 189 N Main St Suite 116 800-746-5518 www.grandvalleylodging.com pets $50/stay nonsmoking studios to 5-bdrm vacation homes and condos, laundry, yards, walking trails	(12) $130– $475	K	T
Locanda Di Fiori (The Inn of Flowers) 208-456-0909 www.rpgwebs.com/locanda, B&B, dogs allowed by advance approval only, completely nonsmoking, private baths-decks-entrances, on 20 acres	(2) $95	FB	T
Pines Motel-Guest Haus 208-354-2774 105 S Main St 800-354-2778 johnnans@tetonvalley.net pets $5/day full breakfast for $10 extra, large yard to walk dogs	(8) $35– $80	C M/F	T
Teton Valley Property Management 208-354-8881 55 N Main St 888-354-8881 www.tetonvalleyidaho.com, private homes, laundry, all linens provided, most properties have yards, close to national forests and hiking trails	(56) $125– $275	K	T

Dubois, Idaho

| Cross Roads Motel   208-374-5258
391 S Reynolds St
open field for walking dogs | (10)
$28–
$40 | | |

Kilgore General Store & Cabins 208-778-5334 26 miles east of Dubois 100 year old rustic cabins, some with kitchens and baths, RV sites, open field	(8) $26– $35	K

Eden, Idaho

Amber Inn Motel 208-825-5200 1132 E 1000 S pets $5/day 1 to 2 dogs only, open walking area behind building	(25) $30– $55	M/F

Elk City, Idaho

Blackwood Manor English Style B & B 208-842-2591 501 Elk Creek Rd www.blackwoodmanor.com completely nonsmoking, laundry, decorated as an English medieval pub on 56 acres, short drive to wilderness areas, $10 discount if you bring your dog!	(2) $75– $125	FB M
Elk City Hotel 208-842-2452 289 Main St www.elkcityhotel.com nonsmoking rooms, dogs allowed with manager's approval only, national forest and walking trails, 25 miles to Red River Hot Springs	(15) $32– $52	C K R
Prospector Lodge & Cabins 208-842-2597 129 Main St www.camasnet.com/~cabins cabins and lodge units, open walking area at lodge, dogs allowed off-leash at cabins (5 miles out of town)	(12) $30– $55	K
Red River Corrals & Cabins Guest Ranch HC 1 Box 18 208-842-2228 fully equipped log cabins sleep 8, no electricity but propane lights-refrigerator-stove, linens provided, horse corrals, open end of May thru Thanksgiving	(3) $55– $115	
Red River Hot Springs 208-842-2587 Elk City www.redriverhotsprings.com 5 rustic sleeping cabins, 4 modern log homes with jacuzzi tubs sleep 12, woods and walking trails	(9) $45– $200	R K	OP T
Sable Trail Ranch 208-842-2672 HC 1 Box 21 Red River Rd sabletrail@valint.net cabin with fully equipped kitchen and bath sleeps 11, bunkhouse sleeps 8, horse accommodations, camp sites, walking trails, 1 mile to Red River Hot Springs	(2) $60– $115	K

C = coffee
CB = continental
    breakfast
F = refrigerator
FB = full breakfast
	IP = indoor pool
	K = full kitchen
	(k) = kitchenette
	L = lounge
	M = microwave
		OP = outdoor pool
		R = restaurant
		S = sauna or
		    steamroom
		T = spa or hot tub
			(# of units)
			& rates
				food
				& drink
					pool, sauna
					& hot tub

### Emmett, Idaho					
Holiday Motel 208-365-4479 1111 S Washington Ave nonsmoking rooms, laundry, lawn area to walk dogs			(20) $32– $47		
### Featherville, Idaho					
Featherville Saloon & Motel 208-653-2310 4437 N Pine-Featherville Rd dogs allowed with advance approval only, nonsmoking rooms, woods and walking trails			(10) $54	C R/L	
### Fruitland, Idaho					
Elm Hollow B & B 208-452-6491 4900 Hwy 95 completely nonsmoking 1-bdrm cottage sleeps 4, laundry, open field to walk dogs			(1) $50– $60	FB K	
### Garden Valley, Idaho					
Garden Valley Motel 208-462-2911 1111 Banks Lowman Rd pets $5/day www.gardenvalleymotel.com, nonsmoking rooms, lawn, walking trails, discount pass for nearby natural hot springs swimming pool at Terrace Lakes			(12) $55– $85	C K	
Silver Creek Plunge 208-739-3400 2345 Silver Creek Rd each pet $5/stay www.silvercreekplunge.com, cabins sleep 4 to 8, hot geothermal swimming pool, forest walking trails			(16) $42– $78		OP
Valley Inn Motel 208-462-2305 486 Middlefork Rd pets $10/stay cabins, linens provided, open field, walking trails			(3) $45– $65	M/F	
Walk on the Wild Side B & B 208-462-8047 69 River Ranch Rd www.wildsidebb.com in-room spa, on 75 riverside acres, lots of walking trails and wildlife			(4) $75– $125	FB	T

Gibbonsville, Idaho

Lost Trail Inn 208-865-2222 3099 Hwy 93 N nonsmoking cabin sleeps 4, linens provided, national forest land, walking trails	(1) $45– $65	C K R
Ramey's Broken Arrow Resort 208-865-2241 3230 Hwy 93 N www.thebrokenarrow.com open May–October, rustic 1926 log cabins sleep up to 7, shared baths in community showerhouse, private bath in 1 cabin, swimming pond, restaurant open Thursday–Sunday	(9) $35– $100	CB R

Glenns Ferry, Idaho

Hanson's Cafe & Motel 208-366-9983 201 E 1st Ave close to public parks	(6) $35– $50	C R
Redford Motel 208-366-2421 601 W 1st Ave redfordmotel@hotmail.com nonsmoking rooms, public parks within 2 blocks	(11) $29– $62	K F

Gooding, Idaho

Historic Gooding Hotel B & B 208-934-4374 112 Main St 888-260-6656 http://goodingbb.hypermart.net pets $10/day dogs allowed by advance reservation and owner's approval only, completely nonsmoking, short walk to several parks	(10) $65– $80	FB M/F
Lincoln Inn 208-934-4423 413 Main St nonsmoking rooms, 2 public parks within 6 blocks	(10) $34– $51	R/L
Skyler Inn 208-934-4055 1331 Main St 800-979-4055 nonsmoking rooms, public park across street	(16) $29– $35	K

Grand View, Idaho

Hillside Motor Inn 208-834-2097 650 Roosevelt open areas for walking dogs, ¼ mile to dirt road along canal bank	(8) $30– $40	M/F

C = coffee IP = indoor pool OP = outdoor pool CB = continental K = full kitchen R = restaurant breakfast (k) = kitchenette S = sauna or F = refrigerator L = lounge steamroom FB = full breakfast M = microwave T = spa or hot tub	(# of units) & rates	food & drink	pool, sauna & hot tub

Grangeville, Idaho

Elkhorn Lodge 208-983-1500 822 SW 1st St nonsmoking rooms, lawn, short drive to public park	(20) $30– $46	C K	
Essential Evergreen B & B 208-983-2587 605 E Main St 888-832-5251 http://evergreenbnb.tripod.com pets $10/day nonsmoking rooms, cabin with kitchen sleeps 6, laundry, RV sites, ½ block to 2 city parks, 20 minute drive to 200 miles of groomed forest service trails	(3) $39– $79	FB K	
Monty's Motel 208-983-2500 700 W Main St 877-983-1463 nonsmoking rooms	(23) $35– $60	CB M/F	OP
Super 8 Motel 208-983-1002, 800-800-8000 801 SW 1st St $10 refundable pet deposit www.super8motel-grangeville.com, nonsmoking rooms, laundry, exercise room, lawn for walking dogs, 2 public parks within ½ mile	(39) $43– $120	CB M/F	IP T

Hagerman, Idaho

Billingsley Creek Lodge & Retreat 208-837-4822 17940 Hwy 30 completely nonsmoking, 6 rooms and 2 cabins with bath and private hot tubs, 1 with kitchenette, dogs by advance approval only	(8) $50– $85	C (k)	T
Hagerman RV Village 208-837-4906 18049 Hwy 30 N 1 to 2 room cabins sleep 4, laundry, RV sites, large lawns, 1 block to public park, 1 mile to Fossil Beds Monument Museum and trail	(4) $25– $29	M/F	S
Hagerman Valley Inn 208-837-6196 State & Hagerman pets $5/stay www.northrim.net/hvimotel, nonsmoking rooms, large grassy walking area, 3 blocks to public park	(16) $37– $50		

Hailey, Idaho

Airport Inn 820 4th Ave S www.taylorhotelgroup.com, dogs allowed in smoking rooms only, laundry, delivered express continental breakfast and dog treats, walking trail	208-788-2477 pets $5/day	(29) $78– $95	CB (k) M/F	T
Hitchrack Motel 619 S Main St nonsmoking rooms, 5 blocks to park and trail	208-788-1696 pets $5/day	(8) $50– $70	C K M/F	
Wood River Inn 603 N Main St www.woodriverinn.com laundry, dogs allowed in smoking rooms only, 3 blocks to public park	208-578-0600 877-542-0600 pets $25/stay	(56) $79– $125	CB K M/F	IP T

Hammett, Idaho

Oasis Ranch Motel 7341 Old Hwy 30 40 acres for walking dogs	208-366-2025	(6) $19– $30	M/F

Hayden Lake, Idaho

Affordable Inn 9986 N Government Way nonsmoking rooms, large lawn for walking dogs	208-772-4414	(19) $40– $80	C M/F
Coeur d'Alene Sonrise Campground & RV Park 5196 E Garwood Rd 208-772-4557, 877-799-2267 cabin sleeps 4, dogs MUST be kept off beds, RV sites, lots of area for walking dogs		(1) $30	C

Heyburn, Idaho

Super 8 Motel 336 S 600 W www.super8.com, nonsmoking rooms, laundry, up to 2 pets per room, open field for walking dogs	208-678-7000 pets $5/day	(68) $47– $60	C	IP T
Tops Motel 310 S 310 W open area for walking dogs	208-436-4724 pets $4/day	(16) $28– $44	M/F	

				# of units) & rates	food & drink	pool, sauna & hot tub
C = coffee	IP = indoor pool	OP = outdoor pool			
CB = continental	K = full kitchen	R = restaurant			
breakfast	(k) = kitchenette	S = sauna or			
F = refrigerator	L = lounge	steamroom			
FB = full breakfast	M = microwave	T = spa or hot tub			

Homedale, Idaho

Sunnydale Motel 208-337-3302	(8)	C	
2 E Colorado Ave walking area behind building,	$35–	(k)	
hunting dogs must be in kept in travel kennels when	$50	M/F	
in the motel room, close to fairgrounds			

Hope, Idaho

Idaho Country Resort 208-264-5505	(6)	K	
141 Idaho Country Rd 800-307-3050	$75–		
www.idahocountryresorts.com, cabins sleep 4 to 10,	$150		
laundry, all linens provided, hot tub with 1 cabin,			
RV sites, open area for walking dogs			

Red Fir Resort 208-264-5287	(12)	K	
1147 Red Fir Rd www.redfirresort.com	$90–		
completely nonsmoking, laundry, linens provided,	$160		
private decks and BBQs, lots of walking area			

Horseshoe Bend, Idaho

Old Riverside Depot B & B Inn 208-793-2330	(3)	CB	T
105 Riverside Dr www.depotinn.com	$49–	K	
dogs allowed by advance approval only, completely	$79		
nonsmoking, lawn and riverfront walking area, less			
than 1 mile to public park			

Idaho City, Idaho

Idaho City Hotel 208-392-4290	(5)	C	
215 Montgomery St idahocityhotel@aol.com	$39–		
½ acre lawn and creek, 2 blocks to walking trail and	$49		
public park			

Prospector Motel 208-392-4290	(6)	K	
507 Main St idahocityhotel@aol.com	$39–		
laundry, large lawn and creek, public park, 2 blocks	$49		
to walking trail			

Idaho Falls, Idaho

Lodging	Phone	Rate		
Best Western Cottontree Inn 900 Lindsay Blvd www.bestwestern.com, dogs under 30 lbs only, laundry, riverside walking path	208-523-6000 800-662-6886	(94) $59– $99	CB	IP T
Best Western Driftwood Inn 575 River Parkway www.bwdriftwood.com pets $10/stay nonsmoking rooms, laundry, lawn areas, close to riverside greenbelt walking path	208-523-2242 800-939-2242	(74) $52– $115	CB M/F	OP
Comfort Inn 208-528-2804, 800-228-5150 195 S Colorado Ave pets $5/stay nonsmoking rooms, 1 mile to greenbelt walking path		(56) $50– $90	CB M/F	IP T
Idaho Falls KOA 208-523-3362, 800-562-7644 1440 Lindsay Blvd sleeping cabins sleep 4, private grills, picnic tables, laundry, BBQ dinners and pancake breakfasts Memorial Day–Labor Day, designated pet rest area and lots of walking areas		(10) $32– $42		T
Littletree Inn 208-523-5993, 800-529-5993 888 N Holmes pets $15/stay nonsmoking rooms, lawn walking area, laundry, beer and wine 5-7 PM, DJ and "Comedy Nights"		(92) $49– $79	CB M/F L	IP T
Motel 6 208-522-0112, 800-466-8356 1448 W Broadway St nonsmoking rooms, laundry, lawn, ½ mile to riverside trails		(79) $38– $60	C	OP
Motel West 208-522-1112, 800-582-1063 1540 W Broadway St $10 refundable pet deposit nonsmoking rooms, laundry, small grassy area for walking dogs, short drive to public park		(80) $38– $75	C R	IP T
National 9 Inn 208-523-6260, 800-852-7829 850 Lindsay Blvd pets $5/stay nonsmoking rooms, laundry, lawn, greenbelt trail		(130) $56– $160	FB R/L	OP T
Shilo Inn 208-523-0088, 800-222-2244 780 Lindsay Blvd pets $10/stay www.shiloinns.com, nonsmoking rooms, laundry, 24 hour pool, next to greenbelt walking path		(161) $79– $179	CB M/F R/L	IP S T

C = coffee IP = indoor pool OP = outdoor pool CB = continental K = full kitchen R = restaurant breakfast (k) = kitchenette S = sauna or F = refrigerator L = lounge steamroom FB = full breakfast M = microwave T = spa or hot tub	(# of units) & rates	food & drink	pool, sauna & hot tub

Idaho Falls, Idaho (continued)

Stardust Inn 208-523-8900 700 Lindsay Blvd pets $15/day nonsmoking rooms, laundry, next to paved greenbelt walking path	(248) $45– $99	CB M/F	IP OP S T
Towne Lodge 208-523-2960 255 E St nonsmoking rooms, laundry, lots of open area for walking dogs	(40) $44– $60	C	
WestCoast Hotel 208-523-8000, 800-325-4000 475 River Pkwy www.westcoasthotels.com nonsmoking rooms, laundry, 24 hour year-round hot tub, riverside greenbelt walking path across street	(138) $49– $109	FB M/F R	OP T
Yellowstone Motel 208-529-9738 2460 S Yellowstone Hwy pets $5/day laundry, grassy area for walking dogs, ¼ mile to park	(20) $32– $36	C M/F	

Island Park, Idaho

A-Bar Motel & Supper Club 208-558-7358 3433 Hwy 20 800-286-7358 riverside access, open field, national forest	(8) $44– $100	R/L	
Anglers Lodge & Riverfront Restaurant 3431 Hwy 20 208-558-9555 nonsmoking, in-room spa, laundry, forest service land and walking trails	(15) $80– $160	(k) M/F R/L	T
Aspen Lodge 208-558-7407 4187 Aspen Ridge Ln cabins with kitchens sleep 6, RV sites, linens provided, open area, forest, trails	(5) $39– $69	K R	T
Elk Creek Ranch 208-558-7404 3906 Loop Rd cabins sleep up to 8, rates include 3 meals/day in main dining hall, forest service land for walking dogs	(8) $85	C R	

Jacobs Island Park Ranch 208-558-0900 3561 Old Kilgore Rd 800-230-9530 www.jacobsranch.com, cabins sleep 4 to 18, private BBQ grills and hot tubs, laundry, walking trails	(14) $80– $350	K (k)	
Pond's Lodge 208-558-7221, 888-731-5153 3757 N Hwy 20 pets $5/day laundry, RV sites, grocery store, bike path, forest	(22) $40– $160	K R/L	
Staley Springs Lodge 208-558-7471 5397 Henry's Lake Rd pets $5/day www.staleysprings.com, 1 to 4-bdrm cabins sleep 8, fully equipped kitchens, linens provided, hiking trails	(19) $64– $199	K R/L	

Jerome, Idaho

Best Western Sawtooth Inn 208-324-9200 2653 S Lincoln Ave $50 refundable pet deposit www.bestwestern.com, nonsmoking rooms, laundry, 24 hour pool, grassy area, 2 miles to trail and park	(57) $54– $89	CB M/F	IP T
Crest Motel 208-324-2670 2545 S Lincoln Ave each pet $4/day nonsmoking rooms, lawn, open field	(18) $43– $60	M/F	
Days Inn 208-324-6400, 800-329-7466 1200 S Centennial Spur pets $10/stay www.daysinn.com, nonsmoking rooms, laundry, lawn for walking dogs, 3 miles to public park	(72) $49– $60	CB M/F	T
Holiday Motel 208-324-2361 401 W Main St pets $5/stay nonsmoking rooms, open area for walking dogs, 4 blocks to fairgrounds	(23) $25– $60	(k) M/F	

Kamiah, Idaho

Clearwater 12 Motel 208-935-2671, 800-935-2671 108 E 3rd St (Hwy 12) pets $5/stay nonsmoking rooms, public park across street	(29) $45– $60	CB (k)	
Lewis-Clark Resort 208-935-2556, 800-264-9943 Hwy 12 (3 miles past Kamiah Bridge) cabins sleep 6, www.lewisclarkresort.com, nonsmoking rooms, RV sites, laundry, woods and trails, linens provided	(43) $44– $102	C F R	OP T

C = coffee IP = indoor pool OP = outdoor pool CB = continental K = full kitchen R = restaurant breakfast (k) = kitchenette S = sauna or F = refrigerator L = lounge steamroom FB = full breakfast M = microwave T = spa or hot tub	(# of units) & rates	food & drink	pool, sauna & hot tub

Kamiah, Idaho (continued)

Sundown Motel 208-935-2568 1004 3rd St (Hwy 12) library in office, laundry, small walking area, ½ mile to large riverside public park and swimming pool, great year-round fishing	(14) $24– $39	M/F	

Kellogg, Idaho

Motel 51 208-786-9441 206 E Cameron Ave small dogs only, alley behind bldg for walking dogs, bike path, 4 blocks to park	(11) $25– $35	C M	
Silverhorn Motor Inn & Restaurant 208-783-1151 699 W Cameron Ave 800-437-643 www.silverhornmotorinn.com, nonsmoking rooms, laundry, RV sites, large yard, 1 block to walking trail	(40) $57– $75	R	T
Super 8 Motel 208-783-1234, 800-785-5443 601 Bunker Ave $20 refundable pet deposit www.super8.com, nonsmoking rooms, laundry, open field and walking trail, 2 blocks to park	(61) $39– $100	CB M/F	IP T
Trail Motel 208-784-1161 206 W Cameron Ave ½ block to walking trails	(24) $31– $43	F	

Ketchum, Idaho

Best Western Tyrolean Lodge 208-726-5336 260 Cottonwood St pets $10/day, 800-333-7912 www.bestwestern.com/tyrolean lodge, nonsmoking rooms, laundry, designated pet area, bike trail	(56) $70– $135	CB M/F L	OP S T
Clarion Inn of Sun Valley 208-726-5900 600 N Main St 800-262-4833 www.resortswest.net/clarion.htm pets $10/day nonsmoking rooms and condos, open walking area, 4 blocks to public park	(58) $74– $250	CB M/F R	IP T

Private Idaho 208-726-7722, 800-249-7722 500 S Main St Suite 103 www.privateidaho.net fully equipped nonsmoking homes and condos, laundry, near parks and walking paths	(30) $140– $1000	K	
Ski View Lodge 208-726-3441 409 S Main St pets $5/day nonsmoking rooms, open walking area, 1½ blocks to walking trails	(8) $50– $80	K	
Smiley Creek Lodge 208-774-3547 37 miles north of Sun Valley dogs allowed in sleeping cabins and Indian teepees, bathhouse, RV sites, trails, www.ruralnetwork.net/~smileyck	(5) $35– $45	R	
Sun Valley Area Reservations 208-726-3660 460 Sun Valley Rd # 202 800-635-1076 1-bdrm 2-bath nonsmoking condo sleeps 5, all linens provided, laundry, 1 block to lake, great walking area	(1) $250– $350	K	OP
Sun Valley Properties 208-788-3005, 800-622-7721 591 3rd Ave S Suite 8 www.kslsunvalley.com nonsmoking fully equipped vacation homes, laundry, most have yards, all are close to walking paths	(3) $275– $500		

Kooskia, Idaho

Looking Glass Inn B & B 208-926-0855 Rt 12 Milepost 84.5 pets $10/day, 888-926-0855 www.lookingglassinn.com, dogs allowed by advance approval only, completely nonsmoking, dining room and living room just for guests, private entrances, 10 acres for walking dogs, including off-leash areas	(7) $75– $85	FB K	
Mount Stuart Inn 208-926-0166 106 S Main St nonsmoking rooms, riverside walking area	(9) $25– $50	K	
Ryan's Wilderness Inn 208-926-4706 Hwy 12 Milepost 97.5 lawn for walking dogs, short drive to hiking trails	(6) $45– $50	R	
Three Rivers Motel 208-926-4430, 888-926-4430 HC 75 Box 61 www.threeriversresort.com motel rooms, cabins sleep 8, open walking areas	(30) $35– $105	CB (k) R	OP T

C = coffee IP = indoor pool OP = outdoor pool CB = continental K = full kitchen R = restaurant breakfast (k) = kitchenette S = sauna or F = refrigerator L = lounge steamroom FB = full breakfast M = microwave T = spa or hot tub	(# of units) & rates	food & drink	pool, sauna & hot tub

Lava Hot Springs, Idaho

Dempsey Creek Lodge 208-776-5000 162 E Main St pets $5/stay dogs allowed with advance approval only, 2 blocks to pools and public park, www.lavahotsprings.org/ DempseyCreek/dempseylodge.html	(2) $35– $50	K	
Lava Hot Springs Inn 208-776-5830, 800-527-5830 94 E Portneuf Ave pets $10/stay www.lavahotspringsinn.com, nonsmoking rooms, in-room spa, lawn and trails for walking dogs, hot mineral pools, 2 blocks to public park	(24) $69– $189	FB M/F	T
Lava Ranch Inn Motel & RV Camping 208-776-9917 9611 E Hwy 30 motel rooms, RV sites, 6½ acres for walking dogs	(10) $30– $60	C M/F	
Oregon Trail Lodge 208-776-5920 196 E Main St pets $5/day park-like walking area, 4 blocks to public park	(8) $35– $65	(k)	
R & R Executive Vacation Rentals 208-776-5021 377 W Fife each pet $5/day www.lavahotsprings.org/r&r_rentals/index.html townhouse and 2-bdrm cottage sleep 6 to 8, mineral pools and olympic swimming pool, riverside path	(2) $89– $179	K	
Riverside Inn & Hot Springs 208-776-5504 255 E Portneuf Ave pets $5/day www.riversideinnhotspring.com, historic hotel, completely nonsmoking, "reservable" hot mineral pools, small lawn and riverside trail for walking dogs	(16) $69– $119	CB M/F R/L	

Leadore, Idaho

Leadore Inn 208-768-2237 Leadore open May–December, large fenced yard	(4) $32– $40	(k)	

Lewiston, Idaho

Bel Air Motel 208-798-4444 2018 North-South Hwy open area for walking dogs, public rose garden across street, 1 mile to paved greenway walking path	(10) $20– $28	K	
Comfort Inn 208-798-8090, 800-228-5150 2128 8th Ave pets $10/day www.comfortinn.com, nonsmoking rooms, laundry, in-room spa, lawn, short drive to public park	(52) $45– $119	CB M/F	IP T
El Rancho Motel 208-743-8517 2240 3rd Ave N nonsmoking rooms, laundry, large lawn, playground, public park, baseball field	(24) $30– $38	C K M/F	OP
Evergreen Motel 208-746-5851 2125 3rd Ave N nonsmoking rooms, small area for walking dogs, 1 block to public park	(18) $32– $38	C M/F	
Hillary Motel 208-743-8514 2030 North-South Hwy pets $5/day open field for walking dogs, 2 blocks to public park	(11) $23– $34	K	
Ho Hum Motel 208-743-2978 2015 North-South Hwy pets $3/day nonsmoking rooms, lawn and open area, public park	(12) $28– $50	(k)	
Howard Johnson Express Inn 208-743-9526 1716 Main St, 800-446-4656 pets $15/stay nonsmoking rooms, laundry, 2 blocks to waterfront walking path	(66) $55– $93	CB K	OP T
Inn America 208-746-4600, 800-469-4667 702 21st St www.innamerica.com, nonsmoking rooms, laundry, close to greenway walking path	(61) $44– $79	CB	OP
Italianna Inn-Anna B & B 208-743-4552, 877-550-2662 2728 11th Ave at Sunset Park www.italiannainn.com dogs allowed with advance approval only, laundry, 5-course Tuscan breakfast, completely nonsmoking, mini-olympic outdoor pool, surrounded by park	(4) $69– $168	FB	OP
Red Lion Lewiston 208-799-1000, 800-232-6730 621 21st Ave www.redlionlewiston.com, nonsmoking rooms, laundry, athletic club, 3 blocks to public park	(183) $79– $400	C M/F R/L	IP T

C = coffee
CB = continental
    breakfast
F = refrigerator
FB = full breakfast
	IP = indoor pool
	K = full kitchen
	(k) = kitchenette
	L = lounge
	M = microwave
		OP = outdoor pool
		R = restaurant
		S = sauna or
		    steamroom
		T = spa or hot tub
			(# of units)
			& rates
				food
				& drink
					pool, sauna
					& hot tub

Lewiston, Idaho (continued)

Riverview Inn 208-746-3311, 800-806-7666 1325 Main St nonsmoking rooms, dog kennels available, close to public park		(75) $40– $61	CB M/F L	OP
Sacajawea Select Inn 208-746-1393, 800-333-1393 1824 Main St each pet $2/day laundry, fitness room, small area for walking dogs, ⅓ block to riverfront walking trail		(90) $48– $80	CB F R/L	T
Sportsman Inn 208-743-9424 3001 North-South Hwy pets $5/day nonsmoking rooms, riverside walking area		(46) $30– $69	CB M/F	OP
Super 8 Motel 208-743-8808, 800-800-8000 3120 North-South Hwy pets $5/day nonsmoking rooms, laundry, riverside park and trail		(62) $47– $66	CB M/F	

Lower Stanley, Idaho

Salmon River Cabins & Motel 208-774-2290 Scenic Hwy 75 pets $5–$7/day, 800-972-4627 completely nonsmoking rooms and cabins, riverside walking area, trails and mineral springs pools in area		(16) $65– $105	C (k)	

Lowman, Idaho

Sawtooth Lodge 208-259-3331 Grandjean pets $25/stay www.sawtoothlodge.com, some cabins have sink and wood cookstove, natural hot springs swimming pool open June–August, RV sites, nature walking trail		(11) $45– $90	(k) R	OP

Lowman, Idaho

Sourdough Lodge 208-259-3326 8406 Hwy 21 pets $10/day www.sourdoughlodge.com, nonsmoking rooms and cabins, RV sites, wooded walking area and trails		(9) $45– $90	R	T

Lucile, Idaho

Acres For Kids B & B 208-628-3569 Between Mileposts 210 & 211 1 to 2-bdrm cottages and mobile home, completely nonsmoking, 8 acre organic farm, safe beach, www.acresforkids.com	(4) $59– $89	CB K	
Steelhead Inn 208-628-3045, 800-331-4445 Hwy 95 Milepost 210 www.steelheadinn.com picnic area, river beach, grassy walking area, ¼ mile to large off-leash area and swimming pond	(10) $50– $55	C K M/F	

Mackay, Idaho

Wagon Wheel Motel & RV Park 208-588-3331 809 W Custer pets $5/day dogs allowed in smoking rooms only, playground, laundry, RV sites, short drive to national forest trails	(16) $33– $70	C K M/F	
White Knob Motel & Trailer Park 208-588-2622 4243 Hwy 93 800-314-2622 nonsmoking rooms, laundry, RV sites, open field	(6) $22– $42	C (k) R	OP

Malad City, Idaho

South Canyon Cabins 208-766-4325 10990 Old Hwy 191 log house, 2-bdrm apt, cabins (with and without bathrooms) sleep 4 to 12, 60 acres, swing and trampoline for children, fishing reservoir	(3) $60– $100	K	T
Village Inn Motel 208-766-4761 50 S 300 E nonsmoking rooms, grassy area and residential streets for walking dogs	(30) $44– $60		

McCall, Idaho

Accommodation Services 208-634-7766 1008 N 3rd St each pet $15/day, 800-551-8234 www.accommodationservices.com, cabins, condos, homes, laundry, private hot tubs, walking trails	(165) $85– $850		S T
Bear Creek Lodge 208-634-3551, 888-634-2327 3492 Hwy 55 pets $10/stay www.bearcreeklodge.com, completely nonsmoking rooms and duplex cabins on 65 acres, in-room spa	(13) $120– $175	FB M/F	T

C = coffee	IP = indoor pool	OP = outdoor pool	(# of units) & rates
CB = continental breakfast	K = full kitchen	R = restaurant	food & drink
F = refrigerator	(k) = kitchenette	S = sauna or steamroom	pool, sauna & hot tub
FB = full breakfast	L = lounge M = microwave	T = spa or hot tub	

McCall, Idaho (continued)

Best Western Inn 208-634-6300, 800-937-8376 415 N 3rd St www.bestwestern.com nonsmoking rooms, laundry, next to wooded area for walking dogs	(79) $55– $100	CB M/F	IP T
Brundage Inn & Bungalows 208-634-8573 1005 W Lake St 800-643-2009 www.brundagevacations.com each pet $10/day completely nonsmoking rooms and bungalows sleep up to 12, laundry, lawn and wooded walking areas	(29) $55– $169	C K R	
Fircrest Condominiums 208-634-4528 300 Washington #107 dogs allowed with advance approval only, completely nonsmoking, linens provided, lawn and woods, 4 blocks to lake	(20) $69– $149	K	
Super 8 Motel 208-634-4637, 800-800-8000 303 S 3rd St each pet $6/day dogs allowed by advance reservation only, laundry, nonsmoking rooms, 1 mile to riverside walking area	(60) $52– $122	CB (k)	T
Woodsman Motel 208-634-7671 402 N 3rd St nonsmoking rooms, undeveloped walking area, 10 minute walk to lake	(60) $46– $56	R	

Montpelier, Idaho

Best Western Clover Creek Inn 208-847-1782 243 N 4th St 800-528-1234 www.bestwestern.com each pet $6/day nonsmoking rooms, 1 to 2 dogs only, grassy walking area, 1 block to public park	(65) $48– $122	CB M/F	T
Budget Motel 208-847-1273 240 N 4th St nonsmoking rooms, grassy pet area, next to park	(24) $20– $35	C M/F	

Fisher Inn 208-847-1772 401 Boise St each pet $5/stay nonsmoking rooms, playground and area for walking dogs, 1 block to public park	(10) $30– $50		OP
Montpelier Creek KOA 208-847-0863, 800-562-7576 28501 Hwy 89 N sleeping cabins sleep 4, outdoor BBQ pit and picnic table for each cabin, laundry, designated dog rest area	(2) $31		
Park Motel 208-847-1911 745 Washington St pets $6/stay nonsmoking rooms, lawn area for walking dogs, 1 block to public park	(24) $35– $50	C M/F	

Moscow, Idaho

Best Western Inn 208-882-0550 1516 W Pullman Rd 800-325-8765 www.uinnmoscow.com pets $25/day nonsmoking rooms, 7-mile paved walking trail	(173) $79– $98	CB M/F R/L	IP S T
Hillcrest Motel 208-882-7579 706 N Main St 800-368-6564 hillcrest@moscow.com pets $5/day nonsmoking rooms, laundry, grassy pet walking area, 1 mile to public park	(35) $36– $80	CB M/F	
Mark IV Motor Inn 208-882-7557, 800-833-4240 414 N Main St pets $10/day www.mark4motorinn.com, nonsmoking rooms, lawn	(86) $49– $125	C M/F R/L	IP T
Palouse Inn 208-882-5511 101 Baker St pets $7/day www.palouseinn.com, nonsmoking rooms, laundry, close to open field for walking dogs	(110) $34– $70	CB M/F	OP
Royal Motor Inn 208-882-2581 120 W 6th St each pet $5/day nonsmoking rooms, lots of walking trails	(38) $25– $65	C (k) M/F	S
Super 8 Motel 208-883-1503, 800-800-8000 175 Peterson Dr each pet $5/day 1 to 2 small dogs allowed with manager's approval only, close to walking trail	(60) $40– $71	CB M	IP T

C = coffee IP = indoor pool OP = outdoor pool CB = continental K = full kitchen R = restaurant breakfast (k) = kitchenette S = sauna or F = refrigerator L = lounge steamroom FB = full breakfast M = microwave T = spa or hot tub	(# of units) & rates	food & drink	pool, sauna & hot tub

Mountain Home, Idaho

Foothills Motor Inn 1080 Hwy 20 www.bestwestern.com nonsmoking rooms, laundry, open field to walk dogs	208-587-8477 800-604-8477 pets $5/day	(76) $55– $125	CB OP K T M/F
Hilander Motel & Steak House 615 S 3rd W nonsmoking rooms, open area behind building for walking dogs, short drive to public park	208-587-3311 pets $4/stay	(34) $35– $49	C M/F R
Maple Cove Motel 700 E Hwy 30 nonsmoking rooms, laundry, open field for walking dogs, cafe serves breakfast and lunch	208-587-2202	(10) $25– $35	FB R
Motel Thunderbird 910 Sunset Strip nonsmoking rooms	208-587-7927 pets $5/stay	(27) $28– $65	OP T
Sleep Inn 1180 Hwy 20 www.sleepinn.com nonsmoking rooms	208-587-9743 800-753-3746 pets $5/day	(60) $54– $77	C M/F R/L
Towne Center Motel 410 N 2nd E nonsmoking rooms, grassy area for walking dogs, 2 blocks to public park	208-587-3373 $20 refundable pet deposit	(31) $34– $40	C OP F

Moyie Springs, Idaho

Hemlocks Country Inn Hwy 2 between Bonners Ferry & Montana Stateline completely nonsmoking rooms sleep up to 4, RV sites, seasonal restaurant, on 6 acres, forest trails and dirt roads for walking dogs	208-267-9822 pets $5/stay	(4) $39– $65	C (k) M/F R

Mullan, Idaho

Lookout Motel 201 W River St nonsmoking rooms, bike rentals, open lot and paved walking path across street	208-744-1601 pets $5/day	(16) $20– $45	M/F	T

Murray, Idaho

Murray House 1884 B & B 6325 Prichard Creek Rd childress@nidlink.com dogs allowed with advance approval only, completely nonsmoking, laundry, forest land and trails	208-682-4653	(4) $45– $65	FB

Nampa, Idaho

Desert Inn 208-467-1161, 800-588-5268 115 9th Ave S each pet $10/day nonsmoking rooms, 1 to 3 pets only, open area for walking dogs		(40) $40– $49	CB M/F	OP
Shilo Inn-Nampa Blvd 208-466-8993, 800-222-2244 617 Nampa Blvd each pet $10/day www.shiloinns.com, nonsmoking rooms, laundry, pet beds and treats, 1½ miles to public park		(61) $60– $82	CB M/F	OP S T
Shilo Inn-Nampa Suites 208-465-3250 1401 Shilo Dr 800-222-2244 www.shiloinns.com each pet $10/day nonsmoking rooms, laundry, pet beds and treats, small area behind building for walking dogs, ½ mile to public park		(84) $70– $110	CB K M/F R	IP
Sleep Inn 208-463-6300 1315 Industrial Rd 800-668-0080 www.sleepinn.com/hotel/id003 pets $10/stay nonsmoking rooms, laundry, 24 hour pool, open field for walking dogs, 1 mile to public park		(81) $61– $90	CB	IP T
Super 8 Motel 208-467-2888 624 Nampa Blvd 800-800-8000 www.super8.com each pet $5/day nonsmoking rooms, laundry, grassy areas for walking dogs, ½ mile to public park		(62) $42– $72	CB	

		(# of units) & rates	food & drink	pool, sauna & hot tub
C = coffee	IP = indoor pool OP = outdoor pool			
CB = continental	K = full kitchen R = restaurant			
breakfast	(k) = kitchenette S = sauna or			
F = refrigerator	L = lounge steamroom			
FB = full breakfast	M = microwave T = spa or hot tub			

New Meadows, Idaho

Hartland Inn 208-347-2114, 888-509-7400 211 Norris St (Hwy 95) dogs allowed in smoking rooms only, vacant lot and dirt road for walking dogs, short drive to mountain hiking trails		(22) $44– $125	C K	T
Meadow's Motel 208-347-2175 302 N Norris St (Hwy 95) nonsmoking rooms, laundry, lawn and dirt roads for walking dogs		(16) $35– $55	C M	
Pinehurst Resort Cottages 208-628-3323 5604 Hwy 95 (13 miles south of Riggins) pets $5/day nonsmoking rooms and cottages, riverside lawn, picnic tables, BBQ, lawn chairs		(6) $40– $60	K	

Nordman, Idaho

Elkins Resort on Priest Lake 208-443-2432 404 Elkins Rd www.elkinsresort.com lakefront cabins, trails pets $15/day		(28) $85– $345	K R/L	
Kaniksu RV Resort & Marina 208-443-2609 485 Jim Low Rd pets $5/day 2-bdrm cabins, kitchens and baths, linens provided, laundry, RV sites, fenced area and walking trails		(10) $125	K R	

North Fork, Idaho

100 Acre Wood B & B And Outfitters 208-865-2165 2356 Hwy 93 N www.100acrewoodresort.com dogs allowed by advance reservation only, laundry, nonsmoking rooms, dinners available Thur–Sat, on Lewis & Clark Trail, guided outdoor adventure tours, catch-and-release fishing on private lake		(8) $55– $115	FB	T
North Fork Store, Cafe, Motel & Campground 2046 Hwy 93 N 208-865-2412 laundry, RV sites, store, riverside lawn and woods		(7) $40– $54	R	

Rivers' Fork Inn 208-865-2301 2036 Hwy 93 N www.riversforkinn.com completely nonsmoking, RV sites, boat ramp, forest land trails for walking dogs	(7) $53– $63	C F	

Orofino, Idaho

Helgeson Place Hotel 208-476-5729 125 Johnson Ave 800-404-5729 www.helgesonhotel.com pets $10/day nonsmoking rooms, private hot tub, ½ block to park	(20) $40– $55	CB K	T
Konkolville Motel 208-476-5584 2000 Konkolville Rd 800-616-1964 konkolvillemotel@clearwater.net each pet $5/day nonsmoking rooms, laundry, grassy pet walking areas, fish cleaning station	(40) $36– $65	CB M/F	OP T
Riverside Motel 208-476-5711 10560 Hwy 12 $15 refundable pet deposit nonsmoking rooms, pet walking area behind building, riverside trails, 1½ miles to public park	(14) $26– $39	M/F	

Palisades, Idaho

Palisades RV Park & Cabins 208-483-4485 3802 Swan Valley Hwy cabins sleep 2 to 4, house sleeps 12, riverside walking area, boat dock	(4) $45– $95	K	
Timberwolf Resort 208-483-3581 3781 Swan Valley Hwy sleeping cabins sleep 2, laundry, RV sites, 110 acres for walking dogs	(4) $48		

Pierce, Idaho

Cedar Inn Lodge 208-464-2704, 800-450-0250 412 S Main St each pet $5/day www.minersshanty.com, completely nonsmoking, creekside walking area, trails, 2 blocks to public park	(10) $28– $58	C K R	
Outback Cabins & Breakfast 208-464-2171 211 S Main St pets $5–$10/stay, 800-538-1754 completely nonsmoking cabins and 2-bdrm suites sleep 11, private hot tub in one cabin, RV sites, 4 acres for walking dogs	(9) $35– $140	CB K	T

C = coffee IP = indoor pool OP = outdoor pool CB = continental K = full kitchen R = restaurant breakfast (k) = kitchenette S = sauna or F = refrigerator L = lounge steamroom FB = full breakfast M = microwave T = spa or hot tub	(# of units) & rates	food & drink	pool, sauna & hot tub

Pierce, Idaho (continued)

| Pierce Motel   208-464-2324, 877-464-2324
509 S Main St   nonsmoking rooms, laundry,
RV sites, lawn, trails and woods for walking dogs | (12)
$30–
$40 | C
M | |

Pine, Idaho

| Nester's Mountain Motel   208-653-2210
54 E Nester's Dr
nonsmoking rooms, lawn and wooded walking area | (12)
$45–
$65 | C | T |

Pinehurst, Idaho

| Kellogg/Silver Valley KOA Resort   208-682-3612
801 N Division   www.koa.com, 800-562-0799
$25 refundable pet deposit, cottage sleeps 4, sleeping
cabins sleep 6, RV sites, dogwalking area, public park | (6)
$46–
$125 | K | OP
T |

Plummer, Idaho

| Hiway Motel   208-686-1310
301 10th St   nonsmoking rooms, lawn
area for walking dogs, 2 blocks to public park | (16)
$35–
$60 | C
M/F | |

Pocatello, Idaho

Best Western Cottontree Inn 208-237-7650 1415 Bench Rd www.cottontree.net, 800-662-6886 nonsmoking rooms, exercise room, pet walking area	(149) $70– $96	CB K L	IP T
Comfort Inn 208-237-8155, 800-424-6423 1333 Bench Rd pets $7/day www.comfortinn.com, nonsmoking rooms, area for walking dogs, ½ mile to fairgrounds and public park	(52) $60– $90	CB M/F	IP T
Econo Lodge-University 208-233-0451, 800-377-0451 835 S 5th Ave $20 refundable pet deposit www.econolodge.com/hotel/id029, nonsmoking rooms, laundry, exercise room, grassy pet areas	(54) $46– $60	CB M/F R	

Holiday Inn 1399 Bench Rd nonsmoking rooms, laundry, workout room, lawn, 5 miles to greenway trail and large public park	208-237-1400, 800-200-8944 www.holidayinnpocatello.com	(190) $65– $79	M/F R/L	IP S T
Motel 6 291 W Burnside Ave nonsmoking rooms, large field for walking dogs	208-237-7880, 800-466-8356 www.motel6.com	(108) $35– $50	C	OP
Ramada Inn 133 W Burnside Ave nonsmoking rooms, laundry, exercise room, 24 hour sauna and hot tub, open field, 2 miles to public park	208-237-0020, 866-237-0020 www.ramada.com	(116) $49– $69	CB M/F R/L	OP S T
Super 8 Motel 1330 Bench Rd www.super8.com, nonsmoking rooms, in-room spa, laundry, area behind building for walking dogs	208-234-0888, 866-378-7378 pets $2–$10/day	(80) $48– $79	CB M/F	T
Thunderbird Motel 1415 S 5th Ave www.thunderbirdmotelid.com nonsmoking rooms, laundry, grassy pet areas	208-232-6330 888-978-2473 pets $5/day	(45) $35– $50	C M/F	OP
WestCoast Pocatello Hotel 1555 Pocatello Creek Rd www.westcoasthotels.com, nonsmoking rooms, large grassy areas and walking trail, 1 mile to public park	208-233-2200 800-527-5202	(150) $62– $89	C M/F R/L	IP S T

Post Falls, Idaho

Holiday Inn Express 3105 E Seltice Way www.6c.com, nonsmoking rooms, exercise room, evening cookies and milk, Centennial walking trail	208-773-8900, 800-465-4329 pets $10/stay	(47) $59– $99	CB M/F	
Howard Johnson Express Inn 3647 W 5th Ave www.hojo.com, nonsmoking rooms, laundry, open walking area, 6 blocks to Centennial trail	208-773-4541 pets $5/day, 800-829-3124	(99) $49– $149	CB M/F	IP T
Sleep Inn 100 N Pleasant View Rd www.choicehotels.com, nonsmoking rooms, laundry, large lawn, Centennial paved walking trail	208-777-9394, 800-851-3178 pets $15/stay	(84) $50– $100	CB	IP T

C = coffee
CB = continental
   breakfast
F = refrigerator
FB = full breakfast
	IP = indoor pool
	K = full kitchen
	(k) = kitchenette
	L = lounge
	M = microwave
		OP = outdoor pool
		R = restaurant
		S = sauna or
		   steamroom
		T = spa or hot tub
			(# of units)
			& rates
				food
				& drink
					pool, sauna
					& hot tub

Post Falls, Idaho (continued)

WestCoast Templin's Resort 414 E 1st Ave www.westcoasthotels.com dogs allowed in smoking rooms only, laundry, RV sites, riverside walking area, 3 blocks to walking trail	208-773-1611 800-283-6754 each pet $5/day		(167) $64– $112	C R/L	IP S T

Powell, Idaho

Lochsa Lodge Hwy 12 Milepost 162 motel rooms and cabins, forest trails and forest service roads, 10 miles to Jerry Johnson Hot Springs	208-942-3405 each pet $5/stay		(14) $38– $80	R/L	

Preston, Idaho

Deer Cliff Inn 2016 N Deer Cliff Rd open May–October, dogs allowed with advance approval only, next to river and national forest	208-852-0643		(4) $32– $35	K R	
Plaza Motel 427 S Hwy 91 laundry, lawn and field for walking dogs	208-852-2020 nonsmoking rooms,		(31) $45– $55		
Riverdale Resort 3696 N 1600 E well-behaved dogs allowed with advance approval only, completely nonsmoking rooms, 2 hot pools, breakfast basket provided, RV sites, country setting	208-852-0266 www.riverdaleresort.com		(8) $70– $80	CB	OP T

Priest Lake, Idaho

Hill's Resort 4777 W Lake Shore Rd pets $25 per day off-season, $150/week in summer, (1 week minimum in summer), motel/condo rooms and cabins sleep 4 to 12, laundry, walking trails	208-443-2551 www.hillsresort.com		(63) $80– $305	K R/L	

Priest River, Idaho

Eagle's Nest Motel 208-448-2000, 800-881-6378 1007 Albeni Hwy (Hwy 2) pets $10/stay nonsmoking rooms, in-room spa, riverside walking area, 2 blocks to public park	(30) $45– $90	C M/F	T
River Country Motel & RV Park 208-448-1100 3566 Hwy 2 866-779-1100 $25 refundable pet deposit, dogs allowed with manager's approval only, lawn and open walking area near Pend Oreille River, RV sites	(6) $25– $95	(k)	
Selkirk Motel 208-448-1112, 800-395-8335 1201 Albeni Hwy pets $6/day dogs allowed with manager's approval only, wooded walking areas near river, designated dog rest area	(6) $45– $60	C (k)	

Rexburg, Idaho

Best Western Cottontree Inn 208-356-4646 450 W 4th S 800-662-6886 www.bestwestern.com, nonsmoking rooms, laundry, fitness room, grassy lot, trail to small nature park	(99) $56– $110	C M/F R	IP T
C J's Motel 208-356-5477 357 W 4th S $10 refundable pet deposit nonsmoking rooms, small grassy area for walking dogs, 2 blocks to public park	(10) $40– $45	C M/F	
Comfort Inn 208-359-1311, 800-228-5150 1565 W Main St nonsmoking rooms, grassy walking area, ¼ mile to public park	(52) $49– $84	CB M/F	IP T
Days Inn 208-356-9222, 800-329-7466 271 S 2nd W www.daysinn.com nonsmoking rooms, ½ block to public park	(42) $37– $66	CB M/F	OP
Sheffield House B & B 208-356-4182 5362 S Hwy 191 pets $5/day sheffieldbb@msn.com, cabin sleeps up to 4, small well-behaved dogs allowed with advance approval only, RV sites, rustic working ranch with 200 acres for walking dogs	(2) $60– $95	FB	

C = coffee IP = indoor pool OP = outdoor pool CB = continental K = full kitchen R = restaurant breakfast (k) = kitchenette S = sauna or F = refrigerator L = lounge steamroom FB = full breakfast M = microwave T = spa or hot tub	# of units & rates	food & drink	pool, sauna & hot tub

Rigby, Idaho

South Fork Inn 208-745-8700	(39)	C
425 Farnsworth Way pets $5/day	$40–	M/F
nonsmoking rooms, bike path around the lake	$70	

Riggins, Idaho

Best Western Salmon Rapids Lodge 208-628-2743	(55)	CB	IP
1010 S Main 877-957-2743	$73–	(k)	T
www.salmonrapids.com pets $15/day	$103	F	
nonsmoking rooms, pet beds provided, laundry, vacant lot and riverside trail for walking dogs, ¼ mile to public park			

Bruce Motel 208-628-3005, 888-517-3005	(20)	C	
515 N Main St www.bruce_motel.tripod.com/	$30–	(k)	
thebrucemotel/index/html, nonsmoking rooms, laundry, lawn area, city park across street	$90	F	

Riggins Motel 208-628-3456	(19)	C	T
615 S Main (Hwy 95) 800-669-6739	$34–	K	
rooms and fully equipped 2-bdrm home, lawn and riverside area for walking dogs	$110		

River View Motel 208-628-3041, 888-256-2322	(16)	C	
704 N Main St www.riverviewmotel.com	$42–	M	
nonsmoking rooms, riverside walking area, 2 blocks to public park, 1 mile to walking trails	$69		

Salmon River Motel 208-628-3025, 888-628-3025	(16)	(k)	
1203 S Hwy 95 www.salmonrivermotel.com	$38–		
nonsmoking rooms, laundry, open walking area	$68		

Rogerson, Idaho

Desert Hot Springs 208-857-2233	(8)	R	OP
Rogerson sleeping cabins sleep up to 6,	$25–		T
RV sites, hot springs pools	$45		

Rupert, Idaho

Flamingo Lodge Motel 208-436-4321 402 E 8th St nonsmoking rooms, large grassy play area, bike trail leads to fairgrounds	(15) $30– $50	(k)

Sagle, Idaho

Bottle Bay Resort & Marina 208-263-5916 115 Resort Rd 866-268-8532 www.bottlebayresort.com each pet $8/day RV sites, open walking area, beach access, boat rentals, restaurant open midMay–midSeptember	(8) $75– $145	K R/L	
Country Inn 208-263-3333 470700 Hwy 95 each pet $5/stay dogs allowed in smoking rooms only, pond and open walking area, 5 miles to lakefront beach	(24) $25– $65	C M/F	T
Midas Inn B & B 208-263-6074 1575 Garfield Bay Rd 877-223-4793 www.povn.com/midas pets $15/stay dogs allowed with advance approval only, completely nonsmoking, fields, trails, 2 blocks to public park and boat ramp	(5) $65– $75	FB M/F	

Salmon, Idaho

Motel Deluxe 208-756-2231 112 S Church St nonsmoking rooms, laundry, lawn area for walking dogs, 4 blocks to public park	(24) $40– $70	C K M/F
Salmon River Lodge Inc. 208-756-6622 16 Lodge Rd 800-635-4717 www.wildidaho.net, 47 miles north of North Fork in wilderness area accessible only by jet boat, rooms and cabins sleep up to 4, family style dining room	(10) $60– $90	C R
Solaas B & B 208-756-3903 3 Red Rock Stage Rd pets $10/stay www.salmonidaho.com/solaas, dogs allowed with advance approval only, 2½ acres for walking dogs, dog run available, nearly 100-year-old home is a former stage coach stop, theme rooms	(7) $35– $50	FB

C = coffee IP = indoor pool OP = outdoor pool CB = continental K = full kitchen R = restaurant breakfast (k) = kitchenette S = sauna or F = refrigerator L = lounge steamroom FB = full breakfast M = microwave T = spa or hot tub	# of units) & rates	food & drink	pool, sauna & hot tub

Salmon, Idaho (continued)

Suncrest Motel 208-756-2294 705 S Challis St $5 refundable pet deposit nonsmoking rooms, open area for walking dogs, horse corral, close to natural hot springs	(21) $39– $59	CB (k)	
Syringa Lodge B & B 208-756-4424 26 S 9th Rd www.geocities.com/syringa_lodge completely nonsmoking, decks, waterfront access, walking trails	(8) $45– $95	FB M/F	
Wagons West Motel 208-756-4281 503 Hwy 93 N www.wagonswestmotel.com nonsmoking rooms, laundry, riverside walking area, ½ mile to public park	(53) $39– $75	C	T

Sandpoint, Idaho

Best Western Edgewater 208-263-3194 56 Bridge St 800-635-2534 www.sandpointhotels.com pets $5/day nonsmoking rooms, RV sites, weight room, lawn area for walking dogs	(54) $70– $160	CB (k) R/L	IP S T
Inn at Sandcreek 208-255-2821, 800-439-5593x415 105 S 1st Ave www.innatsandcreek.com completely nonsmoking, restaurant open for dinner only Wed–Sun, massage therapy available, marina, boardwalk, 6-mile walking path, 2 blocks to park	(3) $125– $195	K R	T
K 2 Inn at Sandpoint 208-263-3441 501 N 4th Ave pets $10/day completely nonsmoking, open lot for walking dogs, walking trail, dog run available	(18) $54– $94	CB K	T
La Quinta Inn & Suites 208-263-9581, 800-531-5900 415 W Cedar St www.laquinta.com exercise room, small park, 2 blocks to lakefront park	(70) $69– $159	CB K M/F	OP T

Lakeside Inn 106 Bridge St 208-263-3717 each pet $5/day www.keokee.com/lakeside/index.html, nonsmoking rooms, laundry, large lawns, close to walking trail	(60) $69– $84	CB	S T
Monarch Mountain Lodge 208-263-1222 Hwy 95 N, 363 Bonner Mall Wy 800-543-8193 nonsmoking rooms, in-room spa, each pet $5/day, laundry, 1½ miles to trails	(48) $39– $90	CB M/F	S T
Motel 16 208-263-5323 317 S Marion (Hwy 2 W) nonsmoking rooms, lawn, close to walking trail	(16) $30– $59	C (k) M/F	
Motel 6 208-263-1883, 800-466-8356 477255 Hwy 95 www.motel6.com nonsmoking rooms, laundry, 24 hour hot tubs, large grassy fields for walking dogs	(70) $35– $61	C M/F	T
Quality Inn 208-263-2111, 800-635-2534 807 N 5th Ave pets $5/day www.sandpointhotels.com, laundry, nonsmoking rooms, short drive to trail and pet-friendly beach	(62) $44– $99	C R/L	IP T
S & W Motel 208-263-5979 31016 Hwy 200 E dogs allowed with manager's approval only, nonsmoking rooms, laundry, lawn	(12) $30– $50	K	
Super 8 Motel 208-263-2210, 800-800-8000 476841 Hwy 95 www.super8.com nonsmoking rooms, lawn, walking trails	(61) $30– $80		T

Shoshone, Idaho

Governor's Mansion B & B 208-886-2858 315 S Greenwood St 2 rooms with private bath, 3 with shared baths, large yard, 4 blocks to park	(5) $30– $65	FB	

Shoup, Idaho

Shoup Store, Cafe & Cabins 208-394-2125 1829 Salmon River Rd 2 cabins sleep 3 to 5, 1 historic schoolhouse sleeps 9 "bunkhouse-style," all have kitchens and baths, large lawn for walking dogs, close to river	(3) $15 per person	K R	

C = coffee IP = indoor pool OP = outdoor pool	(# of units) & rates	food & drink	pool, sauna & hot tub
CB = continental K = full kitchen R = restaurant			
breakfast (k) = kitchenette S = sauna or			
F = refrigerator L = lounge steamroom			
FB = full breakfast M = microwave T = spa or hot tub			

Shoup, Idaho (continued)

Smith House B & B 208-394-2121, 800-238-5915 3175 Salmon River Rd 2 rooms in log home with shared bath, 3-bdrm 2-bath guest house sleeps 10, completely nonsmoking, on 3 acres of vineyard, fruit trees, lawn for walking dogs	(5) $45– $65	FB K	T

Smelterville, Idaho

Sands Motel & Cafe 208-784-1331 605 Washington Ave nonsmoking rooms, open walking area, 1 block to public park and trails	(16) $25– $45	C R	

Soda Springs, Idaho

Brigham Young Lodge & Trailer Park 208-547-3009 120 E 2nd S studios to 3-bdrm house, RV sites, city park across street	(7) $35– $100	(k) M/F	
J & R Inn 208-547-3366 179 W 2nd S pets $5/day nonsmoking rooms, open walking area, 1½ blocks to city park, 5 blocks to walking trail to natural mineral springs and man-made geyser (1 mile roundtrip)	(45) $35– $47	M/F	
Lake View Motel & Trailer Park 208-547-4351 341 W 2nd S nonsmoking rooms, RV sites, lawn, 5 blocks to walking trail to mineral springs	(14) $29– $50	C M/F	

Spencer, Idaho

Spencer B & B 208-374-5376 Main St trailer house sleeps 5, breakfast available on request, close to opal mines, lots of open walking area	(1) $30	C K	
Spencer Stage Station 208-374-5242 Spencer sleeping cabins sleep up to 5, RV sites, open field and walking trails	(2) $30	R/L	

St Anthony, Idaho

Best Western Weston Inn 208-624-3711 115 S Bridge St 800-937-8376 www.bestwestern.com $20 refundable pet deposit nonsmoking rooms, riverside walking area, park	(30) $45– $62	C R

St Maries, Idaho

Birch Tree B & B 208-245-2198 1 Jay Ln small to medium well-behaved dogs only, bedroom and sitting room, in each unit, completely nonsmoking, large yard and grassy walking area	(2) $40– $55	FB
Pines Motel 208-245-2545 1117 Main Ave dogs allowed in smoking rooms only, public park across street	(28) $40– $65	

Stanley, Idaho

Danner's Log Cabin Motel 208-774-3539 1 Wall St each pet $8/day www.stanleycc.org, cabins sleep up to 6, some have kitchens, BBQ and picnic area, lots of walking area	(9) $70– $125	K	
Diamond D Ranch 208-336-9772 38 miles north of Stanley 800-222-1269 www.diamonddranch-idaho.com, 2 to 4-bdrm cabins, lodge rooms and suites, completely nonsmoking, prefer pets to be kept in travel crates while in rooms	(12) $135– $185	R	OP T
Mountain Village Lodge 208-774-3661, 800-843-5475 Hwy 21 & Hwy 75 each pet $8/day www.mountainvillage.com, nonsmoking rooms, laundry, natural hot springs pool, open field	(61) $59– $111	C (k) M/F R/L	
Redwood Cabins 208-774-3531 Hwy 75 www.redwood-stanley.com open May 15–October 1, dogs allowed with advance approval only, open lot for walking dogs	(13) $46– $75	K	
Sunbeam Village Resort 208-838-2211 100 Yankee Fork Rd pets $10/stay www.sunbeamvillage.com, nonsmoking rooms, RV sites, laundry, natural hot springs, near public park	(6) $59– $125	C K	

C = coffee IP = indoor pool OP = outdoor pool CB = continental K = full kitchen R = restaurant breakfast (k) = kitchenette S = sauna or F = refrigerator L = lounge steamroom FB = full breakfast M = microwave T = spa or hot tub	(# of units) & rates	food & drink	pool, sauna & hot tub

Sun Valley, Idaho

High Country Properties 208-726-1256, 800-726-7076 251 S Main St Suite 101 $500 refundable pet deposit www.highcountry-rentals.com, studios, duplexes, townhouses, penthouses, executive homes, some with yards, close to walking paths, fitness center	(200) $125– $900	K	OP T

Terreton, Idaho

B K's Motel 208-663-4578 1073 E 1500 N bkmotel@dcdi.net, nonsmoking rooms, RV sites, open field for walking dogs	(8) $35– $50	M/F	

Tetonia, Idaho

Teton Mountain View Lodge 208-456-2741 510 Egbert Ave 800-625-2232 www.tetonlodging.com each pet $5/day nonsmoking rooms, on 5½ acres with open fields for walking, ½ mile to park	(24) $45– $95	CB M/F	T
Teton Ridge Ranch 208-456-2650 200 Valley View Rd 4,000 acre guest ranch, rate includes 3 meals/day, in-room spa, cross-country skiing, horseback riding	(5) $495– $630		T

Twin Falls, Idaho

Best Western Apollo Motor Inn 208-733-2010 296 Addison Ave W $50 refundable pet deposit nonsmoking rooms, 1 small dog only, grassy walking area, 1½ blocks to public park	(50) $51– $80	CB	OP T
Comfort Inn 208-734-7494, 800-228-5150 1893 Canyon Springs Rd each pet $10/day www.choicehotels.com, nonsmoking rooms, in-room spa, grassy walking area, ¼ mile to public park	(52) $60– $140	CB M/F	IP T

Dunes Motel　　208-733-9141 447 Addison Ave W nonsmoking rooms, canyon trail behind building for walking dogs, 3 blocks to public park	(45) call for rates	M/F	OP
El Rancho Motel　　208-733-4021 380 Addison Ave W　　pets $5/day dogs under 30 lbs only, nonsmoking rooms, open field behind building for walking dogs	(14) $26– $42	CB M/F	
Holiday Motel　　208-733-4330 615 Addison Ave W　　pets $2–$5/day nonsmoking rooms, ½ block to public park	(18) $29– $45	C M/F	
Monterey Motor Inn　　208-733-5151 433 Addison Ave W　　pets $5/day nonsmoking rooms, laundry, dogs under 30 lbs only, open field behind building, riverside walking trail	(28) $30– $65	CB M/F	OP T
Motel 6　　208-734-3993 1472 Blue Lakes Blvd N　　nonsmoking rooms, laundry, lawn, close to walking trail	(132) $36– $56	C	OP
Sands Motel　　208-733-9141 401 Addison Ave W nonsmoking rooms, guests can use swimming pool at Dunes Motel next door, 3 blocks to public park	(16) call for rates	M/F	
Shilo Inn　　208-733-7545 1586 Blue Lakes Blvd N　　each pet $10/day www.shiloinns.com, nonsmoking rooms, laundry, pet beds and treats, fitness center, lawn	(128) $80– $116	CB K M/F	IP S T
Super 7 Motel　　208-733-8770, 888-530-0138 320 Main Ave S　　pets $5/day nonsmoking rooms, laundry, 3 blocks to public park	(40) $30– $50	C M/F	OP
Super 8 Motel　　208-734-5801 1260 Blue Lakes Blvd N　　each pet $5/day laundry, small dogs only, fitness center, in-room spa, grassy walking area, 1 block to campus paths	(94) $40– $80	CB M/F	T
Twin Falls Motel　　208-733-8620 2152 Kimberly Rd　　small dogs allowed with manager's approval only, open field for walking dogs	(8) $43– $64	M/F	

C = coffee CB = continental breakfast F = refrigerator FB = full breakfast	IP = indoor pool K = full kitchen (k) = kitchenette L = lounge M = microwave	OP = outdoor pool R = restaurant S = sauna or steamroom T = spa or hot tub	(# of units) & rates	food & drink	pool, sauna & hot tub

Twin Falls, Idaho (continued)

WestCoast Twin Falls Hotel 208-734-5000 1357 Blue Lakes Blvd N www.westcoasthotels.com, nonsmoking rooms, fitness room, restaurant and espresso shop, large walking area, 1 block to 2-mile long walking trail	(112) $67– $117	CB M/F R	OP S T
Weston Inn 208-733-6095, 800-551-3505 906 Blue Lakes Blvd N pets $5/day nonsmoking rooms, 1 block to walking path	(98) $40– $56	CB F	IP T

Victor, Idaho

Teton Mountain Hideaways 208-787-3094 219 Highland Wy pets $50/stay www.tetonhideaways.com, fully equipped vacation homes, completely nonsmoking, daily and weekly rates, country settings for walking dogs	(4) up to $250		
Teton Valley Campground & Cabins 208-787-2647 128 Hwy 31 dogs allowed with advance approval only, sleeping cabins sleep up to 6, BBQ and picnic table at each cabin, bathhouse, laundry, RV sites, off-leash exercise area	(4) $42– $62	L	OP

Wallace, Idaho

Best Western Wallace Inn 208-752-1252 100 Front St $10 pet deposit, 800-643-2386 nonsmoking rooms, workout room, walking area	(63) $60– $90	C F R/L	IP S T
Brooks Hotel 208-556-1571 500 Cedar St 800-752-0469 2 blocks to public park	(22) $45– $65	(k) R/L	
Molly B'Damm Motel 208-753-2031 60330 Silver Valley Rd nonsmoking rooms, wooded pet area behind building, near walking trail	(20) $36– $46	C (k) M/F	T

Ryan Hotel 208-753-6001 608½ Cedar St ryanhotel@wallaceid.com historic downtown hotel, nonsmoking rooms, private bath in all but 3 rooms, 1 block to walking trail	(14) $23– $55	C M/F	
Stardust Motel 208-752-1213 410 Pine St nonsmoking rooms, guest pass to swimming pool and exercise room at nearby hotel, lawn, 2 blocks to public park	(43) $46– $80	C M/F	

Warm Lake, Idaho

North Shore Lodge 208-632-2000, 800-933-3193 175 N Shoreline Dr each pet $25/stay www.ohwy.com/id/n/nslgres.htm, lakeside cabins, most have kitchens, beach and walking trails	(10) $50– $95	K R/L	

Weiser, Idaho

Colonial Motel 208-549-0150 251 E Main St pets $5/day nonsmoking rooms, large lawn, 3 blocks to city park	(24) $36– $68	C (k)	
State Street Motel 208-414-1390 1279 State St nonsmoking rooms, open pet walking area, 3 blocks to public park	(13) $41– $55	C M/F	

White Bird, Idaho

White Bird Motel 208-839-2308 Bridge & Main St pets $5/day small dogs allowed with advance approval only, RV sites, laundry, open field for walking dogs, less than 1 mile to national monument and public park	(10) $30– $65	(k)	

Winchester, Idaho

Winchester Minnie Motel 208-924-7784 420 Algoma nonsmoking motel rooms and tepees, dogs allowed with advance approval only, large yard, 1 block to state park and trails, 1 mile to Wolf Education Center featuring wild wolves	(4) $25– $55	C F	

	# of units) & rates	food & drink	pool, sauna & hot tub
C = coffee IP = indoor pool OP = outdoor pool CB = continental K = full kitchen R = restaurant breakfast (k) = kitchenette S = sauna or F = refrigerator L = lounge steamroom FB = full breakfast M = microwave T = spa or hot tub			

Worley, Idaho

Coeur d'Alene Casino Resort Hotel 208-686-0248 27068 S Hwy 95 800-523-2464 www.cdacasino.com $25 refundable pet deposit nonsmoking rooms, 24 hour pool and hot tub, large grassy area for walking dogs	(96) $75– $275	C M/F R/L	IP T

Yellow Pine, Idaho

Yellow Pine Lodge 208-633-3377 360 Yellow Pine Ave dogs allowed with advance approval only, large open lot for walking dogs, next to national forest land	(6) $30– $50	C R	

Oregon's Dog-Friendly Lodgings

Agness, Oregon

Cougar Lane Lodge 541-247-7233 04219 Agness Rd pets $3–$5/day laundry, RV and campsites, close to waterfront and walking trail, open midApril–November	(6) $45– $65	K R/L	
Singing Springs Resort 541-247-6162 34501 Agness Illahe Rd singingsprings@gb.wave.net, rooms, cabins, 6-bdrm house, restaurant and lounge open May–October 9½ acres on Rogue River, 1 mile to walking trail	(8) $45– $75	K R/L	

Albany, Oregon

Best Western Pony Soldier Motor Inn 541-928-6322 315 Airport Rd SE 800-634-7669 nonsmoking rooms, laundry, ½ acre fenced pet area, close to fairgrounds, lakeside walking trail	(72) $65– $76	CB	OP T
Budget Inn 541-926-4246 2727 Pacific Blvd SE pets $5/day www.budgetinnofalbany.com, nonsmoking rooms, laundry, large yard, near lakeside walking trail	(47) $35– $60	CB (k)	
Comfort Suites 541-928-2053 100 Opal Ct NE pets $25/stay nonsmoking rooms, exercise room, laundry, RV sites, ½ mile to public park	(86) $69– $129	FB M/F	IP S T
Days Inn & Suites 541-928-5050, 800-329-7466 1100 Price Rd pets $8/stay laundry, next to public park for walking dogs	(71) $49– $72	CB	IP T
La Quinta Inn & Suites 541-928-0921, 800-531-5900 251 Airport Rd SE www.laquinta.com nonsmoking rooms, laundry, large city park and pond across street	(62) $65– $129	CB K	IP S T
Marco Polo Motel 541-926-4401 2410 Pacific Blvd SE nonsmoking rooms, dog allowed for one night only	(18) $30– $35	M/F	

C = coffee
CB = continental
  breakfast
F = refrigerator
FB = full breakfast
	IP = indoor pool
	K = full kitchen
	(k) = kitchenette
	L = lounge
	M = microwave
		OP = outdoor pool
		R = restaurant
		S = sauna or
		  steamroom
		T = spa or hot tub
			(# of units)
			& rates
				food
				& drink
					pool, sauna
					& hot tub

Albany, Oregon (continued)

Motel 6 541-926-4233, 800-466-8356 2735 Pacific Blvd SE www.motel6.com nonsmoking rooms, 1 dog under 50 lbs only, 14 acre park, paved walking path, lighted 24 hours per day	(42) $47– $50	C M/F	T
Relax Inn & Suites 541-926-0170 1212 Price Rd SE 888-321-3352 nonsmoking rooms, laundry, close to public park	(78) $37– $58	C R	OP
Valu Inn 541-926-1538 3125 Santiam Hwy SE pets $5/stay nonsmoking rooms, laundry, near large public park	(60) $33– $46	C K R	OP

Arch Cape, Oregon

Shaw's Oceanfront B & B 503-436-1422 79924 Cannon Rd 888-269-4483 www.shawsoceanfrontbb.com pets $25/stay oceanfront with deck, sleeps 5, nonsmoking, located in "Oregon's Carmel," close to park and walking trail	(1) $135– $195	FB K	

Arlington, Oregon

Arlington Motel 541-454-2077 1300 Locust St pets $3/stay nonsmoking rooms, park area with trees for walking dog, 1 block to public park and pond	(17) $35– $39	M/F	
Village Inn 541-454-2646 410 Beech St pets $6/stay nonsmoking rooms, laundry, beach across street, nearby area for walking dogs	(34) $37– $46	C M/F R/L	

Ashland, Oregon

Ashland Motel 541-482-2561, 800-460-8858 1145 Siskiyou Blvd pets $5/day nonsmoking rooms, laundry, close to public park	(27) $38– $68	K	OP

Ashland Regency Inn & RV Park 541-482-4700 50 Lowe Rd each pet $5/day, 800-482-4701 nonsmoking rooms, RV sites, close to walking trail	(43) $39– $65	CB R	OP
Best Western Bard's Inn 541-482-0049, 800-528-1234 132 N Main St each pet $15/day nonsmoking rooms, 1 block to public park	(91) $125– $155	CB F	OP T
Best Western Windsor Inn 541-488-2330 2520 Ashland St 800-334-2330 www.flagship-inn.com pets $15/day nonsmoking rooms, laundry, 1 mile to walking trails	(92) $55– $159	CB K	OP T
Box R Ranch 541-482-1873 16799 Hwy 66 www.boxrranch.com nonsmoking rooms, laundry, MUST call for advance approval to bring a dog, 2-bdrm 1-bath log houses sleep 10, swimming pond, 1600 acre working ranch	(4) $75– $200	K	
Callahan's Siskiyou Lodge 541-482-12997 7100 Old Hwy 99 South 800-286-050 www.callahanslodge.com pets $10/day completely nonsmoking, in-room spa, RV sites, near Pacific Crest Trail	(12) $65– $135	FB M/F R/L	T
Cedarwood Inn Motel 541-488-2000, 800-547-4141 1801 Siskiyou Blvd pets $10/day nonsmoking rooms, dogs allowed November–April only, 2 miles to off-leash dog park	(64) $56– $148	C K	IP S T
Flagship Inn 541-482-2641, 800-547-6414 1193 Siskiyou Blvd each pet $10/day nonsmoking rooms, coffee in lobby, ¾ mile to Lithia Park, 2½ miles to a 30-mile long greenbelt walkway	(64) $56– $105	C R/L	
Green Springs Inn 541-482-0614 11470 Hwy 66 www.greenspringsinn.net nonsmoking rooms, laundry, in-room spa, located 30 minutes east of Ashland	(8) $59– $99	R/L	T
Howard Prairie Lake Resort 541-482-1979 3249 Hyatt Prairie Rd www.howardprairieresort.com overnight accommodations consist of fully equipped RV rentals, laundry, RV sites and tent sites, marina, boat rentals, on 400 acres for walking dogs	(21) $75– $85	K R	

C = coffee / CB = continental breakfast / F = refrigerator / FB = full breakfast / IP = indoor pool / K = full kitchen / (k) = kitchenette / L = lounge / M = microwave / OP = outdoor pool / R = restaurant / S = sauna or steamroom / T = spa or hot tub	(# of units) & rates	food & drink	pool, sauna & hot tub

Ashland, Oregon (continued)

	(# of units) & rates	food & drink	pool, sauna & hot tub
Hyatt Lake Cabins 541-488-2826 170 Emigrant Lake Rd cabins sleep 6 to 8, fully stocked kitchens, linens, 30 minutes east of Ashland	(2) $150– $175	K	
Hyatt Lake Resort 541-482-3331 7979 Hyatt Prairie Rd nonsmoking cabins, laundry, RV and tent sites, lake swimming	(4) $69	R	
Knight's Inn Motel 541-482-5111, 800-547-4566 2359 Ashland St pets $10/day nonsmoking rooms, large field for walking dogs, 1½ miles to off-leash dog park	(40) $44– $78	C F R/L	OP T
La Quinta Inn & Suites 541-482-6932, 800-531-5900 434 E Valley View Rd www.laquinta.com nonsmoking rooms, laundry, 24 hour pool and spa, exercise room, large field, close to public park	(71) $55– $109	FB K	IP T
Patterson House B & B 541-482-9171, 888-482-9171 639 N Main St nonsmoking rooms and cottage, large yard, 7 blocks to Lithia Park	(4) $90– $125	FB M/F	
Relax Inn 541-482-4423, 888-672-5290 535 Clover Ln $10 refundable pet deposit back yard for walking dogs	(18) $30– $48	C	OP
Super 8 Motel 541-482-8887, 800-800-8000 2350 Ashland St $25 refundable pet deposit nonsmoking rooms, laundry, designated pet area, ¾ mile to greenbelt walking and bike trail	(67) $50– $99	CB K	IP
Timbers Motel 541-482-4242 1450 Ashland St www.ashlandtimberslodging.com nonsmoking rooms, RV sites, park across street	(29) $40– $100	C K	OP
Windmill Inn & Suites 541-482-8310 2525 Ashland St 800-547-4747 nonsmoking rooms, laundry, on 14 acres	(230) $61– $250	CB M/F	OP T

Astoria, Oregon

Astoria Best Western 503-325-2205, 800-621-0641 555 Hamburg Ave pets $10/stay small well-groomed dogs only, 6 blocks to riverside walking trail	(77) $49– $149	CB (k)	IP S T
Bayview Village 503-338-4359 783 W Marine Dr nonsmoking rooms, RV sites, next to park and bay	(19) $30– $60	K	
Clementine's B & B 503-325-2005 847 Exchange St 800-521-6801 www.clementines-bb.com pets $15/stay nonsmoking rooms, in-room spa, laundry, public park across street	(7) $110– $150	FB K	T
Crest Motel 503-325-3141, 800-421-3141 5366 Leif Erickson Dr www.crest-motel.com nonsmoking rooms, laundry, 2½ acres overlooking Columbia River, 1 mile to Astoria River walking trail	(40) $45– $107	CB M/F	T
Lamplighter Motel 503-325-4051, 800-845-8847 131 W Marine Dr pets $5/day nonsmoking rooms, laundry, close to waterfront	(29) $32– $75	CB M/F	
Red Lion Inn 503-325-7373, 800-547-8010 400 Industry St pets $10/day nonsmoking rooms, designated pet area, close to public park and riverfront walkway	(124) $59– $124	C M/F R/L	
Rivershore Motel 503-325-2921, 866-322-8047 59 W Marine Dr pets $10/stay nonsmoking rooms, small dogs only, close to riverfront walking trail	(43) $40– $88	C K	
Rose River Inn B & B 503-325-7175 1510 Franklin Ave 888-876-0028 www.roseriverinn.com pets $10/stay completely nonsmoking, laundry, 3 blocks to Columbia River walking trail, owner has 2 therapy dogs and is a licensed massage therapist for both people and pets	(5) $75– $135	FB M/F	S

C = coffee IP = indoor pool OP = outdoor pool CB = continental K = full kitchen R = restaurant breakfast (k) = kitchenette S = sauna or F = refrigerator L = lounge steamroom FB = full breakfast M = microwave T = spa or hot tub	(# of units) & rates	food & drink	pool, sauna & hot tub

Azalea, Oregon

Havenshire B & B 541-837-3511 1098 Hogum Creek Rd 800-837-3511 completely nonsmoking house with 5 acre park	(2) $65	FB	

Baker City, Oregon

Baker City Motel & RV Park 541-523-6381 880 Elm St 800-931-9229 nonsmoking rooms, small dogs only, pets $7/stay RV sites, laundry, 10 minute walk to public park	(17) $35– $45	C M/F	
Bridge Street Inn 541-523-6571 134 Bridge St 800-932-9220 www.ohwy.com/or/b/bristrin.htm each pet $5/day nonsmoking rooms, next to Leo Adler walkway	(40) $28– $38	CB M/F	
Budget Inn 541-523-6324, 800-547-5827 2205 Broadway St pets $5/day nonsmoking rooms, ½ mile to public park	(36) $38– $44	CB M	OP
Eldorado Inn 541-523-6494, 800-537-5756 695 Campbell St pets $5/day nonsmoking rooms, RV sites, ¾ mile to public park	(56) $42– $81	C F	IP
Geiser Grand Hotel 541-523-1889, 888-434-7374 1996 Main St pets $10/day nonsmoking rooms, guest passes to swimming pool, 3 blocks to city park and Leo Adler parkway	(30) $79– $199	C R/L	
Oregon Trail Motel & Restaurant 541-523-5844 211 Bridge St pets $5/day, 800-628-3982 nonsmoking rooms, laundry, small walking area, greenbelt walkway, 6 blocks to park	(54) $40– $70	CB R	OP S
Powder River B & B 541-523-7143, 800-600-7143 305 Hwy 7 South nonsmoking rooms, can accommodate special dietary needs, 1½ acres, ¼ mile to playground and golf course	(2) $75– $95	FB M/F	

Rodeway Inn 541-523-2242, 800-228-5151 810 Campbell St pets $5/day nonsmoking rooms, ½ mile to public park	(53) $51– $66	C F		
Trail Motel 541-523-4646 2815 10th St pets $2–$5/day ½ block to open area, 2 blocks to river parkway	(4) $30– $45	K		
Western Motel 541-523-3700, 800-481-3701 3055 10th St pets $3–$5/day nonsmoking rooms, RV sites	(14) $25– $30	C M/F		

Bandon, Oregon

Bandon Beach Motel 541-347-4430 1140 Beach Loop Rd pets $5/day nonsmoking rooms	(40) $35– $60	CB K	IP T	
Bandon Wayside Motel & RV Park 541-347-3421 1175 2nd St SE picnic and barbecue facilities, RV sites	(10) $20- $80	C		
Best Western Inn at Face Rock 541-347-9441 3225 Beach Loop Rd pets $15/stay, 800-638-3092 nonsmoking rooms, laundry, beach across street	(74) $69– $234	C K R/L	IP S T	
Driftwood Motel 541-347-9022, 888-374-3893 460 Hwy 101 each pet $5/day nonsmoking rooms, 2 miles to city park	(22) $40– $80	CB		
Dunshee House at Face Rock 541-347-5030 1860 Beach Loop Rd 888-347-5030 nonsmoking apartments, each pet $5/day, private entrances, lawn, beach access, www.dunshee.com	(2) $75– $100	C K		
Gorman Motel at Coquille Point 541-347-9451 1110 11th St SW pets $5/day beachfront nonsmoking rooms, laundry	(24) $50– $115	CB K	T	
La Kris Motel 541-347-5312, 888-496-3610 940 Oregon Ave SW 1 dog per room only, www.bandon.com/page12.html/page3.html, close to playground, ¼ mile to ocean access and park	(12) $44– $89	C F		
Lamplighter Motel 541-347-4477 40 North Ave NE 800-650-8817 nonsmoking rooms, area for walking dogs	(16) $36– $85	C K		

		# of units) & rates	food & drink	pool, sauna & hot tub

C = coffee
CB = continental
    breakfast
F = refrigerator
FB = full breakfast
	IP = indoor pool
	K = full kitchen
	(k) = kitchenette
	L = lounge
	M = microwave
		OP = outdoor pool
		R = restaurant
		S = sauna or
		    steamroom
		T = spa or hot tub		

Bandon, Oregon (continued)

Shooting Star Motel 1640 Oregon Ave SW nonsmoking rooms, large area for walking dogs	541-347-9192	(15) $35– $50	C K	
Sunset Oceanfront Accommodations 1865 Beach Loop Rd nonsmoking rooms and 2-bdrm house, laundry, beach access	541-347-2453 800-842-2407 pets $10/day	(72) $48– $175	C K	IP T
Table Rock Motel 840 Beach Loop Rd completely nonsmoking, pet towel and blanket provided, open field for walking dogs, beach access (please keep dogs away from the bird sanctuary)	541-347-2700 pets $5–$10/day	(15) $40– $105	C K M/F	

Beatty, Oregon

New Beatty Store & Motel 42615 Hwy 140 nonsmoking rooms, laundry, national forest, ½ mile to "Rails to Trails" walkway	541-533-2689	(6) $29– $38		

Beaverton, Oregon

Beaverton Val-U Inn 12255 SW Canyon Rd laundry, small park area for walking dogs	503-646-4131, 800-443-7777 nonsmoking rooms,	(60) $45– $79	CB K	OP
Greenwood Inn 10700 SW Allen Blvd nonsmoking rooms, laundry, fitness center, large open area with trails for walking dogs	503-643-7444, 800-289-1300 pets $20/stay	(250) $69– $89	CB K R/L	OP T
Homestead Studio Suites Hotel 875 SW 158th Ave nonsmoking rooms, laundry ¼ mile to walking trails and nature center	503-690-3600 888-782-9473 pets $75/stay	(142) $54– $84	C K	

Homewood Suites by Hilton 503-614-0900 15525 NW Gateway Ct each pet $10/day dogs under 25 lbs only, nonsmoking rooms, laundry	(123) $149– $179	FB (k)	OP
Peppertree Inn 503-641-7477, 800-453-6219 10720 SW Allen Blvd dogs under 15 lbs only, nonsmoking rooms, laundry, walking path and pond	(73) $50– $79	CB M/F	OP T

Bend, Oregon

Bend Riverside Motel & Suites 541-389-2363 1565 NW Hill St pets $10/day, 800-284-2363 laundry, pet cleanup tools provided, riverfront park	(200) $52– $129	C K	IP S T
Best Western Inn & Suites 541-382-1515 721 NE 3rd St 800-937-8376 nonsmoking rooms each pet $5/day www.bestwestern.com/innsuitesofbend	(102) $69– $109	CB	OP T
Budget Inn 541-389-1448 1300 SE 3rd St pets $5/day nonsmoking rooms, laundry, well-behaved dogs only, public access to riverfront area	(23) $28– $65	C K M/F	
Cascade Lodge 541-382-2612, 800-852-6031 420 SE 3rd St pets $4/day nonsmoking rooms, 5 minute walk to public park	(33) $30– $99	CB M/F	OP
Central Oregon Accommodations 541-617-0179 Inn of the Seventh Mountain 866-617-0179 www.centraloregonaccomm.com, nonsmoking condominiums, laundry, near waterfront and trails	(2) $85– $140		S T
Chalet Motel 541-382-6124 510 SE 3rd St pets $4/day nonsmoking rooms, 2 blocks to public park, 4 blocks to river and walking trails	(22) $28– $40	CB K M/F	OP T
Cimarron Motor Inn 541-382-7711, 800-304-4050 437 NE 3rd St pets $10/stay nonsmoking rooms, 3 blocks to park and pool	(59) $39– $99	CB K R/L	OP
Crane Prairie Resort & RV Park 541-383-3939 PO Box 1171 pets $5/day rustic cabins sleep 4 to 8, bathhouse and laundry, RV sites, leash rules strictly enforced	(3) $40– $50		

C = coffee IP = indoor pool OP = outdoor pool CB = continental K = full kitchen R = restaurant breakfast (k) = kitchenette S = sauna or F = refrigerator L = lounge steamroom FB = full breakfast M = microwave T = spa or hot tub	(# of units) & rates	food & drink	pool, sauna & hot tub

Bend, Oregon (continued)

Cricketwood Country B & B 541-330-0747 63520 Cricketwood Rd 877-330-0747 www.cricketwood.com, fireplace, pets $10/day, dogs allowed in cottage only, laundry, on 10 acres	(3) $115	K	T
Cultus Lake Resort 541-389-3230, 800-616-3230 Hwy 46 Century Dr each pet $10/day www.cultuslakeresort.com, open May–October, lakefront cabins sleep 4 to 8, linens provided, boat and jet ski rentals, close to walking or biking trail	(24) $74– $115	K R	
Econo Lodge 541-318-0848, 877-326-6262 20600 Grandview Dr each pet $7/day nonsmoking rooms, laundry, open field for walking	(50) $59– $99	CB K	IP T
Elk Lake Resort 541-480-7228 Cascade Lakes Hwy pets $7/day www.elklakeresort.com, laundry, dogs allowed in summer only, 1 cabin has private hot tub	(8) $85– $250	K R	T
Entrada Lodge 541-382-4080 19221 SW Century Dr each pet $5/day nonsmoking rooms, laundry, 1 to 2 pets per room, national forest land, lots of walking trails	(79) $69– $129	CB M/F	OP T
Hampton Inn 541-388-4114, 800-426-7866 15 NE Butler Market Rd pets $10/stay nonsmoking rooms, 5 blocks to walking trail	(99) $69– $109	CB	OP T
Holiday Inn Express 541-317-8500 20615 Grandview Dr 888-919-7666 www.rogueweb.com/holidaybend each pet $5/day nonsmoking rooms, laundry, field and vacant lot	(99) $49– $199	CB (k)	IP T
La Quinta Inn & Suites 541-388-2227, 800-642-4258 61200 S Hwy 97 www.laquinta.com nonsmoking rooms, in-room spa, laundry, 24 hour swimming pool	(65) $55– $120	CB (k) M/F	IP T

Motel 6 201 NE 3rd St nonsmoking rooms, ½ mile to public park	541-382-8282 800-466-8356	(60) $35– $80	C M/F	OP
Motel West 228 NE Irving Ave small pet walking area, 10 minute walk to public park	541-389-5577, 800-282-5577 nonsmoking rooms,	(39) $36– $49	C K	
Mt Bachelor Motel 2359 NE Division St laundry, dogs on leash at all times please, riverside park across street	541-382-6365 pets $5/day	(19) $25– $30	M/F	
Plaza Motel 1430 NW Hill St nonsmoking rooms, across street from public park	541-382-1621, 800-300-1621 pets $5/stay	(27) $36– $99	CB K	
Red Lion Bend North 1415 NE 3rd St nonsmoking rooms, laundry, exercise room	541-382-7011, 800-733-5466 www.redlion.com	(75) $64– $169	CB M/F R/L	OP T
Red Lion Bend South 849 NE 3rd St nonsmoking rooms, laundry, exercise room	541-382-8384 800-733-5466	(75) $64– $169	CB M/F	OP T
Riverhouse Resort 3075 N Hwy 97 nonsmoking rooms, in-room spa, laundry, riverfront nature trails, ½ block to public park	541-389-3111, 800-547-3928 www.riverhouse.com	(220) $64– $225	CB (k) M/F R/L	IP S T
Rodeway Inn 3705 N Hwy 97 nonsmoking rooms, laundry, close to public park and walking trail	541-382-2211, 800-507-2211 pets $5/day	(36) $35– $89	CB M/F	OP T
Scandia Pines Lodge 61405 S Hwy 97 completely nonsmoking facility	541-389-5910 pets $5/day	(13) $39– $69	C K	
Shilo Inn 3105 O B Riley Rd www.shiloinns.co nonsmoking rooms, pet beds and treats, exercise room, designated pet walking area, riverside walking trails, 4 blocks to park	541-389-9600 800-222-2244 each pet $10/day	(151) $109– $225	C K M/F R	IP S T

C = coffee IP = indoor pool OP = outdoor pool CB = continental K = full kitchen R = restaurant breakfast (k) = kitchenette S = sauna or F = refrigerator L = lounge steamroom FB = full breakfast M = microwave T = spa or hot tub	(# of units) & rates	food & drink	pool, sauna & hot tub

Bend, Oregon (continued)

Sleep Inn 541-330-0050, 800-627-5337 600 NE Bellevue pets $8/stay nonsmoking rooms, 10 acre field for walking dogs, 3 blocks to Pilot Butte State Park	(59) $59– $98	CB M/F	OP T
Sonoma Lodge 541-382-4891 450 SE 3rd St pets $5/day www.sonomalodge.com, nonsmoking, laundry	(17) $39– $79	CB K	
Super 8 Motel 541-388-6888, 800-800-8000 1275 SE 3rd St $25 refundable pet deposit nonsmoking rooms, 2 miles to riverfront park	(79) $52– $66	CB	IP T
Swallow Ridge B & B 541-389-1913 65711 Twin Bridges Rd each pet $5/day http://home.teleport.com/~bluesky, dogs allowed by advance arrangement only, 6 acres, riverside trails	(1) $50– $75	CB K	
Westward Ho Motel 541-382-2111, 800-999-8143 904 SE 3rd St pets $3/stay nonsmoking, laundry, ¼ mile to park and trails	(65) $32– $99	CB M/F	IP T

Biggs Junction, Oregon

Biggs Motel 541-739-8255 91413 Biggs-Rufus Hwy pets $5/stay nonsmoking rooms, close to public park, 5 miles to Deschutes National Park	(7) $32– $48	M/F	
Dinty's Motor Inn at Biggs Junction 541-739-2596 91581 Biggs-Rufus Hwy 800-218-5913 nonsmoking rooms, 3 miles to public parks	(26) $35– $45	C	OP
Nu Vu Motel 541-739-2525 91495 Biggs-Rufus Hwy pets $5/stay nonsmoking rooms, close to public park, 5 miles to Deschutes National Park	(16) $42– $51	C M/F	

Travelodge Motel 541-739-2501, 800-944-4156 91484 Biggs-Rufus Hwy pets $10/day nonsmoking rooms, small dogs only, must be kept in travel crates when in the room, river and trails	(40) $50– $76	CB M/F	OP

Blue River, Oregon

Belknap Resort & Hot Springs 541-822-3512 59296 N Belknap Springs Rd nonsmoking rooms, RV sites, hot springs pools, massage therapist	(3) $55– $80	K	

Boardman, Oregon

Dodge City Inn 541-481-2451 100 1st & Front Sts www.dodgecityinn.com grassy area across street, 4 blocks to riverside trail	(40) $43– $65	CB M/F	
Econo Lodge 541-481-2375 105 Front St SW 800-336-4485 nonsmoking rooms, in-room spa, ¼ mile to park	(51) $49– $79	C M/F	OP T

Bridgeport, Oregon

Bruno Ranch B & B 541-446-3468 19518 Bridgeport Ln nonsmoking rooms, barn, can accommodate horses	(2) $30– $40	FB K	

Brightwood, Oregon

Oregon Ark Motel 503-622-4911 61716 Hwy 26 nonsmoking rooms, woodstoves, laundry, rustic setting on 20 acres with 5 acres of pasture and 5 ponds	(15) $30– $40	(k)	

Brookings, Oregon

Beaver State Motel 541-469-5361 437 Chetco Ave 1 dog up to 30 lbs only, nonsmoking rooms, 4 blocks to public park, 1 mile to beach access	(17) $39– $85	C M/F	
Best Western Beachfront Inn 541-469-7779 16008 Boat Basin Rd 800-468-4081 nonsmoking rooms, each pet $5/day laundry, beach access	(102) $94– $165	C K	OP T

C = coffee IP = indoor pool OP = outdoor pool CB = continental K = full kitchen R = restaurant breakfast (k) = kitchenette S = sauna or F = refrigerator L = lounge steamroom FB = full breakfast M = microwave T = spa or hot tub	(# of units) & rates	food & drink	pool, sauna & hot tub

Brookings, Oregon (continued)

Bonn Motel 541-469-2161 1216 Chetco Ave pets $5/day nonsmoking rooms, dogs under 10 lbs only, small yard, biking trail, ¼ mile to beach access	(37) $28– $85	C K	IP S
Harbor Inn Motel 541-469-3194, 800-469-8444 15991 Hwy 101 S each pet $8/day www.harborinnmotel.com, field, ¼ mile to beach	(30) $50– $99	C M/F	
Pacific Sunset Inn 541-469-2141 1144 Chetco Ave 800-469-2141 nonsmoking rooms each pet $5/day	(40) $37– $85	C K	
Sea Dreamer Inn B & B 541-469-6629, 800-408-4367 15167 McVay Ln each pet $10/day nonsmoking rooms, ½ acre yard, ½ mile to beach	(4) $50– $80	FB	

Burns, Oregon

Best Inn 541-573-1700, 800-237-8466 999 Oregon Ave pets $5/day, refundable deposit nonsmoking rooms, open field, ½ mile to public park	(38) $38– $70	CB M/F	IP S
Bontemps Motel 541-573-2037 74 W Monroe St 800-229-1394 nonsmoking rooms pets $5/day	(15) $30– $50	CB K	
City Center Motel 541-573-5100 73 W Monroe St $10 refundable pet deposit nonsmoking rooms, 5 blocks to public park	(20) $30– $55	C K	
Days Inn Ponderosa Inn 541-573-2047, 800-303-2047 577 W Monroe St pets $10/stay small dogs only, open field across street	(52) $38– $68	CB M/F	OP
Silver Spur Motel 541-573-2077, 800-400-2077 789 N Broadway Ave pets $5/day nonsmoking rooms, popcorn every evening, guest pass to health club, 1 block to public park	(26) $40– $66	CB M/F	

Camp Sherman, Oregon

Black Butte Resort Motel & RV Park 541-595-6514 25635 SW Forest Service Rd 1419 877-595-6514 www.blackbutte-resort.com pets $5/day next to Metolius River and forest service land	(6) $65– $85	C (k)	
Cold Springs Resort & RV Park 541-595-6271 25615 Cold Springs Resort Ln pets $8/day www.coldsprings-resort.com, rustic or modern cabins sleep 6, linens provided, 1 acre lawn, trails	(5) $103– $128	K	
Lake Creek Lodge 541-595-6331, 800-797-6331 13375 SW Forest Service Rd 1419 pets $10/day nonsmoking rooms, laundry, cabins sleep 2 to 9, summer rate includes dinner, wooded trails	(16) $100– $550	K R	OP

Canby, Oregon

Econo Lodge 503-266-5400 463 SW 1st Ave well-behaved dogs only, nonsmoking rooms, 1 mile to public park	(35) $54– $69	CB	

Cannon Beach, Oregon

Cannon Beach Ecola Creek Lodge 503-436-2776 208 5th St 800-873-2749 nonsmoking rooms, 1–2 dogs only, each pet $10/day laundry, public park across street, 600 yards to beach	(22) $89– $199	C K	
Cannon Village Motel 503-436-2317 3163 S Hemlock St pets $5/stay nonsmoking 1 to 2-bdrm suites, laundry, designated pet walking area, 1 block to beach	(6) $50– $200	C K	
Guest House Motel 503-436-0630, 800-585-0630 1016 S Hemlock pets $5–$10/day nonsmoking motel rooms and 4-bdrm 2-bath home, full kitchens in all units, in-room spa, laundry, beach	(3) $99– $259	C K	T
Hallmark Resort 503-436-1566, 888-448-4449 1400 S Hemlock St each pet $12/day www.hallmarkinns.com, nonsmoking rooms, next to beach, laundry, "Pet Basket" includes dog blankets, treats, Dispoz-a-Scoops	(141) $99– $329	C K M/F R/L	IP S T

C = coffee　　IP = indoor pool　OP = outdoor pool CB = continental　K = full kitchen　R = restaurant 　　breakfast　(k) = kitchenette　S = sauna or F = refrigerator　L = lounge　　steamroom FB = full breakfast　M = microwave　T = spa or hot tub	(# of units) & rates	food & drink	pool, sauna & hot tub

Cannon Beach, Oregon (continued)

Haystack Resort　　　　　　　　503-436-1577 3339 S Hemlock St　　　　　　　800-499-2220 www.haystackresort.com　　　　pets $10/day completely nonsmoking, 1½ blocks to beach	(23) $99– $189	C (k)	IP T
Inn at Cannon Beach　　　　　　503-436-9085 3215 S Hemlock St　　　　　　　800-321-6304 www.atcannonbeach.com　　　　pets $10/day completely nonsmoking, 1 to 2 dogs only, in-room spa, 1 block to park and beach	(40) $159– $209	CB (k)	T
Land's End Motel　　　503-436-2264, 800-793-1477 263 W 2nd St at Oceanfront　　each pet $10/stay nonsmoking rooms, laundry, fireplaces, beach	(14) $95– $205	C K	T
Ocean Lodge　　　　　　　　　503-436-2241 2863 Pacific St　　　　　　　　888-777-4047 www.theoceanlodge.com　　each pet $10/day nonsmoking rooms, in-room spa, 1 to 2 dogs only	(46) $130– $269	CB K M/F	T
Quiet Cannon Lodgings　　　　　503-436-1405 372 N Spruce St　　　　　　each pet $5/stay nonsmoking oceanfront units, fireplaces, sheltered patios overlooking beach and Ecola Creek	(2) $95	(k)	
Sandcastle Motel Condominiums　　503-436-1577 3507 S Hemlock St　　pets $10/day, 800-547-6100 nonsmoking rooms, laundry, 1½ blocks to beach	(8) $209– $239	K	IP T
Surfsand Resort　　　　　　　　503-436-2274 1315 S Hemlock St　　　　　　　800-547-6100 www.surfsand.com　　　　　　pets $12/day completely nonsmoking, laundry, close to beach and walking trails	(83) $135– $269	C K R/L	IP T
Tasha's Garden Vacation Rental for People with Pets 168 Sunset Blvd　　　　　　　503-436-9610 fully equipped cottage, yard, 3 blocks to beach	(1) $75– $95	K	

Tolovana Inn 3400 S Hemlock St www.tolovanainn.com nonsmoking rooms, laundry, fitness center, licensed massage therapist, next to beach	503-436-2211 800-333-8890 each pet $10/day	(96) $75– $165	C K R/L	IP S T

Canyonville, Oregon

Leisure Inn 554 SW Pine nonsmoking rooms, 1 block to public park	541-839-4278 pets $5/day	(37) $40– $45	C K	OP
Riverside Lodge 1786 Stanton Park Rd nonsmoking rooms, close to public park	541-839-4557 pets $10/stay	(16) $39	C M/F	
Valley View Motel 1926 Stanton Park Rd nonsmoking rooms, riverside area for walking dogs, ⅛ mile to Stanton Park	541-839-4550 pets $10/stay	(11) $39– $54	C	

Cascade Locks, Oregon

Best Western Columbia River Inn 735 NW Wanapa St nonsmoking rooms, exercise room, each pet $10/day open grassy area for walking dogs, close to hiking trails, www.bestwestern.com/columbiariverinn	541-374-8777 800-595-7108	(62) $59– $129	CB M/F	IP T
Bridge of the Gods Motel & RV Park 630 Wanapa St nonsmoking rooms, laundry, 1½ blocks to walking trails, 2½ blocks to public park	541-374-8628 small dogs only,	(15) $30– $64	C (k)	
Econo Inn 25 Oneonta St nonsmoking rooms, laundry, 1 block to public park	541-374-8417 pets $3–$5/day	(30) $32– $48	C M/F	

Cave Junction, Oregon

Country Hills Resort 7901 Caves Hwy nonsmoking rooms and cabins, laundry, tent and RV sites, 22 acres with creek and trails, 12 miles to Oregon Caves National Park	541-592-3406, 800-997-8464 pets $5/stay	(11) $45– $69	CB K	

C = coffee / CB = continental breakfast / F = refrigerator / FB = full breakfast	IP = indoor pool / K = full kitchen / (k) = kitchenette / L = lounge / M = microwave	OP = outdoor pool / R = restaurant / S = sauna or steamroom / T = spa or hot tub	(# of units) & rates	food & drink	pool, sauna & hot tub

Cave Junction, Oregon (continued)

Junction Inn 406 S Redwood Hwy 1 mile to public park		541-592-3106 800-592-4466 pets $5/day	(60) $50– $62	M/F R	OP

Charleston, Oregon

Captain John's Motel 63360 Kingfisher Dr nonsmoking rooms, 2 miles to public park		541-888-4041 each pet $10/day	(47) $42– $46	CB	

Chemult, Oregon

Chemult Motel S Hwy 97 nonsmoking rooms, 3 acres for walking dogs, snowmobile and walking trail		541-365-2228 pets $5/stay	(16) $30– $40		
Crater Lake Motel 109482 Hwy 97 N nonsmoking rooms, 2 miles to public park, 5 lakes within 15 miles, 20 miles to Crater Lake		541-365-2241	(20) $32– $95	C K	
Dawson House Lodge 1st St and Hwy 97 completely nonsmoking, in-room spa, ¼ mile to public park, ½ mile to walking trails		541-365-2232 www.dawsonhouse.net	(9) $45– $95	CB K	T
Feather Bed Inn 108915 Hwy 97 N www.thefeatherbedinn.com, nonsmoking rooms and 2-bdrm house, in-room spa, laundry, on 5 acres next to national forest land		541-365-2235 pets $5/stay	(14) $25– $120	CB K	T
Holiday Village Motel Beaver Marsh (Hwy 97) nonsmoking rooms, open area by airport for walking dogs, next to national forest land and trails		541-365-2394 pets $5/stay	(8) $30– $76	C K M/F	

Whispering Pines Motel Hwy 97 & Hwy 138 nonsmoking rooms, close to national forest land, 14 miles to Crater Lake north entrance	541-365-2259 pets $5/day	(11) $35– $55	C K

Chiloquin, Oregon

Sportsman Motel 27627 Hwy 97 N nonsmoking rooms, large field for walking dogs	541-783-2867 each pet $5/day	(8) $29– $42	C K
Spring Creek Ranch Motel 47600 Hwy 97 N nonsmoking rooms and cabins sleep 8, 25 wooded acres on a trout creek, ½ mile to Collier State Park	541-783-2775 $25 refundable pet deposit	(10) $40– $80	K

Christmas Valley, Oregon

Christmas Valley Desert Inn Christmas Valley Rd # 1 nonsmoking rooms, lake and open area for walking dogs, 1 mile to public park	541-576-2262 pets $5/stay	(16) $30– $45	K
Lakeside Terrace Motel #1 Spruce nonsmoking rooms, patios, RV sites, bathhouse	541-576-2309 $20 refundable pet deposit	(10) $34– $49	M/F R

Clackamas, Oregon

Clackamas Inn 16010 SE 82nd Dr www.clackamasinn.com nonsmoking rooms, laundry, 1 block to walking trail	503-650-5340 800-874-6560 pets $10/day	(44) $49– $119	CB M/F	OP

Cloverdale, Oregon

Raines Resort 33555 Ferry St fully equipped cabins, RV sites, 1 mile to beach	503-965-6371 pets $5/stay	(7) $45– $65	K

Condon, Oregon

Condon Motel 216 N Washington St laundry, completely nonsmoking, open walking area	541-384-2181 pets $5/stay	(18) $38– $50	C M/F

C = coffee CB = continental 　breakfast F = refrigerator FB = full breakfast	IP = indoor pool K = full kitchen (k) = kitchenette L = lounge M = microwave	OP = outdoor pool R = restaurant S = sauna or 　steamroom T = spa or hot tub	# of units & rates	food & drink	pool, sauna & hot tub

Condon, Oregon (continued)

	# of units & rates	food & drink	pool, sauna & hot tub
Hotel Condon　　　　541-384-4624, 800-201-6706 202 S Main St　　　　$25 refundable pet deposit small dogs only, 3 blocks to public park, 5 minute drive to outdoor museum	(18) $70– $95	CB F R/L	

Coos Bay, Oregon

	# of units & rates	food & drink	pool, sauna & hot tub
Best Western Holiday Motel　　　　541-269-5111 411 N Bayshore Dr　each pet $10/day, 800-228-8655 dogs under 35 lbs only, nonsmoking rooms, laundry, open field for walking dogs, ½ block to walking path	(83) $69– $104	CB F	IP T
Coos Bay Manor B & B　　　　541-269-1224 955 S 5th St　　　　pets $10/stay, 800-269-1224 nonsmoking rooms, 3 blocks to bayfront area, ½ mile to city park	(3) $85– $100	FB	
Edgewater Inn　　　　541-267-0423, 800-233-0423 275 E Johnson Ave　　　　each pet $8/day www.edgewater-inns.com, nonsmoking rooms, in-room spa, close to waterfront and walking trail	(82) $80– $92	CB M/F	IP S T
Motel 6　　　　541-267-7171, 800-466–8356 1445 N Bayshore Dr　nonsmoking rooms, laundry, grassy areas for walking dogs, 1 mile to public park	(94) $44– $54	C K	S T
Old Tower House B & B　　　　541-888-6058 476 Newmark Ave　　　　pets $10/day www.towerbnb.go.to　　dogs allowed in carriage house suite only, ½ acre yard, 1 block to waterfront	(5) $80	FB K	
Pacific Empire Motel　　　　541-888-3281 155 S Empire Blvd　　　　nonsmoking rooms, open field for walking dogs, 1 block to bayfront	(51) $33– $49	(k) R	
Red Lion Inn　　　541-267-4141, 800-547-8010 1313 N Bayshore Dr # 1　　　　www.redlion.com nonsmoking rooms, laundry, close to bayfront	(143) $62– $99	C M/F R/L	OP T

This Olde House B & B 541-267-5224 202 Alder Ave pets $15/stay www.bnbweb.com/thisoldehouse.html rooms and suite, 3 blocks to bayfront and boardwalk, evening hors d'oeuvres and wine, complimentary gourmet dinner for guests staying 3 nights or more	(5) $85– $155	FB	T
Timber Lodge Motel 541-267-7066, 800-782-7592 1001 N Bayshore Dr pets $5/stay nonsmoking rooms, open field, ½ mile to boardwalk	(53) $39– $90	C M/F R/L	

Coquille, Oregon

Myrtle Lane Motel 541-396-2102 787 N Central St pets $4/day nonsmoking rooms, 1 mile to public park	(25) $35– $55	C K M/F	

Corvallis, Oregon

At Home In Oregon.com 541-929-3059 6120 SW Country Club Dr a booking service for dog-friendly B & Bs and vacation rentals in Corvallis area and statewide, see www.athomeinoregon.com	(24) $59 and up		
Corvallis Budget Inn 541-752-8756 1480 SW 3rd St pets $5/stay nonsmoking rooms, small dogs only, public park	(24) $32– $55	K	
Holiday Inn Express 541-752-0800, 800-465-4329 781 NE 2nd St pets $10/day laundry, nonsmoking, walking trail to public park	(93) $69– $129	CB M/F	IP T
Econo Lodge 541-752-9601, 800-553-2666 345 NW 2nd St pets $5/day nonsmoking, laundry, in-room spa, riverside trail	(61) $38– $58	C M/F	T
Hanson Country Inn B & B 541-752-2919 795 SW Hanson St 2 suites with private decks and 2-bdrm cottage, completely nonsmoking, on 6 acres for walking dogs	(3) $95– $145	FB K	
Jason Inn 541-753-7326, 800-346-3291 800 NW 9th St pets $4/day ½ mile from OSU campus for walking dogs	(51) $36– $75	R/L	OP

C = coffee, CB = continental breakfast, F = refrigerator, FB = full breakfast, IP = indoor pool, K = full kitchen, (k) = kitchenette, L = lounge, M = microwave, OP = outdoor pool, R = restaurant, S = sauna or steamroom, T = spa or hot tub	(# of units) & rates	food & drink	pool, sauna & hot tub

Corvallis, Oregon (continued)

Motel Orleans 541-758-9125 935 NW Garfield Ave 800-626-1900 nonsmoking rooms, laundry, 2 blocks to public park	(61) $47– $73	C M/F	T
Shanico Inn 541-754-7474, 800-432-1233 1113 NW 9th St each pet $10/day nonsmoking rooms, bike path for walking dogs	(76) $63– $82	CB F	OP
Super 8 Motel 541-758-8088, 800-800-8000 407 NW 2nd $25 refundable pet deposit nonsmoking rooms, laundry, riverside walking trail	(101) $56– $76	CB M/F	IP T
Towne House Motor Inn 541-753-4496, 800-898-4496 350 SW 4th St pets $5–$7/day 1 to 2 dogs only, nonsmoking rooms, laundry, 2 blocks to walking trail, 3 blocks to public park	(85) $32– $49	C K R/L	
Travel Inn 541-752-5917 1562 SW 3rd St 1 block to public park	(15) $28– $49	K	

Cottage Grove, Oregon

Best Western Village Green Inn 541-942-2491 725 Row River Rd 800-343-7666 nonsmoking rooms, laundry, 1 block to jogging trails	(96) $59– $119	CB	
City Center Motel 541-942-8322 737 Hwy 99 S pets $5/day small dogs only, nonsmoking rooms, public park	(15) $35– $45	C K	
Cottage Grove Comfort Inn 541-942-9747 845 Gateway Blvd 800-944-0287 nonsmoking rooms, laundry each pet $10/day open field across street, walking trail nearby	(64) $54– $119	CB M/F	OP T
Holiday Inn Express 541-942-1000, 800-465-4329 1601 Gateway Blvd pets $10/stay nonsmoking rooms, exercise room, ¼ mile to park	(41) $69– $99	CB M/F	IP T

Relax Inn 541-942-5132 1030 N Pacific Hwy 99 pets $5/day nonsmoking rooms, yard, 1 mile to public park	(24) $28– $45	C K	

Crescent Lake, Oregon

Crescent Creek Cottages & RV Park 541-433-2324 Hwy 58 Milepost 71 pets $5/stay creekside cabins, all linens provided, RV sites, on 4 acres with trails for walking dogs	(5) $45– $75	K	
Crescent Lake Lodge & Resort 541-433-2505 NE Shore each pet $10/day www.crescentlakeresort.com, 1 to 2 dogs per cabin only, kitchens in most cabins, all linens provided, laundry, boat rentals, national forest trails	(18) $55– $195	K R/L	
Odell Lake Resort 541-433-2540, 800-432-2540 Hwy 58 East Odell Lake Exit each pet $5/day www.odelllakeresort.com, cabins sleep 4 to 16, seasonal restaurant, national forest land and trails	(19) $80– $230	K R	
Willamette Pass Inn & RV Park 541-433-2211 19821 Hwy 58 nonsmoking rooms and chalet sleep up to 8, laundry, RV sites, bathhouse, wilderness trails, 2 miles to lake	(13) $58– $120	C (k)	

Creswell, Oregon

Creswell Inn 541-895-3341, 877-895-3341 345 E Oregon Ave www.creswellinn.com nonsmoking rooms pets $5/day	(69) $39– $99	C M/F	OP

Curtin, Oregon

Stardust Motel 541-942-5706 455 Bear Creek Rd pets $5/day nonsmoking rooms, 5 minute walk to small park	(18) $28– $35	C K	

Dallas, Oregon

Best Western Dallas Inn & Suites 503-623-6000 250 Orchard Dr pets $10/stay www.bestwestern.com/dallasinnandsuites, exercise room, dogs under 30 lbs only, 1½ acre open field	(42) $63– $90	CB M/F	T

C = coffee IP = indoor pool OP = outdoor pool CB = continental K = full kitchen R = restaurant breakfast (k) = kitchenette S = sauna or F = refrigerator L = lounge steamroom FB = full breakfast M = microwave T = spa or hot tub	# of units & rates	food & drink	pool, sauna & hot tub

Dallas, Oregon (continued)

Riverside Inn & Suites 503-623-8163 517 Main St pets $5–$10/day nonsmoking rooms, ½ mile to public park	(20) $48– $78	C K	

Depoe Bay, Oregon

Crown Pacific Inn 541-765-7773, 888-845-5131 Hwy 101 & NE Bechill St pets $5/day www.crownpacificinn.com, nonsmoking rooms, small dogs only, in-room spa, great view of ocean and Spouting Horn from balconies, 2 miles to beach	(31) $65– $115	CB M/F	T
Four Winds Motel 541-765-2793, 888-875-2936 356 Hwy 101 nonsmoking rooms, laundry, ocean access 1 block	(22) $39– $49	CB K M/F	
Gracie's Landing Inn B & B 541-765-2322 235 SE Bay View Ave pets $7/day, 800-228-0448 completely nonsmoking, patio doors open onto lawn for walking dogs, next to public park	(13) $90– $135	FB	
Homestead B & B 541-765-3363, 877-321-3363 614 NE Hwy 101 each pet $10/day completely nonsmoking home, advance reservation recommended for dog-friendly rooms, dogs MUST be on leash at all times, oceanview sun porch, open area for walking dogs, 1½ miles to public beach	(8) $45– $75	FB	
Inn at Arch Rock 541-765-2560, 800-767-1835 70 NW Sunset St pets $10/day dogs under 20 lbs only, nonsmoking, beach access	(15) $85– $129	CB	
Trollers Lodge 541-765-2287, 800-472-9335 355 SW Hwy 101 each pet $7/day www.trollerslodge.com, completely nonsmoking rooms and oceanfront cottage, 1½ blocks to park and harbor, 1¼ miles north to beach access	(12) $59– $150	C K	

Whale Cove Inn 541-765-2255, 866-364-9159 2345 S Hwy 101 www.whalecoveinn.com small dogs only, completely nonsmoking, public park	(7) $50– $95	R/L	

Detroit, Oregon

All Seasons Motel 503-854-3421 130 Breitenbush Rd well-behaved quiet dogs only, rooms and 2-bdrm house, dogsitting service, lakefront and trails www.open.org/~tomvuyo/allseas.htm	(15) $35– $125	K	
Detroit Motel 503-854-3344 175 Detroit Ave $25 refundable pet deposit nonsmoking rooms, grassy area, ½ block to lakefront	(10) $45– $60	K	

Diamond, Oregon

Hotel Diamond 541-493-1898 10 Main St dogs allowed at manager's discretion only, nonsmoking rooms and 3-bdrm house, open March–October, next to Malheur wildlife refuge	(9) $65– $105	CB R	

Diamond Lake, Oregon

Diamond Lake Resort 541-793-3333, 800-733-7593 350 Resort Dr each pet $5/day www.diamondlake.net, nonsmoking rooms and cabins sleep up to 6, 5 miles north of Crater Lake	(92) $75– $200	K R/L	

Elgin, Oregon

Minam Motel 541-437-4475 72601 Hwy 82 riverfront area for walking dogs	(8) $26– $29	K	
Pinewood B & B 541-437-4010, 888-731-8889 72333 Darr Rd www.pinewoodbb.com secluded log house with 2-bdrm suite sleeps 4, fenced dog run and horse paddock, next to Boise Cascade forest area for walking dogs	(1) $85– $115	FB (k)	T
Stampede Inn 541-437-2441 51 S 7th Ave each pet $5/day nonsmoking rooms, 3 blocks to park and public pool	(14) $38– $48	M/F	

C = coffee IP = indoor pool OP = outdoor pool CB = continental K = full kitchen R = restaurant breakfast (k) = kitchenette S = sauna or F = refrigerator L = lounge steamroom FB = full breakfast M = microwave T = spa or hot tub	(# of units) & rates	food & drink	pool, sauna & hot tub

Elkton, Oregon

Big K Guest Ranch 541-584-2295, 800-390-2445 20029 Hwy 138 W pets $10/day www.big-k.com, B&B, nonsmoking rooms, laundry, 2,500 acre working ranch so dogs must be on leash	(20) $125– $339	FB M/F R	T

Enterprise, Oregon

Ponderosa Motel 541-426-3186 102 E Greenwood St pets $5–$10/day nonsmoking rooms, 2 blocks to park and trails	(33) $46– $107	CB M/F	
Wallowa Lake Vacation Rentals 541-426-2039 405 SW Thorpe Lane pets $10/day nonsmoking homes and cabins, most are located within 5 blocks of walking trails or public parks	(8) $80– $250	K	T
Wilderness Inn Motel 541-426-4535, 800-965-1205 301 W North St each pet $5/day nonsmoking rooms, in-room spa, 2 blocks to public park and open field at fairgrounds	(29) $46– $74	C K	T

Estacada, Oregon

Olallie Lake Resort 541-504-1010 Mount Hood National Forest www.olallielake.com close to Pacific Crest hiking trail, campsites, fishing	(16) $30– $105		

Eugene, Oregon

A-1 Krumdieck Kottage B & B 541-688-9406 858 Washington St 2-story completely nonsmoking house sleeps 2, 3 blocks to public park, 4 blocks to riverside trail	(1) $75	FB K	
Best Western Greentree Inn 541-485-2727 1759 Franklin Blvd 800-528-1234 www.bestwestern.com/greentreeinneugene next to public walking paths	(65) $62– $92	CB K R/L	OP T

Best Western New Oregon Motel 1655 Franklin Blvd nonsmoking rooms, laundry, exercise facility, next to public walking paths	541-683-3669 800-528-1234	(128) $62– $92	CB	IP S T
Boon's Red Carpet Motel 1055 W 6th Ave open area for walking dogs, 2 blocks to public park, 6 blocks to downtown and fairgrounds	541-345-0579 pets $5/stay	(24) $32– $45	M/F	
Budget Host Motor Inn 1190 W 6th Ave www.budhostinn.com nonsmoking rooms, 6 blocks to public park	541-342-7273 800-554-9822 pets $5/day	(77) $35– $55	M/F	
Campbell House B & B 252 Pearl St www.campbellhouse.com, cottage and 2 dog-friendly rooms with private entrances, laundry, masseuse, natural park area, 2 blocks to riverside walking paths	541-343-1119 each pet $50/day	(19) $109– $345	FB F R	
Classic Residence Inn 1140 W 6th Ave www.classicresidenceinn.com, nonsmoking rooms, laundry, large yard, ½ mile to riverside paths and public park, close to fairgrounds and Hult Center	541-343-0730 pets $5–$7/day	(39) $30– $85	K F	
Country Squire Inn 33100 Van Duyn Rd nonsmoking rooms, laundry, large yard and quiet road for walking dogs, 1½ miles to public park	541-484-2000 each pet $5/day	(105) $35– $100	C	
Courtesy Inn 345 W 6th Ave www.courtesyinneugene.com nonsmoking rooms, short walk to public park	541-345-3391 888-259-8481 each pet $10/day	(34) $49– $69	CB M/F	
Days Inn Eugene/Springfield 1859 Franklin Blvd nonsmoking rooms, walking distance to public park	541-342-6383 800-444-6383	(60) $53– $96	CB M/F R	S T
Eugene Motor Lodge 541-344-5233, 800-876-7829 476 E Broadway nonsmoking rooms, across street to riverfront park	pets $8/day	(49) $35– $55	C M/F	OP

C = coffee	IP = indoor pool	OP = outdoor pool			
CB = continental	K = full kitchen	R = restaurant			
breakfast	(k) = kitchenette	S = sauna or	(# of units) & rates	food & drink	pool, sauna & hot tub
F = refrigerator	L = lounge	steamroom			
FB = full breakfast	M = microwave	T = spa or hot tub			

Eugene, Oregon (continued)

		# of units & rates	food & drink	pool, sauna & hot tub
Executive House Motel	541-683-4000	(36)	F	
1040 W 6th Ave	nonsmoking rooms,	$30–		
5 minute walk to Rose Garden and walking paths		$45		
Hilton Eugene	541-342-2000	(273)	R/L	IP
66 E 6th Ave	800-937-6660	$95–		T
www.eugene.hilton.com	pets $25/stay	$170		
nonsmoking rooms, fitness center, close to waterfront and walking trail				
La Quinta Inn & Suites 541-344-8335, 800-531-5900		(73)	FB	IP
155 Day Island Rd	www.laquinta.com	$79–	K	T
nonsmoking rooms, laundry, in-room spa, 24 hour pool, spa, fitness center, public park and trail		$170		
Motel 6 Eugene South 541-687-2395, 800-466-8356		(59)	C	OP
3690 Glenwood Dr	nonsmoking rooms,	$40–	M/F	
area for walking dogs, 1½ miles to Prefontaine Trail		$50		
Nite Inn	541-686-2060	(25)	K	
1522 W 6th Ave	www.niteinnmotel.com	$33–	M/F	
laundry, open field for walking dogs		$50		
Quality Inn & Suites	541-342-1243	(79)	CB	OP
2121 Franklin Blvd	800-456-6487	$50–	K	S
exercise room, next to public park		$116		T
Ramada Inn	541-342-5181	(148)	CB	IP
225 Coburg Rd	800-917-5500	$55–	M/F	T
www.ramada.com	pets $15/stay	$140	R/L	
laundry, area for walking dogs, ¼ mile to public park with riverside trails				
Red Lion Inn	541-342-5201	(137)	R/L	OP
205 Coburg Rd	800-733-5466	$59–		
www.redlion.com/properties/eugene.html		$99		
nonsmoking rooms, exercise room, courtyard for walking dogs, laundry, 1 mile to park and trails				

Residence Inn by Marriott 541-342-7171 25 Club Rd 800-331-3131 www.residenceinn.com/eugri pets $50/stay complimentary dinner Monday–Thursday, laundry, public park and riverside walking trails	(84) $109– $139	FB K	OP T
Sixty-Six Motel 541-342-5041 755 E Broadway $25 refundable pet deposit nonsmoking rooms, 100 yards to riverfront path	(66) $32– $48		
Timbers Motel 541-343-3345, 800-643-4167 1015 Pearl St well-behaved quiet dogs only, nonsmoking rooms, 8 blocks to riverside trails	(55) $39– $59	CB M/F	S
Valley River Inn 541-687-0123, 800-543-8266 1000 Valley River Way www.valleyriverinn.com nonsmoking rooms, dogs allowed in ground floor rooms only, close to paved walking path along river	(257) $89– $200	C R/L	OP S T
Value Inn Motel 541-688-2733 595 Hwy 99 N pets $5/day 1 dog only per room	(25) $30– $50	C	

Fields, Oregon

Fields General Store & Motel 541-495-2275 22276 Fields Dr open area for walking dogs	(4) $40– $85	R	

Florence, Oregon

Lighthouse Inn 541-997-3221 155 Hwy 101 each pet $5/day http://members.tripod.com/lighthouseinn nonsmoking rooms, 1 block to riverfront	(28) $55– $125	C M/F	
Mercer Lake Resort 541-997-3633, 800-355-3633 88875 Bayberry Ln pets $5/day laundry, RV sites, on 5 acres, trails from cabins to lake for walking dogs	(11) $45– $100	K	
Money Saver Motel 541-997-7131 170 Hwy 101 pets $7/stay www.moneysaverflorence.com, nonsmoking rooms ½ block to public park, 6 miles to beach access	(40) $45– $81	C	

C = coffee IP = indoor pool OP = outdoor pool CB = continental K = full kitchen R = restaurant breakfast (k) = kitchenette S = sauna or F = refrigerator L = lounge steamroom FB = full breakfast M = microwave T = spa or hot tub	(# of units) & rates	food & drink	pool, sauna & hot tub

Florence, Oregon (continued)

Ocean Breeze Motel 541-997-2642, 800-753-2642 85165 Hwy 101 S pets $8–$10/stay nonsmoking rooms, large yard for walking dogs, ½ mile to the dunes, 1 mile to beach access	(14) $35– $89	C K M/F	
Park Motel 541-997-2634, 800-392-0441 85034 Hwy 101 each pet $8/day www.parkmotel.florenceor.com, nonsmoking rooms, and separate chalet, 2½ acres for walking dogs	(17) $38– $160	C K R	
Villa West Motel 541-997-3457 901 Hwy 101 pets $10/day, refundable deposit dogs under 15 lbs only, close to waterfront and trail	(22) $28– $63	C M/F	

Forest Grove, Oregon

| Holiday Motel 503-357-7411 3224 Pacific Ave pets $7/day nonsmoking rooms | (14) $45– $65 | (k) | |

Fort Klamath, Oregon

Aspen Inn 541-381-2321 52250 Hwy 62 pets $10/day completely nonsmoking, open area for walking dogs, walking distance to Wood River	(12) $45– $75	C M/F	
Crater Lake Resort 541-381-2349 50711 Hwy 62 each pet $5/day completely nonsmoking, RV sites, wooded areas for walking dogs	(9) $45– $75	C K	
Horseshoe Ranch B & B 541-381-2297, 866-658-5933 52909 Hwy 62 www.thehorseshoeranch.com 65 acre ranch, wine and hors d'oeuvres, laundry, river access, walking trails, "horse hotel"—barn, corral, pasture, riding trails—each horse $15/day	(6) $79– $150	FB K	

Wilson's Cottages 541-381-2209 57997 Hwy 62 fully equipped 2 to 3-bdrm cottages sleep up to 7, 130 wooded acres with walking trails	(10) $50– $80	K		

Fossil, Oregon

Bridge Creek Flora Inn B & B 541-763-2355 828 Main St completely nonsmoking facility, lots of open area for walking dogs	(5) $60– $65	FB		
Fossil Motel & Trailer Park 541-763-4075 105 First St nonsmoking rooms, RV sites, next to public park, lots of open area for walking dogs	(10) $34– $57	CB K		

Garibaldi, Oregon

Bayshore Inn 503-322-2552 227 Garibaldi Ave pets $7/stay laundry, close to walking trail and Tillamook Bay	(22) $64– $110	C M/F K		
Harbor View Inn & RV Park 503-322-3251 302 S 7th St pets $5/day nonsmoking rooms, RV sites, bayfront access, trails	(20) $45– $50	M/F		
Western Royal Inn 503-322-3338, 800-624-2912 502 E Garibaldi Ave pets $10/day nonsmoking rooms, laundry, open area for walking dogs, 5 minute drive to beach	(50) $45– $125	C M/F	IP S T

Gates, Oregon

Oak Park Motel & Trailer Park 503-897-3420 119 E Central St RV sites, lots of area for walking dogs	(7) $55– $60	M/F		

Gearhart, Oregon

Gearhart Ocean Inn 503-738-7373, 800-352-8034 67 N Cottage Ave each pet $10/day www.oregoncoastlodgings.com/gearhart 1 to 2 dogs only, yard with barbecue, croquet, 3 blocks to beach access, 1 block to historic ridge path and tennis court	(11) $45– $129	C K F		

C = coffee IP = indoor pool OP = outdoor pool CB = continental K = full kitchen R = restaurant breakfast (k) = kitchenette S = sauna or F = refrigerator L = lounge steamroom FB = full breakfast M = microwave T = spa or hot tub	(# of units) & rates	food & drink	pool, sauna & hot tub

Gearhart, Oregon (continued)

Gearhart-by-the-Sea 503-738-8331, 800-547-0115 1157 N Marion Ave each pet $11/day nonsmoking fully equipped condominiums, laundry, beachfront access, close to public golf course	(85) $113– $174	C K	IP
Lodge at Gearhart's Little Beach 503-288-7318 715 H St 888-502-5588 8-bdrm 4-bath lodge sleeps 26, 4 blocks to beach	(1) $725– $1215		

Gilchrist, Oregon

Gilchrist Inn 541-433-2878 3 Mississippi Dr pets $10/stay 2 to 3-bdrm units, completely nonsmoking, fenced yard for walking dogs, close to bike and walking path	(6) $53– $80	C K	

Gladstone, Oregon

Oxford Suites 503-722-7777, 877-558-7710 75 82nd Dr pets $15/stay completely nonsmoking, complimentary cocktails and hors d'oeuvres, laundry, racquetball club passes, next to riverside walking trail and public park	(99) $69– $99	FB	IP T

Glendale, Oregon

Glendale Inn 541-832-2662 127 Pacific Ave pets $5/stay nonsmoking rooms, open area for walking dogs, 1 block to public park	(16) $48– $52		

Gleneden Beach, Oregon

Beachcombers Haven 541-764-2252, 800-428-5533 7045 NW Glen Ave pets $25/stay www.beachcombershaven.com, oceanfront homes and condominiums, hot tubs, easy beach access	(13) $125– $225	K	T

Salishan Lodge & Golf Resort 541-764-2371 7760 Hwy 101 N 800-890-9316 completely nonsmoking, fitness center, pets $25/day 3 miles of private beach for walking dogs	(205) $119– $269	C R/L	IP T

Glide, Oregon

Steelhead Run B & B 541-496-0563, 800-348-0563 23049 N Umpqua Hwy pets $10/stay completely nonsmoking, laundry, 5 acres of woods and walking trails, river swimming	(5) $58– $125	FB K	

Gold Beach, Oregon

Clear Sky Lodgings 541-247-6456 29350 Clear Sky Ln www.clearskylodging.com dogs allowed with manager's approval only, 2-bdrm luxury townhouses and 2 to 3-bdrm homes, laundry, decks, 3 wooded acres, 3 minute walk to beach	(8) $128– $225	K	S T
Drift In Motel 541-247-4547, 800-424-3833 94250 N Port Dr pets $5/stay nonsmoking rooms, miniature golf course, area for walking dogs, 10 minute walk to beach	(23) $25– $62	C (k)	
Econo Lodge 541-247-6606 29171 Ellensburg Ave 800-503-0833 www.econolodgegoldbeach.com each pet $5/stay nonsmoking rooms, walking trail, easy beach access	(38) $40– $125	CB K	
Half Moon Bar Lodge 541-247-6968, 888-291-8268 94181 4th St dogs allowed by advance reservation, completely nonsmoking, room rate includes meals, accessible by 54-mile boat ride or 11-mile hike, www.southcoastlodging.com/HalfMoonBar.htm	(16) $110– $120	R	S
House at Kissing Rock 541-247-5037, 800-495-9067 94181 4th St dogs allowed by advance reservation, fully equipped home sleeps 8, overlooking ocean, www.southcoastlodging.com/KissingRock.htm	(1) $165– $200	K	T
Inn of the Beachcomber 541-247-6691, 888-690-2378 29266 Ellensburg Ave pets $25/stay www.beachcomber-inn.com, dogs under 20 lbs only, nonsmoking rooms, lawn, next to the beach	(48) $65– $125	CB K	IP T

C = coffee CB = continental breakfast F = refrigerator FB = full breakfast	IP = indoor pool K = full kitchen (k) = kitchenette L = lounge M = microwave	OP = outdoor pool R = restaurant S = sauna or steamroom T = spa or hot tub	(# of units) & rates	food & drink	pool, sauna & hot tub

Gold Beach, Oregon (continued)

		& rates	food & drink	pool
Ireland's Rustic Lodges 541-247-7718 29330 Ellensburg Ave $5–$10/day nonsmoking rooms, ocean view, yard, beach access		(40) $55– $65	C M/F	
Jot's Resort 541-247-6676, 800-367-5687 94360 Wedderburn Lp pets $10–$25/day www.jotsresort.com, nonsmoking rooms, laundry, large area for walking dogs, ½ mile to beach		(140) $50– $315	C K R/L	IP S T
Motel 6 541-247-4533, 800-759-4533 94433 Jerry's Flat Rd www.motel6goldbeach.com nonsmoking rooms, in-room spa, laundry, walking trail to viewpoint at water tower, 2 blocks to beach		(50) $36– $68	C K	T
Oregon Coast Vacation Rentals 541-247-4114 32716 Miller Ranch Rd pets $35/stay, 800-775-4114 www.oregoncoastrentals.com, fully equipped homes, dogs allowed by advance reservation only		(4) $160– $240	C	T
Oregon Trail Lodge 541-247-6030 29855 Ellensburg Ave pets $5/stay nonsmoking rooms, 2 blocks to harborfront and jetties for walking dogs		(18) $23– $62	C M/F	
Paradise Wilderness Lodge 541-247-6022 29116 11th St 800-525-2161 www.paradise-lodge.com, located 52 miles upriver, accessible by jetboat/helicopter/hiking trail/raft, dogs allowed by advance reservations only		(13) $95– $200		
Rogue Autel Motel 541-247-7444 29450 Ellensburg Ave rooms-cottages-homes, RV sites, grassy area behind motel, trail to beach		(11) $35– $95	K	
Sand 'n' Sea Motel 541-247-6658, 800-808-7263 29362 Ellensburg Ave pets $5/day www.sandnseamotel.com, 1 to 2-bdrm nonsmoking units, walking trails, ¾ mile to public beach		(43) $62– $99	CB K M/F	T

Sanddollar Inn　　　　　541-247-9685, 866-726-3657 29399 Ellensburg Ave　　　　　　　　　pets $5/day nonsmoking rooms, beach access 100 yards across the fairgrounds	(25) $31– $55	CB (k) M/F	
Tranidu Lodge　　　　　　541-247-5037, 800-495-9067 94181 4th St　　　　　　　www.southcoastlodging.com 6-bdrm 5½-bath home sleeps 22, dogs allowed by advance reservation only	(1) $700	K	IP

Gold Hill, Oregon

Flycaster Motel　　　　　　　　　　　541-855-7178 1356 Rogue River Hwy nonsmoking rooms, ¼ mile to public park	(5) $25– $40	K	
Rogue River Guest House B & B　　　541-855-4485 41 Rogue River Hwy　　　　　　　　877-764-8322 nonsmoking rooms, dinners available on request, in-room spa, friendly resident dog, large fenced yard, 100 yards to river and trails	(3) $65– $125	FB	T

Government Camp, Oregon

Mount Hood Inn　　　　　503-272-3205, 800-443-7777 87450 E Government Camp Lp　　　each pet $10/day nonsmoking rooms, laundry, walking trails	(56) $89– $169	CB M/F	T
Summit Meadow Cabins　　　　　　　1-503-272-3494 Summit Meadow　　　　　　www.summitmeadow.com cabins and chateaus, linens provided, surrounded by national forest, ski right out the front door	(5) $125– $220	K	
Trillium Lake Basin Cabins　　　　　503-297-5993 32798 E Mineral Creek Dr　　　2-bdrm rustic cabin, 3-bdrm chalet, cross-country ski in 1½ miles to the cabins, 1 mile to lake, healing@chiroenergy.com	(2) $95– $225	K	S
View House LLC　　　　　　　　　　503-272-3295 Government Camp　　www.oregontrail.net/~viewhse 2-bdrm 1-bath cabin, fully equipped kitchen, linens provided, national forest land for walking dogs	(1) $168	K	

	# of units & rates	food & drink	pool, sauna & hot tub
C = coffee IP = indoor pool OP = outdoor pool CB = continental K = full kitchen R = restaurant breakfast (k) = kitchenette S = sauna or F = refrigerator L = lounge steamroom FB = full breakfast M = microwave T = spa or hot tub			

Grand Ronde, Oregon

Grand B & B 503-879-1100 8635 Grand Ronde Rd pets $20/stay completely nonsmoking, 1½ fenced acres for walking dogs, 1½ miles to casino, dogsitting service available	(7) $65– $125	FB K	

Granite, Oregon

Granite Lodge 541-755-5200 1525 McCann St nonsmoking rooms, pet walking area, www. grantcounty.cc/business.php/190	(9) $52– $132	CB	

Grants Pass, Oregon

Best Western Grants Pass Inn 541-476-1117 111 NE Agness Ave 800-553-7666 www.bestwestern.com/prop_38102 pets $5/day nonsmoking rooms, laundry	(84) $65– $135	C R/L	OP T
Best Western Inn at the Rogue 541-582-2200 8959 Rogue River Hwy 800-238-0700 www.bestwestern.com/prop_38118 pets $10-20/day nonsmoking rooms, 1 acre lawn, riverside park	(54) $72– $100	CB M/F	OP T
Comfort Inn 541-479-8301 1889 NE 6th St 800-626-1900 nonsmoking rooms, laundry, ½ mile to public park	(59) $65– $95	CB M/F	OP
Discovery Inn 541-476-7793 748 SE 7th St small to medium sized dogs only, nonsmoking rooms, 2 blocks to public park	(35) $32– $55	C	
Flamingo Inn 541-476-6601 728 NW 6th St pets $3/day dogwalking area, 5 minute walk to public park	(33) $25– $35	K	OP
Holiday Inn Express 541-471-6144, 800-838-7666 105 NE Agness Ave each pet $5/day www.hiexpress.com, grassy pet walking area	(81) $68– $84	CB	OP T

Knights Inn Motel 541-479-5595, 800-826-6835 104 SE 7th St pets $5/stay nonsmoking rooms, walking area, 3 blocks to park	(32) $38– $45	C K		
La Quinta Inn & Suites 541-472-1808, 800-527-1133 243 NE Morgan Ln www.laquinta.com nonsmoking rooms, laundry, 24 hour pool	(59) $69– $150	CB K	IP T	
Mahoney Resorts: Rod & Reel/Rogue Valley Motels 7799 Rogue River Hwy 541-582-1516 river frontage, woods and walking trail pets $10/day	(20) $45– $85	K	OP T	
Motel 6 541-474-1331, 800-466-8356 1800 NE 7th St www.motel6.com nonsmoking rooms, laundry, area behind motel for walking dogs, 3 miles to public park, near river dock	(122) $40– $56	C M/F	OP	
Motel Del Rogue 541-479-2111 2600 Rogue River Hwy 866-479-2111 www.moteldelrogue.com each pet $5/day nonsmoking rooms, decks overlooking Rogue River, lawns and riverside trails	(16) $55– $95	C K M/F		
Redwood Motel 541-476-0878 815 NE 6th St 888-535-8824 www.redwoodmotel.com pets $10/day nonsmoking rooms, pool open May–September, year-round hot tub, 10 blocks to public park	(28) $50– $175	CB (k)	OP T	
Riverside Inn Resort 541-476-6873, 800-334-4567 971 SE 6th St pets $15/stay www.riverside-inn.com, nonsmoking rooms, bridge and trail from resort to riverside public park	(159) $59– $275	C K R/L	OP T	
Rogue River Inn 541-582-1120 6285 Rogue River Hwy nonsmoking rooms, laundry, across street from riverside park and trails	(21) $45– $85	C K	OP	
Royal Vue Motor Hotel 541-479-5381 110 NE Morgan Ln 800-452-1452 laundry	(60) $35– $68	C R/L	OP S T	
Shilo Inn 541-479-8391, 800-222-2244 1880 NW 6th St each pet $10/day www.shiloinns.com, pet beds and treats, small lawn for walking dogs, 2 blocks to public parks	(70) $60– $95	CB M/F	OP S	

C = coffee
CB = continental
    breakfast
F = refrigerator
FB = full breakfast
	IP = indoor pool
	K = full kitchen
	(k) = kitchenette
	L = lounge
	M = microwave
		OP = outdoor pool
		R = restaurant
		S = sauna or
		    steamroom
		T = spa or hot tub
			(# of units)
			& rates
				food
				& drink
					pool, sauna
					& hot tub

Grants Pass, Oregon (continued)

Super 8 Motel 541-474-0888, 800-800-8000 1949 NE 7th St $25 refundable pet deposit www.super8.com, nonsmoking rooms, laundry, open lot behind motel for walking dogs	(80) $46– $75	CB K	IP T
Sweet Breeze Inn 541-471-4434, 800-349-4434 1627 NE 6th St www.sweetbreezeinn.com completely nonsmoking, open area for walking dogs	(21) $45– $60	CB M/F	
Travelodge 541-479-6611, 800-578-7878 1950 NW Vine St each pet $5/day www.travelodge.com, dogs under 35 lbs only, large open area for walking, 5 blocks to park	(61) $59– $69	CB M/F	OP

Gresham, Oregon

Best Value Carlton Inn 503-666-9545, 888-315-2378 1572 NE Burnside St pets $10/stay www.bestvalueinn.com, nonsmoking rooms, laundry, open field for walking dogs, 5 minute walk to park	(73) $69– $79	CB R	OP
Best Western Pony Soldier Motor Inn 503-665-1591 1060 NE Cleveland Ave 800-634-7669 www.bestwestern.com, nonsmoking rooms, open area behind motel for walking dogs, 1 mile to park	(78) $69– $95	CB (k) M/F R/L	OP S T
Shilo Inn 503-907-1777, 800-222-2244 2752 NE Hogan each pet $10/day www.shiloinns.com, nonsmoking rooms, pet beds and treats, fitness center, 1 block to public park	(167) $69– $99	K M/F	IP T

Halfway, Oregon

Birch Leaf B & B 541-742-2990 47830 Steele Hill Rd pets $10/stay completely nonsmoking, 40 acres, swimming pond, 3 miles to Eagle Cap Wilderness trailhead	(4) $50– $150	CB K	

Halfway Motel & RV Park 541-742-5722 170 S Main St www.halfwayor.com/motel-rvpark nonsmoking rooms, RV sites, open yard for walking dogs, 4 blocks to public park	(31) $35– $55	C K M/F		
Pine Valley Lodge 541-742-2027 163 N Main St pets $10/stay skyhawk@pinetail.com, gourmet restaurant open to overnight guests only, national forest and trails	(8) $75– $150	CB K R		

Halsey, Oregon

Best Western Pioneer Lodge 541-369-2804 33180 Hwy 228 each pet $5/day 38143@hotelbestwestern.com, nonsmoking rooms, laundry, lawn and open field for walking dogs	(60) $61– $75	CB R/L	OP T	

Hammond, Oregon

South Jetty Inn 503-861-2500 984 Pacific Dr pets $5/stay jettyinn@pacifier.com, nonsmoking rooms, 2 blocks to marina, 1 mile to state park	(9) $35– $95	C (k)		

Heppner, Oregon

Northwestern Motel & RV Park 541-676-9167 389 N Main St 888-851-8436 nonsmoking rooms, RV sites each pet $5/day across street from public park and open field	(16) $45– $50	C F		

Hermiston, Oregon

Economy Inn 541-567-5516, 888-567-9521 835 N First St each pet $5/day nonsmoking rooms, RV sites, walking area and park	(39) $38– $75	CB M/F	OP	
Oxford Inn 541-567-7777, 888-729-7848 655 N First St pets $20/stay www.oxfordsuites.com, nonsmoking rooms, laundry, open lot behind building for walking dogs	(90) $55– $69	CB M/F	OP	
Oxford Suites 541-564-8000 1050 N First St pets $20/stay www.oxfordsuites.com, laundry, exercise room	(127) $75– $109	CB M/F	IP T	

C = coffee
CB = continental
       breakfast
F = refrigerator
FB = full breakfast
	IP = indoor pool
	K = full kitchen
	(k) = kitchenette
	L = lounge
	M = microwave
		OP = outdoor pool
		R = restaurant
		S = sauna or
		       steamroom
		T = spa or hot tub
			(# of units)
			& rates
				food
				& drink
					pool, sauna
					& hot tub

Hermiston, Oregon (continued)

Way Inn 541-567-5561, 888-564-8767 635 S Hwy 395 each pet $2/day nonsmoking rooms, open area for walking dogs	(30) $44– $46	C M/F	OP

Hillsboro, Oregon

Candlewood Suites Hotel 503-681-2121 3133 NE Shute Rd 800-946-6200 www.candlewoodsuites.com pets $75/stay nonsmoking rooms, laundry, next to private park for walking dogs	(126) $109– $129	CB K	T
Dunes Motel 503-648-8991 452 SE 10th Ave 800-547-5550 nonsmoking rooms, laundry, 2 blocks to public park	(44) $44– $70	C M/F	
Residence Inn Portland West 503-531-3200 18855 NW Tanasbourne Dr 800-331-3131 www.residenceinn.com/pdxhb each pet $10/day nonsmoking rooms, fitness center, designated area for walking dogs, close to walking paths	(122) $99– $179	FB K	OP T
Towneplace Suites by Marriott 503-268-6000 6550 NE Brighton St 800-257-6000 www.towneplacesuites.com pets $10/day nonsmoking rooms, laundry, exercise room, lawn, across street from community park	(136) $69– $109	CB K	OP T
Travelodge 503-640-4791 622 SE 10th Ave 800-548-0163 www.travelodge-hillsboro.com pets $10/stay nonsmoking rooms, laundry, park across street	(58) $45– $75	C	
Wellesley Inn & Suites 503-439-0706, 800-444-8888 19311 NW Cornell Rd dogs under 35 lbs only, laundry, large open field for walking dogs, close to walking trails, www.wellesleyinnandsuites.com	(139) $75– $105	CB K	OP

WestCoast Hillsboro Hotel 503-648-3500 3500 NE Cornell Rd each pet $5/day, 800-325-4000 www.westcoasthotels.com, nonsmoking rooms, laundry, open area for walking dogs, 1 mile to park	(123) $69– $105	C M/F R/L	OP T

Hines, Oregon

Comfort Inn 541-573-3370, 800-228-5150 504 N Hwy 20 nonsmoking rooms, laundry, vacant lot for walking dogs, ¼ mile to public park	(51) $55– $64	CB	IP T

Hood River, Oregon

Beryl House B & B 541-386-5567 4079 Barrett Dr completely nonsmoking, rural area for walking dogs, 1 mile to river	(4) $65– $90	FB	
Best Western Hood River Inn 541-386-2200 1108 E Marina Way 800-828-7873 www.hoodriverinn.com pets $12/day nonsmoking rooms, laundry, riverside walking paths	(149) $55– $179	M/F R/L	OP T
Columbia Gorge Hotel 541-386-5566, 800-345-1921 4000 Westcliff Dr pets $25/stay www.columbiagorgehotel.com, room rate includes champagne and caviar plus full country breakfast, dog treats, landscaped grounds for walking dogs	(40) $159– $279	R/L FB	
Hood River Hotel 541-386-1900, 800-386-1859 102 Oak Ave pets $15/day www.hoodriverhotel.com, ground floor rooms with private outside entrances, exercise room, marina	(41) $139– $159	C K R/L	S T
Lost Lake Resort & Campground 541-386-6366 Mt. Hood National Forest dogs allowed in cabins but not main lodge, swimming in lake, hiking trails	(7) $50– $125	K	
Meredith Motel 541-386-1515 4300 Westcliff Dr pets $10/stay http://lodging.gorge.net/meredith, nonsmoking rooms, yard with picnic table, ¼ mile to public park	(21) $49– $79	CB M/F	
Vagabond Lodge 541-386-2992, 877-386-2992 4070 Westcliff Dr www.vagabondlodge.com in-room spa, nonsmoking, 5 acres for walking dogs	(42) $39– $99	C K M/F	T

C = coffee IP = indoor pool OP = outdoor pool CB = continental K = full kitchen R = restaurant breakfast (k) = kitchenette S = sauna or F = refrigerator L = lounge steamroom FB = full breakfast M = microwave T = spa or hot tub	# of units) & rates	food & drink	pool, sauna & hot tub

Huntington, Oregon

Farewell Bend Motor Inn 541-869-2211 5945 Hwy 30 nonsmoking rooms, open area for walking dogs, ½ mile to state park	(42) $39– $50	CB R	

Idleyld Park, Oregon

Dogwood Motel 541-496-3403 28866 N Umpqua Hwy log cabin duplexes sleep 4, 3 acres with picnic area, badminton, croquet, river access, near hiking trails	(6) $55– $70	K	
Idleyld Lodge B & B 541-496-0088 23834 N Umpqua Hwy pets $10/stay www.ibbp.com/or/idleyldlodge.html 120-year old lodge and cabin, gift and antique shop, 2-bdrm theme-decorated suites sleep 4, river access, 1 mile to 17-mile hiking trail to Crater Lake	(4) $49– $100	K R CB FB	
North Umpqua Resort 541-496-0149 23885 N Umpqua Hwy 800-350-1028 riverfront motel rooms and cabin with full kitchen, national forest land for walking dogs, www.northumpquaresort.com	(7) $29– $59	C K	

Ione, Oregon

Woolery House B & B 541-422-7218 170 E 2nd completely nonsmoking, 2 blocks to public park	(5) $45– $75	FB	

Jacksonville, Oregon

Stage Lodge 541-899-3953 830 N 5th St 800-253-8254 www.stagelodge.com each pet $10/day nonsmoking rooms, in-room spa, small yard for walking dogs, 2 blocks to public park	(27) $79– $150	CB	T

John Day, Oregon

Best Western John Day Inn 541-575-17008 315 W Main St each pet $5/day, 800-243-262 laundry, exercise room, open area behind building for walking dogs, 2 blocks to public park	(39) $53– $100	CB M/F	IP T
Dreamers Lodge Motel 541-575-0526, 800-654-2849 144 N Canyon Blvd nonsmoking rooms, close to public park and waterfront	(25) $50– $63	C K M/F	
John Day Sunset Inn 541-575-1462, 800-452-4899 390 W Main St each pet $4/day nonsmoking rooms, open field, 1 block to park	(44) $41– $66	C M/F	IP T
Little Pine Inn 541-575-2100 250 E Main St each pet $5/day nonsmoking rooms, open area, 4 blocks to park	(14) $36– $41	FB	
Sonshine B & B 541-575-1827 210 NW Canton St completely nonsmoking, city park for walking dogs	(2) $45– $65	FB	
Traveler's Motel 541-575-2076 755 S Canyon Blvd laundry, open areas nearby for walking dogs	(14) $27– $42	C M/F	

Jordan Valley, Oregon

Basque Station Motel 541-586-2244 801 Main St 4 blocks to public park	(16) $39– $49		
Sahara Motel 541-586-2500 607 Main St pets $5/day nonsmoking rooms, open area for walking dogs	(22) $37– $57	C	

Joseph, Oregon

Collett's Cabins & Fine Arts 541-432-2391 84681 Ponderosa Ln 866-432-2391 www.eoni.com/~smcollet each pet $6/day art by resident artist displayed in onsite art gallery and completely nonsmoking cabins, area for walking dogs, walking distance to lake and trails	(12) $53- $68	K	

C = coffee IP = indoor pool OP = outdoor pool	(# of units) & rates	food & drink	pool, sauna & hot tub
CB = continental K = full kitchen R = restaurant			
breakfast (k) = kitchenette S = sauna or			
F = refrigerator L = lounge steamroom			
FB = full breakfast M = microwave T = spa or hot tub			

Joseph, Oregon (continued)

Eagle Cap Chalets 541-432-4704 59879 Wallowa Lake Hwy www.eaglecapchalets.com nonsmoking rooms-cabins-condos, pets $6–$10/day, dogs allowed Sept–May only, riverfront walking area	(34) $60– $115	K R	IP T
Indian Lodge Motel 541-432-2651 201 S Main St 888-286-5484 www.eoni.com/~gingerdaggett pets $10–$15/stay nonsmoking rooms, pet walking area, 2 blocks to park, 1 mile to lake	(16) $37– $53	C F	
Mountain View Motel & RV Park 541-432-2982 83450 Joseph Hwy 866-262-9891 mountainviewmotel@yahoo.com each pet $5/day nonsmoking rooms, RV sites, pet walking area	(9) $35– $65	C K	
Ninebark Outfitters & Lodge 541-426-4855 65881 Dobbin Rd 877-646-3275 www.ninebark.com, 2-bdrm lodge and bunkhouse sleep combined total of 9, private wilderness setting	(1) call for rates	K M/F	
Strawberry Wilderness B & B 541-432-3125 406 W Wallowa completely nonsmoking, outside entrances, covered porches, 1 mile to lake	(3) $50– $90	FB	

Junction City, Oregon

Guest House Inn 541-998-6524 1335 Ivy St pets $5/stay nonsmoking rooms, dogs allowed in ground floor units only, area for walking dogs, 2 blocks to park	(22) $49– $69	C M/F	

Klamath Falls, Oregon

A-1 Budget Motel 541-884-8104 3844 Hwy 97 N nonsmoking rooms, laundry, yard for walking dogs	(32) $30– $60	C K	IP

Best Western Klamath Inn 4061 S 6th St nonsmoking rooms, yard, biking and walking trail	541-882-1200 877-882-1200	(52) $69– $99	CB M/F	IP
Cimarron Motor Inn 541-882-4601, 800-742-2648 3060 S 6th St pets $5/stay www.oxfordsuites.com, nonsmoking rooms, laundry, walking path, 7 minute drive to public park		(163) $49– $69	CB M/F	OP
Crystalwood Lodge B & B 38625 Westside Rd www.crystalwoodlodge.com, historic lodge on 133 acres, pond, wildlife refuge and national forest, rates include breakfast and gourmet dinner, in-room pet crates provided, dog washing facility, pet daycare service, guided canoe-snowshoe-flyfishing trips	541-381-2322 888-381-2322	(7) $105– $245	CB R/L	
Econo Lodge 541-884-7735, 800-553-2666 75 Main St www.econolodge.com nonsmoking rooms, next to public park and lake		(51) $25– $80	CB M/F	
Golden West Motel 541-882-1758, 888-840-8180 6402 S 6th St nonsmoking rooms, on ½ acre for walking dogs, 2 blocks to 5-mile long hiking trail		(14) $35– $48	M/F	
Hill View Motel 541-883-7771 5543 S 6th St nonsmoking rooms, yard for walking dogs, ¾ mile to public park		(16) $34– $85	C K	
Holiday Inn Express 541-884-9999 2500 S 6th St $20 refundable pet deposit nonsmoking rooms, laundry, 24 hour pool, open area for walking dogs, 1 block to walking trail		(57) $83– $149	CB M/F	IP T
La Vista Motor Lodge 541-882-8844 3939 Hwy 97 N nonsmoking rooms, laundry, large yard for walking dogs		(24) $28– $45	CB M/F	OP T
Lake of the Woods Resort 541-949-8300 950 Harriman Rt pets $5/stay www.lakeofthewoodsresort.com, cabins, screened porches, tent sites, swimming beach, hiking trails		(15) $139– $219	C K R/L	
Maverick Motel 541-882-6688, 800-404-6690 1220 Main St pets $10/stay nonsmoking rooms, small grassy walking area		(49) $39– $59	CB M/F	OP

C = coffee IP = indoor pool OP = outdoor pool CB = continental K = full kitchen R = restaurant breakfast (k) = kitchenette S = sauna or F = refrigerator L = lounge steamroom FB = full breakfast M = microwave T = spa or hot tub	(# of units) & rates	food & drink	pool, sauna & hot tub
## Klamath Falls, Oregon (continued)			
Motel 6 541-884-2110, 800-466-8356 5136 S 6th St www.motel6.com nonsmoking rooms, laundry, mowed walking area, 6 blocks to public park and walking path	(62) $50– $63	C	OP
Olympic Lodge 541-883-8800 3006 Green Springs Dr nonsmoking rooms, walking trails, 1 mile to park	(32) $30– $40	CB K	OP
Oregon 8 Motel & RV Park 541-883-3431 5225 N Hwy 97 nonsmoking rooms, RV sites, pet walking area	(29) $37– $47	C	
Quality Inn 541-882-4666, 800-228-5151 100 Main St www.qualityinn.com, nonsmoking rooms, laundry, exercise room, ½ block to park	(80) $49– $109	CB R/L	OP T
Red Lion Inn 541-882-8864 3612 S 6th St nonsmoking rooms, laundry, walking path	(108) $73– $109	C R/L	OP T
Running Y Ranch Resort 541-850-5500 5500 Running Y Rd pets $20/stay, 888-850-0275 www.runningy.com, laundry, 8-mile walking trail	(83) $119– $269	CB K R/L	IP T
Shilo Inn 541-885-7980, 800-222-2244 2500 Almond St each pet $10/day www.shiloinns.com, pet beds and treats, fitness center, designated pet walking area, walking path	(143) $99– $129	R	
South Entrance Motel 541-883-1994 9339 Hwy 97 S nonsmoking rooms, lawn for walking dogs, across street to game refuge	(12) $27– $48	C K	
Super 8 Motel 541-884-8880, 800-800-8000 3805 Hwy 97 N super8kf@cdf.com nonsmoking rooms, laundry, lawn and open lot for walking dogs, 2 blocks to park and paved trail	(61) $47– $53	CB F	T

La Grande, Oregon

Greenwell Motel 541-963-4134 305 Adams Ave pets $5/day 1 dog only, nonsmoking rooms, 2 blocks to park	(33) $30– $45	CB	OP
Howard Johnson Inn 541-963-7195, 800-446-4656 2612 Island Ave pets $10/stay www.hojo.com, laundry, weight room, grassy area for walking dogs, ½ mile to public park	(146) $67– $87	CB M/F	OP S T
Moon Motel 541-963-2724 2116 Adams Ave pets $5/day nonsmoking rooms, public park across street	(9) $30– $38	C	
Orchard Motel 541-963-6160 2206 E Adams Ave completely nonsmoking, 2 blocks to public park	(12) $35– $55	CB K	
Royal Motor Inn 541-963-4154, 800-990-7575 1510 Adams Ave pets $10/stay nonsmoking rooms, small dogs only, yard	(43) $32– $58	C M/F	
Stardust Lodge 541-963-4166 402 Adams Ave each pet $17/day www.stardustlodge.com, nonsmoking rooms, lawn for walking dogs, 2 miles to public park	(32) $25– $45	CB M/F	OP
Super 8 Motel 541-963-8080 2407 E R Ave pets $7–$10/stay www.super8motel.com, nonsmoking rooms, laundry, lawn for walking dogs, ½ mile to public park	(64) $49– $83	CB K	IP T
Travelodge 541-963-7116, 800-578-7878 2215 Adams Ave pets $10/stay nonsmoking rooms, grassy area for walking dogs, 1 mile to public park	(35) $44– $54	CB M/F	

La Pine, Oregon

Best Western Newberry Station 541-536-5130 16515 Reed Rd 800-210-8616 dogs under 25 lbs only $25 refundable pet deposit nonsmoking rooms, forested park-like walking area, 4 blocks to public park	(40) $62– $132	CB M/F	IP T

C = coffee / CB = continental breakfast / F = refrigerator / FB = full breakfast / IP = indoor pool / K = full kitchen / (k) = kitchenette / L = lounge / M = microwave / OP = outdoor pool / R = restaurant / S = sauna or steamroom / T = spa or hot tub	(# of units) & rates	food & drink	pool, sauna & hot tub

La Pine, Oregon (continued)

Diamondstone Guest Lodge & Gallery 541-536-6263 16693 Sprague Loop 800-600-6263 www.diamondstone.com, pets $20/day completely nonsmoking B&B, 5 acres for walking dogs, ½ mile to river, swimming, fishing	(3) $80– $135	FB	T
East Lake Resort & RV Park 541-536-2230 22430 E Paulina Lake Rd pets $5/day www.eastlakeresort.com, nonsmoking rooms, RV sites, laundry, boat rentals, in heart of Newberry National Monument, lots of trails for walking dogs	(16) $45– $125	K	
Highlander Motel 541-536-2131 51511 Hwy 97 nonsmoking rooms, RV sites, open area for walking dogs, 3 blocks to public park	(9) $34– $55	C K M/F	
Paulina Lake Lodge 541-536-2240 La Pine pets $7/day nonsmoking rooms, only 1 dog per cabin, general store, boat rentals, lots of trails for walking dogs	(14) $55– $155	K R	
Timbercrest Inn 541-536-1737 52560 Hwy 97 pets $10/stay nonsmoking rooms, close to Paulina Lake and trails	(21) $35– $95	CB K	
West View Motel 541-536-2115 51371 Hwy 97 dogs allowed in smoking rooms only, open area for walking dogs	(9) $34– $54	C K	

Lake Oswego, Oregon

Best Western Sherwood Inn 503-620-2980 15700 SW Upper Boones Ferry Rd 800-528-1234 nonsmoking rooms, pet walking area pets $10/day	(101) $64– $74	CB R/L	IP S
Crowne Plaza Hotel 503-624-8400, 800-227-6963 14811 Kruse Oaks Dr nonsmoking rooms, laundry, paved paths, www.crowneplaza.com/lakeoswegoor	(161) $69– $175	CB M/F R/L	IP T

Residence Inn by Marriott-Portland South 15200 SW Bangy Rd 503-684-2603 www.residenceinn.com 800-331-3131 nonsmoking rooms, laundry pets $10/day designated area for walking dogs, ¼ mile to park	(112) $69– $149	CB K	OP T

Lakeside, Oregon

Lakeshore Lodge 541-759-3161 290 S 8th St pets $5–$10/day www.lakeshorelodgeor.com, laundry, RV sites, boat rentals, private dock, walking trails	(20) $45– $81	C M/F R/L	

Lakeview, Oregon

Best Western Skyline Motor Lodge 541-947-2194 414 North G St 800-528-1234 dogs allowed in smoking rooms only pets $10/day laundry, 4 blocks to public park	(38) $60– $120	CB M/F	
Budget Inn Lakeview 541-947-2201 411 North F St nonsmoking rooms, open areas for walking dogs, across street from public park	(16) $28– $38	CB K	T
Interstate 8 Motel 541-947-3341 354 North K St $20 refundable pet deposit nonsmoking rooms	(32) $32– $55	CB M/F	
Lakeview Lodge Motel 541-947-2181 301 North G St 888-315-2378 nonsmoking rooms, exercise room, 4 blocks to public park	(40) $50– $90	C K M/F	S T
Rim Rock Motel 541-947-2185 727 South F St rim_rock_motel@msn.com nonsmoking rooms, large yard for walking dogs, 1 block to small public park	(27) $32– $42	C K	

Lebanon, Oregon

Cascade City Center Motel 541-258-8154 1296 S Main St pets $5/day nonsmoking rooms, laundry, small area for walking dogs, 1 mile to public park	(16) $30– $52	K M/F	

C = coffee
CB = continental
  breakfast
F = refrigerator
FB = full breakfast
	IP = indoor pool
	K = full kitchen
	(k) = kitchenette
	L = lounge
	M = microwave
		OP = outdoor pool
		R = restaurant
		S = sauna or
		  steamroom
		T = spa or hot tub
			(# of units)
			& rates
				food
				& drink
					pool, sauna
					& hot tub

Lebanon, Oregon (continued)

Shanico Inn 541-259-2601, 888-815-4408 1840 S Main St pets $10–$15/day www.lebanonoregon.net, nonsmoking rooms, open area for walking dogs	(40) $44– $74	C (k) M/F	
Valley Inn 541-258-8184 2885 S Santiam Hwy pets $10/day nonsmoking rooms, lawn area for walking dogs, short drive to public park	(11) $32– $85	C K	

Lincoln City, Oregon

All Seasons Vacation Rentals 541-996-3549 1116 SW 51st St pets $10/stay, 800-362-5229 www.allseasonsvacation.com, small dogs only, 1-bdrm nonsmoking suites, across street from beach	(2) $55– $110	C K	
Anchor Motel 541-996-3810, 800-582-8611 4417 SW Hwy 101 pets $5–$10/day nonsmoking rooms, walking area, 1 block to beach	(29) $25– $75	C K	
Beach Cottage Rentals 866-994-7026, 541-994-7028 4741 SW Hwy 101 $100 refundable pet deposit www.cottagesbythebeach.com, vacation homes	(1+) call for rates		
Beachfront Garden Inn 541-994-2324, 866-994-2324 3313 NW Inlet Ave pets $10/day www.beachfrontgardeninn.com, in-room spa, fully equipped kitchens, nonsmoking, beach access	(12) $75– $250	C K	T
Budget Inn 541-994-5281 1713 NW 21st St pets $10/day nonsmoking rooms, undeveloped area for walking dogs, 1 block to beach	(50) $30– $80	C M/F	
Captain Cook Inn 541-994-2522, 800-994-2522 2626 NE Hwy 101 pets $5-10/day www.captaincookinn.com, close to waterfront	(17) $50– $69	C K	

City Center Motel 541-994-2612 1014 NE Hwy 101 pets $5/day nonsmoking rooms, small dogs only, beach 5 blocks	(15) $29– $59	C K	
Coast Inn B & B 541-994-7932, 888-994-7932 4507 SW Coast Ave $25 refundable pet deposit www.oregoncoastinn.com, nonsmoking rooms, fireplaces, decks, 2 blocks to beach	(4) $95– $125	FB	
Coho Inn 541-994-3684, 800-848-7006 1635 NW Harbor Ave each pet $7/day www.thecohoinn.com, adult dogs under 25 lbs only, nonsmoking rooms, walking area, beach access	(50) $72– $136	C K	S T
Dolphin Motel 541-994-2124 1018 SE Hwy 101 yard for walking dogs, ¾ mile to beach	(10) $35– $50	(k) M/F	
Edgecliff Motel 541-996-2055 3733 SW Hwy 101 888-750-3636 www.lincolncity.com/edgecliff pets $5/stay nonsmoking rooms, ½ block to beach access	(28) $50– $125	CB K M/F	
Ester Lee Motel 541-996-3606, 888-996-3606 3803 SW Hwy 101 each pet $7/day www.esterlee.com, nonsmoking rooms, in-room spa, designated pet walking area, paved path to beach	(53) $49– $151	C K M/F	T
Hide-A-Way Motel 541-994-8874 810 SW 10th St pets $10/day completely nonsmoking, overlooking ocean, 1 block to beach access	(6) $40– $140	C K	
Lincoln City Inn 541-996-4400, 800-870-7067 1091 SE 1st St pets $10/stay nonsmoking rooms, laundry, in-room spa, small area for walking dogs, across highway from beach	(59) $39– $119	CB M/F	T
O'Dysius Hotel B & B 541-994-4121, 800-869-8069 120 NW Inlet Ave each pet $10/day www.odysius.com, 1 dog under 20 lbs only, in-room spa, private decks, nonsmoking, close to waterfront	(30) $149– $299	CB	T
Orca Inn 541-996-3996, 800-843-4940 861 SW 51st St pets $7/day dogs under 25 lbs only, across street from beach	(40) $49– $135	C K	

C = coffee IP = indoor pool OP = outdoor pool CB = continental K = full kitchen R = restaurant breakfast (k) = kitchenette S = sauna or F = refrigerator L = lounge steamroom FB = full breakfast M = microwave T = spa or hot tub	(# of units) & rates	food & drink	pool, sauna & hot tub

Lincoln City, Oregon (continued)

Overlook Motel 541-996-3300 3521 SW Anchor Dr each pet $10/day www.skybusiness.com/overlookmotel, nonsmoking rooms, area for walking dogs, stairs to the beach	(8) $88– $215	K	
Sailor Jack Oceanfront Motel 541-994-3696 1035 NW Harbor Ave pets $10/stay, 888-432-8346 www.sailorjack.com, nonsmoking rooms, in-room spa, sundecks, easy beach access	(40) $50– $129	C M/F	S T
Sea Horse Oceanfront Lodging 541-994-2101 2039 NW Harbor Dr 800-662-2101 www.seahorsemotel.com, 1 to 2 dogs, pets $10/day miles of open sandy beaches, dogs must NEVER be left alone in rooms and must be on leash at all times	(54) $64– $139	C K	IP T
Seagull Beach Front Motel 541-994-2948 1511 NW Harbor Ave 800-422-0219 www.seagullmoteloregon.com $20 pet deposit well-behaved adult dogs only, nonsmoking rooms, in-room spa, open walking area across street, lighted handicapped-accessible walkway to beach	(25) $45– $90	C K M/F	T
Shilo Inn 541-994-3655, 800-222-2244 1501 NW 40th Pl each pet $15/day www.shiloinns.com, nonsmoking rooms, laundry, fitness center, pet beds and treats, next to beach	(247) $80– $280	C M/F R	IP S T
Sweetwater Inn 541-994-4708 4006 W Devils Lake Rd pets $10/day dogs under 35 lbs only, on lakefront with natural areas for walking dogs, 1 mile to Regatta State Park	(8) $40– $170	C (k)	
Whistling Winds Motel 541-994-6155 3264 NW Jetty Ave pets $10/stay in-room spa, nonsmoking rooms, open pet walking area, ½ block to beach access	(16) $32– $79	C K M/F	T

Madras, Oregon

Best Western Rama Inn 541-475-6141, 888-726-2466 12 SW 4th St pets $10/stay nonsmoking rooms, walking area, 2 blocks to park	(47) $60– $75	CB M/F	OP T
Budget Inn 541-475-3831 133 NE 5th St pets $6/day nonsmoking rooms, grassy area for walking dogs, 1 block to public park	(30) $40– $74	CB K M/F	
Hoffy's Motel 541-475-4633, 800-227-6865 600 N Hwy 26 each pet $5/day hoffys@quicknet.com, nonsmoking rooms, laundry, lawn and open field for walking dogs	(99) $42– $225	CB M/F	IP
Juniper Motel 541-475-6186 414 N Hwy 26 800-244-1399 3 blocks to public park pets $15/stay	(22) $35– $75	C K M/F	
Royal Dutch Motel 541-475-2281 1101 SW Hwy 97 nonsmoking rooms, pet walking area, county fairgrounds across street	(10) $30– $50	C M/F	
Sonny's Motel 541-475-7217, 800-624-6137 1539 SW Hwy 97 pets $10/stay www.sonnysmotel.com, nonsmoking rooms, laundry, pet walking area, 1 mile to public park	(44) $42– $110	CB K R	OP T

Manzanita, Oregon

Coast Cabins 503-368-7113 635 Laneda Ave pets $10/day www.coastcabins.com, completely nonsmoking, all linens provided, laundry, 5 blocks to beach	(4) $90– $155	C K	
Manzanita Beach Fireside Inn 503-368-1001 114 Laneda Ave 800-368-1001 www.neahkahnie.net/fireside.html, pets $5–$15/day nonsmoking rooms, 1 block to beach, 1 mile to trail	(14) $40– $90	C K	
Manzanita Rental Co 503-368-6797, 800-579-9801 686 Manzanita Ave each pet $10–$15/day www.manzanitarentals.com, nonsmoking homes, some with yards or fenced dog run, beach access	(75) $75– $295	K	T

C = coffee　　IP = indoor pool　　OP = outdoor pool CB = continental　　K = full kitchen　　R = restaurant 　　breakfast　　(k) = kitchenette　　S = sauna or F = refrigerator　　L = lounge　　　steamroom FB = full breakfast　　M = microwave　　T = spa or hot tub	# of units) & rates	food & drink	pool, sauna & hot tub

Manzanita, Oregon (continued)

Ocean Inn　　　　　　　503-368-7701, 866-368-7701 32 Laneda Ave　　　　　　　　　each pet $10/day www.oceaninnatmanzanita.com, nonsmoking rooms, in-room spa, laundry, beach for walking dogs	(10) $85– $145	K	T
Sunset Surf Motel　　　　503-368-5224, 800-243-8035 248 Ocean Rd　　　　　　　　　each pet $10/day across road from ocean, close to walking trails	(40) $50– $127	K M/F	OP

Maupin, Oregon

Imperial River Company　541-395-2404, 800-395-3903 304 Bakeoven County Rd　　　　each pet $10/day www.deschutesriver.com, several undeveloped acres along Deschutes River for walking dogs (PLEASE clean up after rest stops), next to public park	(12) $75– $110	CB R	
Oasis Resort　　　　　　　　　　　541-395-2611 609 Hwy 197 S　　　　　　　　　　pets $5/day www.deschutesriveroasis.com, nonsmoking, next to Deschutes River and public walking areas	(11) $35– $69	C M/F R	

McKenzie Bridge, Oregon

Caddisfly Resort　　　　　　　　　541-822-3556 56404 McKenzie Hwy　　　　　　each pet $10/day nonsmoking riverside cottages sleep 2 to 10, national forest trails for walking dogs	(3) $70– $126	K R	

McMinnville, Oregon

Baker Street B & B　　　　503-472-5575, 800-870-5575 129 SE Baker St　　　　　　　www.bakerstreetinn.com nonsmoking rooms, laundry, 2 blocks to city park	(1) $95– $125	FB K	
Paragon Motel　　　　　　503-472-9493, 800-525-5469 2065 S Hwy 99 W　　　　　　　　　pets $6/day nonsmoking rooms, laundry, open walking area	(55) $39– $60	CB M/F	OP

Red Lion Inn & Suites 2535 NE Three Mile Ln www.redlion.com nonsmoking rooms, laundry, field for walking dogs	503-472-1500 888-489-1600 pets $10/day	(67) $99	CB M/F	IP T
Tuscan Estate B & B 809 NE Evans St www.a-tuscanestate.com completely nonsmoking, laundry, 6 blocks to park	503-434-9016 800-441-2214 pets $35/stay	(4) $125– $225	FB	

Medford, Oregon

Best Inn & Suites 1015 S Riverside Ave www.bestinn.com $100 refundable pet deposit nonsmoking rooms, laundry, exercise room, open area for walking dogs	541-773-8266 800-237-8466	(105) $49– $79	CB M/F	OP
Capri Motel 250 E Barnett Rd pets $5/day nonsmoking rooms, 1 acre fenced area for dogs to run loose, 3 blocks to public park	541-773-7796	(36) $32– $37	C M/F	OP
Cedar Lodge Motor Inn 518 N Riverside Ave www.oregonfishing.com $25 refundable deposit nonsmoking rooms, picnic tables, walking paths, 1½ blocks to public park	541-773-7361 800-282-3419	(80) $38– $68	CB K M/F R/L	OP
Fish Lake Resort Hwy 140 Mile Marker 30 each pet $15/day laundry, RV sites, rustic cottages and larger modern cabins, lakeside hiking trails	541-949-8500	(11) $50– $175	K F R	
Motel 6 North 2400 Biddle Rd www.motel6.com, nonsmoking rooms, laundry, dogwalking area, 1 mile to bike and walking trails	541-779-0550 800-466-8356	(116) $40– $52	C M/F	OP
Motel 6 South 950 Alba Dr www.motel6.com, nonsmoking rooms, laundry, next to public park and off-leash dog park	541-773-4290 800-466-8356	(101) $40– $59	C M/F	OP

C = coffee
CB = continental
    breakfast
F = refrigerator
FB = full breakfast
	IP = indoor pool
	K = full kitchen
	(k) = kitchenette
	L = lounge
	M = microwave
		OP = outdoor pool
		R = restaurant
		S = sauna or
		    steamroom
		T = spa or hot tub
			(# of units)
			& rates
				food
				& drink
					pool, sauna
					& hot tub

Medford, Oregon (continued)

Pear Tree Motel 541-535-4445, 800-645-7332 300 Pear Tree Ln pets $10/day advance reservations recommended, nonsmoking rooms, laundry, RV sites, designated pet rest area, lots of open area for walking dogs	(46) $54– $69	CB	OP T
Red Lion Hotel 541-779-5811, 800-733-5466 200 N Riverside Ave www.redlion.com nonsmoking rooms and suites, in-room spa, laundry, area for walking dogs, bike path and public park	(185) $69– $99	C R/L	OP T
Reston Hotel 541-779-3141, 800-779-7829 2300 Crater Lake Hwy pets $20/stay www.restonhotel.com, nonsmoking rooms, laundry, close to citywide walking paths	(164) $48– $82	CB M/F L	IP
Rogue Regency Inn 541-770-1234, 800-535-5805 2345 Crater Lake Hwy www.rogueregency.com dogs allowed by advance reservation only, laundry, nonsmoking rooms, close to creekside walking trail	(203) $84– $105	C M/F R/L	OP T
Rogue Valley Inn 541-772-2800 2800 E Barnett Rd pets $6/day nonsmoking rooms, private patios, open field, near public park, ¾ mile to off-leash dog park	(15) $54– $74	C (k) R	
Shilo Inn 541-770-5151, 800-222-2244 2111 Biddle Rd each pet $10/day www.shiloinns.com, nonsmoking rooms, pet beds and treats, walking paths, ¾ mile to public park	(48) $70– $100	CB M/F	S T
Travelodge 541-773-1579, 800-578-7878 954 Alba Dr www.travelodge.com 1 small dog only, close to public park and trail	(60) $45– $75	CB	OP
Valli Hai Motel 541-772-6183 1034 Court St nonsmoking rooms, grassy area behind building for walking dogs, park across street	(20) $30– $85	(k)	

Waverly Cottage & Suites 541-779-4716 305 N Grape St dogs allowed at owner's discretion only, in-room spa, laundry, completely nonsmoking, close to walking trails	(4) $45– $95	K	T
Windmill Inn 541-779-0050 1950 Biddle Rd 800-547-4747 www.windmillinns.com, nonsmoking rooms, laundry, grassy walking area, bicycles, continental breakfast delivered to room–including dog biscuits	(123) $77– $107	CB (k) M/F R	OP S T

Merlin, Oregon

Doubletree Ranch 541-476-0120 6000 Abegg Rd www.doubletree-ranch.com dogs allowed at manager's discretion only, riverfront area and trails for walking dogs	(4) $85– $125	C K	
Galice Resort 541-476-3818 11744 Galice Rd dogs allowed in cabins only, riverside trails, 4 miles to park, www.galice.com	(6) $65	F R	

Merrill, Oregon

Wild Goose Motel 541-798-5826 105 Court Dr nonsmoking rooms, RV sites, dog kennel, riverfront walking area, 1 block to park	(11) $30– $60	C K	

Mill City, Oregon

Morrison Cottage 503-897-3371, 800-699-5937 418 NW Alder St www.morrisoncottage.com nonsmoking rooms, large yard, 3 blocks to walking trail through town, 1 mile to large state park	(1) $65– $75	CB (k)	T

Milton-Freewater, Oregon

Morgan Inn 541-938-5547, 800-533-4017 104 N Columbia St pets $10/stay nonsmoking rooms, laundry, grassy walking area, 5 blocks to public park	(34) $43– $71	CB K	
Out West Motel 541-938-6647 84040 Hwy 11 800-881-6647 nonsmoking rooms, area for walking dogs	(12) $35– $48	C M/F	

C = coffee
CB = continental
  breakfast
F = refrigerator
FB = full breakfast
	IP = indoor pool
	K = full kitchen
	(k) = kitchenette
	L = lounge
	M = microwave
		OP = outdoor pool
		R = restaurant
		S = sauna or
		  steamroom
		T = spa or hot tub
			# of units)
			& rates
				food
				& drink
					pool, sauna
					& hot tub

Mitchell, Oregon

Oregon Hotel 104 Main St www.wheelercountyoregon.com/adds/oh.html nonsmoking rooms, public park across street		541-462-3027 pets $10/stay	(11) $35– $45	CB K	
Sky Hook Motel 101 Hwy 26 rooms and 2-bdrm suites, completely nonsmoking, pet walking area, public park across highway		541-462-3569 pets $5/day	(6) $40– $65	C K	

Molalla, Oregon

Stage Coach Inn Motel 415 Grange Ave nonsmoking rooms, open field for walking dogs, 2 blocks to public parks		503-829-4382 pets $5/day	(32) $45– $60	C K M/F	

Monmouth, Oregon

College Inn 235 Pacific Ave S 5 blocks to public park		503-838-1711 each pet $5/day	(12) $35– $60	K M/F	
Courtesy Inn 270 N Pacific Ave 1 dog under 30 lbs only, ½ mile to public park		503-838-4438 pets $10/day	(35) $49– $69	C M/F R	

Moro, Oregon

Tall Winds Motel 301 Main St (Hwy 97) nonsmoking rooms, next to public park		541-565-3519 $20 refundable pet deposit	(12) $38– $60	C F	

Mount Vernon, Oregon

Blue Mountain Lodge 150 W Main St nonsmoking rooms, 1 block to public park		541-932-4451, 877-668-8919 pets $3/day	(14) $25– $64	M/F	

Mount Vernon Motel & Trailer Park 541-932-4712 195 N Mountain Blvd pets $2/day nonsmoking rooms, laundry, shaded yard for walking dogs, 2 blocks to public park	(5) $30– $47	K

Mt Hood-Parkdale, Oregon

Mt Hood Hamlet B & B 541-352-3574, 800-407-0570 6741 Hwy 35 www.mthoodhamlet.com dogs allowed by advance reservation only, 9 acres of fields and woods for walking dogs	(3) $105– $145	FB

Myrtle Creek, Oregon

Rose Motel 541-863-3581 316 N Main St fenced yard for exercising dogs, next to city park, walking distance to Umpqua River	(4) $28– $38	M/F

Myrtle Point, Oregon

Myrtle Trees Motel 541-572-5811 1010 8th St pets $5/day small dogs only, picnic tables, BBQ grill, 2½ acres for walking dogs	(29) $43– $48	C M/F

Neskowin, Oregon

Neskowin Vacation Rentals 503-392-4850 48990 Hwy 101 S www.neskowinvacationrentals.com, laundry, studios, 1 to 2-bdrm condos, all linens provided, completely nonsmoking, grassy area and beach for walking dogs	(6) $59– $159	K
Proposal Rock Inn 503-392-3115 PO Box 70 pets $15/stay nonsmoking rooms and 1-bdrm suite, small grassy area for walking dogs, 1 block to beach	(38) $44– $109	C K
The Breakers Condominiums 503-392-3417 48060 Breakers Blvd pets $10/stay www.breakersoregon.com, completely nonsmoking 3-bdrm condominiums, fireplaces, full kitchens, beachfront location for walking dogs	(11) $105– $235	K

C = coffee IP = indoor pool OP = outdoor pool CB = continental K = full kitchen R = restaurant breakfast (k) = kitchenette S = sauna or F = refrigerator L = lounge steamroom FB = full breakfast M = microwave T = spa or hot tub	# of units & rates	food & drink	pool, sauna & hot tub

Netarts, Oregon

| Edgewater Motel 503-842-1300 1020 W 1st St pets $10/stay overlooking ocean, full kitchens, dog blankets and towels provided, pet walking area, beach access | (6) $79– $114 | C K | |
| Terimore Lodging by the Sea 503-842-4623 5105 Crab Ave pets $7/day, 800-635-1821 www.oregoncoast.com/terimore, laundry, open walking area, easy beach access, nonsmoking rooms | (26) $40– $100 | C K | |

Newberg, Oregon

Avellan Inn B & B 503-537-9161 16900 NE Hwy 240 www.avellaninn.com nonsmoking rooms, covered deck, private entrance, fenced area and 12 acres for walking dogs	(2) $115	FB	
Shilo Inn 503-537-0303, 800-222-2244 501 Sitka Ave each pet $10/day www.shiloinns.com, nonsmoking rooms, laundry, pet beds and treats, fitness center, grassy area for walking dogs, 1½ blocks to public park	(60) $60– $100	CB K M/F	OP S T
Towne & Country Motel 503-538-2800, 888-538-2800 1864 Portland Rd (99W) each pet $7/day nonsmoking rooms, open field, 3 blocks to park	(22) $40– $56	(k)	

Newport, Oregon

| Best Western Agate Beach Inn 541-265-9411 3019 N Coast Hwy 800-547-3310 www.newportbestwestern.com each pet $10/stay nonsmoking rooms, short walking trail to beach | (148) $74– $149 | C R/L | |
| Driftwood Village Motel 541-265-5738 7947 N Coast Hwy pets $10/day www.newportnet.com/driftwood, designated pet walking area, trail to beach, dog towels provided | (12) $45– $95 | K | |

Econo Lodge 541-265-7723 606 SW Coast Hwy 866-211-5107 nonsmoking rooms, laundry, 2 blocks to the beach	(43) $29– $95	CB M/F	
Hallmark Resort of Newport 541-265-2600 744 SW Elizabeth St each pet $5/day, 888-448-4449 www.hallmarkinns.com, fitness center, laundry, pet walking area, easy beach access	(158) $79– $189	C K M/F R/L	IP S T
La Quinta Inn & Suites 541-867-7727 45 SE 32nd St each pet $5/day, 800-527-1133 www.laquinta.com, laundry, grassy area for walking dogs, 1 mile to beach access	(71) $69– $150	CB K	IP
Money Saver Motel 541-265-2277, 877-428-4393 861 SW Coast Hwy $15 refundable pet deposit www.newportoregonmotel.com, nonsmoking rooms	(42) $45– $55	K	
Newport Bay Motel 541-265-4533 1823 N Coast Hwy each pet $5–$10/day nonsmoking rooms, 4 blocks to park, beach access	(50) $35– $115	CB	
Newport City Center Motel 541-265-7381 538 SW Coast Hwy 800-687-9099 www.pacificonline.net/citycenter pets $10/stay nonsmoking rooms, open area for walking dogs, 1½ blocks from beach	(30) $40– $70	C K	
Newport Motor Inn 541-265-8516 1311 N Coast Hwy pets $5/stay www.wavesofnewport.com/newportmotorinn.cfm nonsmoking rooms, dog biscuits provided, laundry, open field for walking dogs, facilities for cleaning fish and cooking crabs, 6 blocks to beach	(39) $24– $48	C M/F	
Park Motel 541-265-2234 1106 SW 9th St pets $7/day sasha@actionet.net, small dogs only, nonsmoking rooms, 4 minute walk to public park, near waterfront and walking trails	(13) $45– $78	C K F	
Penny Saver Motel 541-265-6631, 800-477-3668 710 N Coast Hwy pets $10/day nonsmoking rooms, small to medium dogs only, yard for walking dogs, 7 blocks from beach	(46) $32– $72	C K	

C = coffee IP = indoor pool OP = outdoor pool CB = continental K = full kitchen R = restaurant breakfast (k) = kitchenette S = sauna or F = refrigerator L = lounge steamroom FB = full breakfast M = microwave T = spa or hot tub	(# of units) & rates	food & drink	pool, sauna & hot tub

Newport, Oregon (continued)

Shilo Inn 541-265-7701, 800-222-2244 536 SW Elizabeth each pet $10/day www.shiloinns.com, nonsmoking rooms, laundry, pet beds and treats, small grassy walking areas, stairs to beach, 4 blocks to small park and picnic area	(179) $79– $399	C M/F R	IP
Starfish Point 541-265-3751 140 NW 48th St 800-870-7795 www.newportnet.com/starfishpoint pets $8/day 2-bdrm 2-bath condos overlooking the ocean, 1 dog only, in-room spas, lawn, private trail to beach	(6) $155– $190	K	T
Val-U Inn 541-265-6203 531 SW Fall St pets $5/day, 800-443-7777 www.valuinn.com, nonsmoking rooms, laundry, designated pet walking area, across street to beach	(71) $49– $120	CB K	
Vikings Cottages & Condos 541-265-2477 729 NW Coast St 800-480-2477 www.vikingsoregoncoast.com, large yard for walking dogs, stairs to beach	(14) $65– $120	K	
Waves Motel 541-265-4661, 800-282-6993 820 NW Coast St pets $5/day www.wavesofnewport.com, nonsmoking rooms, small dogs only, large grassy area, 2 blocks to beach	(27) $48– $78	CB M/F	
Whaler Motel 541-265-9261, 800-433-9444 155 SW Elizabeth St www.whalernewport.com 1 small dog only, fitness room, across street to beach	(73) $99– $129	CB	IP T

North Bend, Oregon

City Center Motel 541-756-5118 750 Connecticut St pets $5/stay nonsmoking rooms, vacant lot behind building for walking dogs, 2 blocks to public park	(18) $32– $40	CB M/F	

Itty Bitty Inn B & B Motel 1504 Sherman nonsmoking rooms, ½ block to public park	541-756-6398 pets $5/stay	(5) $33– $42	M/F	
Parkside Motel 1480 Sherman Ave small dogs only, nonsmoking rooms, fully equipped apartments, laundry, area for walking dogs, close to public park	541-756-4124	(16) $36– $45	K M/F	

North Powder, Oregon

Powder River Motel 850 2nd St www.powderrivermotel.com, nonsmoking rooms, laundry, 1½ blocks to riverfront for walking dogs	541-898-2829 each pet $6/day	(12) $35– $48	C F	

O'Brien, Oregon

Madrone Motel 32429 Redwood Hwy laundry, open field for walking dogs	541-596-2498	(5) $22– $40	C (k)	

Oakland, Oregon

Best Western Rice Hill Inn 621 Long John Rd www.bestwestern.com nonsmoking rooms, fitness center	541-849-2500 877-633-3196 pets $10/day	(48) $64– $79	CB M/F	IP T
Ranch Motel 581 John Long Rd area for walking dogs	541-849-2126	(25) $33– $65	C	OP

Oakridge, Oregon

Arbor Inn Motel 48229 Hwy 58 nonsmoking rooms, laundry, RV sites, area for walking dogs near creek, close to walking trails	541-782-2611 800-505-9047	(15) $28– $38	C (k) M/F	
Best Western Oakridge Inn 47433 Hwy 58 each pet $5/day, 800-528-1234 nonsmoking rooms, grassy area for walking dogs	541-782-2212	(40) $59– $67	CB K M/F	OP T

C = coffee CB = continental 　breakfast F = refrigerator FB = full breakfast	IP = indoor pool K = full kitchen (k) = kitchenette L = lounge M = microwave	OP = outdoor pool R = restaurant S = sauna or 　steamroom T = spa or hot tub	# of units) & rates	food & drink	pool, sauna & hot tub

Oakridge, Oregon (continued)

Cascade Motel　　　　　　541-782-2489 47487 Hwy 58　　www.vacationsdirect.com nonsmoking rooms, laundry, open alley behind the building for walking dogs, 6 blocks to river and trails	(11) $35– $48	C (k)	
Oakridge Motel　　　　　　541-782-2432 48197 Hwy 58 E　　nonsmoking rooms, laundry, open area and trails for walking dogs, ½ mile to park, http://hometown.aol.com/theoakridgemotel	(10) $29– $44	C M/F	

Ontario, Oregon

Best Western Inn　　541-889-2600, 800-828-0364 251 Goodfellow Ln　　$50 refundable pet deposit nonsmoking rooms, laundry	(61) $64– $150	CB M/F	IP T
Budget Inn　　　　541-889-3101, 800-905-0024 1737 N Oregon St　　　　　　　pets $5/stay nonsmoking rooms, laundry, open lot to walk dogs, 3 blocks to state park	(26) $38– $65	C K	OP
Carlile Motel　　　　541-889-8658, 800-640-8658 589 N Oregon St　　　　　　each pet $5/day www.carlilemotel.com, dogs allowed by advance reservation only, lawn, 1½ miles to riverside park	(18) $38– $67	K	
Colonial Inn　　　　541-889-9615, 800-727-5014 1395 Tapadera Ave　　　　　　pets $5/stay nonsmoking rooms, area for walking dogs, 2 miles to riverside public park	(89) $36– $75	CB	IP T
Creek House B & B　　　　　541-823-0717 717 SW 2nd St　　completely nonsmoking, in-room spa, 2 blocks to college campus for walking dogs	(4) $69– $99	FB F	T
Economy Inn　　　　　　　541-889-6449 88 N Oregon St　　$10 refundable pet deposit nonsmoking rooms, walking area, 1 block to park	(30) $25– $45	C M/F	OP

Holiday Inn 541-889-8621, 800-525-5333 1249 Tapadera Ave pets $10/stay www.hi-ontario.com, open area for walking dogs	(98) $72– $82	C R/L	OP T
Holiday Motel 541-889-9188 615 E Idaho Ave nonsmoking rooms, area for walking dogs, 2 miles to public park	(72) $38– $59	C R	OP
Motel 6 541-889-6617, 800-466-8356 275 NE 12th St www.motel6.com nonsmoking rooms, laundry, field for walking dogs	(103) $36– $52	C M/F	OP
Oregon Trail Motel 541-889-8633 92 E Idaho Ave 800-895-7945 nonsmoking rooms, lawn, 3 blocks to public park	(30) $28– $65	C K	
Sleep Inn 541-881-0007 1221 SE 1st Ct pets $5/day www.choicehotels.com, nonsmoking rooms, laundry, gravel area behind building, 5 miles to park	(65) $45– $75	CB	IP T
Stockman's Motel 541-889-4446 81 SW 1st St $10 refundable pet deposit nonsmoking rooms, alley behind building for walking dogs, across street to public park	(28) $30– $45	C M/F	

Oregon City, Oregon

Rivershore Hotel 503-655-7141, 800-443-7777 1900 Clackamette Dr each pet $5/day www.hemstreet.com, nonsmoking rooms, riverfront walking area, 2 minute walk to large public park	(117) $67– $113	FB M/F R/L	OP T

Otter Rock, Oregon

Alpine Chalets 541-765-2572, 800-825-5768 7045 Otter Crest Loop each pet $10/day www.lincolncity.com/achalet, nonsmoking, private park on premises with picnic area, beach access	(11) $80– $90	C K	

Oxbow, Oregon

Hells Canyon RV Park & Cabins 541-785-3393 HC 59 Box 80 800-453-3393 fully equipped cottages, RV sites, creekside walking area, 2 miles to public park	(6) $45– $60		

		# of units) & rates	food & drink	pool, sauna & hot tub
C = coffee IP = indoor pool OP = outdoor pool CB = continental K = full kitchen R = restaurant breakfast (k) = kitchenette S = sauna or F = refrigerator L = lounge steamroom FB = full breakfast M = microwave T = spa or hot tub				

Pacific City, Oregon

Anchorage Motel 503-965-6773, 800-941-6250 6585 Pacific Ave each pet $3/day www.oregoncoast.com/anchorage, 1 and 2-bdrm suites, area for walking dogs, 4 blocks to beach	(10) $37– $84	C K		
Inn at Cape Kiwanda 503-965-7001, 888-965-7001 33105 Cape Kiwanda Dr each pet $15/day www.innatcapekiwanda.com, laundry, in-room spa, completely nonsmoking, day spa with massage, warm water pet washing facility, lawn, beach access	(35) $109– $219	C R/L	T
Inn at Pacific City 503-965-6366, 888-722-2489 35215 Brooten Rd pets $9/day www.innatpacificcity.com, nonsmoking rooms, open area for walking dogs, 5 blocks to beach	(16) $39– $99	C K	
Pacific City Lodging 503-965-6464, 888-722-2489 35280 Brooten Rd pets $9/day www.innatpacificcity.com, nonsmoking rooms, dogs under 50 lbs only, park, 5 minute walk to beach	(34) $39– $99	C K M/F	
Riverview Lodge & RV Park 503-965-6000 36220 Resort Dr each pet $5/day nonsmoking 2-bdrm units, laundry, RV sites, 5 acres on the Nestucca River, open field, fishing dock	(5) $55– $75	K	
Sea View Vacation Rentals 503-965-7888 6335 Pacific Ave 888-701-1023 www.seaview4u.com each pet $10/stay fully equipped nonsmoking homes, laundry, hot tubs, close to beach for walking dogs	(11) $85– $260	K	T

Pendleton, Oregon

7 Inn 541-276-4711, 800-734-7466 I-84 Barnhart Rd Exit 202 pets $5/day www.7inn.com, nonsmoking rooms, field, trails	(50) $91– $97	C M/F	

Lodging	Contact	Rooms/Price	Col1	Col2
Best Western Pendleton Inn 400 SE Nye Ave www.bestwestern.com nonsmoking rooms, laundry, open walking area	541-276-2135 800-937-8376 pets $10/stay	(69) $60– $82	CB M/F	OP T
Budget Inn 1807 SE Court Ave nonsmoking rooms, laundry, grassy walking area	541-276-4521 pets $5/day	(30) $31– $51	C M/F	
Econo Lodge 620 SW Tutuilla Rd www.choicehotels.com, nonsmoking rooms, creekside pet walking area, close to walking trail	541-276-8654 pets $5/day	(51) $47– $110	CB K	
Economy Inn 201 SW Court Ave nonsmoking rooms, laundry, riverfront walking area	541-276-5252, 800-522-1555 pets $5/day	(51) $31– $57	CB M/F	OP
Holiday Inn 600 SE Nye Ave nonsmoking rooms, large field for walking dogs	541-966-6520, 800-465-4329 pets $10/stay	(64) $59– $69	CB	IP T
Motel 6 325 SE Nye Ave nonsmoking rooms, laundry, open field for walking	541-276-3160, 800-466-8356 www.motel6.com	(92) $36– $49	C	OP
Oxford Suites 2400 SW Court Pl www.oxfordsuites.com, nonsmoking rooms, laundry, lawn and field, 1 mile to public park and trails	541-276-6000, 877-545-7848 pets $15/stay	(87) $69– $139	FB M/F	IP T
Parker House B & B 311 N Main St dog must be small enough to carry upstairs, please bring dog's own bed, large back yard, neighborhood of historic homes, ½ block to river walkway	541-276-8581, 800-700-8581 www.parkerhousebnb.com	(6) $75– $135	FB	
Pillars Motel 1816 SE Court Ave nonsmoking rooms, dogs allowed by advance reservation only, open pet walking area, 3 blocks to riverside park with paved walking trails	541-276-6241 pets $2/day	(14) $25– $37	C M/F	
Red Lion Hotel 304 SE Nye Ave www.redlion.com, nonsmoking rooms, lawn	541-276-6111, 800-733-7663 $20 refundable pet deposit	(170) $59– $79	C M/F R/L	OP T

C = coffee CB = continental breakfast F = refrigerator FB = full breakfast	IP = indoor pool K = full kitchen (k) = kitchenette L = lounge M = microwave	OP = outdoor pool R = restaurant S = sauna or steamroom T = spa or hot tub	(# of units) & rates	food & drink	pool, sauna & hot tub

Pendleton, Oregon (continued)

Relax Inn 205 SE Dorion Ave nonsmoking rooms, laundry, 4 blocks to public park	541-276-3293 pets $5/day	(36) $25– $40	C M/F	
Super 8 Motel 601 SE Nye Ave nonsmoking rooms, in-room spa, lawn	541-276-8881, 800-800-8000 pets $10/stay	(50) $55– $100	CB M/F	T
Tapadera Inn 105 SE Court Ave nonsmoking rooms, dogs under 30 lbs only, ½ block to public park for walking dogs	541-276-3231, 877-722-8277 pets $5/stay	(46) $41– $63	C F R/L	
Travelodge 411 SW Dorion Ave www.travelodge.com nonsmoking rooms, laundry, 1 block to riverfront trail for walking dogs	541-276-7531 800-578-7878 pets $10/stay	(36) $52– $110	CB M/F	
Wildhorse Resort & Casino Hotel 72777 Hwy 331 www.wildhorseresort.com nonsmoking rooms, laundry, RV sites, walking trails	541-278-2274 800-654-9453 pets $10/stay	(99) $65– $80	CB R/L	IP S T

Philomath, Oregon

Galaxie Motel 104 S 20th St nonsmoking rooms, area for walking dogs, 1 block to public park	541-929-4334 pets $7/day	(15) $30– $65	M/F	

Phoenix, Oregon

Phoenix Motel 510 N Main St www.stayatphoenix.com, nonsmoking rooms, small dogs only, grassy area for walking pets	541-535-1555 pets $5–$8/day	(21) $35– $55	M/F	OP

Pilot Rock, Oregon

Pilot Rock Motel 326 NE 4th St open area for walking dogs, close to creekside park	541-443-2851 pets $5/stay	(8) $30– $53	K M/F

Port Orford, Oregon

Castaway-by-the-Sea Motel 545 W 5th St www.castawaybythesea.com, nonsmoking rooms, 1 block to beach	541-332-4502 pets $5/day	(13) $45– $85	C K
Holly House Inn 600 Jackson St nonsmoking 2-bdrm apartment sleeps 6, private entrance, large yard, hiking trails, 1 block to beach	541-332-7100	(1) $80– $120	CB K
Humbug Mountain Lodge 39292 Hwy 101 rooms and cabins, lakeside walking area, fishing and hiking trails nearby	541-332-1021	(9) $30– $65	K M/F
Port Orford Inn 1035 Oregon St nonsmoking rooms, coffee bar, fenced back yard, 2½ blocks to beach	541-332-0212	(12) $38– $48	K R
Sea Crest Motel 541-332-3040, 888-332-3040 44 Hwy 101 S www.seacrestoregon.com no pet fee for 1 dog, each additional dog $5/day, nonsmoking rooms overlooking ocean, next to large field that is lighted at night, ¼ mile to beach access		(18) $42– $88	C M/F
Shoreline Motel 206 6th St nonsmoking rooms, across street from beach	541-332-2903 pets $75/stay	(13) $36– $46	C K

Portland, Oregon

5th Avenue Suites Hotel 503-222-0001, 800-711-2971 506 SW Washington www.5thavenuesuites.com nonsmoking rooms, evening wine tasting, exercise room, 5 blocks to Waterfront Park		(221) $99– $189	C M/F R/L
6th Avenue Motel 2221 SW 6th Ave nonsmoking rooms	503-226-2979 800-686-7199 pets $10/day	(29) $45– $66	C M/F

C = coffee
CB = continental
    breakfast
F = refrigerator
FB = full breakfast
	IP = indoor pool
	K = full kitchen
	(k) = kitchenette
	L = lounge
	M = microwave
		OP = outdoor pool
		R = restaurant
		S = sauna or
		    steamroom
		T = spa or hot tub
			# of units)
			& rates
				food
				& drink
					pool, sauna
					& hot tub

Portland, Oregon (continued)

Airport Inn Econo Lodge 503-252-6666 9520 NE Sandy Blvd nonsmoking rooms, well-mannered quiet dogs only, laundry, across street from walking and biking path	(37) $45– $54	CB M/F	S T
Aladdin Motor Inn 503-246-8241, 800-292-4466 8905 SW 30th Ave pets $5/day laundry, small dogs only, lawn area for walking dogs	(52) $44– $50	C K	
Banfield Motel 503-280-1400 1525 NE 37th Ave pets $5/day nonsmoking rooms, laundry, well-behaved dogs only	(53) $51– $56	C	OP
Benson Hotel 503-228-2000 309 SW Broadway 888-523-6766 www.bensonhotel.com pets $50/stay complimentary wine tasting, 3 blocks to Park Blocks for walking dogs, 7 blocks to Waterfront Park, dog beds-bowls-treats provided, valet dogwalking service	(287) $119– $255	C R/L	
Best Inn & Suites 503-661-5100, 888-599-5100 121 NE 181st Ave each pet $10/day www.bestinn.com, laundry, bark dust area for walking dogs, short walk to public park	(44) $49– $73	CB M/F	T
Best Western Inn at the Convention Center 420 NE Holladay St 503-233-6331, 800-937-8376 www.bestwestern.com pets $7/day dogs under 20 lbs allowed on smoking floors only, 4 blocks to public park	(97) $65– $119	CB	
Best Western Inn at the Meadows 503-286-9600 1215 N Hayden Meadows 800-937-8376 www.bestwestern.com pets $22/stay nonsmoking rooms, laundry, small walking area, 2 blocks to public park, 6 blocks to walking trail, pet-friendly shuttle to airport and surrounding area	(146) $69– $150	CB M/F	T

Best Western Northwind Inn 503-431-2100 16105 SW Pacific Hwy (King City) pets $10/stay www.bestwestern.com, small dogs only, nonsmoking rooms, laundry, grassy areas for walking dogs, short drive to public park with walking trails	(72) $69– $140	CB M/F	IP T
City of Roses Motel 503-285-4626 8310 N Interstate Ave pets $5/day nonsmoking rooms, close to public park	(13) $45– $65	K	
Clyde Hotel 503-224-8000 1022 SW Stark St pets $10/day nonsmoking rooms, laundry, close to Park Blocks	(32) $70– $100	CB	
Coliseum Budget Inn 503-288-4489 109 NE San Rafael St small dogs only, laundry, 5 minute walk to park	(23) $40– $45	K	
Crown Motel 503-288-5277 5226 N Interstate Ave small dogs only, next to public park	(22) $40– $55		
Days Inn-Portland North 503-289-1800, 800-833-1800 9930 N Whitaker Rd pets $15/stay www.the.daysinn.com/portland11544, nonsmoking rooms, laundry, exercise room, next to public park	(211) $60– $85	CB (k)	
Days Inn-Airport 503-253-1151 1530 NE 82nd Ave 800-329-7466 nonsmoking rooms, ½ mile to public park	(40) $55– $75	CB K	
Doubletree Hotel Portland Downtown 503-221-0450 310 SW Lincoln St 800-222-8733 nonsmoking rooms $25 refundable pet deposit courtyard walking area, 2 blocks to waterfront park	(235) $69– $139	M/F R/L	OP
Doubletree Hotel Columbia River 503-283-2111 1401 N Hayden Island Dr 800-222-8733 www.doubletree.com pets $35/stay nonsmoking rooms, laundry, riverside walking paths	(352) $85– $160	R/L	OP T
Doubletree Hotel Jantzen Beach 503-283-4466 909 N Hayden Island Dr 800-222-8733 www.doubletree.com pets $35/stay nonsmoking rooms, laundry, tennis courts, exercise room, riverside walking paths	(320) $89– $179	C K R/L	OP T

C = coffee IP = indoor pool OP = outdoor pool CB = continental K = full kitchen R = restaurant breakfast (k) = kitchenette S = sauna or F = refrigerator L = lounge steamroom FB = full breakfast M = microwave T = spa or hot tub	(# of units) & rates	food & drink	pool, sauna & hot tub

Portland, Oregon (continued)

Downtown Value Inn 503-226-4751 415 SW Montgomery St pets $10/day www.downtownvalueinn.com, nonsmoking rooms, laundry, 2 blocks to public park	(36) $45– $55		
Econo Lodge 503-460-9000 3800 NE Sandy Blvd 800-424-6423 pets $5/day	(58) $49– $54	CB M	
Four Points Portland Sheraton 503-221-0711 50 SW Morrison St 800-325-3535 www.fourpointsportland.com, nonsmoking rooms, well-behaved dogs only, next to Waterfront Park	(140) $89– $160	C K R/L	
Hawthorn Inn & Suites 503-666-4785, 800-527-1133 2323 NE 181st Ave pets $10/stay www.hawthorn.com, nonsmoking rooms, laundry, exercise room, bike path and lawn for walking dogs	(70) $69– $130	FB K	IP S T
Heathman Hotel 503-241-4100, 800-551-0011 1001 SW Broadway pets $25/day nonsmoking rooms, 1 dog only under 50 lbs, fitness center, swimming pool across street, next to Park Blocks for walking dogs	(150) $99– $650	C F R/L	
Holiday Inn Express East 503-252-7400 9707 SE Stark St pets $20/stay small dogs only, nonsmoking rooms, in-room spa, exercise room, 1 block to walking/biking path	(84) $69– $89	CB M	T
Hotel Lucia 503-228-7221, 877-225-1717 400 SW Broadway www.hotellucia.com nonsmoking rooms, 2 blocks to public park	(128) $115– $165	C R/L	
Hotel Vintage Plaza 503-228-1212, 800-243-0555 422 SW Broadway www.vintageplaza.com nonsmoking rooms, complimentary wine tasting, designated pet area, 8 blocks to Waterfront Park	(107) $109– $300	C F R/L	T

Howard Johnson Airport Hotel 503-255-6722 7101 NE 82nd Ave 800-345-3896 www.hojo.com, nonsmoking rooms, pets $15/stay, 24 hour hot tub and sauna, courtyard to walk dogs	(137) $62– $95	C M/F R/L	OP S T
Kings Row Motel 503-246-3349 8715 SW Barbur Blvd pets $10/day nonsmoking rooms	(25) $35– $40	K	
La Quinta Inn & Suites 503-382-3820, 877-620-1002 11207 NE Holman St www.laquinta.com dogs under 50 lbs only, completely nonsmoking, 24 hour pool, laundry, lawn, walking and biking path	(98) $70– $91	CB	IP
La Quinta Inn & Suites 503-233-7933, 800-531-5900 431 NE Multnomah St pets $10/day www.laquinta.com, 24 hour laundry and pool, fitness room, 2 blocks to public park	(79) $79– $109	CB M/F	IP
La Quinta Inn & Suites 503-497-9044, 800-527-1133 4319 NW Yeon Ave pets $7/stay www.laquinta.com, nonsmoking rooms, laundry, 24 hour exercise room-spa-pool, small lawn for walking dogs, 3 miles to Waterfront Park	(84) $59– $150	CB K	IP S T
Mallory Hotel 503-223-6311, 800-228-8657 729 SW 15th Ave pets $10/stay www.malloryhotel.com, 90 year old European-style hotel, nonsmoking rooms, 2 blocks to open area for walking dogs, 15 blocks to Waterfront Park	(130) $95– $165	CB F R/L	
Mark Spencer Hotel 503-224-3293 409 SW 11th Ave 800-548-3934 www.markspencer.com pets $25/stay nonsmoking rooms, afternoon tea, laundry, discount pass to health club and pool, 2 blocks to public park	(101) $69– $109	CB (k)	
Marriott Portland Hotel 503-226-7600, 800-228-9290 1401 SW Naito Parkway pets $50/stay www.marriotthotels.com, nonsmoking rooms, fitness center, laundry, next to Waterfront Park	(503) $149– $169	CB F R/L	IP S T
Mel's Motor Inn 503-285-2556 5205 N Interstate Ave small dogs only, nonsmoking rooms, across street from public park	(40) $40– $55	K	

C = coffee IP = indoor pool OP = outdoor pool	(# of units) & rates	food & drink	pool, sauna & hot tub
CB = continental K = full kitchen R = restaurant breakfast (k) = kitchenette S = sauna or F = refrigerator L = lounge steamroom FB = full breakfast M = microwave T = spa or hot tub			

Portland, Oregon (continued)

Motel 6-Portland Central 503-238-0600 3104 SE Powell Blvd www.motel6.com nonsmoking rooms, next to school field and track	(69) $46– $62	C	OP
Oxford Suites-Jantzen Beach 503-283-3030 12226 N Jantzen Dr 800-548-7848 www.oxfordsuites.com pets $15/stay nonsmoking rooms, laundry, exercise room, trails	(203) $69– $129	FB M/F	IP S T
Park Lane Suites 503-226-628 809 SW King Ave 800-532-9543 www.parklanesuites.com pets $5/day laundry, 4 blocks from Washington Park	(44) $89– $129	C (k)	
Portlander Inn 503-283-1111, 800-523-1193 10350 N Vancouver Way pets $10–$35/stay www.portlanderinn.com, nonsmoking rooms, 24 hour convenience store, laundry, walking paths	(100) $65– $100	C R/L	
Quality Inn-Airport 503-256-4111, 800-246-4649 8247 NE Sandy Blvd pets $15/stay www.qualityinn.com, nonsmoking rooms, laundry, lawn area for walking dogs, across street to park	(120) $58– $115	CB M/F R/L	OP
Red Lion-Airport 503-252-6397, 877-666-3456 5019 NE 102nd Ave pets $25/stay area for walking dogs	(68) $69– $110	CB M/F	
Residence Inn-Lloyd Center 503-288-1400 1710 NE Multnomah St 800-331-3131 pets $10/day plus $50 cleaning fee, nonsmoking rooms and suites, complimentary dinner buffet, 4 blocks to park, www.residenceinnportland.com	(168) $99– $259	CB K	OP T
Residence Inn-Riverplace 503-552-9500 2115 SW River Parkway each pet $10/day www.residenceinn.com/pdxri, nonsmoking rooms, laundry, exercise room, next to Waterfront Park	(258) $69– $209	FB K	IP T

Riverplace Hotel 503-228-3233, 800-227-1333 1510 SW Harbor Way pets $45/stay www.riverplacehotel.com, nonsmoking rooms, guest pass to athletic club next door, laundry, pet amenities provided, next to Waterfront Park	(84) $189– $709	CB K R/L	S T
Rodeway Inn-Mall 205 503-255-0808, 888-773-6222 9225 SE Stark St pets $10/day nonsmoking rooms, laundry, 1 block to walking trail and public park	(63) $49– $120	CB M/F	T
Rose Manor Inn 503-236-4175, 800-252-8333 4546 SE McLoughlin Blvd pets $5/day nonsmoking rooms, 1 block to public park with walking trail to river	(76) $40– $79	C (k)	OP
Sheraton Portland Airport Hotel 503-281-2500 8235 NE Airport Way 800-325-3535 www.sheratonportland.com pets $25/stay	(213) $69– $175	R/L	IP S T
Shilo Inn-Portland/Beaverton 503-297-2551 9900 SW Canyon Rd 800-222-2244 www.shiloinns.com each pet $10/day nonsmoking rooms, laundry, pet beds and treats, fitness center, grassy walking area, 2½ miles to park	(142) $85– $115	CB K M/F R	OP T
Sleep Inn-Gresham 503-618-8400, 800-753-3746 2261 NE 181st Ave each pet $10/day www.sleepinn-portland.com, nonsmoking rooms, laundry, walking area, 3 miles to Blue Lake Park	(76) $55– $79	CB M/F	IP
Staybridge Suites 503-262-8888, 800-238-8000 11936 NE Glenn Widing Dr www.staybridge.com pets $10/day plus $25 cleaning fee, nonsmoking rooms and suites, hors d'oeuvres, 24 hour fitness center, wetlands area and path for walking dogs	(106) $99– $159	FB K	IP S T
Sullivan's Gulch B & B 503-331-1104 1744 NE Clackamas St www.sullivansgulch.com completely nonsmoking, 4 blocks to public park	(4) $75– $90	CB F	
Super 8 Motel 503-257-8988, 800-800-8000 11011 NE Holman St $25 refundable pet deposit nonsmoking rooms, laundry, small dogwalking area, close to walking and biking path	(80) $47– $59	C K M/F	

C = coffee IP = indoor pool OP = outdoor pool CB = continental K = full kitchen R = restaurant 　breakfast (k) = kitchenette S = sauna or F = refrigerator L = lounge 　steamroom FB = full breakfast M = microwave T = spa or hot tub	(# of units) & rates	food & drink	pool, sauna & hot tub

Portland, Oregon (continued)

Travelodge　　　　503-244-0151, 800-578-7878 10450 SW Barbur Blvd　　　　　　pets $10/stay nonsmoking rooms, laundry, 1½ miles to parks	(42) $40– $69	C K R/L	OP T
Travelodge Convention Center　　　503-231-7665 1506 NE 2nd Ave　　　　　　　　800-578-7878 www.travelodge-portland.com　pets $10–$15/day nonsmoking rooms, laundry, area for walking dogs	(43) $59– $89	CB M/F	S
Travelodge Portland Airport　　　　503-255-1400 9727 NE Sandy Blvd　　　　　　　800-578-7878 nonsmoking rooms, in-room spa, pets $15/day, open area for walking dogs, laundry, 3 blocks to park	(166) $39– $89	CB M/F R/L	OP T
Travelodge Suites I-205　503-788-9394, 800-578-7878 7740 SE Powell Blvd　　　　　　　pets $10/stay nonsmoking rooms, laundry, small area for walking dogs, 2 blocks to public park	(39) $66– $78	CB M/F	
Tudor House B & B　　　503-287-9476, 800-786-9476 2321 NE 28th Ave　　　　$25 refundable pet deposit 1 dog only, completely nonsmoking, large back yard, 4 blocks to public park and jogging track	(4) $85– $125	FB	
Viking Motel　　　　503-285-6687, 800-308-5097 6701 N Interstate Ave　　　　　　　pets $8/stay nonsmoking, lawn, 5 minute walk to public park	(25) $40– $52	C K	OP
Washington Park Inn　　503-226-6288, 800-532-9543 809 SW King Ave　　　　　　　　　pets $5/day nonsmoking rooms, dogs under 25 lbs only, 4 blocks to Washington Park	(44) $49– $59	CB M/F	
Westin Portland Hotel　　　　　503-294-9000 750 SW Alder St　　　　　　　　pets $25/stay www.westinportland.com, nonsmoking rooms, dog treats, fitness center, 3 blocks to public park	(205) $99– $265	C R/L	

Prairie City, Oregon

Sag's Motel 541-820-4515 69117 Hwy 26 well-behaved dogs allowed by advance reservation only, nonsmoking rooms, laundry, lawn and open walking areas, hiking trails, 3 miles to city park	(12) $40– $60	C K M	

Prineville, Oregon

Best Western Prineville Inn 541-447-8080 1475 NE 3rd St pets $15/stay www.bestwestern.com, nonsmoking rooms, laundry, lawn for walking dogs, 2 blocks to public park	(67) $70– $80	C M/F R	IP T
City Center Motel 541-447-5522 509 NE 3rd St www.at-e.com/ccm1.html nonsmoking rooms, laundry, open lot for walking dogs, next to public swimming pool and parks	(20) $35– $52	C M/F	
Executive Inn 541-447-4152 1050 NE 3rd St each pet $5/stay www.executiveinnonline.com, laundry, creekside area for walking dogs, close to park and waterfall	(26) $35– $60	CB K M/F	
Little Pine Motel 541-447-3440 251 NW Deer St nonsmoking rooms, grassy area for walking dogs, 4 blocks to public park	(8) $29– $40		
Ochoco Inn 541-447-6231 123 E 3rd St 888-800-9948 www.ochocoinn.com pets $5/day nonsmoking rooms, laundry, small pet walking area, 3 blocks to public park	(34) $38– $65	CB M/F	
Rustler's Inn 541-447-4185 960 W 3rd St pets $5/day nonsmoking rooms, close to riverfront and open field for walking dogs	(20) $41– $63	CB K M/F R/L	
Stafford Inn 541-447-7100 1773 NE 3rd St pets $20/stay www.staffordinn.com, laundry	(63) $79– $109	CB M/F	IP T

C = coffee CB = continental 　　breakfast F = refrigerator FB = full breakfast	IP = indoor pool K = full kitchen (k) = kitchenette L = lounge M = microwave	OP = outdoor pool R = restaurant S = sauna or 　　steamroom T = spa or hot tub	# of units) & rates	food & drink	pool, sauna & hot tub

Prospect, Oregon

Prospect Historical Hotel & Motel　541-560-3664 391 Mill Creek Dr　　　　　　　800-944-6490 www.prospecthotel.com, completely nonsmoking, 5 acres with field and paths for walking dogs, walking distance to several waterfalls			(24) $50– $85	C (k) R	
Union Creek Resort　　541-560-3565, 866-560-3565 56484 Hwy 62　　　　　　　　　　　pets $5/day cabins with fully equipped kitchens, riverside trails			(23) $40– $95	K R	

Rainier, Oregon

Budget Inn　　　　　　　　　　　503-556-4231 120 A St W　　　　　　　　　　　pets $5/day nonsmoking rooms, 1 block to public park			(26) $35– $85	K M/F	

Redmond, Oregon

Hub Motel & Restaurant　541-548-2101, 800-784-3482 1128 N Hwy 97　　　　　　　　　　pets $5/day nonsmoking rooms, area for walking dogs, close to walking trail			(30) $38– $48	C K M/F R	
Motel 6　　　　　　　541-923-2100, 800-466-8356 2247 S Hwy 97　　　　　　　　　www.motel6.com nonsmoking rooms, laundry, open field for walking dogs, close to walking trails			(83) $46– $72	C F	T
Redmond Inn　　　　　541-548-1091, 800-833-3259 1545 Hwy 97 S　　　　　　　　　　pets $5/day www.redmondinn.net, nonsmoking rooms, laundry, large pet walking area, 1 block to park			(46) $40– $70	CB K R/L	OP
Super 8 Motel　　　　　541-548-8881, 800-800-8000 3629 SW 21st Pl　　　　$25 refundable pet deposit www.super8.com, nonsmoking rooms, laundry, open field for walking dogs, 1 mile to public park			(85) $42– $78	CB	IP T

Village Squire Motel 541-548-2105 629 SW 5th St dogs allowed in smoking rooms only, small pet walking area, 1 block to public park	(24) $30– $55	C M/F	

Reedsport, Oregon

Anchor Bay Inn 541-271-2149 1821 Winchester Ave 800-767-1821 www.ohwy.com/or/a/anchobin.htm pets $7/day nonsmoking rooms, laundry, 1 block to riverside area for walking dogs	(21) $39– $63	CB M/F	OP
Best Budget Inn 541-271-3686 1894 Winchester Ave pets $5/day nonsmoking rooms, 1 block to public park	(23) $30– $85	CB K M/F	
Best Western Salbasgeon Inn 541-271-4831 1400 Hwy 101 S pets $5/day www.salbasgeon.com, nonsmoking rooms, laundry, fitness center, grassy area near the river for walking dogs, 4 miles to a public park	(57) $76– $180	CB K	IP S T
Economy Inn 541-271-3671, 800-799-9970 1593 Hiway Ave pets $3/day nonsmoking rooms, open area for walking dogs, 5 minute walk to public park	(41) $32– $85	CB K	OP
Fir Grove Motel 541-271-4848 2178 Winchester Ave (Hwy 101 at 2nd) pets $5/stay nonsmoking rooms, laundry, area behind building for walking dogs, 1 block to public park	(19) $38– $95	CB K	OP
Pacific Sands Inn 541-271-4894 76347 Hwy 101 nonsmoking rooms, area for walking dogs, ½ mile to beach	(35) $40– $65	C K	
Salbasgeon Inn of the Umpqua 541-271-2025 45209 State Hwy 38 pets $5/day nonsmoking rooms, large riverside pet walking area	(14) $60– $98	C K	
Salty Seagull Motel 541-271-3729 1806 Winchester Ave www.saltyseagull.com nonsmoking rooms and 2 to 3-room suites, fenced area for walking dogs, ½ block to public park and walking trails, ¾ mile to bike trail	(9) $35– $58	C K	

C = coffee IP = indoor pool OP = outdoor pool	(# of units) & rates	food & drink	pool, sauna & hot tub
CB = continental K = full kitchen R = restaurant			
breakfast (k) = kitchenette S = sauna or			
F = refrigerator L = lounge steamroom			
FB = full breakfast M = microwave T = spa or hot tub			

Richland, Oregon

Hitching Post Motel 541-893-6176	(18)	C	
1st & Main each pet $5/day	$42–	(k)	
rooms and cabins sleep 6, area for walking dogs, close to public park, 1 mile from river	$100		

Rockaway Beach, Oregon

Beachway Motel 503-355-2525	(7)	C	
421 N Miller St pets $15/stay	$35–	K	
nonsmoking rooms, trails for walking dogs, 1 block to beach, 4 blocks to public park	$115	F	

Getaway Oceanfront Lodging 503-355-2501	(13)	K	
621 S Pacific Dr 800-756-5552	$45–		
www.getawayoceanfront.com pets $15/stay	$115		
completely nonsmoking beachfront condominiums, easy beach access, ping pong table, volleyball			

Inn on Manhattan Beach 503-355-2301, 800-368-6499	(10)	CB	T
105 NW 23rd Ave pets $10/day	$69–	K	
www.river-inn.com, nonsmoking rooms, next to public park and walking trails, 100 feet to beach	$149		

Ocean Locomotion Motel 503-355-2093	(10)	C	
19130 Alder Ave pets $3–$5/day	$48–	K	
www.ohwy.com/or/o/oceanloc.htm	$115	M/F	
nonsmoking rooms, RV sites, picnic tables, BBQ, crab cooker, walking area, 1 mile to public park			

Ocean Spray Motel 503-355-2237	(8)	C	
505 N Pacific St pets $5–$10/day	$45–	K	
completely nonsmoking, 2 small or 1 large dog only, next to beach for walking dogs	$85		

Sea Treasures Inn 503-355-8220, 800-444-1864	(14)	C	
301 N Miller St each pet $6/stay	$48–	K	
nonsmoking rooms, ½ block to beach	$78	M/F	

Silver Sands Motel 503-355-2206, 800-457-8972 215 S Pacific Ave pets $5/stay www.oregonsilversands.com, dogs allowed in smoking rooms only, easy beach access	(64) $108– $146	C (k) F	IP S T
Surfside Oceanfront Resort Motel 503-355-2312 101 NW 11th Ave 800-243-7786 nonsmoking beachfront rooms pets $10/day	(80) $49– $121	K	IP
Tradewinds Motel 503-355-2112, 800-824-0938 523 N Pacific St pets $5–$10/day www.tradewinds-motel.com, nonsmoking rooms, in-room spa, pet walking area, next to beach	(19) $58– $237	C K	T
Twin Rocks Motel 503-355-2391 7925 S Minnehaha St pets $2–$5/day nonsmoking fully equipped beachfront cabins	(5) $74– $119	K	

Roseburg, Oregon

Best Western Douglas Inn 541-673-6625 511 SE Stephens St 877-368-4466 www.bestwestern.com/douglasinn pets $6/day nonsmoking rooms, laundry, fitness room, 2 blocks to small public park, ½ mile to large park	(52) $55– $85	CB M/F	S T
Best Western Garden Villa Motel 541-672-1601 760 NW Garden Valley Blvd 800-547-3446 www.bestwestern.com pets $10/day dogs under 10 lbs only, nonsmoking rooms, laundry, across street to park with walking trails	(121) $54– $102	CB M/F	OP T
Budget 16 Motel 541-673-5556 1067 NE Stephens St $20 refundable pet deposit nonsmoking rooms, designated pet walking area, 4 blocks to public park	(48) $35– $68	C K M/F	OP
Comfort Inn 541-957-1100 1539 NW Mulholland Dr pets $10/day www.comfortinn.com/hotel/or410 nonsmoking rooms, laundry, walking area, ¼ mile to trail and park	(50) $59– $99	CB M/F	IP T
Dunes Motel 541-672-6684, 800-260-9973 610 W Madrone St www.roseburgmall.com/dunes/ ½ block to public park	(43) $40– $60	CB M/F	

C = coffee CB = continental breakfast F = refrigerator FB = full breakfast	IP = indoor pool K = full kitchen (k) = kitchenette L = lounge M = microwave	OP = outdoor pool R = restaurant S = sauna or steamroom T = spa or hot tub	# of units) & rates	food & drink	pool, sauna & hot tub

Roseburg, Oregon (continued)

Holiday Inn Express 541-673-7517, 800-898-7666 375 W Harvard Ave pets $5/day www.hiexpress.com, nonsmoking rooms, laundry, designated pet area, close to biking trails	(100) $59– $99	CB F	IP T
Holiday Motel 541-672-4457, 800-446-4656 444 SE Oak Ave pets $6/day nonsmoking rooms, next to public park	(40) $30– $40	C F	
Howard Johnson 541-673-5082 978 NE Stephens St pets $7/day www.the.hojo.com/roseburg02132 nonsmoking rooms, laundry, guest pass to Gold's gym, small pet walking area, 2½ blocks to park	(31) $45– $110	CB K M/F	
Motel 6 541-464-8000, 800-466-8356 3100 NW Aviation Dr nonsmoking rooms, laundry, grassy area for walking dogs, ½ mile to public park	(82) $40– $55	C	
New Vista Motel 541-673-2736 1183 NE Stephens St pets $5/day nonsmoking rooms, laundry, area for walking dogs, 1 mile to public park	(15) $25– $69	M/F	
Quality Inn 541-673-5561, 800-626-1900 427 NW Garden Valley Blvd $100 pet deposit www.meyercrest.com, nonsmoking rooms, laundry, exercise room, 1 mile to waterfront park and trails	(70) $50– $90	CB (k) M/F	OP
Riverview B & B 541-677-0492, 800-861-5655 5601 Sunshine Rd nonsmoking rooms with private outside entrances sleep 2-3, deck overlooking river, wooded country setting, riverside walking area	(2) $65	FB K	
Rose City Motel 541-673-8209 1142 NE Stephens St $20 refundable pet deposit completely nonsmoking, large field for walking dogs, close to bike trail and several public parks	(11) $35– $75	K M/F	

Shady Oaks Motel 541-672-2608 2954 Old Hwy 99 S nonsmoking rooms, open area for walking dogs, large yard with BBQ, picnic tables	(12) $37– $48	C M/F	
Shamrock Motel 541-672-9183 2484 Old Hwy 99 S pets $5/day large lawn area for walking dogs	(14) $35– $45	K	
Sleep Inn 541-464-8338, 800-753-3746 2855 Edenbower Blvd pets $7/stay www.sleepinn.com, nonsmoking rooms, laundry, fitness room, open field, 1 mile to public park	(109) $47– $74	CB M/F R/L	IP T
Super 8 Motel 541-672-8880, 800-800-8000 3200 NW Aviation Dr $25 refundable deposit www.super8.com, open fields for walking dogs	(88) $50– $61	CB M	IP T
Travel Inn 541-672-3354 1627 SE Stephens St small dogs only, nonsmoking rooms, dirt road for walking dogs	(12) $33– $55	K	
Travelodge 541-672-4836, 800-578-7878 315 W Harvard Ave each pet $10/day nonsmoking rooms, private riverside park and picnic area, 1 block to public park and walking trails	(40) $55– $85	CB F	OP
Windmill Inn 541-673-0901, 800-547-4747 1450 NW Mulholland Dr nonsmoking rooms, www.windmillinns.com, laundry, pet treats, breakfast delivered to room each morning, fitness room, open field, walking trail, 2 blocks to public park	(128) $61– $83	CB M/F R	OP S T

Rufus, Oregon

Tyee Motel 541-739-2310 304 E 1st St pets $10/stay nonsmoking rooms, laundry, arcade and pool table, area for walking dogs, 1 mile to public park	(18) $42– $63	C K M/F	

Salem, Oregon

Best Western Mill Creek Inn 503-585-3332 3125 Ryan Dr SE 800-346-9659 www.bestwestern.com/millcreekinn pets $10/day nonsmoking rooms, dogs under 20 lbs only, laundry, ¼ mile to walking trail, 2 miles to public park	(109) $81– $92	FB M/F R/L	OP S T

C = coffee　　　IP = indoor pool　　OP = outdoor pool CB = continental　K = full kitchen　　R = restaurant 　　breakfast　(k) = kitchenette　S = sauna or F = refrigerator　L = lounge　　　　steamroom FB = full breakfast　M = microwave　　T = spa or hot tub	(# of units) & rates	food & drink	pool, sauna & hot tub
Salem, Oregon (continued)			
Best Western New Kings Inn　　　　503-581-1559 1600 Motor Ct NE　　　pets $10/stay, 877-594-1110 www.bestwestern.com, nonsmoking rooms, laundry, exercise room, open field for walking dogs	(101) $62– $85	CB M/F	IP S T
Best Western Pacific Highway Inn　　503-390-3200 4646 Portland Rd NE　　pets $10/day, 800-832-8905 www.bestwestern.com/pacifichighwayinn, laundry, nonsmoking rooms, residential pet walking area	(52) $59– $83	CB M/F	IP T
City Center Motel　　　503-364-0121, 800-289-0121 510 Liberty St SE　　　　　　pets $5–$15/stay nonsmoking rooms, laundry, small area for walking dogs, 3 blocks to public park, 6 blocks to waterfront	(30) $35– $65	C M/F	
Economy Inn　　　　　　　　　　　503-589-8010 2250 Mission St SE　　nonsmoking rooms, open field for walking dogs, 5 blocks to public park	(75) $40– $60	C M/F	OP
Holiday Inn Express　　　503-391-7000, 800-465-4329 890 Hawthorne Ave SE　　　　　pets $15/stay www.hiexpress.com, nonsmoking rooms, laundry, exercise room, next to walking trail	(113) $79– $115	CB M/F	IP
Holiday Lodge　　　　　503-585-2323, 800-543-5071 1400 Hawthorne Ave NE　　　　　pets $7/day small to medium dogs only, proof of vaccinations required, large open walking area, 1 mile to park	(54) $39– $59	CB M/F	OP
Motel 6　　　　　　　503-371-8026, 800-466-8356 1401 Hawthorne Ave NE　　　　www.motel6.com nonsmoking rooms, laundry, grassy walking areas, 8 blocks to public park	(115) $38– $56	C M/F	OP
Oregon Capital Inn　　　　　　　　503-363-2451 745 Commercial St SE　　　　　pets $10/stay laundry, children's play area, designated pet walking area, next to riverfront park	(109) $35– $40	F	

Phoenix Inn Suites North Salem 1590 Weston Ct NE www.phoenixinnsuites.com nonsmoking rooms, laundry, exercise room, lawn, close to fairgrounds	503-581-7004 888-239-9593 pets $10/stay	(80) $74– $129	CB M/F	IP T
Phoenix Inn Suites South Salem 4370 Commercial St SE www.phoenixinnsuites.com nonsmoking rooms, laundry, exercise room, 2 blocks to public park	503-588-9220 800-445-4498 pets $10/day	(89) $69– $99	CB M/F	IP T
Red Lion Hotel 3301 Market St NE www.redlionsalem.com nonsmoking rooms, laundry, 1 mile to public park	503-370-7888 800-248-6273 pets $10/stay	(150) $49– $119	M/F R/L	IP T
Salem Inn 1775 Freeway Ct NE www.saleminn.net, nonsmoking rooms, in-room spa, laundry, exercise room, 3 blocks to public park	503-588-0515, 888-305-0515 pets $10/day	(63) $59– $119	CB M/F	IP T
Super 8 Motel 1288 Hawthorne Ave NE www.super8.com, nonsmoking rooms, laundry, lawn and bark dust areas for walking dogs	503-370-8888, 800-800-8000 $25 refundable deposit	(80) $45– $71	CB K	IP T
Tiki Lodge Motel 3705 Market St NE field for walking dogs, short drive to public park	503-581-4441 nonsmoking rooms, open	(50) $33– $65	C K	OP
Travelodge Salem Capitol 1555 State St www.travelodge.com, nonsmoking rooms	503-581-2466 each pet $20/day, 800-578-7878	(42) $58– $90	CB	OP

Sandy, Oregon

Best Western Sandy Inn 37465 Hwy 26 nonsmoking rooms, laundry, close to nature trail	503-668-7100, 800-528-1234 pets $10/day	(45) $61– $89	CB M/F	IP T
Brookside B & B 45232 SE Paha Loop completely nonsmoking, dogs allowed by owner's approval only, rural area for walking dogs	503-668-4766 www.brooksidebandb.com	(5) $50– $70	FB	

C = coffee IP = indoor pool OP = outdoor pool CB = continental K = full kitchen R = restaurant breakfast (k) = kitchenette S = sauna or F = refrigerator L = lounge steamroom FB = full breakfast M = microwave T = spa or hot tub	# of units & rates	food & drink	pool, sauna & hot tub

Sandy, Oregon (continued)

| Shamrock Forest Inn   503-622-4911
59550 E Hwy 26   20 motel units plus a
2-story "recreation house" that sleeps 20 with private
hot tub, laundry, 3 miles to parks and hiking trails | (21)
$50–
$135 | CB
K | |

Scappoose, Oregon

| Barnstormer Inn B & B   503-543-2740, 888-875-1670
53758 W Lane Rd   pets $20/stay
www.barnstormerinn.com, small dogs only, in-room
spa, back road and lots of open area for walking dogs | (6)
$59–
$115 | FB
M/F | T |
| Malarkey Ranch Inn B & B   503-543-5244
55948 Columbia River Hwy   nonsmoking rooms,
large walking area, trails and horseback riding | (4)
$60–
$80 | FB | OP
T |

Seaside, Oregon

Best Western Oceanview Resort 503-738-3334 414 N Prom each pet $15/day, 800-234-8439 www.oceanviewresort.com, nonsmoking rooms, laundry, 2-mile long beach promenade for walking	(104) $60– $300	C (k) M/F R/L	IP T
Budget Inn 503-738-5221, 800-479-5191 521 Beach Dr each pet $5/day laundry, ½ block to beach for walking dogs	(24) $40– $140	C K	
City Center Motel 503-738-6377, 800-479-5191 250 1st Ave pets $5/day nonsmoking rooms, 1½ blocks to beach	(40) $35– $180	C K	IP T
Coast River Too 503-738-8474, 800-479-5191 800 S Holladay Dr each pet $5/day studios, 1 to 2-bdrm units, house, 5 blocks to beach	(5) $50– $100	K M/F	
Comfort Inn 503-738-3011, 800-226-9815 545 Broadway St pets $7/day 24 hour pool, boardwalk, river, 3 blocks to beach	(65) $68– $189	CB K	IP S T

Driftwood Motel 503-717-0331, 800-479-5191 825 N Holladay Dr pets $5/day area for walking dogs, 7 blocks to beach	(13) $37– $86	C K	
Guest House B & B 503-717-0495, 800-340-8150 486 Necanicum Dr dogs allowed in fenced yard and heated garage at B&B, pet-friendly cottage and condominium also available, 2 blocks to beach	(4) $60– $95	FB	
Lanai Oceanfront Condominiums 503-738-6343 3140 Sunset Blvd pets $10/stay, 800-738-2683 www.seasidelanai.com, dogs under 20 lbs only, fully equipped nonsmoking condominiums, lawn and beach for walking dogs, pool open May–September	(6) $60– $96	K	OP
Motel 6 503-738-6269, 800-466-8356 2369 S Roosevelt Dr www.motel6.com dogs allowed by manager's approval, advance reservation recommended, nonsmoking rooms, laundry, wetlands walking area, ⅓ mile to beach	(53) $39– $79	C M/F	
Riverside West Cottages 503-738-3251, 800-903-3251 445 Avenue G pets $10/day nonsmoking rooms, 1 dog under 30 lbs only, open lot for walking dogs, 3 blocks to ocean	(12) $45– $165	C K	
Rogers Inn 503-738-7367, 888-717-7367 436 S Downing St pets $30/stay www.rogersinn.com, completely nonsmoking, fully equipped cottages and vacation homes, laundry, some have in-room spas or yards for walking dogs	(27) $85– $375		T
Seaside Convention Center Inn 503-738-9581 441 2nd Ave pets $10/day, 800-699-5070 www.seasideccinn.com, nonsmoking rooms, laundry, 2 blocks to beach and promenade	(48) $69– $169	CB M/F	IP T
Seasider II Motel 503-738-7622, 800-305-3718 210 N Downing St pets $5/day nonsmoking rooms, laundry, area for walking dogs, 2 blocks to beach	(12) $45– $75	C M/F	
Seasider Motel 503-738-7764, 888-870-6544 110 5th Ave pets $10/stay nonsmoking rooms, next to beach for walking dogs	(9) $49– $79	M/F	

C = coffee IP = indoor pool OP = outdoor pool CB = continental K = full kitchen R = restaurant breakfast (k) = kitchenette S = sauna or F = refrigerator L = lounge steamroom FB = full breakfast M = microwave T = spa or hot tub	# of units) & rates	food & drink	pool, sauna & hot tub

Seaside, Oregon (continued)

Seaview Inn 503-738-5371, 800-479-5191 120 9th Ave pets $5/day nonsmoking rooms, ½ block to boardwalk and beach for walking dogs	(23) $35– $140	C K	
Shilo Inn-Seaside East 503-738-0549 900 S Holladay Dr 800-222-2244 www.shiloinns.com each pet $10/day nonsmoking rooms, laundry, pet beds and treats, pet walking area behind building, 4 blocks to beach	(58) $55– $125	CB K M/F	IP S T
Windjammer Motel 503-738-3250, 800-479-5191 4253 Hwy 101 N pets $5/day nonsmoking rooms, quiet Gearhart location, area for walking dogs, 1 mile to beach	(24) $40– $135	C K	

Shady Cove, Oregon

Edgewater Inn 541-878-3171 7800 Rogue River Dr 888-811-3171 www.edgewater-inns.com each pet $7/day nonsmoking rooms, deck overlooking river, exercise room, designated pet walking area, laundry, next to county park, close to trails	(54) $49– $155	CB K M/F	IP T
Royal Coachman Motel 541-878-2481 21906 Hwy 62 nonsmoking rooms, lawn area for walking dogs, 2 blocks to public park	(15) $39– $59	C K M/F	

Silverton, Oregon

Egg Cup Inn B & B 503-873-5497, 877-417-1461 11920 Sioux Rd NE ground floor 1-bdrm with sitting room and 1 suite with kitchenette, completely nonsmoking, well-behaved dogs only, resident pets, on 4 acres with walking paths	(2) $65– $75	FB (k)

Sisters, Oregon

Australian Outback Country Lodge 541-549-4312 68733 Junipine Lane www.sisterslodging.com B&B, private entrances, decks, RV sites, 9 creekside acres with trails for walking dogs	(5) $99– $149	FB M/F	T
Best Western Ponderosa Lodge 541-549-1234 505 Hwy 20 W each pet $10/day, 888-549-4321 nonsmoking rooms, laundry, large grassy area, resident llamas, forest service land with trails	(49) $84– $99	CB M/F	OP T
Black Butte Accommodations 541-549-3433 Black Butte Ranch 866-549-3433 nonsmoking rooms to fully equipped 3-bdrm 2-bath houses, laundry, miles of paved walking paths	(2+) $160– $250	R/L	OP
Sisters Comfort Inn 541-549-7829 540 Hwy 20 W nonsmoking rooms, dogs allowed at manager's discretion only, laundry, large pet walking areas	(50) $69– $95	CB K	IP T
Sisters Motor Lodge 541-549-2551 511 W Cascade Ave pets $5/day dogs allowed by manager's approval only, completely nonsmoking, next to forest service land and trails	(11) $59– $100	FB K	
Suttle Lake Resort 541-595-6662 13300 Hwy 20 www.suttlelake.com camping cabins sleep 6, some have kitchens and baths, all have covered porches-picnic table-firepit, bathhouse with toilets and showers; walking trails	(12) $45– $55	K R	

Spray, Oregon

Spray Asher Motel 541-468-2053 106 Willow St dogs MUST be kept off beds and furniture, open walking area, close to public park	(4) $30– $40		

Springfield, Oregon

Comfort Suites 541-746-5359, 877-746-5359 969 Kruse Way each pet $10/day dogs allowed in smoking rooms only, exercise room, laundry, in-room spa	(77) $59– $89	CB M/F	IP T

C = coffee IP = indoor pool OP = outdoor pool CB = continental K = full kitchen R = restaurant 　　breakfast (k) = kitchenette S = sauna or F = refrigerator L = lounge 　　steamroom FB = full breakfast M = microwave T = spa or hot tub	# of units) & rates	food & drink	pool, sauna & hot tub

Springfield, Oregon (continued)

Doubletree Eugene/Springfield　　　541-726-8181 3280 Gateway Rd　　　　　　　　800-222-8733 www.doubletreeeugene.com, nonsmoking rooms, laundry, exercise room, large walking area, 5 blocks to walking paths, short drive to off-leash dog park	(234) $89– $156	C M/F R/L	OP T
Gateway Inn　　　　541-726-1212, 800-392-3035 3540 Gateway St　　　　　　each pet $15/stay nonsmoking rooms, laundry, small lawn area	(91) $43– $69	CB M/F R/L	OP
Holiday Inn Express　　　　　　　541-746-8471 3480 Hutton St　　　　　　　　800-465-4329 www.hiexpress.com/eugeneor　　pets $10/day dogs allowed in smoking rooms only, laundry, large open field, ¾ mile to public park	(58) $59– $109	CB M/F	IP
Motel 6 Eugene/Springfield　　　　541-741-1105 3752 International Ct　　　　　　800-466-8356 www.motel6.com, nonsmoking rooms, laundry, open field for walking dogs, 1 mile to public park	(131) $36– $50	C	OP
Motel Orleans　　　　541-746-1314, 800-626-1900 3315 Gateway St　　　　$100 refundable pet deposit nonsmoking rooms, laundry, lawn, 3 miles to park	(71) $42– $72	C M/F	IP T
Shilo Inn-Eugene/Springfield　　　541-747-0332 3350 Gateway　　　　　　　　　800-222-2244 www.shiloinns.com　　　　　each pet $10/stay nonsmoking rooms, laundry, pet beds and treats, open area for walking dogs, 4 blocks to citywide system of walking trails	(140) $60– $110	C K R	OP
Village Inn Motel　　　　　　　　541-747-4546 1875 Mohawk Blvd　　　　　　　800-327-6871 nonsmoking rooms, laundry, area for walking dogs	(67) $62– $72	CB K R/L	OP T

St Helens, Oregon

Best Western Inn 503-397-3000, 800-937-8376 585 S Columbia River Hwy pets $10/stay www.bestwestern.com, nonsmoking rooms, laundry, lawn, open field, 3 miles to public park	(50) $69– $109	CB M/F	IP T
Village Inn Motel 503-397-1490 535 S Columbia River Hwy each pet $3/day nonsmoking rooms, laundry, RV sites, open fields, 1½ miles to public park	(52) $44– $51	K R/L	

Stayton, Oregon

Bird & Hat Inn B & B 503-769-7817 717 N 3rd Ave www.wvi.com/~dhull/bird&hat.html completely nonsmoking, 2 rooms open onto veranda, large yard for walking dogs, 1 block to public park	(3) $45– $65	FB	
Gardner House B & B 503-769-5478 633 N 3rd Ave completely nonsmoking, ground floor suite sleeps 3, 2 blocks to public park	(2) $75– $93	FB (k)	

Sublimity, Oregon

Best Western Sunrise Inn 503-769-9579 300 SW Sublimity Blvd pets $25/stay, 800-528-1234 small dogs only, nonsmoking rooms, laundry, large open field for walking dogs, 1 mile to city parks, 15 miles to Silver Creek Falls	(50) $59– $99	CB M/F	IP T

Summer Lake, Oregon

Lodge at Summer Lake 541-943-3993, 866-943-3993 53460 Hwy 31 pets $5/stay www.thelodgeatsummerlake.com, nonsmoking rooms and 3-bdrm house, 20 acres with designated pet walking area and horse pasture, bird sanctuary	(12) $44– $100	C K M/F R	
Summer Lake Inn 541-943-3983, 800-261-2778 31501 Hwy 31 each pet $10/stay www.summerlakeinn.com, 1 to 2 dogs per cabin, fully equipped kitchens, in-room spa, meals available, 150 acres, pond, swimming dock, off-leash play areas	(9) $105– $165	C K	T

C = coffee IP = indoor pool OP = outdoor pool CB = continental K = full kitchen R = restaurant breakfast (k) = kitchenette S = sauna or F = refrigerator L = lounge steamroom FB = full breakfast M = microwave T = spa or hot tub	# of units) & rates	food & drink	pool, sauna & hot tub

Sumpter, Oregon

| Depot Inn   541-894-2522, 800-390-2522
179 Mill St S   pets $5/stay
www.thedepotinn.com, nonsmoking rooms, open
area for walking dogs, next to state park and trails | (14)
$50–
$75 | C | |

Sunriver, Oregon

Discover Sunriver Vacation Rentals 541-593-2482 www.discoversunriver.com 800-544-0300 nonsmoking homes, some with hot tubs, laundry, guest pass to community swimming pool	(150) $81– $350	K M/F	OP T
Showroom Inn 541-593-2156 17919 Spring River Rd www.showroominns.com completely nonsmoking apartment and large home, 1 acre of lawn and woods for walking dogs	(2) $75– $250	C K	T
Sunray Vacation Rentals 541-593-3225 56890 Venture Lane 800-531-1130 www.sunrayinc.com, nonsmoking homes-condos, laundry, in-room spa, RV sites, paved walking trails	(50) $110– $290		T
Twin Lakes Resort 541-593-6526 11200 S Century Dr pets $5/day lakefront cabins, RV sites, laundry, national forest	(14) $90– $155	K R	
Village Properties 541-593-1653, 1-800-786-7483 #2 Country Mall Suite I www.village-properties.com VIP pass to 2 community swimming pools, fully equipped nonsmoking 2 to 4-bdrm homes, trails	(6) $100– $350	K	T

Sutherlin, Oregon

| Best Budget Inn   541-459-4236
181 Hutchins St $15 refundable pet deposit
dogs allowed with manager's approval only,
nonsmoking rooms, open field for walking dogs | (48)
$30–
$45 | C
F | |

Sutherlin Inn 541-459-6800, 800-635-5425 1400 Hospitality Way pets $10/stay www.cloud9inns.com/cloud9_009.htm, nonsmoking rooms, laundry, large walking area, close to parks	(80) $40– $65	CB M/F	
Town & Country Motel 541-459-9615, 800-459-9615 1386 W Central Ave pets $5/day nonsmoking rooms, walking area, ½ block to park	(18) $40– $59	C K	

Sweet Home, Oregon

Sweet Home Inn 541-367-5137 805 Long St pets $10/stay sweethomeinn@yahoo.com, laundry, pet walking area, 2 blocks to public park	(31) $59– $69	M/F	S T

The Dalles, Oregon

American Hospitality Inn 541-296-9111 200 W 2nd St pets $5/day nonsmoking rooms, laundry, small area for walking dogs, 2 blocks to public park	(54) $39– $49	C M/F	
Best Western Inn 541-296-9107 112 W 2nd St 888-935-2378 www.bestwesternoregon.com pets $10/day nonsmoking rooms, laundry, field, 4 blocks to park	(65) $49– $114	FB F R/L	OP
Budget Inn 541-296-5464 118 W 4th St pets $7/day nonsmoking rooms, area for walking dogs, walking distance to public park	(24) $32– $48	M/F	
Days Inn 541-296-1191, 800-991-0801 2500 W 6th St pets $20/day nonsmoking rooms, laundry, open area for walking dogs, short drive to public park	(70) $51– $69	CB F	OP
Inn at the Dalles 541-296-1167, 800-982-3496 3550 SE Frontage Rd pets $5/day nonsmoking, open field, ½ mile to riverside park	(45) $28– $70	C K	IP
Oregon Trail Motel 541-296-2473 3830 W 6th St completely nonsmoking, laundry, open field for walking dogs, 1 mile to public park	(14) $30	K	

C = coffee	IP = indoor pool	OP = outdoor pool	(# of units) & rates	food & drink	pool, sauna & hot tub
CB = continental	K = full kitchen	R = restaurant			
breakfast	(k) = kitchenette	S = sauna or			
F = refrigerator	L = lounge	steamroom			
FB = full breakfast	M = microwave	T = spa or hot tub			

The Dalles, Oregon (continued)

Quality Inn 2114 W 6th St www.qualityinn-thedalles.com nonsmoking rooms, laundry, athletic club pass, lawn, short drive to park	541-298-5161 800-848-9378 pets $10/day	(93) $50– $99	C K R/L	OP T
Shilo Inn 3223 Bret Clodfelter Way www.shiloinns.com nonsmoking rooms, laundry, fitness center, pet beds and treats, small pet walking area, 1½ miles to park	541-298-5502 800-222-2244 each pet $10/day	(112) $70– $130	M/F	OP S T
Super 8 Motel 541-296-6888, 800-800-8000 609 Cherry Heights Rd each pet $10/day nonsmoking rooms, laundry, in-room spa, grassy area and open field for walking dogs, 1 block to park		(73) $65– $100	CB M/F	OP T

Tigard, Oregon

Embassy Suites Hotel 9000 SW Washington Square Rd www.embassysuites.com nonsmoking suites, complimentary cocktails, pet walking area, close to park and trails	503-644-4000 800-362-2779 pets $25/stay	(354) $99– $149	FB M/F R/L	IP S T
Homestead Studio Suites Hotel 13009 SW 68th Pkwy www.homesteadhotels.com nonsmoking suites, laundry, guest pass at athletic club, large lawn, close to park	503-670-0555 888-782-9473 pets $75/stay	(136) $64– $109	C K	
Motel 6-Portland South 503-620-2066, 800-466-8356 17950 SW McEwan Ave www.motel6.com nonsmoking rooms, laundry, 1 dog per room, grassy pet walking areas, short drive to public parks		(117) $35– $61	C M/F	OP

Ramada Limited 503-620-2030 17993 SW Lower Boones Ferry Rd pets $10/stay www.ramada.com, nonsmoking mini-suites, laundry, exercise room, ½ mile to public park	(68) $45– $69	CB (k) R/L	OP S T
Red Roof Inn 503-684-0760, 800-733-7663 17959 SW McEwan Rd www.redroof.com 1 small dog only, laundry, grassy walking area	(80) $43– $59	C	OP
Shilo Inn-Portland I-5 South 503-639-2226 7300 SW Hazelfern Rd 800-222-2244 www.shiloinns.com each pet $10/day nonsmoking rooms, laundry, dog beds and treats, fitness center, pet walking area, short drive to park	(117) $70– $100	CB	OP S T
Shilo Inn-Washington Square 503-620-4320 10830 SW Greenburg Rd 800-222-2244 www.shiloinns.com each pet $10/day nonsmoking rooms, fitness center, pet beds and treats, walking area, 1 mile to park	(77) $70– $110	CB K M/F	S T

Tillamook, Oregon

Mar-Clair Inn 503-842-7571, 800-331-6857 11 Main Ave pets $6/day nonsmoking rooms, huge open lot for walking dogs, across street to small park, ½ mile to larger park	(47) $38– $80	C K	OP S T
Sea Lion Motel 503-842-5477 4951 Netarts Hwy W apartments with full kitchens, open field for walking dogs, 2 blocks to beach	(7) $49– $69	C K	
Shilo Inn-Tillamook 503-842-7971, 800-222-2244 2515 N Main St each pet $10/day www.shiloinns.com, nonsmoking rooms, pet beds and treats, pet walking area, 1 mile to city park	(101) $70– $130	C K M/F R	IP S T
Three Capes Inn at Netarts 503-842-4003 4800 Netarts Hwy W pets $5/day nonsmoking rooms, fish cleaning station, large yard and hiking trails, 1½ blocks to bay, ¼ mile to park	(8) $50– $65	C K	
Western Royal Inn 503-842-8844 1125 N Main St 800-624-2912 laundry, open field for walking dogs pets $5/stay	(40) $55– $105	C M/F	

C = coffee IP = indoor pool OP = outdoor pool CB = continental K = full kitchen R = restaurant breakfast (k) = kitchenette S = sauna or F = refrigerator L = lounge steamroom FB = full breakfast M = microwave T = spa or hot tub	(# of units) & rates	food & drink	pool, sauna & hot tub

Troutdale, Oregon

Motel 6 Portland/Troutdale 503-665-2254 1610 NW Frontage Rd 800-466-8356 www.motel6.com, nonsmoking rooms, laundry, open field for walking dogs, 1 mile to public park	(123) $38– $55	C	OP
Phoenix Inn Troutdale 503-669-6500 477 NW Phoenix Dr 800-824-6824 www.phoenixinnsuites.com pets $10/stay nonsmoking rooms, dog treats, ½ mile to park, 1 mile to walking trail	(73) $59– $120	CB M/F	IP T
Travelodge-Portland/Troutdale 503-666-6623 23705 NE Sandy Blvd pets $5/day, 800-578-7878 www.greshamtravelodge.com, nonsmoking rooms, laundry, large lawn for walking dogs, ¼ mile to park	(44) $39– $65	CB K M/F R/L	

Tualatin, Oregon

La Quinta Inn & Suites 503-612-9952, 800-531-5900 7640 SW Warm Springs St pets $5/day www.laquinta.com, laundry, workout room, lawn and open field for walking dogs, short drive to park	(59) $59– $120	FB K M/F	IP T
Sweetbrier Inn 503-692-5800, 800-551-9167 7125 SW Nyberg Rd www.sweetbrier.com laundry, 24 hour fitness center, lawn and wooded area for walking dogs, close to public park	(131) $74– $110	CB M/F R/L	OP

Ukiah, Oregon

Antlers Inn 541-427-3492 Main & Alba pets $5/stay next to public park for walking dogs	(12) $30– $60	C	
Stage Stop Motel & RV Park 541-427-3352 501 E Main St cabins, showerhouse, RV sites, open walking areas	(5) $45	M/F	

Umatilla, Oregon

Desert River Inn 541-922-1000, 877-922-1500 705 Willamette Ave pets $10/day www.desertriverinn.com, nonsmoking rooms, nature trails, 1½ blocks to Columbia River	(67) $60– $81	C K M/F R/L	OP T
Tillicum Motor Inn 541-922-3236 1481 6th St pets $10/day dogs under 20 lbs only, nonsmoking rooms, laundry, lawn area for walking dogs	(79) $39– $62	C K	OP
Umatilla Inn & Suites 541-922-3271, 800-423-9913 1370 6th St each pet $5/day nonsmoking rooms, 3 blocks to public park	(36) $38– $110	C K	

Unity, Oregon

Unity Motel & RV Park 541-446-3431 302 Main nonsmoking rooms, laundry, RV sites, pet walking area, short drive to national forest and wilderness	(7) $30– $70	C K	

Vale, Oregon

Golden Wheel Motel 541-473-3024 350 A St E grassy area for walking dogs, next to river and trails	(14) $20– $30	M/F	

Vernonia, Oregon

Vernonia Inn 503-429-4006 900 Madison Ave 800-354-9494 nonsmoking rooms, private decks, in-room hot tubs, 2 blocks to paved walking trail, 2 public parks and lake within 2 blocks	(15) $45– $80	CB M/F	T

Vida, Oregon

Adventure River Center 541-822-3888 49701 McKenzie Hwy 888-547-5565 www.adventurerivercenter.com, 3-bdrm 2-bath lodge with full kitchen sleeps up to 12, laundry, fenced yard, close to McKenzie River hiking trail, rafting trips available	(1) $140– $220	K	

				(# of units) & rates	food & drink	pool, sauna & hot tub
C = coffee	IP = indoor pool	OP = outdoor pool				
CB = continental	K = full kitchen	R = restaurant				
breakfast	(k) = kitchenette	S = sauna or				
F = refrigerator	L = lounge	steamroom				
FB = full breakfast	M = microwave	T = spa or hot tub				

Vida, Oregon (continued)

Bliss' McKenzie River Inn	541-896-3218	(4)	R/L	
45441 McKenzie Hwy (Milepost 26)		$67		
riverside pet walking area, national forest and trails				
Eagle Rock Lodge B & B	541-822-3630	(8)	FB	T
49198 McKenzie Hwy	888-773-4333	$55–	K	
www.eaglerocklodging.com		$195	M/F	
completely nonsmoking, in-room spa, on 8 wooded acres along river for walking dogs				
McKenzie River Inn	541-822-6260	(6)	CB	T
49164 McKenzie Hwy www.mckenzieriverinn.com		$75–	K	
lodge rooms and cabins sleep up to 6, in-room spa,		$125	R	
private decks, gourmet breakfast served in lodge,				
trails for walking dogs				
Wayfarer Resort	541-896-3613	(13)	K	
46725 Goodpasture Rd	800-627-3613	$65–		
www.wayfarerresort.com	pets $10/day	$230		
cabins sleep 3 to 10, river swimming, private hot tub in 1 unit, 10 acres for walking dogs				

Wagontire, Oregon

Wagontire Motel & Cafe	541-493-2317	(6)	R	
53358 S Hwy 395 dogs allowed at manager's		$35–		
discretion only, nonsmoking rooms, RV sites, store,		$45		
service station, landing strip, designated pet area				

Waldport, Oregon

Alsea Bay Evening Star Resort	541-563-7700	(83)	CB	OP
902 NW Bayshore Dr	877-327-6500	$45–	F	
www.eveningstarresort.com	pets $10/day	$180		
dogs allowed in smoking rooms only, laundry,				
exercise room, bay shore access for walking dogs,				
5 minute walk to ocean				

Alsea Manor Motel 541-563-3249 190 SW Arrow (Hwy 101) pets $5/day nonsmoking rooms, small dogs only, fenced area for walking dogs, 1 block to beachfront	(16) $49– $95	C	
Edgewater Cottages 541-563-2240 3978 SW Pacific Coast Hwy pets $5–$10/day nonsmoking rooms, 8 miles of beach to walk dogs	(9) $85– $150	K	
Sundown Motel 541-563-3018, 800-535-0192 5050 SW Hwy 101 pets $4–$7/day direct beach access for walking dogs	(8) $41– $105	C K M/F	

Wallowa, Oregon

Mingo Motel 541-886-2021 102 N Alder St www.mingomotel.com unique nonsmoking theme rooms, close to park	(11) $42– $75	C M/F	

Wamic, Oregon

Pine Hollow Lakeside Resort 541-544-2271 34 N Mariposa Dr pets $5/day www.pinehollowlakeside.com cabins sleep 2 to 8, open walking area and trails	(7) $40– $50	(k)	

Warrenton, Oregon

Ray's Tavern & Motel 503-861-2566 45 NE Skipanon Dr nonsmoking rooms, lawn and undeveloped area to walk dogs, short drive to beach	(8) $38– $48	C M/F	
Shilo Inn 503-861-2181 1609 E Harbor St 800-222-2244 www.shiloinns.com each pet $10/day nonsmoking rooms, fitness center, pet beds and treats, open pet walking area, 2 miles to public park	(63) $69– $99	C K M/F	IP S T

Welches, Oregon

Old Welches Inn B & B 503-622-3754 26401 E Welches Rd www.mthoodlodging.com dogs allowed in 2-bdrm riverfront cottage only, fully equipped kitchens, all linens, pet beds-bowls-towels, fenced yard, short drive to hiking trails	(5) $163– $203	C K	

C = coffee IP = indoor pool OP = outdoor pool CB = continental K = full kitchen R = restaurant breakfast (k) = kitchenette S = sauna or F = refrigerator L = lounge steamroom FB = full breakfast M = microwave T = spa or hot tub	(# of units) & rates	food & drink	pool, sauna & hot tub

West Linn, Oregon

Riverbend House B & B 503-557-1662 949 Willamette Falls Dr www.riverbendhouse.com dogs allowed by advance reservation only, laundry, completely nonsmoking, huge riverside lawn, pet agility equipment available, next to wilderness park	(2) $90– $125	FB F	T

Westlake, Oregon

Siltcoos Lake Resort & Motel 541-997-3741 82855 Fir St area for walking dogs, kennels and dog run, pet-sitting service available	(8) $30– $50	K	
Westlake Resort 541-997-3722 4785 Laurel Ave www.westlakeresort.com cabins, laundry, lakefront area for walking dogs	(9) $50– $70	K	

Weston, Oregon

Tamarack Inn B & B 541-566-9348, 800-662-9348 62388 Hwy 204 small dogs allowed by advance approval only, 2 acres in mountain recreational area, forest roads and trails, 4 miles to ski area	(4) $75– $110	FB	T

Westport, Oregon

Westport Motel 503-455-2212 49238 Hwy 30 pets $3/day BBQ, picnic table, walking area, close to playground	(8) $45– $80	K	

Wheeler, Oregon

Maggie's Guestrooms B & B 503-368-6881 47 Gregory St www.stayatmaggies.com dogs allowed by advance approval only, nonsmoking rooms, close to public park and walking trail	(3) $55– $85	CB	

Wheeler on the Bay Lodge & Marina 503-368-5858 580 Marine Dr 800-469-3204 www.wheeleronthebay.com pets $6/day dogs under 20 lbs only, completely nonsmoking, in-room spa, mowed area for walking dogs, 4 miles to state parks-ocean beaches-hiking trails	(11) call for rates	C M/F	T

Wilsonville, Oregon

Best Western Willamette Inn 503-682-2288 30800 SW Parkway Ave 888-682-0101 www.bestwesternoregon.com, nonsmoking rooms, laundry, exercise room, dogs under 25 lbs only, large walking area, 5 minute walk to public park	(63) $70– $98	CB (k)	OP T
Comfort Inn 503-682-9000, 888-522-6122 8855 SW Citizens Dr pets $10/day www.comfortinn.com, nonsmoking rooms, laundry, grassy pet area and walking paths	(65) $59– $109	CB M/F	IP T
Days Inn & Suites 503-682-3184, 800-329-7466 8815 SW Sun Pl pets $10/day www.daysinn.com, nonsmoking rooms, laundry, lawn for walking dogs, 1½ miles to public park	(79) $49– $79	CB M/F	OP T
Holiday Inn 503-682-2211, 800-465-4329 25425 SW 95th Ave pets $10/day nonsmoking rooms, laundry, area for walking dogs, close to public park	(169) $59– $125	C CB M/F R/L	IP S T
Snooz Inn 503-682-2333, 800-343-1553 30245 SW Parkway Ave each pet $5/day www.snoozeinn.com, nonsmoking rooms, near park	(57) $39– $45	CB M/F	OP
Super 8 Motel 503-682-2088, 800-800-8000 25438 SW Parkway Ave $25 refundable deposit nonsmoking rooms, laundry, open area for walking dogs, 1½ miles to public park	(72) $40– $56	C M/F	

Winchester Bay, Oregon

Discovery Point Resort 541-271-3443 242 Discovery Point Lane pets $5/day fully equipped bayfront cabins, laundry, RV sites, across street from beach and jetty	(7) $68– $98		

C = coffee IP = indoor pool OP = outdoor pool CB = continental K = full kitchen R = restaurant breakfast (k) = kitchenette S = sauna or F = refrigerator L = lounge steamroom FB = full breakfast M = microwave T = spa or hot tub	(# of units) & rates	food & drink	pool, sauna & hot tub

Winchester Bay, Oregon (continued)

| Harbor View Motel   541-271-3352
540 Beach Blvd   pets $2/day
waterfront area for walking dogs, 1 block to park | (14)
$34–
$47 | K | |
| Winchester Bay Inn   541-271-4871, 800-246-1462
390 Broadway   pets $3/day
www.winbayinn.com, nonsmoking rooms, grassy
pet walking area, 1 block to harbor, 1 mile to beach | (50)
$55–
$105 | CB
K | T |

Winston, Oregon

| Safari Inn   541-679-6736
101 NE Main St   nonsmoking rooms, laundry,
area for walking dogs, 3 blocks to public park | (18)
$36–
$49 | M/F | |
| Sweet Breeze Inn   541-679-2420, 888-672-2420
251 NE Main St   pets $5/stay
completely nonsmoking, open fields for walking
dogs, 7 blocks to park, near Wildlife Safari entrance | (32)
$54–
$80 | CB
M/F | |

Wolf Creek, Oregon

| Sunny Valley Motel   541-476-9217
352 Sunny Valley Loop
nonsmoking rooms, open area for walking dogs | (10)
$35–
$45 | C
K | |

Woodburn, Oregon

| Best Western Inn   503-982-6515, 800-766-6433
2887 Newberg Hwy   pets $10/day
www.bestwestern.com, laundry, dogs allowed in
smoking rooms only, lawn and field for walking dogs | (81)
$49–
$79 | CB
M/F | OP
T |
| Fairway Inn Motel   503-981-3211
2450 Country Club Ct   800-981-2466
nonsmoking rooms, laundry, lawn and open field
for walking dogs | (46)
$36–
$55 | C
M/F | OP |

La Quinta Inn & Suites 503-982-1727, 800-531-5900 120 N Arney Rd pets $5/day www.laquinta.com, nonsmoking rooms, laundry, exercise room, lawn and open field, 2 miles to park	(60) $49– $120	CB K M/F	OP T
Super 8 Motel 503-981-8881, 800-800-8000 821 Evergreen Rd $25 refundable pet deposit www.super8.com, nonsmoking rooms, laundry, lawn and fields for walking dogs	(81) $42– $72	CB	IP T
Woodburn Inn 503-982-9741 1025 N Pacific Hwy www.woodburninn.com laundry, small dogs only, pet walking area	(20) $40– $55	CB K	

Yachats, Oregon

Adobe Resort 541-547-3141 1555 Hwy 101 N 800-522-3623 www.adoberesort.com each pet $10/day nonsmoking rooms, laundry, fitness room, beach and walking trail, "pet packs" include dog towel, sheet to cover bed, dog treats and pooper scooper	(100) $65– $150	C K M/F R/L	IP S T
Ambrosia Gardens B & B 541-547-3013 95435 Hwy 101 S www.ambrosia-gardens.com dogs allowed in 1 room at owner's discretion only, completely nonsmoking, open meadow for walking dogs, 1 block to beach access	(3) $115	FB	T
Beachcombers Motel 541-547-3432 95500 Hwy 101 S each pet $6/day cabins with fully equipped kitchens, pet walking area, easy beach access	(5) $40– $95	C K	
Fireside Resort Motel 541-547-3636 1881 Hwy 101 N 800-336-3573 www.overleaflodge.com/fireside.htm pets $7/day nonsmoking rooms, in-room spa, walking trail, 10 minute walk to beach	(44) $45– $115	C K	T
Holiday Inn Market & Motel 541-547-3120 5933 Hwy 101 N pets $5/day www.holidayinyachats.com, cabins with full kitchens, fireplaces, next to beach for walking dogs	(7) $65– $90	C K	

C = coffee
CB = continental
   breakfast
F = refrigerator
FB = full breakfast
	IP = indoor pool
	K = full kitchen
	(k) = kitchenette
	L = lounge
	M = microwave
		OP = outdoor pool
		R = restaurant
		S = sauna or
		   steamroom
		T = spa or hot tub
			(# of units)
			& rates
				food
				& drink
					pool, sauna
					& hot tub

Yachats, Oregon (continued)

See Vue Motel 541-547-3227 95590 Hwy 101 S pets $5/day www.seevue.com, completely nonsmoking theme-decorated rooms—The Santa Fe, The Crow's Nest, The Princess & The Pea, etc.—large yard for walking dogs, beach access		(10) $57– $85	C K F	
Shamrock Lodgettes 541-547-3312 105 Hwy 101 S 800-845-5028 www.shamrocklodgettes.com pets $5/day nonsmoking, area for walking dogs, easy beach and river access		(19) $80– $131	C K M/F	S T
Silver Surf Motel 541-547-3175 3767 Hwy 101 N 800-281-5723 www.silversurf-motel.com pets $5/day nonsmoking rooms, laundry, beachfront access for walking dogs		(25) $79– $89	C (k)	IP T
Yachats Inn 541-547-3456 331 Hwy 101 S 888-270-3456 www.yachatsinn.com pets $5/day completely nonsmoking, fireplaces, oceanfront area and wayside road for walking dogs		(36) $49– $98	C K	IP T

Yamhill, Oregon

Flying M Ranch 503-662-3222 23029 NW Flying M Rd www.flying-m-ranch.com nonsmoking motel units and cabins, some with full kitchens, lots of pet walking area, private airstrip, swimming pond, horseback trail rides		(31) $60– $200	K R/L	

Washington's Dog-Friendly Lodgings

Aberdeen, Washington

Flamingo Hotel 360-532-4103 1120 E Wishkah St each pet $5/day nonsmoking rooms, grassy area, 1 block to park	(20) $35– $85	C	
GuestHouse International Inn & Suites 360-537-7460 701 E Heron St pets $10/day www.guesthouseintl.com, nonsmoking rooms, 1½ mile-long riverside walking path	(60) $83– $150	CB (k)	IP T
Nordic Inn Motel 360-533-0100 1700 S Boone St pets $10/day nonsmoking rooms, wooded area for walking dogs	(66) $40– $80	C M/F	
Olympic Inn 360-533-4200, 800-562-8618 616 W Heron St pets $5/day nonsmoking rooms, laundry, 9 blocks to park	(55) $39– $92	CB (k) M/F	
Red Lion Inn 360-532-5210 521 W Wishkah St www.westcoasthotels.com nonsmoking rooms, fitness gym with hydromassage bed, grassy areas for walking dogs	(67) $55– $109	CB F	
Thunderbird Motel 360-532-3153 410 W Wishkah St ramatb@techline.com laundry, close to open fields, 1 mile to riverfront park	(36) $48– $74	C M/F	
Trave-Lure Motel 360-532-3280 623 W Wishkah St pets $5/day nonsmoking rooms, laundry	(24) $35– $55	C M/F	

Airway Heights, Washington

Lantern Park Motel 509-244-3653 West 13820 Sunset Hwy pets $10/day nonsmoking rooms, lawn, ½ mile to public park	(11) $28– $58	C K M/F	
Microtel Inns & Suites 509-242-1200, 888-819-0131 1215 S Garfield Rd pets $15/stay dogs under 25 lbs only, in-room spa, nonsmoking rooms, lawn and field for walking dogs	(60) $39– $79	CB (k)	

C = coffee IP = indoor pool OP = outdoor pool CB = continental K = full kitchen R = restaurant breakfast (k) = kitchenette S = sauna or F = refrigerator L = lounge steamroom FB = full breakfast M = microwave T = spa or hot tub	(# of units) & rates	food & drink	pool, sauna & hot tub

Airway Heights, Washington (continued)

Solar World Estates Motel Alternative 509-244-3535 1832 S Lawson St pets $5/day, 800-650-9484 nonsmoking rooms and 4-plex suites, in-room spa, laundry, grassy dogwalking areas, 3 blocks to park	(93) $57– $67	K	T

Amanda Park, Washington

Amanda Park Motel 360-288-2237, 800-410-2237 8 River Dr each pet $10/day 2 acres of grassy open area for off-leash exercising	(8) $45– $60	F	
Lochaerie Resort 360-288-2215 638 N Shore Rd pets $25/stay www.lochaerie.com, dogs allowed with advance approval only, fully equipped lakeside cottages, completely nonsmoking, free canoes	(6) $90– $100	K	

Anacortes, Washington

Anaco Inn 360-293-8833, 888-293-8833 905 20th St pets $10/day www.anacoinn.com, completely nonsmoking rooms and suites, dog allowed by advance reservation only, in-room spa, laundry, waterfront walking paths	(14) $59– $149	CB K M/F	T
Anacortes Inn 360-293-3153, 800-327-7976 3006 Commercial Ave pets $10/stay www.anacortesinn.com, nonsmoking rooms, next to park and playground	(44) $55– $120	C M/F	OP
Fidalgo Country Inn 360-293-3494, 800-244-4179 7645 Hwy 20 pets $10/day www.nwcountryinns.com, nonsmoking rooms, open lot for walking dogs, 10 minute drive to state park	(50) $89	CB (k)	OP T

Guemes Island Resort 360-293-6643 4268 Guemes Island Rd 800-965-6643 guemesresort@juno.com pets $5/day well-mannered dogs only, completely nonsmoking, fully furnished beachfront cabins, one of the island's longest walking beaches	(7) $95– $230	K	OP	
Holiday Motel 360-293-6511 2903 Commercial Ave pets $3/day nonsmoking rooms, public park across street	(10) $30– $70	M/F		
Islands Inn 360-293-4644, 866-331-3328 3401 Commercial Ave pets $5/day www.islandsinn.com, nonsmoking rooms, Dutch hot breakfast, 2 blocks to public park	(36) $60– $120	FB R/L	OP T	
Lake Campbell Lodging 360-293-5314 6676 Hwy 20 pets $10/day nonsmoking rooms, continental breakfast served in summer only, large area for walking dogs, 4 miles to state park	(10) $45– $90	CB (k) M/F		
Old Brook Inn B & B 360-293-4768, 800-503-4768 7270 Old Brook Ln www.oldbrookinn.com each room sleeps 2 to 4, completely nonsmoking, 10 acres of forest trails for walking and birdwatching	(2) $90– $100	CB		
San Juan Motel 360-293-5105, 800-533-8009 1103 6th St refundable pet deposit nonsmoking rooms, open lot behind building for walking dogs, 1 block to public park, 3 miles to ferry	(29) $40– $65	K		
Ship Harbor Inn 360-293-5177, 800-852-8568 5316 Ferry Terminal Rd pets $5/day www.shipharborinn.com, in-room spa, nonsmoking rooms, laundry, lawn for walking dogs, 1 mile to park	(26) $65– $95	CB M/F	T	

Anderson Island, Washington

August Inn 253-884-4011 14117 Lyle Point Rd www.augustinn.com beachfront house sleeps 6, dogs allowed by advance arrangement only, completely nonsmoking, private gated deck, beach access	(3) $219– $400	CB K		

C = coffee CB = continental breakfast F = refrigerator FB = full breakfast	IP = indoor pool K = full kitchen (k) = kitchenette L = lounge M = microwave	OP = outdoor pool R = restaurant S = sauna or steamroom T = spa or hot tub	(# of units) & rates	food & drink	pool, sauna & hot tub

Anderson Island, Washington (continued)

Inn at Burg's Landing B & B 253-884-9185 8808 Villa Beach Rd 800-431-5622 small dog allowed in 1 room only, beachfront access, 1 to 2 miles to walking trail and public parks	(4) $80– $125	FB	T

Arlington, Washington

Arlington Motor Inn 360-652-9595 2214 Hwy 530 NE pets $25/stay arlington1@foxinternet.com, nonsmoking rooms, laundry, lawn for walking dogs, 2 miles to trails	(42) $50– $65	CB M/F	T
Crossroads Inn 360-403-7222, 877-856-3751 5200 172nd St NE #E pets $20/stay nonsmoking rooms, lawn, ¼ mile to park and trail	(52) $69– $79	CB F	T
Smokey Point Motor Inn 360-659-8561 17329 Smokey Point Dr pets $8/day www.smokey-point.com, nonsmoking rooms, open field, ½ mile to county park on the lake	(54) $44– $65	C (k) F	OP T

Ashford, Washington

Four Paws Paradise 360-569-0047 PO Box 27, Ashford, WA refundable pet deposit 6-sided log cabin with loft sleeps up to 3, fireplace, stained glass windows, 7 forested acres on Nisqually River, riverside picnic and exercise area, fenced yard for "doggie daycare"	(1) $95	K	
Stormking Spa B & B at Mt Rainier 360-569-2964 37311 Hwy 706 E pets $20/day www.stormkingspa.com, dogs allowed by advance approval only, completely nonsmoking rooms and cabins, deluxe vegetarian continental breakfast, massage therapy, country setting for walking dogs	(3) $80– $110	CB	T

Auburn, Washington

Auburn Days Inn 253-939-5950, 800-446-4656 1521 D St NE pets $25/stay www.daysinn.com, small dogs only, nonsmoking rooms, laundry, short drive to public park	(66) $65– $100	CB M/F	OP T
Auburn Val-U Inn 253-735-9600, 800-443-7777 9 14th St NW pets $5/day www.valuinn.com, small dogs only, nonsmoking rooms, laundry, open field for walking dogs	(96) $60– $105	CB K M/F	T
Microtel Inn & Suites 253-833-7171, 888-771-7171 9 16th St NW pets $10/day www.microtelinn.com, nonsmoking rooms, trail	(95) $50– $87	CB M/F	
Nendels Valu Inn 253-833-8007, 866-833-8007 102 15th St NE pets $5/day small dogs only, nonsmoking rooms, open area behind building for walking dogs	(33) $40– $75	CB M/F	

Bainbridge Island, Washington

Bainbridge House 206-842-1599 5257 Lynwood Center Rd NE 1-bdrm and 2-bdrm apartments, completely nonsmoking, laundry, lawn, ¼ mile to waterfront, www.bainbridgehouse.com	(2) $125– $150	K	
Holly Lane Gardens 206-842-8959 9432 Holly Farm Ln NE dusb2@aol.com completely nonsmoking suites and cottage, kitchens, 8 acres with walking trails, short drive to public park	(3) $100– $125	FB K	T
Island Country Inn 206-842-6861 920 Hildebrand Ln NE 800-842-8429 www.nwcountryinns.com/island pets $10/day nonsmoking rooms, open field for walking dogs, 1 mile to park	(46) $89– $169	CB K M/F	OP T
Kellerman Creek B & B 206-855-8081 10220 NE Roberts Rd www.kellermancreek.com dogs allowed by advance reservation only, separate studio, 1 acre English garden, 10 minute drive to state park, walking distance to dog-friendly beach	(1) $100– $125	FB (k)	

C = coffee IP = indoor pool OP = outdoor pool CB = continental K = full kitchen R = restaurant breakfast (k) = kitchenette S = sauna or F = refrigerator L = lounge steamroom FB = full breakfast M = microwave T = spa or hot tub	(# of units) & rates	food & drink	pool, sauna & hot tub

Bainbridge Island, Washington (continued)

Monarch Manor Estates B & B 206-780-0112 7656 Madrona Dr NE pets $10/stay www.monarchmanor.com, laundry, full kitchens, breakfast and snacks basket, beachfront access	(4) $125– $250	FB K	OP T
Old Mill Guest House 206-842-8543 6159 Old Mill Rd NE www.oldmillguesthouse.com dogs allowed with advance approval only, completely nonsmoking 1-bdrm house sleeps 4, lawn, 1½ miles to state park and beach	(1) $155	CB K	

Bay Center, Washington

Blue Heron Motel & Restaurant 360-875-5130 2nd & Bridge St fully equipped apartments sleep 4 to 8, RV sites, 2 waterfront acres for walking dogs, 4 blocks to county park	(2) $46– $125	R	

Beaver, Washington

Bear Creek Motel & Cafe 360-327-3660 PO Box 236 pets $10/stay lawn for walking dogs, 1 block to public park	(10) $45– $80	(k) R	

Belfair, Washington

Belfair Motel 360-275-4485 23322 NE Hwy 3 each pet $10/day laundry, lawn area behind building	(28) $50– $66	C K	

Bellevue, Washington

Bellevue Redmond Residence Inn 425-882-1222 14455 NE 29th Pl 800-331-3131 www.marriott.com each pet $15/day nonsmoking rooms, kitchens, designated pet walking area, next to jogging trail	(120) $89– $189	FB K	OP T

Doubletree Bellevue Center 818 112th Ave NE www.doubletreehotels.com nonsmoking rooms, 1 block to jogging path, 3 blocks to public park, 20 minute drive to off-leash park	425-455-1515 800-222-8733 pets $20/stay	(208) $59– $159	C K F R/L	OP T
La Residence Suite Hotel 475 100th Ave NE 1 to 2-bdrm nonsmoking suites, close to 2 public parks, www.lopezislander.com/laresidencesuite	425-455-1475 pets $50/stay	(24) $120– $160	K	

Bellingham, Washington

Aloha Motel 315 N Samish Way nonsmoking rooms, large garden, 1 mile to park	360-733-4900 pets $5/day	(28) $35– $65	C K	
Bellingham Days Inn 125 E Kellogg Rd www.daysinn.com, nonsmoking rooms, laundry, small lawn for walking dogs, 1 mile to public park	360-671-6200, 800-831-0187 pets $7/day	(70) $45– $120	CB K	OP T
Bellingham Inn 202 E Holly St www.bellinghaminn.com dogs under 15 lbs only, nonsmoking rooms, laundry, ½ block to public park	360-734-1900	(50) $40– $54	CB M/F	
Best Western Lakeway Inn 714 Lakeway Dr www.bestwesternwashington.com pets $10/day nonsmoking rooms, laundry, grassy pet walking area, several public parks within 8 blocks	360-671-1011 888-671-1011	(132) $79– $119	C M/F R/L	IP S T
Cascade Inn 208 N Samish Way nonsmoking rooms, laundry, 6 blocks to public park	360-733-2520 pets $4/day	(44) $35– $50	C K M/F	T
Coachman Inn 120 N Samish Way nonsmoking rooms, grassy areas for walking dogs, jogging trails, 15 minute drive to lakes and trails	360-671-9000, 800-962-6641 pets $10/stay	(60) $37– $56	CB M/F	OP
Evergreen Motel 1015 Samish Way dogs allowed in 1 unit only, large yard to walk dogs	360-734-7671	(10) $35– $40		

C = coffee CB = continental 　　breakfast F = refrigerator FB = full breakfast	IP = indoor pool K = full kitchen (k) = kitchenette L = lounge M = microwave	OP = outdoor pool R = restaurant S = sauna or 　　steamroom T = spa or hot tub	(# of units) & rates	food & drink	pool, sauna & hot tub

Bellingham, Washington (continued)

Fairhaven Village Inn　360-733-1311, 877-733-1100 1200 10th St　　　　　　　　　each pet $20/day www.nwcountryinns.com/fairhaven, nonsmoking, walking trail, 3 blocks to off-leash dog park			(22) $109– $159	CB F	
Holiday Inn Express　　360-671-4800, 800-465-4329 4160 Meridian St　　　　　　　　　pets $10/stay nonsmoking rooms, grassy area behind building			(101) $71– $105	CB M/F	IP T
Hotel Bellwether　　360-392-3100, 877-411-1200 1 Bellwether Way　　　　　　　　pets $65/stay www.hotelbellwether.com, completely nonsmoking, spas in all rooms, waterfront walking trails and lawn, ½ mile to public park			(66) $129– $229	C K F R/L	
Lions Inn　　　　　　　　　　　360-733-2330 2419 Elm St　　　　　　　　　　pets $5/day 2 blocks to public park			(15) $30– $45	C (k) M/F	
Mac's Motel　　　　　　　　　　360-734-7570 1215 E Maple St grassy area across street for walking dogs			(30) $27– $42		
Motel 6　　　　　　360-671-4494, 800-466-8356 3701 Byron St　　　　　　　　　www.motel6.com nonsmoking rooms, laundry, small lawn, close to trails, 5 miles to state park and Eastsound waterfront			(60) $44– $68	C	OP
Quality Inn-Baron Suites　360-647-8000, 800-900-4661 100 E Kellogg Rd　　　　　　　　pets $25/stay www.hotelchoice.com, nonsmoking rooms, laundry, in-room spa, lawn, 1 mile to public park			(86) $60– $100	CB	OP T
Ramada Inn　　　　　　360-734-8830, 800-272-6232 215 N Samish Way　　　　　　　　pets $10/day www.ramada.com, dogs under 25 lbs only, lawn behind building for walking dogs			(66) $59– $112	CB M/F	OP

Rodeway Inn 3710 Meridian St www.choicehotels.com nonsmoking rooms, laundry, 2 blocks to large public park and trail	360-738-6000 800-476-5413 pets $10/stay	(74) $38– $95	CB M/F	T
Shangri-La Downtown Motel 611 E Holly St nonsmoking rooms, lawn, 3 blocks to walking trail, 10 blocks to waterfront, 1 mile to public park	360-733-7050 pets $5/day	(19) $35– $65	C (k) M/F	
Travel House Inn 3750 Meridian St nonsmoking rooms, laundry, 6 blocks to public park and trails	360-671-4600 pets $5/day	(124) $44– $109	CB M/F	OP T
Val-U Inn Bellingham 805 Lakeway Dr valu-inn-res@qwest.net nonsmoking rooms, laundry, lawn behind building, 1½ miles to large public park	360-671-9600 800-443-7777 pets $5/day	(82) $54– $80	CB F	T
Villa Inn 212 N Samish Way nonsmoking rooms, lawn and road behind building for walking dogs, 2 miles to public park	360-714-1996, 888-714-1996 pets $10/day	(40) $38– $95	C (k)	OP

Bingen, Washington

City Center Motel 208 W Steuben St nonsmoking rooms, laundry, 2 blocks to city park, 4 blocks to riverfront walking area	509-493-2445 pets $3/day	(9) $34– $64	(k)	

Birch Bay, Washington

Birch Bay Vacation Weekly Rental Cottages 8068 Birch Bay Dr 206-329-9288, 877-222-1031 3+bdrm home (Fairview Lodge) and guest house sleep a combined total of 14, rented to one group at a time, minimum 7 night stay, walking path leads to bayfront beach, duplex and apartment (Hillview) also available to sleep a combined total of 20 people		(2) $107– $129	K	

C = coffee IP = indoor pool OP = outdoor pool CB = continental K = full kitchen R = restaurant breakfast (k) = kitchenette S = sauna or F = refrigerator L = lounge steamroom FB = full breakfast M = microwave T = spa or hot tub	(# of units) & rates	food & drink	pool, sauna & hot tub

Blaine, Washington

Bev's Beach Resort 360-371-2756 8126 Birch Bay Dr bevclamshells@aol.com small 2-bdrm apartments, 2 night min stay, laundry, fenced yard, across street to beach	(4) $95– $145	(k)	
Motel & Cafe International 360-332-8222 758 Peace Portal Dr refundable pet deposit laundry, 3 blocks to Peace Arch State Park, 4 blocks to walking trails	(23) $45– $70	C R	
Resort Semiahmoo 360-371-2000 9565 Semiahmoo Pkwy 800-770-7992 www.semiahmoo.com pets $50/stay nonsmoking rooms, laundry, rooms and suites, walking paths, rocky beaches	(198) $99– $399	C F R/L	OP S T
Westview Motel 360-332-5501 1300 Peace Portal Dr westviewmotel@attbi.com nonsmoking rooms, lawn for walking dogs, pet daycare facilities coming in July 2003	(13) $30– $40	(k) M/F	

Bothell, Washington

Residence Inn by Marriott 425-485-3030 11920 NE 195th St 800-331-3131 pets $10/day plus onetime $50 cleaning fee, nonsmoking rooms, laundry, complimentary dinner Monday-Thursday, 1½ mile walking trail around pond and business park, www.residenceinn.com	(120) $89– $189	FB K	OP

Bremerton, Washington

Flagship Inn 360-479-6566, 800-447-9396 4320 Kitsap Way pets $6/day www.flagship-inn.com, nonsmoking rooms, small dogs only, small wooded area for walking dogs	(29) $69– $101	CB M/F	OP

Howard Johnson Plaza Hotel 360-373-9900 5640 Kitsap Way pets $25/stay, 800-446-4656 www.hojo.com, dogs under 25 lbs only, nonsmoking rooms, laundry, ¼ mile to public park	(145) $102– $172	C M/F R/L	IP T
Illahee Manor 360-698-7555, 800-693-6680 6680 Illahee Rd NE refundable pet deposit www.illaheemanor.com, dogs allowed in 3 cabins, breakfast $7.50 additional, completely nonsmoking, in-room spa, 6 bayfront acres, trail to off-leash beach	(3) $175– $250	FB K	T
Midway Inn 360-479-2909, 800-231-0575 2909 Wheaton Way refundable pet deposit www.midway-inn.com, nonsmoking rooms, laundry, dogs under 20 lbs only, lawn, 1 mile to public park	(60) $55– $70	CB (k) M/F	
Oyster Bay Inn 360-377-5510 4412 Kitsap Way 800-393-3862 www.oysterbaymotel.com pets $20/stay dogs allowed by advance approval only, nonsmoking rooms, laundry, enclosed lawn for walking dogs	(78) $63– $130	CB K M/F R/L	
Super 8 Motel 360-377-8881, 800-800-8000 5068 Kitsap Way pets $10/stay www.super8.com, nonsmoking rooms, laundry, open area for walking dogs, 1 mile to public park	(77) $64– $86	C M/F	

Brewster, Washington

Apple Avenue Motel 509-689-3000 16 Hwy 97 N open field for walking dogs, 1 mile to public park	(17) $50– $80	C M/F	

Brinnon, Washington

Bayshore Motel 360-796-4220, 800-488-4230 306142 Hwy 101 bayshoremotel@jupitercity.com open field for walking dogs	(12) $40– $50	C	

Buckley, Washington

Alpine Cabins 360-829-4200 456 Sorensen St each pet $20/day www.alpinecabinrentals.com, fully equipped kitchen, 2-bdrm 2-bath modern cabin, river and state forest	(1) $145	C K	

C = coffee IP = indoor pool OP = outdoor pool CB = continental K = full kitchen R = restaurant breakfast (k) = kitchenette S = sauna or F = refrigerator L = lounge steamroom FB = full breakfast M = microwave T = spa or hot tub	(# of units) & rates	food & drink	pool, sauna & hot tub

Buckley, Washington (continued)

Mountain View Inn 360-829-1100, 800-582-4111 29405 Hwy 410 E pets $20/stay nonsmoking rooms, laundry, small dogs only, across highway to walking trail	(41) $65– $75	CB M/F	OP T
West Main Motor Inn 360-829-2400 466 W Main St pets $5/day	(14) $43– $53		

Burlington, Washington

Cocusa Motel 360-757-6044, 800-628-2257 370 W Rio Vista Ave pets $10/stay www.cocusamotel.com, nonsmoking rooms, laundry, lawn and open lot for walking dogs	(63) $52– $82	CB (k) M/F	OP

Carlton, Washington

Country Town Motel & RV Park 509-997-3432 2266 Hwy 153 pets $5/day, 800-598-6591 laundry, RV sites, miniature golf course, 2 acres lawn and trees, river access	(23) $37– $82	C K R/L	OP T

Carnation, Washington

Alexandra's River Inn B & B 425-333-6000 4548 Tolt River Rd NE www.joylodge.com completely nonsmoking, kitchen open for guest use, most rooms have private decks, steam room, beach, 1½ miles to McDonald Park	(5) $145– $225	FB K	S T

Carson, Washington

Carson Mineral Hot Springs Resort 509-427-8292 372 St. Martin Rd 800-607-3678 www.skamania.org pets $25/stay completely nonsmoking, RV sites, walking trails	(14) $48– $64	C R	

Sandhill Cottages 509-427-3464, 800-914-2178 932 Hot Springs Ave www.sandhillcottages.com historic cottages, fully equipped kitchenettes, open field and golf course, walking trails	(4) $45– $65	C K R/L	
Wind River Cabins & Lodging 509-427-7777 1261 Wind River Rd pets $10/day, 877-816-7908 www.windrivercabins.com, completely nonsmoking, open fields to walk dogs, 1 mile to Columbia River	(11) $45– $65	C K M/F	

Cashmere, Washington

Grandview Orchard Inn B & B 509-782-2340 5105 Moody Rd nonsmoking rooms, quiet country roads and open orchards for walking dogs	(3) $60– $70	FB	T
Village Inn Motel 509-782-3522, 800-793-3522 229 Cottage Ave pets $5/day 1 small dog only, nonsmoking rooms, 2 blocks to riverside public park	(21) $45– $65	C M/F	

Castle Rock, Washington

7 West Motel 360-274-7526 864 Walsh Ave NE nonsmoking rooms, laundry, ½ acre lawn, 4 blocks to riverfront trail	(24) $36– $58	C	
Timberland Inn & Suites 360-274-6002, 888-900-6335 1271 Mt Saint Helens Way NE each pet $5/day www.timberland-inn.com, in-room spa, nonsmoking rooms, undeveloped walking area, 5 miles to park	(40) $55– $145	C M/F	

Cathlamet, Washington

Nassa Point Motel 360-795-3941 851 E Hwy 4 pets $10/stay dogs allowed with advance approval only, wooded walking area, 3 miles to public park and marina	(6) $35– $40	C (k)	

Centralia, Washington

Ferryman's Inn 360-330-2094 1003 Eckerson Rd pets $5/day nonsmoking rooms, laundry, across street from open field for walking dogs, 2 public parks within 2 blocks	(84) $48– $57	CB K M/F	OP T

C = coffee
CB = continental
    breakfast
F = refrigerator
FB = full breakfast
	IP = indoor pool
	K = full kitchen
	(k) = kitchenette
	L = lounge
	M = microwave
		OP = outdoor pool
		R = restaurant
		S = sauna or
		   steamroom
		T = spa or hot tub
			(# of units)
			& rates
				food
				& drink
					pool, sauna
					& hot tub

Centralia, Washington (continued)

Inn at Centralia 360-736-2875, 800-459-0035 702 W Harrison Ave each pet $10/day dogs under 50 lbs only, laundry, RV sites, next to public park, 1 mile to state park with lake and trails	(89) $38– $69	CB M/F	OP
Motel 6 360-330-2057, 800-466-8356 1310 Belmont Ave www.motel6.com nonsmoking rooms, laundry, 6 blocks to public park	(122) $36– $56	C	OP
Park Motel 360-736-9333 1011 Belmont Ave pets $2/day nonsmoking rooms, 1 block to public park	(30) $33– $41	K	
Travelodge 360-736-9344, 800-600-8701 1325 Lakeshore Dr pets $5/day www.travelodge.com, nonsmoking rooms, laundry, all rooms open onto a grassy area and lake, close to fairgrounds for dog shows	(40) $55– $75	CB M/F	

Chehalis, Washington

Howard Johnson Inn 360-748-0101, 800-446-4656 122 Interstate Ave pets $10/stay www.howardjohnson.com, nonsmoking rooms, lawn for walking dogs, 1 block to public park	(71) $50– $100	CB M/F	OP T
ParkPlace Inn & Suites 360-748-4040, 877-748-0008 201 SW Interstate Ave pets $10/day wwww.bestwesternseattleportland.com, dogs under 20 lbs only, exercise room, laundry, small yard, walking path around perimeter of property, close to playground	(61) $67– $92	CB M/F	IP T
Relax Inn 360-748-8608, 800-843-6916 550 SW Parkland Dr pets $5/day nonsmoking rooms, lawn for walking dogs, across street from park	(29) $32– $65	CB M/F	

Chelan, Washington

Best Western Lakeside Lodge 509-682-4396 2312 W Woodin Ave 800-468-2781 www.lakesidelodge.net pets $10/day nonsmoking rooms, laundry, 2 outdoor spas, next to public park that allows leashed pets September–May	(65) $55– $259	CB K	IP T
Cabana Motel 509-682-2233, 800-799-2332 420 Manson Rd W www.cabanamotel.com near public park that allows pets September–May	(12) $38– $160	C (k)	OP
Kelly's Resort 509-687-3220 12801 S Lakeshore Rd 800-561-8978 www.kellysresort.com pets $10/day 20 acre resort on Lake Chelan, nonsmoking cottages with full kitchens, espresso bar, laundry, trails	(16) $150– $275	C K	OP
Midtowner Motel 509-682-4051 721 E Woodin Ave each pet $5–$10/day www.midtowner.com, nonsmoking rooms, laundry, small dogwalking area, 6 blocks to public park	(46) $40– $75	C M/F	IP T

Cheney, Washington

AAA Inn 509-235-4058, 888-303-4058 12 Columbia St & First St aaainn@aol.com laundry, community kitchen, exercise room, BBQ and picnic area, pet walking area behind building, near walking trail that leads to lake and nature park	(12) $45	K	
Chapman Lake Resort 509-523-2221 11011 W Chapman Lake Rd rustic cabins with stove and refrigerator, no kitchen sink, bring your own cooking utensils and bedding, community bathhouse, forest trails for walking dogs	(2) $20		
Willow Springs Motel 509-235-5138 5 B St pets $5/day nonsmoking rooms, laundry, open lot for walking dogs, ½ mile to beginning of "Rails to Trails" walking path that leads 4½ miles to Fish Lake	(42) $39– $54	CB K	

C = coffee CB = continental 　　breakfast F = refrigerator FB = full breakfast	IP = indoor pool K = full kitchen (k) = kitchenette L = lounge M = microwave	OP = outdoor pool R = restaurant S = sauna or 　　steamroom T = spa or hot tub	(# of units) & rates	food & drink	pool, sauna & hot tub

Chewelah, Washington

49er Motel & RV Park 311 S Park St www.theofficenet.com/~49er nonsmoking rooms, RV sites, open field to walk dogs	509-935-8613 888-412-1994 pets $4/day	(13) $38– $68	C K M/F	IP T
Nordlig Motel 101 W Grant Ave www.nordlig.com, nonsmoking rooms, lawn areas, picnic tables, city park across street	509-935-6704 pets $3/stay	(14) $42– $58	CB M/F	T

Clallam Bay, Washington

A-View Mobile Home Park 122 8th St laundry, RV sites, lawn, woods, 3 blocks to the water	360-963-2394 pets $5/stay	(2) $25– $75	K	
Winters' Summer Inn B & B 16651 Hwy 112　　www.northolympic.com/winters rooms with half-baths and shared shower, 1 with private bath and jacuzzi tub, 800 sq ft studio suite with kitchen sleeps 8, deck overlooking river and bird estuary (a 5 minute walk away), beach access	360-963-2264	(4) $75	FB K	

Clarkston, Washington

Astor Motel 1201 Bridge St nonsmoking rooms, RV sites, 10 blocks to riverfront walking trails	509-758-2509 each pet $5/day	(8) $30– $60	(k)	
Golden Key Motel 1376 Bridge St　　dogs allowed with advance approval only, lawn, 3 blocks to riverside public park	509-758-5566	(16) $29– $41	C M/F	
Hacienda Lodge　　509-758-5583, 888-567-2287 812 Bridge St　　nonsmoking rooms, lawn, 5 blocks to walking path along riverside dikes		(31) $32– $48	C (k) M/F	

Highland House 707 Highland Ave completely nonsmoking, 2 blocks to riverside trail, 4 blocks to public park	509-758-3126 pets $5/day	(5) $55– $85	FB	T
Motel 6 222 Bridge St nonsmoking rooms, laundry, riverside greenbelt trail	509-758-1631, 800-466-8356 www.motel6.com	(85) $38– $50	C F	OP
Quality Inn & Suites 700 Port Dr dogs allowed with advance approval only, laundry, nonsmoking rooms, exercise room, espresso stand, riverside walking path and public park	509-758-9500 www.qualityinnclarkston.com	(97) $73– $139	C M/F R/L	OP T
Sunset Motel 1200 Bridge St large lawn, ¼ mile to walking trails and public park	509-758-2517	(10) $30– $60	K	

Cle Elum, Washington

Aster Inn 521 E 1st St nonsmoking rooms, in-room spa, 1 block to walking trail that leads to river	509-674-2551, 888-616-9722 www.asterinn.com	(10) $40– $85	C K M/F	T
Cascade Mountain Inn 906 E 1st St nonsmoking rooms, in-room spa, laundry, large open field for walking dogs, 1 mile to public park	509-674-2380, 888-674-3975 pets $10/day	(43) $50– $125	CB K	T
Chalet Motel 800 E 1st St nonsmoking rooms, large field and woods for walking dogs	509-674-2320 pets $5/day	(11) $35– $50	M/F	
Stewart Lodge 805 W 1st St nonsmoking rooms, laundry, walking trail, 1 block to public park	509-674-4548, 877-233-5358 pets $5/stay	(36) $43– $73	CB M/F	OP T
Timber Lodge Inn 301 W 1st St #3 nonsmoking rooms, laundry, large undeveloped area, 2 blocks to walking trail on old railroad bed	509-674-5966, 800-584-1133 pets $10/stay	(35) $45– $70	CB M/F	T

C = coffee IP = indoor pool OP = outdoor pool CB = continental K = full kitchen R = restaurant breakfast (k) = kitchenette S = sauna or F = refrigerator L = lounge steamroom FB = full breakfast M = microwave T = spa or hot tub	(# of units) & rates	food & drink	pool, sauna & hot tub

Cle Elum, Washington (continued)

Traveler's Inn 509-674-5535 1001 E 1st St pets $5/day nonsmoking rooms, lawn for walking dogs	(33) $35– $65	CB M/F	
Wind Blew Inn Motel 509-674-2294, 888-674-2294 811 Hwy 970 pets $5/day nonsmoking rooms, lawn for walking dogs, 1 mile to hiking trail and public park	(10) $40– $70	C K	

Clinton, Washington

B's Getaway B & B 360-341-4721, 877-220-7622 4750 Orr Rd pets $25/stay dogs allowed by advance reservation only, 2½ view acres, nonsmoking rooms, ½ mile to public park	(1) $85– $95	FB	
Home by the Sea Cottages 360-321-2964 2388 E Sunlight Beach Rd www.frenchroadfarm.com or www.homebytheseacottages.com, nonsmoking beachfront cottages, in-room spa, trails to state park	(2) $145– $185	CB K	T
Lapis Lane Guest House 360-579-2009 3645 Lapis Ln pets $15/day dogs allowed by advance reservation only, 2-bdrm house sleeps 6, deck, quiet yard, next door to artist's glass studio, 1 mile to public beach, near golf course	(1) $139– $199	K	S T
Sweetwater Cottage 360-341-1604 6111 S Cultus Bay Rd pets $10/day nonsmoking rooms, breakfast supplies provided, 22 acres of lawn and woods for walking dogs	(1) $135	FB K	S T
Whidbey Island Beach Cottage 425-641-2765 7485 Humphrey Rd pets $10/day www.vacationrentalsonline.com (item # waw101) small dogs preferred, rustic beachfront cabin with loft sleeps 4	(1) $100	K	

Colville, Washington

Beaver Lodge Resort 509-684-5657 2430 Hwy 20 E laundry, wooded trails, fishing and swimming in lake	(7) $45– $65	(k) R	
Benny's Colville Inn 509-684-2517 915 S Main St 800-680-2517 www.colvilleinn.com pets $6/day nonsmoking rooms, ½ block to public park	(106) $40– $105	CB M/F R/L	IP T
Centsible Inn 509-684-2565 369 S Main St pets $5/day nonsmoking rooms, grassy area behind building for walking dogs, 1½ blocks to public park	(18) $37– $46	C M/F	
Comfort Inn 509-684-2010, 800-228-5150 166 NE Canning Dr pets $5/day www.comfortinn.com, nonsmoking rooms, laundry, grassy area for walking dogs, 2½ miles to public park	(53) $52– $115	CB M/F	IP T
Whitetail Inn 509-684-8856 1140 Basin Rd dogs allowed by advance reservation only, 1-room cottage with kitchen and sleeping loft sleeps 4, 20 acres with resident animals, www.inntravels.com/usa/wa/whitetail.html	(1) $55– $85	FB (k)	

Conconully, Washington

Gibson's North Fork Lodge 509-826-1475 100 W Boone 800-555-1690 www.omakchronicle.com/gibsons, fully equipped cabins, all linens provided, creekside walking trail	(2) $55– $65	K
Jack's RV Park & Motel 509-826-0132 116 Avenue A 800-893-5668 www.jacksrv.com, nonsmoking rooms, dogs allowed with advance approval only, fully equipped kitchens, RV sites, riverfront trails	(6) $69– $85	K
Kozy Kabins & RV Park 509-826-6780 111 E Broadway Ave 888-502-2246 kozykabins@televar.com, cabins, RV and tent sites, walking trails, across street from state park, several lakes within 2 blocks	(8) $35– $45	K

C = coffee	IP = indoor pool	OP = outdoor pool	(# of units) & rates	food & drink	pool, sauna & hot tub
CB = continental breakfast	K = full kitchen (k) = kitchenette	R = restaurant S = sauna or steamroom			
F = refrigerator FB = full breakfast	L = lounge M = microwave	T = spa or hot tub			

Concrete, Washington

Ovenell's Heritage Inn Log Cabins	360-853-8494		(12)	C	
46276 Concrete Sauk Valley Rd	866-464-3414		$75–	FB	
www.ovenells-inn.com	pets $10/day		$115		
fully equipped cabins sleep 4, linens, full breakfast available for additional fee, 600 acre ranch, trails and pond, near national parks					

Connell, Washington

M & M Motel	509-234-8811, 800-353-9981		(43)	CB	
730 S Columbia Ave	nonsmoking rooms, laundry,		$39–	M/F	
open lot across street for walking dogs, 2 blocks to walking trail, 4 blocks to public park			$55		
Tumbleweed Motel	509-234-2081		(20)	C	OP
433 S Columbia Ave nonsmoking rooms, large lawn,			$30–		
walking trail, 2 blocks to public park			$50		

Conway, Washington

South Fork Marina & House Boat	360-445-4803		(2)	CB	
21357 Mann Rd	each pet $10/day		$75–	(k)	
www.virtualcities.com/wa/southfork.htm			$90		
nonsmoking houseboats with full galley sleep 3, dogs allowed with advance approval only, lots of shoreline for off-leash dogwalking					

Copalis Beach, Washington

Beachwood Resort	360-289-2177		(18)	K	OP
3009 Hwy 109	pets $10/day		$75–		S
beach and dunes for walking dogs			$85		T
Iron Springs Resort	360-276-4230		(28)	C	IP
3707 Hwy 109	pets $10/day		$72–	K	
www.ironspringsresort.com, rooms and cottages with full kitchens and fireplaces, beachfront access			$150		

Linda's Low Tide Motel 360-289-3450 14 McCullough Rd pets $6/day nonsmoking rooms, beach access for walking dogs	(12) $55– $125	C K M/F	

Coulee City, Washington

Ala Cozy Motel 509-632-5703 9988 Hwy 2 E nonsmoking rooms, mini-golf, lakefront park ½ mile	(14) $40– $67	C F	OP
Blue Lake Resort 509-632-5364 31199 Hwy 17 N pets $5/day rustic cabins, RV sites, open field for walking dogs, 5 miles to public park	(10) $36– $74	K F	
Blue Top Motel & RV Park 509-632-5596 109 N 6th St pets $5/stay nonsmoking rooms, RV sites, lawn, 3 blocks to lakeside park, 5 miles to state park with hiking trails and Interpretive Center	(13) $40– $43	C (k) F	

Coulee Dam, Washington

Coulee House Motel 509-633-1101, 800-715-7767 110 Roosevelt Way pets $15/day www.couleehouse.com, laundry, overlooking Grand Coulee Dam, near walking trails	(61) $54– $120	C K	OP T
Victoria's Cottage B & B 509-633-2908 209 Columbia www.reitpro.com/victoriascottage romantic 3-room suite, BBQ, private hot tub, fenced yard, walking trail along Columbia River	(1) $110– $150	CB M/F	T

Coupeville, Washington

Eagle's Aerie 360-678-2217 www.eagleaerie.net, nonsmoking room sleeps 4, 14 acres surrounded by park land, beach access	(1) $125	CB	
Tyee Motel & Restaurant 360-678-6616 405 S Main St pets $10/stay www.tyeehotel.com, lawn, 2 blocks to walking trail, 1 mile to waterfront	(9) $45– $54	R/L	

C = coffee IP = indoor pool OP = outdoor pool CB = continental K = full kitchen R = restaurant breakfast (k) = kitchenette S = sauna or F = refrigerator L = lounge steamroom FB = full breakfast M = microwave T = spa or hot tub	(# of units) & rates	food & drink	pool, sauna & hot tub

Coupeville, Washington (continued)

Victorian B & B 360-678-5305 602 N Main St pets $10/stay www.whidbeyvictorianbandb.com, dogs allowed in cottage only, full breakfast provided in main house, close to beach access, 3 blocks to riverfront trail	(3) $80– $100	FB K R	
Willow Pond Lodge and Lake House 206-283-0746 www.willowpondlodge.com, dogs allowed with advance approval only, 5-bdrm houses sleep 15-20, fireplace, 60 acres with meadow, ponds, trails	(2) $350– $600	K	T

Curlew, Washington

Blue Cougar Motel 509-779-4817 2141 N Hwy 21 open field for walking dogs, close to riverside trails	(6) $32– $50		
Curlew Motel 509-779-4260, 800-797-4260 23 Boulder Creek Rd pets $10/stay www.northregion.org, kayaks, canoes, fishing rods, bicycles available for free use, riverside walking area	(7) $40– $60	C K	T
Wolfgang's Riverview Inn 509-779-4252 2320 N Hwy 21 pets $5/stay www.televar.com/wolfgang, laundry, open field, trail to Kettle River, 2 miles to sandy beach on river	(4) $45– $60	C (k) M/F	

Darrington, Washington

Stagecoach Inn 360-436-1776 1100 Seemann St pets $6/day nonsmoking rooms, laundry, designated dogwalking area, public park across street	(20) $45– $65	CB (k) M/F	

Davenport, Washington

Davenport Motel 509-725-7071 1205 Morgan St dogs allowed with manager's permission only, open field for walking dogs	(9) $41– $61	C	
Deer Meadows Motel 509-725-8425 RR 1 Box 201 refundable pet deposit nonsmoking rooms, laundry, loop road around golf course for walking dogs	(16) $45– $60	C K R	S

Dayton, Washington

Blue Mountain Motel 509-382-3040 414 W Main St pets $10/stay designated dogwalking area behind building, 1 block to fairgrounds, 3 blocks to 2 mile-long walking trail	(23) $36– $80	M/F	
Dayton Motel 509-382-4503 110 S Pine St nonsmoking rooms, open area for walking dogs	(17) $34– $65	C K	
Purple House B & B 509-382-3159, 415 E Clay St 800-486-2574 small dogs only, 2 rooms with shared bath, 2 with private baths, 1 suite with kitchen and Japanese soaking tub, dinners and picnic lunches available by special arrangement, lawn, 4 blocks to park	(4) $85– $125	FB K	OP T
Weinhard Hotel 509-382-4032 235 E Main St each pet $20/stay www.weinhard.com, Victorian hotel, in-room spa, nonsmoking rooms, walking trail, 5 blocks to city park, 5 miles to state park	(15) $75– $150	CB R	

Deer Harbor, Washington

Deer Harbor Inn B & B 360-376-4110 Deer Harbor Rd 877-377-4110 www.deerharborinn.com each pet $10/day dogs allowed in cottages only, 1-room to 2-bdrm cottages all have full kitchens and in-room spas, orchard and quiet country roads for walking dogs, ½ mile to beach	(12) $119– $299	CB K M/F	T

C = coffee
CB = continental
   breakfast
F = refrigerator
FB = full breakfast
	IP = indoor pool
	K = full kitchen
	(k) = kitchenette
	L = lounge
	M = microwave
		OP = outdoor pool
		R = restaurant
		S = sauna or
		   steamroom
		T = spa or hot tub
			# of units)
			& rates
				food
				& drink
					pool, sauna
					& hot tub

Deer Harbor, Washington (continued)

Maggie's Manor & Gnome House 360-376-4223 www.orcasrec.com, 4-bdrm 2-bath Manor sleeps 8, 1 small dog allowed by advance reservation only, Gnome house is an alpine-style chalet with loft that sleeps 4 to 6, on 150 acres with wildlife preserve	(2) $135– $395	K	T
The Place at Cayou Cove 360-376-3199, 888-596-7222 Olympic Lodge Ln pets $25/stay www.cayoucove.com, dogs allowed in 2 cottages by advance approval only, fireplaces and kitchens, full breakfast for additional fee, on 3½ waterfront acres	(5) $125– $255	CB K	T

Deer Park, Washington

Love's Victorian B & B 509-276-6939 31317 N Cedar Rd country setting for walking dogs, hot cocoa-tea-sparkling cider served each evening, www.lovesvictorianbedandbreakfast.com	(3) $75– $135	FB	T

Deming, Washington

The Guest House 360-592-2343 5723 Schornbush Rd WeissSmith@aol.com rural area for walking dogs, less than 1 mile to river	(1) $50	C K	T
The Logs Resort 360-599-2711 9002 Mt Baker Hwy pets $5/day www.telcomplus.net/thelogs, 2-bdrm rustic log cabins with bath and fireplace, 2 miles west of Glacier, on 68 forested acres along river	(5) $85– $175	(k)	OP

East Wenatchee, Washington

Cedars Inn 509-886-8000 80 9th St NE 800-358-2074 www.cedarshotels.com pets $6/day nonsmoking rooms, laundry, trail for walking dogs	(94) $61– $122	CB M/F	IP T

Easton, Washington

C B's Motel & General Store 509-656-2248 1781 Railroad St each pet $5/day, 800-347-2336 nonsmoking rooms, dogs allowed with manager's approval only, lawn, less than 1 mile to state park	(4) $55– $65	M	
Silver Ridge Ranch B & B 509-656-0275 182 Silver Ridge Ranch Rd dogs allowed in 1 lodge room only, completely nonsmoking, group kitchen, RV sites, walking trail, www.silverridgeranch.com	(7) $55– $135	FB K	

Eastsound, Washington

Abode 360-376-6247 257 Geer Lane pets $10/day fully equipped vacation apartment, dogs allowed by advance approval only, rural roads for walking dogs, 5 minutes to bay, www.sanjuanweb.com/abode	(1) $75	C (k)	
Bartwood Lodge & Estates 360-376-2242 178 Fossil Bay Dr 866-666-2242 www.bartwoodlodge.com pets $20/day private beach, short drive to 2 state parks	(16) $59– $189	C (k) M/F R	
Cabins on the Point–Highland House–Sunset House Rt 1 Box 70 pets $50/stay, 360-376-4114 dogs allowed with advance approval only, 1-room cabins to 3-bdrm 2-bath house, full kitchens, private beach, short drive to dog-friendly state park	(6) $205– $395	FB K	T
Hollyhock Inn B & B 360-376-3745 252 Deer Harbor Rd 7 wooded acres, fields and woods for walking dogs	(2) $85– $100	FB	
North Beach Inn 360-376-2660 650 Gibson Rd each pet $10/day www.northbeachinn.com, fully equipped 1 to 3-bdrm cottages, fireplaces, ⅓ mile of sand and pebble beach frontage, 90 acres of woods and fields	(12) $115– $200	(k)	
North Shore Cottages 360-376-5131 271 Sunset Ave refundable pet deposit www.northshore4kiss.com, nonsmoking rooms, fully equipped cottages, private hot tubs, lawn and woods	(3) $165– $275	C (k) M/F	S T

C = coffee　　IP = indoor pool　　OP = outdoor pool CB = continental　K = full kitchen　　R = restaurant 　　breakfast　　(k) = kitchenette　　S = sauna or F = refrigerator　L = lounge　　　　　steamroom FB = full breakfast　M = microwave　T = spa or hot tub	(# of units) & rates	food & drink	pool, sauna & hot tub

Eastsound, Washington (continued)

Outlook Inn on Orcas Island　　　　360-376-2200 Main St #171　　　　　pets $10/day, 888-688-5665 www.outlook-inn.com, guest discount at health club, completely nonsmoking, large lawn with ponds for walking dogs, 4 blocks to public park	(49) $44– $275	R/L	
West Beach Resort　　　360-376-2240, 877-937-8224 190 Waterfront Way　　　　　　　pets $15/day www.westbeachresort.com, completely nonsmoking waterfront cabins, RV and tent sites, beach access	(18) $90– $210	K M/F	T

Edmonds, Washington

Edmonds Harbor Inn & Suites　　　425-771-5021 130 W Dayton St　　　　　　　　800-441-8033 www.nwcountryinns.com/harbor　each pet $10/day nonsmoking rooms, laundry, athletic club, wetlands area and greenbelt trail, close to pet-friendly beach	(92) $79– $169	CB K	IP S T
Hudgens Haven B & B　　　　　　425-776-2202 9313 190th SW　　　　　　　　pets $2/day patio and fenced yard, 1 block to nature path, 1 mile to off-leash area	(1) $65– $75	FB	
K & E Motor Inn　　　　　　　　425-778-2181 23921 Hwy 99　　　　　　　　pets $10/day laundry, 5 minute drive to public park	(32) $52– $67	CB (k)	
Travelodge-Seattle North　　　　425-771-8008 23825 Hwy 99　　pets $25/stay, 800-771-8009 www.travelodge.com, nonsmoking rooms, laundry, 5 minute drive to Edmonds waterfront	(58) $59– $119	CB M/F	T

Elk, Washington

Jerry's Landing Resort　　　　　509-292-2337 41114 N Lake Shore Rd RV sites, 2 cabins, lake swimming, wooded trails	(2) $35– $70	(k)	

Ellensburg, Washington

Comfort Inn 509-925-7037 1722 Canyon Rd 800-228-5150 www.comfortinn.com, pets $10/stay nonsmoking rooms, laundry, lawn for walking dogs, ½ mile to lakeside park	(52) $69– $120	CB M/F	IP T
Ellensburg Inn 509-925-9801, 800-321-8791 1700 Canyon Rd pets $6/day nonsmoking rooms, courtyard for walking trails, ½ mile to public park	(105) $43– $77	C F	IP S T
Majestic Country B & B 509-962-6605, 866-625-3785 2830 Thorp Hwy S www.majestic-country.com completely nonsmoking, dogs allowed by advance reservation only, 3½ acres for walking dogs	(3) $70– $85	FB	
Nites Inn Motel 509-962-9600 1200 S Ruby St pets $8/stay www.televar.com/~nites, laundry, RV sites, ½ mile to public park, riverfront walking trail	(32) $48– $62	CB M/F	
Super 8 Motel 509-962-6888, 800-800-8000 1500 Canyon Rd refundable pet deposit www.super8.com, nonsmoking rooms, laundry, open field for walking dogs, 1 mile to public park	(102) $53– $89	C	IP T
Thunderbird Motel 509-962-9856 403 W 8th Ave pets $10/day nonsmoking rooms, 10 minute drive to waterfront	(72) $40– $60	C M R	OP

Elma, Washington

Gray's Harbor Hostel 360-482-3119 6 Ginny Ln ghhostel@techline.com dogs allowed by advance reservation only and they MUST be kept in travel crates in the rooms, 8 acres next to field and fairgrounds, shared kitchen facilities	(3) $15 per person	C K	
Parkhurst Motel 360-482-2541 208 E Main St laundry, open grassy area for walking dogs, ¼ mile to public park, close to fairgrounds	(14) $50– $65	K	

C = coffee IP = indoor pool OP = outdoor pool CB = continental K = full kitchen R = restaurant breakfast (k) = kitchenette S = sauna or F = refrigerator L = lounge steamroom FB = full breakfast M = microwave T = spa or hot tub	# of units & rates	food & drink	pool, sauna & hot tub

Enumclaw, Washington

Best Western Park Center Hotel　360-825-4490 1000 Griffin Ave　　　pets $10/day, 800-238-7234 www.bestwesternwashington.com, nonsmoking rooms, laundry, public park across street	(40) $80– $90	CB M/F R	T
King's Motel　　　　360-825-1626, 888-886-5118 1334 Roosevelt Ave E　　　　　　　pets $10/day www.kingsmotel.com, nonsmoking rooms, laundry, next to fairgrounds, 1 mile to hiking trails	(44) $49– $79	C (k)	OP

Ephrata, Washington

Lariat Motel　　　　　　　　　　　509-754-2437 1639 Basin St SW　　　　　　　　　pets $5/stay nonsmoking rooms, grassy walking area, 3 blocks to public park	(42) $22– $55	K	OP

Everett, Washington

Best Western Cascadia Inn　　　　425-258-4141 2800 Pacific Ave　　　pets $25/stay, 800-822-5876 www.bestwesterncascadia.com, nonsmoking rooms, laundry, open walking area, 4 miles to public park	(134) $69– $149	CB M/F	OP T
Days Inn　　　　　　425-252-8000, 800-329-7466 1122 Broadway　　　　　　　　　　pets $5/day www.daysinn.com, laundry, dogs allowed by advance approval only, 8 blocks to public park	(51) $49– $89	CB M/F	
Everett Inn　　　　　　425-347-9099, 800-434-9204 12619 4th Ave W　　　　　　　　　pets $10/day www.everettinn.com, nonsmoking rooms, in-room spa, walking trail	(72) $50– $105	CB M/F	OP
Holiday Inn　　　　　　425-337-2900, 800-465-4329 101 128th St SE　　　　　　　　　　pets $50/stay www.holidayinn.com, nonsmoking rooms, walking area behind building, short drive to several parks	(249) $89– $129	M/F R/L	IP T

Inn at Port Gardner 1700 W Marine View Dr www.innatportgardner.com refundable pet deposit dogs allowed with advance reservation only, nonsmoking rooms, lawn, waterfront boardwalk	425-252-6779 888-252-6779	(33) $79– $185	CB M/F	
Motel 6-Everett North 10006 Evergreen Way lawn for walking dogs	425-347-2060 800-466-8356 www.motel6.com	(118) $43– $60	C M/F	OP
Motel 6-Everett South 425-353-8120, 800-466-8356 224 128th St SW www.motel6.com laundry, lawn, 4 blocks to public park		(100) $49– $62	C	
Royal Motor Inn 952 N Broadway pets $7/day nonsmoking rooms, lawn, 2 blocks to state park	425-259-5177	(35) $37– $43	C (k) M/F	
Sunrise Motor Inn 425-347-1100, 888-222-2112 8421 Evergreen Way pets $10/day dogs under 10 lbs only, area for walking dogs, 1½ miles to a public park		(68) $45– $50	C K	
Travelodge 425-259-6141, 800-578-7878 3030 Broadway pets $10/stay nonsmoking rooms, 1 block to public park		(28) $45– $75	C M/F	
Welcome Motor Inn 425-252-8828, 800-252-5512 1205 N Broadway pets $20/stay www.welcomemotorinn.com, nonsmoking, lawn		(42) $43– $62	CB (k) M/F	

Federal Way, Washington

Comfort Inn 253-529-0101, 800-648-3311 31622 Pacific Hwy S pets $20/stay www.choicehotels.com, nonsmoking rooms, park		(118) $59– $140	CB (k) M/F	IP T
Siesta Motel 35620 Pacific Hwy S pets $5/day laundry, RV sites, 2½ acres of open field and woods, 1½ miles to public park, 5 miles to waterfront	253-927-2157	(9) $33– $35	C M/F	
Super 8 Motel 253-838-8808, 800-800-8000 1688 S 348th St refundable pet deposit www.super8.com, nonsmoking rooms, laundry, lawn, 1½ miles to aquatic center with walking paths		(90) $49– $68	CB F	

		# of units) & rates	food & drink	pool, sauna & hot tub
C = coffee	IP = indoor pool	OP = outdoor pool		
CB = continental breakfast	K = full kitchen (k) = kitchenette	R = restaurant S = sauna or steamroom		
F = refrigerator	L = lounge			
FB = full breakfast	M = microwave	T = spa or hot tub		

Ferndale, Washington

Scottish Lodge Motel 360-384-4040 5671 Riverside Dr pets $5/day nonsmoking rooms, laundry, lawn, 2 miles to park	(94) $38– $50	C	OP
Slater Heritage House B & B 360-384-4273 1371 W Axton Rd 888-785-0706 www.sleepinginn.com, completely nonsmoking, 2 acres with open fields for walking dogs, 1½ miles to public park, 3 miles to waterfront	(4) $65– $95	FB M/F	
Super 8 Motel 360-384-8881, 800-800-8000 5788 Barrett Rd refundable pet deposit nonsmoking rooms, laundry, large yards	(78) $54– $68	CB M/F	IP T

Fife, Washington

Best Inn & Suites 253-922-9520, 877-982-3781 3100 Pacific Hwy E pets $20–$30/day www.bestinn.com, dogs under 30 lbs only, in-room spa, pet walking area, 3 miles to waterfront park	(108) $49– $80	CB M/F	OP
Days Inn 253-922-3500, 866-922-3500 3021 Pacific Hwy E pets $5/day www.daysinn.com, nonsmoking rooms, dogs under 25 lbs only, open lot for walking dogs, list of local parks available at front desk	(185) $49– $90	CB K	OP
Econo Lodge 253-922-0550, 800-424-4777 3518 Pacific Hwy E pets $10/day www.choicehotels.com, nonsmoking rooms, laundry, small lawn, 15 minute drive to state park	(81) $36– $65	CB M/F	
Ramada Inn 253-926-1000 3501 Pacific Hwy E pets $10/day ramfife@juno.com, nonsmoking rooms, laundry, parking lot area for walking dogs, ½ mile to waterfront, 3 miles to public park	(96) $44– $69	CB M/F	T

Sunshine Motel 3801 Pacific Hwy E small dogs only	253-926-0937 pets $5/day	(36) $40– $44	K	

Forks, Washington

Bagby's Town Motel 1080 S Forks Ave www.bagbystownmotel.com laundry, close to beaches-rivers-trails	360-374-6231 800-742-2429 pets $5/day	(20) $35– $44	C (k) M/F	
Brightwater House B & B 440 Brightwater Dr www.brightwaterhouse.com nonsmoking, 60 acres, ¾ mile Sol Duc River frontage	360-374-5453	(2) $85	FB K	
Dew Drop Inn 100 Fernhill Rd www.dewdropinnmotel.com, field for walking dogs	360-374-4055, 888-433-9376 pets $11/stay	(24) $43– $60	CB M/F	
Forks Motel 351 S Forks Ave www.forksmotel.com, nonsmoking rooms, laundry, ¾ mile to public park, 20 minute drive to beaches	360-374-6243, 800-544-3416 pets $10/day	(73) $68– $75	C (k) M/F	OP
Hoh Humm Ranch B & B 171763 Hwy 101 www.olypen.com/hohhumm, nonsmoking rooms, large pet walking area along Hoh River, dogs must be kept on leash because of resident farm animals	360-374-5337 pets $5/day	(3) $35– $70	FB	
Klaloch Lodge 157151 Hwy 101 cabins with fireplaces, tent spaces, beach for walking dogs (they must be kept on leash at all times)	360-962-2271 pets $14/day	(64) $175– $294	FB (k) R	
Manitou Lodge B & B 813 Kilmer Rd www.manitoulodge.com, completely nonsmoking, 10 forested acres for walking dogs, 4 miles to Rialto Beach (the only pet-friendly beach in the area)	360-374-6295 pets $10/day	(7) $85– $135	FB	
Miller Tree Inn B & B 360-374-6806, 800-943-6563 654 E Division St www.millertreeinn.com, completely nonsmoking, back yard for walking dogs	pets $10/day	(8) $95– $135	FB (k)	T

C = coffee IP = indoor pool OP = outdoor pool CB = continental K = full kitchen R = restaurant breakfast (k) = kitchenette S = sauna or F = refrigerator L = lounge steamroom FB = full breakfast M = microwave T = spa or hot tub	(# of units) & rates	food & drink	pool, sauna & hot tub

Forks, Washington (continued)

Olson's Vacation Cabins 360-374-3142 2423 Mora Rd pets $10/day fully equipped cabin with fenced yard and BBQ, also 1 travel trailer in secluded 4 acre meadow, 2 miles to beach and park	(2) $60– $70	K	
Olympic Suites 360-374-5400 800 Olympic Dr 800-262-3433 www.olympicsuitesinn.com pets $5/day completely nonsmoking 1 to 2-bdrm suites, 1 mile to walking trails and parks, 14 miles to ocean	(30) $49– $99	C K	
Three Rivers Resort 360-374-5300 7764 La Push Rd pets $5/day www.northolympic.com/threerivers, cabins, RV and tent sites, groceries and gasoline, laundry, 1 block to river, 4 miles to ocean beaches	(5) $39– $59	(k) R	
Westward Hoh Resort 360-374-6657 5692 Upper Hoh Rd www.hohriver.com rustic cabins with fully equipped kitchenettes, tent spaces and teepee, bathhouse and showers, off-leash dogwalking area, 12 miles to park, 20 miles to ocean	(2) $40	C (k)	

Freeland, Washington

Blue Willow by the Sea B & B 360-331-7420 6342 Apple Ln www.bluewillowbythesea.com completely nonsmoking, lawn and woods for walking dogs, close to dog-friendly beach	(2) $125– $135	FB	T
Harbour Inn Motel 360-331-6900 1606 E Main St pets $15/day www.harbourinnmotel.com, nonsmoking rooms, 1 to 2 dogs only, 2 acre lawn, picnic tables, 3 blocks to waterfront park, 2 miles to off-leash beach, weekdays are especially good for traveling with pets	(20) $62– $90	CB (k) M/F	

Knickerbockers Harbor Holiday 360-331-5479 5304 Bercot Rd pets $10/day friendly dogs allowed by advance reservation only, studio with loft sleeps 8, pool table, waterfront open lot for walking dogs, across street to harbor	(1) $75– $95	K		
Mutiny Bay Cabin 360-321-2135 1-bdrm cabin sleeps 4, open May–October, 2 miles to off-leash beach, 4 miles to wooded off-leash park	(1) $85	K		
Serenity Pines Cottages 360-321-2575 www.serenitypines.com pets $20/stay laundry, fully equipped waterfront vacation homes, private beaches for walking dogs	(4) $145– $170	C K	T	
Tara Vacation Rentals 360-331-7100 18205 Hwy 525 Suite 5 800-260-4156 www.whidbeyvacation.com pets $30/stay fully equipped nonsmoking vacation homes, laundry, most on waterfront, beach access for walking dogs	(9) $100– $350			

Friday Harbor, Washington

Beaverton Valley Farmhouse B & B 360-378-3276 4144 Beaverton Valley Rd 877-378-3276 nonsmoking rooms and log cabin, 3 partially fenced acres, large meadow for walking dogs	(5) $100– $145	CB (k)		
Blair House B & B 360-378-5907, 800-899-3030 345 Blair Ave www.fridayharborlodging.com dogs allowed in fully equipped guest cottage only, large yard for walking dogs	(8) $95– $175	FB K	OP T	
Harrison House Suites 360-378-3587, 800-407-7933 235 C St www.san-juan-lodging.com suites sleep 2 to 12, pet fee depends on size of dog, fully stocked kitchens, guests have use of organic vegetable garden, 3 private outdoor jacuzzi tubs, communal hot tub, laundry, 1 block to park and ferry	(5) $79– $300	CB K R	T	
Inns at Friday Harbor 360-378-4000, 410 Spring St 800-752-5752 www.theinns.com pets $50/stay nonsmoking rooms, laundry, exercise room, lawn, 4 blocks to harbor	(72) $189	C M/F	IP S T	

C = coffee IP = indoor pool OP = outdoor pool CB = continental K = full kitchen R = restaurant breakfast (k) = kitchenette S = sauna or F = refrigerator L = lounge steamroom FB = full breakfast M = microwave T = spa or hot tub	(# of units) & rates	food & drink	pool, sauna & hot tub

Friday Harbor, Washington (continued)

Sandpiper Condominiums 360-378-5610 570 Jensen Alley www.sandpiper-condos.com completely nonsmoking studios and 1-bdrm condos, laundry, vacant lot for walking dogs	(8) $85– $125	K	OP T
Snug Harbor Marina Resort 360-378-4762 1997 Mitchell Bay Rd pets $5/day www.snugresort.com, nonsmoking waterfront cabins, BBQ, lawn, trails, beach for walking dogs	(10) $95– $209	C (k) M/F	
Tucker House B & B 360-378-2783 260 B St 800-965-0123 www.tuckerhouse.com pets $15/day dogs allowed in 3 cottages, prefer pets to be kept in travel crates when indoors	(6) $75– $225	FB (k) M/F	T
Windermere Vacation Rentals 360-378-5060 520 Spring St 800-391-8190 ask for #70 Karamar Cove: 3-bdrm waterfront vacation home on 78 acres, laundry, outdoor kennel, private cove, www.windermerevacationrentals.com	(1) $1150– $1350 per week	K	

Fruitland, Washington

White Willow Motel & Camp 509-722-3640 6161 Hwy 25 S pets $10/stay laundry, RV sites, teepee rentals, 5 miles to Fort Spokane and riverfront	(15) $50	C	

Garfield, Washington

R C McCroskey House B & B 509-635-1459 803 N Forest St dogs allowed by advance reservation only, nonsmoking rooms, lawn, field and rural roads for walking dogs, 4 blocks to public park	(2) $90	FB	

Gig Harbor, Washington

Best Western Wesley Inn 253-858-9690 6575 Kimball Dr pets $10/day, 888-462-0002 www.wesleyinn.com, nonsmoking rooms, exercise room, in-room spa, dog treats, walking trail, ½ mile to local park, 1 mile to harbor	(53) $89– $179	CB M/F	OP T
Gig Harbor Motor Inn 253-858-8161, 888-336-8161 4709 Point Fosdick Dr NW pets $5/day www.gigharbormotorinn.com, nonsmoking rooms, woods and meadow, walking trails, pond, off-leash exercise area, 2 miles to harbor and public parks	(21) $87– $97	C (k) M/F	
Inn at Gig Harbor 253-858-1111, 800-795-9980 3211 56th St NW pets $5/day plus $15 cleaning fee www.innatgigharbor.com, nonsmoking rooms, fitness center, massage studio, lawn, 2 miles to city park and waterfront	(64) $99– $195	CB (k) M/F R/L	T
No Cabbages' B & B 253-858-7797 10319 Sunrise Beach Dr NW beach access for walking dogs, "prayer labyrinth" meditation path through woods, www.gigharbor.com/nocabbages	(3) $80– $110	FB	
Olde Glencove Hotel B & B 253-884-2835 9418 Glencove Rd www.glencovehotel.com waterfront location, close to walking areas	(4) $65– $85	FB	
Westwynd Motel 253-857-4047, 800-468-9963 6703 144th St NW www.westwyndmotel.com nonsmoking rooms, lawn, ¼ mile to public beach	(24) $44– $72	(k)	

Glacier, Washington

Glacier Creek Lodge 360-599-2991 10036 Mt Baker Hwy 800-719-1414 www.glaciercreeklodge.com pets $5/day nonsmoking lodge rooms and cabins, playground, picnic area, BBQ, creeks and walking trails	(21) $44– $170	K	T
Mt Baker Cabin Country 360-599-9395 6979 Shuksan Dr each pet $5/day www.cabincountrybb.com, cabin and condominium in wooded "back to nature" setting, walking trails	(2) $85– $180	K M/F	IP T

C = coffee IP = indoor pool OP = outdoor pool CB = continental K = full kitchen R = restaurant breakfast (k) = kitchenette S = sauna or F = refrigerator L = lounge steamroom FB = full breakfast M = microwave T = spa or hot tub	(# of units) & rates	food & drink	pool, sauna & hot tub

Glacier, Washington (continued)

	(# of units) & rates	food & drink	pool, sauna & hot tub
Mt Baker Chalet 360-599-2405, 800-258-2405 9857 Mt Baker Hwy www.mtbakerchalet.com completely nonsmoking modern cabins and condos, laundry, walking trails, playground, picnic area	(33) $75– $250	K	IP S T
Mt Baker Lodging 360-599-2453, 800-709-7669 7463 Mt Baker Hwy www.mtbakerlodging.com 1 to 4-bdrm vacation homes, next to national forest	(18) $119– $220		T

Glenwood, Washington

Flying L Ranch Country Inn B & B 509-364-3488 25 Flying L Lane each pet $10/stay, 888-682-3267 www.mt-adams.com, dogs allowed with advance approval only, cabins sleep 4 to 6, off-leash area, on 80 acres with miles of trails, pond, picnic area	(14) $125– $190	FB K	

Goldendale, Washington

Barchris Motel 509-773-4325 128 N Academy Ave pets $5/day suites, full kitchens, BBQ, lawn, 1 block to park	(9) $37– $49	K	
Pine Springs Resort 509-773-4434 2471 Hwy 97 (Status Pass) pets $5–$25/stay nonsmoking cottages, RV sites, wooded setting, next to state park and hiking trails	(3) $50	K	
Ponderosa Motel 509-773-5842 775 E Broadway St pets $7/day nonsmoking rooms, riverside trail, 2 blocks to park	(28) $49– $61	C (k) M/F	

Graham, Washington

SkySong B & B Retreat 253-875-7775 10006 255th Street Ct E http://hometown.aol.com/ skysongbandb/myhomepage/business.html, 6 acres for walking dogs, 2 miles to county park	(3) $75	FB M/F	

Grand Coulee, Washington

Center Lodge Motel 509-633-0770 404 Spokane Way 877-633-2860 www.centerlodge.com pets $10/day nonsmoking rooms, wooded walking area, 2 state parks within 5 miles, 1½ miles to Grand Coulee Dam	(17) $32– $80	C K M/F	
Grand Coulee Motel 509-633-2860, 877-633-2860 404 Spokane Way pets $10/day www.grandcouleemotel.com, nonsmoking rooms, wooded walking area, close to parks and dam	(14) $32– $80	C K M/F	
Trail West Motel 509-633-3155, 866-633-8157 108 Spokane Way pets $5/stay www.trailwestmotel.com, undeveloped area for walking dogs, 1½-mile trail to Grand Coulee Dam	(26) $39– $75	C K	OP

Grandview, Washington

Grandview Motel 509-882-1323 522 E Wine Country Rd pets $5/day nonsmoking rooms, 3 blocks to walking trails	(20) $28– $45	M/F	

Granite Falls, Washington

Mountain View Inn 360-691-6668 32005 Mountain Loop Hwy pets $5/day 1 mile to forest service land and trails	(6) $45– $48	C R	

Grayland, Washington

Grayland Motel & Cottages 360-267-2395 2013 Hwy 105 each pet $10/stay, 800-292-0845 www.westportwa.com/graylandmotel, secluded setting, covered picnic area and BBQ, private path to beach for walking dogs	(8) $49– $75	K	
Ocean Spray Motel 360-267-2205 1757 Hwy 105 pets $5/day nonsmoking rooms, paved road to beach for walking	(10) $55– $80	K	
Surf Motel & Cottages 360-267-2244 2029 Hwy 105 pets $5/day rooms and cottages, dog towels, short path to beach	(7) $39– $67	C K	

C = coffee
CB = continental
   breakfast
F = refrigerator
FB = full breakfast
	IP = indoor pool
	K = full kitchen
	(k) = kitchenette
	L = lounge
	M = microwave
		OP = outdoor pool
		R = restaurant
		S = sauna or
		   steamroom
		T = spa or hot tub
			(# of units)
			& rates
				food
				& drink
					pool, sauna
					& hot tub

Grayland, Washington (continued)

Walsh Motel 360-267-2191 1593 Hwy 105 pets $10/stay in-room spa, beach frontage for walking dogs			(24) $38– $100	C K	

Greenacres, Washington

Alpine Motel 509-928-2700 18815 Barker Rd each pet $5/day nonsmoking rooms, 1 to 2 dogs only, designated pet walking area, 2 blocks to walking trail			(15) $46– $60	F	

Hoodsport, Washington

Sunrise Motel 360-877-5301, 866-736-1484 24520 N Hwy 101 www.hctc.com/~sunrise nonsmoking rooms, waterfront location, lawn and beach access for walking dogs, espresso bar			(15) $60– $120	C K	

Hoquiam, Washington

Sandstone Motel 360-533-6383 2424 Aberdeen Ave pets $7/day nonsmoking rooms, laundry, 10 blocks to waterfront walking area			(24) $45– $75	C (k) M/F	
Snore & Whisker Motel 360-532-5060 3031 Simpson Ave each pet $5/day 2 blocks to school field and playground to walk dogs			(11) $35– $50	K	
Timberline Inn 360-533-8048 415 Perry Ave pets $5/day open areas for walking dogs, 1½ miles to public park, 30 minute drive to beaches			(25) $50– $60	C (k) M/F	
Westwood Inn 360-532-8161, 866-532-8161 910 Simpson Ave pets $5–$10/day nonsmoking rooms, laundry, grassy area for walking dogs, across street to park and walkway			(65) $45– $150	C K	

Husum, Washington

Husum's Riverside B & B and European Cafe 866 Hwy 141 509-493-8900 yard and lots of trails for walking dogs	(7) $62– $120	FB R

Ilwaco, Washington

101 Haciendas 360-642-8459 101 Brumbach St (Hwy 101), laundry, patio and BBQ, 4 blocks to city park, www.101haciendas.com	(7) $40– $150	C K M/F
Coho Motel & Charters 360-642-3333, 800-339-2646 237 Howerton Way www.cohocharters.com dogs under 30 lbs only, area for walking dogs, salmon and sturgeon charter fishing service	(6) $54– $80	
Columbia-Pacific Motel 360-642-3177 214 S 1st St pets $5/day small dogs allowed at owner's discretion only, open area for walking dogs, 1½ miles to beach	(16) $60	C
Harbor Lights Motel & Restaurant 360-642-3196 147 SE Howerton Way pets $10/stay nonsmoking rooms, in-room spa, located on port docks, close to beach and local parks, lighthouses and museums nearby	(19) $38– $69	R/L
Heidi's Inn 360-642-2387, 800-576-1032 126 E Spruce St pets $5/day nonsmoking rooms, laundry, small wooded area for walking dogs, 3 blocks to Port of Ilwaco	(25) $35– $115	C K T

Inchelium, Washington

Hartman's Log Cabin Resort 509-722-3543 178 Twin Lakes Rd pets $6/day motel rooms and log cabins, laundry, RV and tent sites, natural wooded area for walking dogs	(59) $36– $55	(k) R
Rainbow Beach Resort 509-722-5901, 888-862-0978 18 N Twin Lakes Rd pets $10/stay lakefront cabins, laundry, RV sites, walking trails and swimming in lake	(26) $39– $141	K

C = coffee
CB = continental
    breakfast
F = refrigerator
FB = full breakfast
	IP = indoor pool
	K = full kitchen
	(k) = kitchenette
	L = lounge
	M = microwave
		OP = outdoor pool
		R = restaurant
		S = sauna or
		    steamroom
		T = spa or hot tub
			(# of units)
			& rates
				food
				& drink
					pool, sauna
					& hot tub

Index, Washington

Wild Lily Cabins B & B 360-793-2103 www.wildlilyranch.com pets $10/day cedar log cabins, BBQ, outdoor showers, forested riverfront location, surrounded by wilderness	(3) $75– $105	CB	S T

Ione, Washington

Box Canyon Motel 509-442-3728, 800-676-8883 8612 Hwy 31 pets $3/day nonsmoking rooms, river frontage, hiking trails, 1 mile to campground and recreation area	(9) $42– $57	C K
Ione Motel & Trailer Park 509-442-3213 301 S 2nd St dogs allowed by advance reservation only, nonsmoking rooms to 2-bdrm suite, RV sites, 500 ft river frontage, close to public park	(11) $40– $85	C (k) M/F

Issaquah, Washington

Motel 6-Seattle/Issaquah 425-392-8405 1885 15th Pl NW www.motel6.com, 800-466-8356 nonsmoking rooms, across street from state park	(103) $60– $67	C	OP

Kelso, Washington

Best Western Aladdin Motor Inn 360-425-9660 310 Long Ave pets $10/stay, 800-764-3778 www.bestwesternwashington.com, nonsmoking rooms, laundry, field, 2 blocks to Cowlitz River trail	(78) $49– $90	CB M/F R/L	IP T
Guesthouse International Inn 360-414-5953 501 Three Rivers Dr 800-214-8378 www.guesthouseintl.com pets $10/stay nonsmoking rooms and 1 to 2-bdrm suites, laundry, in-room spa, weight room, grassy pet walking area, ¼ mile to waterfront trail, ½ mile to public park	(60) $72– $175	CB K M/F	IP T

Motel 6 360-425-3229, 800-466-8356 106 N Minor Rd www.motel6.com nonsmoking rooms, laundry, open field and lawn for walking dogs, 2 blocks to public park	(63) $43–$59	C	OP	
Red Lion Hotel 360-636-4400, 800-733-5466 510 Kelso Dr pets $10/stay www.redlion.com, nonsmoking rooms, laundry, weight room, park and riverfront trail behind hotel	(162) $68–$150	C M/F R/L	OP T	
Super 8 Motel 360-423-8880 250 Kelso Dr 800-800-8000 www.super8.com refundable pet deposit nonsmoking rooms, laundry, next to Tam O'Shanter Park for walking dogs	(84) $50–$80	C M/F	IP T	

Kennewick, Washington

Best Western Kennewick Inn 509-586-1332 4001 W 27th Ave pets $10/stay pet rooms on ground floor have outside entrances to pet walking area, 24 hour pool-sauna-hot tub	(87) $67–$139	CB M/F	IP S T	
Comfort Inn 509-783-8396, 800-221-2222 7801 W Quinault Ave pets $10/day www.choicehotels.com, nonsmoking rooms, in-room spa, laundry, lawn for walking dogs, ½ mile to park	(56) $45–$55	CB M/F	IP T	
Green Gable Motel 509-582-5811 515 W Columbia Dr pets $5/day nonsmoking rooms, across street to river and park	(23) $25–$40	(k) M/F		
La Quinta Inn & Suites 509-736-3326, 800-531-5900 4220 W 27th Ave www.laquinta.com nonsmoking rooms, laundry, lawn for walking dogs, close to public park	(53) $69–$149	CB K M/F	IP S T	
Nendels Inn 509-735-9511, 800-547-0106 2811 W 2nd Ave pets $5/day nonsmoking rooms, lawn, 1 mile to public park	(106) $43–$66	CB	OP	
Super 8 Motel 509-736-6888, 800-800-8000 626 N Columbia Center Blvd pets $10/stay www.super8.com, nonsmoking rooms, laundry, grassy pet walking area, 7 blocks to riverside park	(95) $40–$65	CB F	IP T	

C = coffee IP = indoor pool OP = outdoor pool CB = continental K = full kitchen R = restaurant breakfast (k) = kitchenette S = sauna or F = refrigerator L = lounge steamroom FB = full breakfast M = microwave T = spa or hot tub	(# of units) & rates	food & drink	pool, sauna & hot tub

Kennewick, Washington (continued)

Tapadera Inn 509-783-6191, 800-722-8277 300 N Ely St #A pets $5/day nonsmoking rooms, laundry, open area for walking dogs, 1 mile to Columbia Park	(61) $38– $90	CB M/F	OP
Travelodge 509-735-6385, 800-578-7878 321 N Johnson St pets $5–$10/day www.travelodge.com, nonsmoking rooms, laundry, fully equipped kitchens, lawn, 3 blocks to open field and park, 5 minute drive to Columbia Park	(45) $45– $75	CB K M/F	OP
WestCoast Hotel-Kennewick 509-783-0611 1101 N Columbia Center Blvd 800-325-4000 www.westcoasthotels.com pets $25/day nonsmoking rooms, fitness center, lawn and open pet walking area, 1½ mile to Columbia Park	(162) $69– $150	C M/F R/L	OP

Kent, Washington

Best Western Plaza by the Green 253-854-8767 24415 Russell Rd pets $25/stay, 800-648-3311x4 www.bestwestern.com/plazabythegreen, laundry, nonsmoking rooms, exercise room, ½ block to park	(97) $69– $79	CB M/F R	S T
Century Motel 206-878-1840 23421 Military Rd S pets $5/stay lawn for walking dogs	(23) $39– $45	C M/F	
Comfort Inn 253-872-2211 22311 84th Ave S pets $10/day nonsmoking rooms, dogs allowed at manager's discretion only, laundry, small lawn, 3 miles to park	(101) $85– $129	CB M/F	IP T
Days Inn-South Seattle/Kent 253-854-1950 1711 W Meeker St pets $10/stay, 877-520-7697 www.daysinn.com, nonsmoking rooms, laundry, open field, 1 block to riverside park and trail	(80) $53– $119	CB M	

Golden Kent Motel 253-872-8372 22203 84th Ave S pets $25/stay laundry, lawn and open field for walking dogs, ½ mile to Green River walking trail	(21) $50– $60	(k)		
Howard Johnson Inn 253-852-7224, 800-446-4656 1233 Central Ave N each pet $10/day www.hojo.com, nonsmoking rooms, laundry, lawn for walking dogs, 2 blocks to public park	(85) $65– $150	CB M/F	OP T	
Kent Val-U Inn 253-872-5525 22420 84th Ave S 800-443-7777 www.valuinn.com/kent.htm pets $5/day nonsmoking rooms, laundry, dogwalking area	(94) $63– $90	CB	T	
La Quinta Inn 253-520-6670, 800-238-7234 25100 74th Ave S pets $25/stay www.laquinta.com, nonsmoking rooms, in-room spa, laundry, area for walking dogs, next to bike trail	(60) $73– $130	CB K	IP S T	
TownePlace Suites by Marriott 253-796-6000 18123 72nd Ave S 800-257-3000 www.marriott.com pets $10/day nonsmoking rooms, laundry, year-round hot tub, seasonal pool, exercise room, across street from Green River walking trail	(144) $89– $109	CB K	OP T	

Kettle Falls, Washington

Grandview Inn Motel & RV Park 509-738-6733 978 Hwy 395 N pets $2–$3/day, 888-488-6733 nonsmoking rooms, laundry, RV sites, ½ mile to public park, dogwalking area up the hill	(13) $36– $55	C (k) M/F	OP T	
Kettle Falls Inn 509-738-6514 205 E 3rd Ave (Hwy 395) 888-315-2378 www.bestvalueinn.com pets $5/day nonsmoking rooms, laundry, open field for walking dogs, close to city park and swimming pool	(24) $38– $68	C (k) M/F	S	

Kingston, Washington

Smiley's Colonial Motel 360-297-3622 11067 Hwy 104 dogs allowed in 1 unit, ½ block to baseball field for walking dogs	(17) $49– $54	M/F	

C = coffee IP = indoor pool OP = outdoor pool CB = continental K = full kitchen R = restaurant breakfast (k) = kitchenette S = sauna or F = refrigerator L = lounge steamroom FB = full breakfast M = microwave T = spa or hot tub	(# of units) & rates	food & drink	pool, sauna & hot tub

Kirkland, Washington

Best Western Kirkland Inn 425-822-2300 12223 NE 116th St 800-332-4200 www.bestwesternwashington.com, nonsmoking rooms, laundry, lawn, 10 minute drive to public park	(110) $74– $97	CB M/F	OP T
La Quinta Inn-Bellevue/Kirkland 425-828-6585 10530 NE Northup Way 800-531-5900 www.lq.com, nonsmoking rooms, laundry, 24 hour fitness center, walking trails, 3 miles to off-leash park	(119) $82– $165	CB M/F	OP
Motel 6-Seattle/Kirkland 425-821-5618, 800-466-8356 12010 120th Pl NE www.motel6.com nonsmoking rooms, laundry, parks within 1 mile	(123) $50– $67	C	OP

La Conner, Washington

Art's Place B & B 360-466-3033 511 Talbott separate guest house with full kitchen, short drive to public park	(1) $60– $65	CB K	
La Conner Country Inn 360-466-3101, 888-466-4113 107 S 2nd St pets $25/stay www.laconnerlodging.com, nonsmoking rooms, lawn for walking dogs, ¼ mile to public park	(28) $95– $170	CB R/L	

La Push, Washington

La Push Ocean Park Resort 360-374-5267 700 Main St 360-374-6488, 800-487-1267 www.ocean-park.org pets $10/stay 1 to 2-bdrm rustic cabins, laundry, RV sites, beach	(55) $62– $175	K R	

Lacey, Washington

Days Inn 360-493-1991, 800-282-7028 120 College St SE www.daysinn.com laundry, dogs under 100 lbs only, exercise room, public park and wooded trails for walking dogs	(83) $49– $75	CB M/F	S

Super 8 Motel 4615 Martin Way E www.super8.com nonsmoking rooms, laundry, 1 block to public park	360-459-8888 800-800-8000 refundable pet deposit	(100) $53– $74	CB	IP

Lakewood, Washington

Colonial Motel 12117 Pacific Hwy SW designated pet walking area, 5 minute drive to park	253-589-3261 in-room spa, laundry,	(34) $40– $85	M/F R	

Langley, Washington

Angel Cottage B & B 616 Edgecliff Dr Sound, dogs allowed by advance reservation only, 10 minute walk to public park and beach	360-221-3676 cottage overlooking Puget	(1) $95	CB K	
Barn Guest House B & B www.barnguesthouse.com, dogs allowed by advance reservation only, studio apartment sleeps 3, kitchen stocked with breakfast supplies, 20 acres pasture and trails through woods for walking dogs	360-321-5875	(1) $120– $130	FB K	
Country Cottage of Langley 215 6th St www.countrycottage.com cottages, private decks, breakfast delivered to your door, in-room spa, 1½ acre lawn, garden, near beach	360-221-8709 800-713-3860 refundable pet deposit	(6) $129– $179	FB M/F	
Crabtrapper Beach House 5941 Norton Ln www.thecrabtrapper.com, 2-bdrm beachfront house sleeps 6, beach for walking dogs	360-321-4353 pets $100/stay	(1) $120– $150	K	
Island Tyme B & B 4940 S Bayview Rd dogs allowed in 1 room only, 20 acres with trails and wildlife, 2 miles to Langley Park, 3½ miles to Double Bluff Off-Leash Park	360-221-5078, 800-898-8963 www.moriah.com/island-tyme	(5) $95– $140	FB	
Langley Motel 526 Camano Ave www.langleymotel.com, completely nonsmoking rooms and suites, patio, open lot, 4 blocks to marina	360-221-6070, 866-276-8292 pets $10/day	(4) $95	C K	

C = coffee
CB = continental
    breakfast
F = refrigerator
FB = full breakfast
	IP = indoor pool
	K = full kitchen
	(k) = kitchenette
	L = lounge
	M = microwave
		OP = outdoor pool
		R = restaurant
		S = sauna or
		    steamroom
		T = spa or hot tub
			(# of units)
			& rates
				food
				& drink
					pool, sauna
					& hot tub

Langley, Washington (continued)

Primrose Path Properties 360-730-3722 3191 SE Harbor Rd pets $20/day www.primrosepath.net, dogs allowed by advance reservation only, cottages sleep 2 to 6, on or close to the waterfront, one cottage has fenced yard	(4) $139– $229	C (k) M/F	T
Rabbit on the Green B & B 360-321-7254 3018 E Quigley Rd 800-366-0645 cottage with fireplace, 10 acres, pond, ¼ mile to lake	(1) $100– $150	CB K	T
Sunset Cottage 360-579-1590 7359 S Maxwelton Beach Rd pets $20/day dogs allowed by advance arrangement only, fully equipped nonsmoking beachfront cottages, large fenced yard, doghouses, low bank beach access	(3) $85– $175	C K	

Leavenworth, Washington

Alpine Rivers Inn 509-548-5875, 800-873-3960 1505 Alpensee Strasse St pets $10/day www.alpineriversinn.com, nonsmoking rooms, walking trails to river, 6 blocks to city parks	(26) $69– $99	C	OP T
Blackbird Lodge 509-548-5800 305 8th St 800-446-0240 www.blackbirdlodge.com pets $8/day dogs under 40 lbs only, close to walking trail	(21) $109– $145	CB M/F	T
Der Ritterhof Motor Inn 509-548-5845, 800-255-5845 190 Hwy 2 pets $10/day www.derritterhof.com, completely nonsmoking, large yard, BBQ, 3 blocks to waterfront park	(51) $76– $98	CB K	OP T
Destination Leavenworth 509-548-4230 940 Hwy 2 #A1 www.destinationleavenworth.com nonsmoking cabins-condos-vacation homes, some with acreage, dogwalking areas, near public parks	(20) $100– $140	K	

Evergreen Motor Inn 1117 Front St www.evergreeninn.com completely nonsmoking, private park for walking dogs, 2½ blocks to riverfront walking trails	509-548-5515 800-327-7212 pets $10/stay	(40) $75– $135	CB (k) M/F	T
Howard Johnson 405 Hwy 2 nonsmoking rooms, across street to park and trails	509-548-4326 pets $12/day	(40) $89– $129	CB M/F	OP T
Lake Wenatchee Hide-A-Ways 19944 Hwy 207 www.bluegrouse.com completely nonsmoking riverfront cabins with full kitchens, wooded area and trails for walking dogs	509-763-0108 800-883-2611 each pet $5/stay	(13) $100– $185	K	T
Natapoc Lodging 12338 Bretz Rd www.natapoc.com completely nonsmoking lodges sleep 2 to 22, private hot tubs, fireplaces, lawn and riverfront wooded area for walking dogs	509-763-3313 888-628-2762 pets $25/day	(7) $180– $300	C K	T
Obertal Motor Inn 509-548-5204, 800-537-9382 922 Commercial St pets $10/day www.obertal.com, nonsmoking rooms, public park		(27) $69– $139	CB M/F	T
Phippen's B & B 509-548-7755, 800-666-9806 10285 Ski Hill Dr completely nonsmoking, 2 fenced yards for walking dogs, ¾ mile to park		(2) $70– $80	FB M/F	OP T
River's Edge Lodge 8401 Hwy 2 nonsmoking rooms, large lawns for walking dogs	509-548-7612 800-451-5285	(23) $67– $78	C K	OP T
Rodeway Inn & Suites 185 Hwy 2 www.leavenworthwa.com nonsmoking rooms, laundry, near Riverfront Park and 1½ mile-long trail that loops through town	509-548-7992 800-693-1225 pets $12/day	(33) $79– $134	CB M/F	IP T
Saimons Hide-A-Way 509-763-3213, 800-845-8638 16408 River Rd www.saimons.com completely nonsmoking cabins with private hot tubs, walking trails, 1 block to river		(6) $135– $185	C K	T

C = coffee IP = indoor pool OP = outdoor pool			
CB = continental K = full kitchen R = restaurant breakfast (k) = kitchenette S = sauna or F = refrigerator L = lounge steamroom FB = full breakfast M = microwave T = spa or hot tub	# of units & rates	food & drink	pool, sauna & hot tub

Leavenworth, Washington (continued)

Tyrolean Ritz Hotel 509-548-5455 633 Front St 800-854-6365 www.tyrolritz.com pets $10/day completely nonsmoking facility, close to walking trail	(16) $70– $150	C R	

Lilliwaup, Washington

Mike's Beach Resort 360-877-5324 38470 N Hwy 101 800-231-5324 www.mikesbeachresort.com pets $10/stay waterfront cabins, motel rooms, laundry, RV sites, 2,000 ft beachfront, walking trails, diving supplies	(20) $45– $95	C (k) M/F	

Long Beach, Washington

Anchorage Cottages 360-642-2351 2209 Boulevard North 800-646-2351 www.theanchoragecottages.com each pet $10/day completely nonsmoking cottages sleep 2-9, tennis court, playground, lawn, Lewis & Clark walking trail	(10) $65– $120	K	
Anthony's Home Court 360-642-2802 1310 Pacific Hwy N 888-787-2754 www.anthonyshomecourt.com pets $5/day laundry, RV sites, beach access across street	(8) $20– $125	C (k) M/F	
Beach It Rentals 360-642-4697 11409 Pacific Way www.vacationparadise.com nonsmoking 2-bdrm vacation homes sleep 6 to 8, oceanfront or close to beach, laundry, beach access	(3) $95– $190	K	
Boulevard Motel 360-642-2434, 888-454-0346 301 N Ocean Blvd pets $5/stay motel rooms and cottages sleep up to 6, 3 minute walk to public park and beach	(22) $50– $105	K	IP

Breakers Hotel 26th & Hwy 103 www.breakerslongbeach.com nonsmoking rooms, laundry, designated dogwalking areas, beach access	360-642-4414 800-219-9833 pets $10/day	(116) $59– $225	C (k) M/F	IP T
Chautauqua Lodge Resort Motel 304 14th St N www.chautauqualodge.com therapy pool, recreation room, paved dune trails	360-642-4401 800-869-8401 pets $8/day	(180) $55– $160	K R/L	IP T
Edgewater Inn 409 SW 10th St nonsmoking rooms, boardwalk and walking trails, www.funbeach.com/partners/edgewater.html	360-642-2311, 800-561-2456 each pet $8/day	(84) $49– $139	C M/F R	
Lighthouse Motel 12415 Pacific Way www.lighthousemotel.net nonsmoking rooms, beach access for walking dogs	360-642-3622 877-220-7555 pets $5–$10/day	(30) $55– $184	K	
Long Beach Motel 1200 Pacific Hwy S guest pass to use swimming pool at nearby hotel, RV sites, large lawn, next to "garden golf" facility	360-642-3500 each pet $7/day	(8) $39– $85	C (k)	
Ocean Lodge 208 Bolstad Ave W nonsmoking rooms, fireplaces, ocean view, easy beach access for walking dogs	360-642-5400, 888-886-9111 pets $5/stay	(64) $45– $110	CB K	OP S T
Our Place at the Beach 1309 S Ocean Beach Blvd www.willapabay.org/~opatb nonsmoking rooms, cabins and oceanview rooms, fitness room, field and beach for walking dogs	360-642-3793 800-538-5107 each pet $5/day	(25) $42– $86	CB (k) M/F	S T
Pacific Realty Properties 102 Bolstad Ave NE condos and vacation homes, on or close to the beach	888-879-5479 www.pacreal.com	(18) $65– $225		
Pacific View Motel 205 Bolstad Ave W www.willapabay.org/~pacvu, nonsmoking rooms, fenced play area, easy beach access for walking dogs	360-642-2415, 800-238-0859 pets $5/day	(19) $56– $140	C K	

C = coffee IP = indoor pool OP = outdoor pool CB = continental K = full kitchen R = restaurant breakfast (k) = kitchenette S = sauna or F = refrigerator L = lounge steamroom FB = full breakfast M = microwave T = spa or hot tub	(# of units) & rates	food & drink	pool, sauna & hot tub

Long Beach, Washington (continued)

Sand-Lo Motel & Trailer Park 360-642-2600 1910 Pacific Ave N each pet $10/stay, 800-676-2601 laundry, RV sites, open field, 4 blocks to beach	(10) $42– $80	R	
Sands Motel 360-642-2100 12211 Pacific Way pets $5/stay rooms and apartments, open space for walking dogs, off-leash exercise area, private beach access	(10) $40– $45	(k)	
Shaman Motel 360-642-3714 115 3rd St SW 800-753-3750 www.shamanmotel.com pets $5/stay nonsmoking rooms, dunes walking path and boardwalk within 3 blocks	(42) $54– $109	CB (k) M/F	OP
Super 8 Motel 360-642-8988, 888-478-3297 500 Ocean Beach Blvd S pets $10/day dunes area for walking dogs, 5 minute walk to beach	(50) $27– $109	C	
Thunderbird Motel 360-642-5700 201 N Ocean Beach Blvd each pet $7/day 1 to 2-bdrm suites sleep 6, open walking area, 2 blocks to beach and boardwalk	(15) $39– $89	CB (k)	IP
Whale's Tale 360-642-3455 620 S Pacific Hwy 800-559-4253 www.thewhalestale.com, nonsmoking rooms, no fee for 1 dog, each additional dog $5/day, recreation room with ping pong and pool table, close to dunes for walking dogs	(9) $29– $99	C K	S T
Yett Beach House 360-642-8069 601 N Ocean Beach Blvd 888-642-8069 www.boreasinn.com, pets $25/stay plus $25 cleaning fee, 110-year old nonsmoking 3-bdrm beachfront cottage sleeps 8, fenced lawn, walking path through dunes to beach, ask about off-season rates	(1) $115	K	

Longview, Washington

Budget Inn 360-423-6980 1808 Hemlock St pets $5–$15/stay nonsmoking rooms, area for walking dogs	(34) $35– $45	C (k)	
Hudson Manor Motel 360-425-1100 1616 Hudson St pets $3/day nonsmoking rooms, open field for walking dogs	(25) $40– $49	CB M/F	
Monticello Hotel 360-425-9900 1405 17th Ave pets $10/day suites, close to public park	(20) $60	(k)	
Ramada Ltd (formerly Patrician Inn) 360-414-1000 723 7th Ave pets $15/stay, 877-566-4843 www.patricianinn.com, nonsmoking rooms, laundry, open field for walking dogs, 1 mile to Lake Sacajawea and walking trail	(50) $59– $99	CB M/F	IP T
Town Chalet Motor Hotel 360-423-2020 1822 Washington Way pets $3/day nonsmoking rooms, lawn, 2 blocks to public park	(24) $30– $53	(k)	
Town House Motel 360-423-7200 744 Washington Way pets $5/day www.townhousemotel.com, nonsmoking rooms, lawn for walking dogs, 1 block to fairground	(28) $32– $50	C M/F	OP

Loomis, Washington

Chopaka Lodge 509-223-3131, 866-651-2120 1995 Loomis Oroville Rd fully equipped cabins, RV and tent sites, next to park on Palmer Lake	(3) $50– $58	K	

Loon Lake, Washington

Inn at White Pine Bed & Barn 509-233-2971 3848 White Pine Rd www.whitepineinn.com beach and dock access, 10 acres for walking dogs, horseback riding, dogs and horses welcome	(2) $75– $85	FB	T
Lakeside Motel 509-233-9060 3849 3rd Ave pets $10/stay sumharv@aol.com, in-room spa, RV sites, area for walking dogs, 1 mile to lake beaches	(13) $40– $80	C M/F R/L	

C = coffee IP = indoor pool OP = outdoor pool CB = continental K = full kitchen R = restaurant breakfast (k) = kitchenette S = sauna or F = refrigerator L = lounge steamroom FB = full breakfast M = microwave T = spa or hot tub	# of units & rates	food & drink	pool, sauna & hot tub

Loon Lake, Washington (continued)

| Robbins Cottages 509-276-2839
40750 Robbins Rd lakefront 2-bdrm cottages
sleep 6, weekly rates also available, quiet country
road for walking dogs, walking trail around lake | (2)
$80 | K | |

Lopez Island, Washington

Fen Wold Cottage & Gardens B & B 360-468-3062 80 Fort Stanley Rd www.fenwoldcottage.com 1 suite sleeps 3, private bath and outside entrance, 2¼ acres for off-leash exercising, across street from county park with trails and beach	(1) $75– $85	FB F	T
Lopez Islander Resort & Marina 360-468-2233 2864 Fisherman Bay Rd 800-736-3434 www.lopezislander.com pets $10/day completely nonsmoking rooms and 3-bdrm suites, access to clamming beach, grassy pet walking areas, kayak and bicycle rentals	(30) $79– $129	K	OP T
Lopez Properties 360-468-5055 308 Lopez Rd 888-772-9735 www.lopezisproperties.com pets $50/stay nonsmoking 1 to 5-bdrm vacation homes, some are on waterfront, laundry, close to parks and trails	(42) $85– $250	K	
MacKaye Harbor Inn 360-468-2253 949 MacKaye Harbor Rd 888-314-6140 www.mackayeharborinn.com, suites sleep 3 to 5, 5 acres for walking dogs, close to golf course	(5) $79– $195		

Lyle, Washington

| Lyle Hotel 509-365-5953
100 7th St pets $5/day
www.lylehotel.com, nonsmoking 100+year old hotel,
shared baths, 28 open acres for walking dogs | (10)
$49–
$59 | CB | |

Lynden, Washington

Windmill Inn	360-354-3424	(15)	C
8022 Guide Meridian Rd	pets $5/day	$35–	K
small dogs only, rooms and 2-bdrm suites, lawn		$90	

Lynnwood, Washington

Lynnwood Landmark Inn	425-775-7447	(103)	CB	IP
4300 Alderwood Mall Blvd	800-775-0805	$59–		T
www.lynnwoodlandmarkinn.com	pets $25/day	$99		
nonsmoking rooms, walking distance to public park				

Residence Inn by Marriott-Lynnwood/Seattle North		(120)	CB	OP
18200 Alderwood Mall Pkwy	425-771-1100	$119–	K	T
each pet $10/day	800-331-3131	$239		
nonsmoking rooms, close to school field for walking dogs, list of local off-leash parks available				

Rodeo Inn	425-774-7700	(52)	CB
20707 Hwy 99	pets $10/day	$39–	(k)
nonsmoking rooms, lawn area for walking dogs		$55	

Rose Motel	425-744-5616	(10)	(k)
20222 Hwy 99	each pet $5/day	$40	
laundry, large back yard, 2 blocks to public park			

Mansfield, Washington

Jameson Lake Resort	509-683-1929	(14)	(k)
580 N Jameson Lake Rd	mobile home and travel	$25–	R
trailers sleep 2 to 6, open April–July 4 and October, RV sites, paddleboat rentals, desert walking area		$85	

Maple Falls, Washington

Thurston House B & B	360-599-2261	(2)	FB	T
9512 Silver Lake Rd		$50–	(k)	
suite and guest house with kitchenette, lakeside area for walking dogs, RV sites, 2 miles to county park		$65		

Yodeler Inn	360-599-1716, 800-642-9033	(4)	K	T
7485 Mt Baker Hwy	www.yodelerinn.com	$65–		
room and cabins sleep 2 to 10, open fields, 3½ miles to public park, 8 miles to national forest land		$150		

C = coffee IP = indoor pool OP = outdoor pool CB = continental K = full kitchen R = restaurant breakfast (k) = kitchenette S = sauna or F = refrigerator L = lounge steamroom FB = full breakfast M = microwave T = spa or hot tub	(# of units) & rates	food & drink	pool, sauna & hot tub

Marysville, Washington

Best Western Tulalip Inn 360-659-4488 6128 Marine Dr NE 800-481-4804 www.bestwestern.com pets $25/day gravel walking area, 5 miles to waterfront and park	(69) $69– $159	CB M/F R	IP T
Village Motor Inn 360-659-0005, 877-659-0005 235 Beach Ave pets $12/day small pets only, 1 block to field for walking dogs	(45) $52– $130	CB M/F	

Mazama, Washington

Lost River Resort 509-996-2537 681 Lost River Rd each pet $10/day well-behaved dogs only, rustic log cabins with full kitchens, RV sites, wooded off-leash exercise areas	(6) $65– $125	K	
Mazama Country Inn 509-996-2681, 800-843-7951 15 Country Rd www.mazamacountryinn.com cabins sleep 6 to 8, wooded areas for walking dogs	(11) $135– $150	K	

Mercer Island, Washington

Travelodge 206-232-8000 7645 Sunset Hwy 800-578-7878 www.mercerislandhotel.com each pet $10/day walking trails, close to parks and waterfront	(35) $69– $96	CB (k) M/F	

Metaline Falls, Washington

Circle Motel 509-446-4343 15802 Hwy 31 each pet $5/day 2 miles north of town, 20 country acres with views and trails for walking dogs, RV sites	(8) $32– $38	C M/F	T
Historic Miners Hotel & Apartments 509-446-4802 101 W 4th Ave dogs allowed with manager's approval only, studios and 1-bdrm suites, laundry, open field, 1 block to public park and riverfront	(4) $39– $49	(k) M/F	

Washington Hotel 509-446-4415 225 E 5th Ave historic building with antique furnishings, across street from public park	(18) $35	

Moclips, Washington

Hi-Tide Ocean Beach Resort 360-276-4142 4890 Railroad Ave each pet $12/day, 800-662-5477 1 to 2 dogs only, grassy area, 100 yards to beach	(25) $95– $175	C K M/F
Moclips Motel 360-276-4228, 866-548-5777 4852 Pacific Ave pets $3–$6/day nonsmoking rooms, 100 feet to the beach	(11) $40– $75	K
Moonstone Beach Motel 360-276-4346, 888-888-9063 4849 Pacific Ave pets $7/day yard and beach for walking dogs	(8) $50– $80	K
Ocean Crest Resort 360-276-4465, 800-684-8439 4651 Hwy 109 pets $15/day www.oceancrestresort.com, nonsmoking rooms, on bluff overlooking ocean, staircase to sandy beach	(45) $39– $150	C IP K S M/F T R/L

Monroe, Washington

Best Western Baron Inn 360-794-3111 19233 Hwy 2 pets $25/stay www.bestwesternwashington.com, nonsmoking rooms, laundry, fitness center, field for walking dogs	(58) $60– $120	CB OP K T M/F
Fairgrounds Inn 360-794-5401 18950 Hwy 2 each pet $5/day nonsmoking rooms, laundry, open area for walking dogs, 10 minute walk to public park	(60) $45– $50	CB T M/F
Monroe Motel 360-794-6751 20310 Old Owen Rd pets $20/stay dogs allowed with manager's approval only, nonsmoking rooms, 7 acres for walking dogs	(22) $40– $60	K

Montesano, Washington

Monte Square Motel 360-249-4424 1000 Brumfield Ave W pets $10/stay www.montesquaremotel.com, nonsmoking facility, designated dogwalking area, 2 miles to state park	(36) $54– $87	C K

C = coffee CB = continental 　　breakfast F = refrigerator FB = full breakfast	IP = indoor pool K = full kitchen (k) = kitchenette L = lounge M = microwave	OP = outdoor pool R = restaurant S = sauna or 　　steamroom T = spa or hot tub	(# of units) & rates	food & drink	pool, sauna & hot tub

Morton, Washington

Evergreen Motel 121 Front St across street from public park		360-496-5407	(12) $35– $50	K	
Seasons Motel 200 Westlake Ave www.whitepasstravel.com nonsmoking rooms, 2½ blocks to a public park, ½ mile to riverfront park		360-496-6835 877-496-6835 pets $10/stay	(49) $55– $70	CB M/F R	
Stiltner Motel 250 Hwy 7 lawn and field for walking dogs		360-496-5103	(7) $40– $50	K	

Moses Lake, Washington

Best Value El Rancho Motel 1214 S Pioneer Way www.bestvaluemoseslake.com grassy area for walking dogs, picnic area with BBQ		509-765-9173 800-341-8000	(20) $38– $65	C K	OP
Heritage Suites　　509-765-7707, 800-457-0271 511 S Division St　　　　www.heritagesuites.com nonsmoking rooms, laundry, grassy area for walking dogs, 5 blocks to public park			(24) $40– $79	K	
Holiday Inn Express　509-766-2000, 800-576-7500 1745 E Kittleson Rd　　　　www.hiexpress.com laundry, exercise room, lawn area for walking dogs			(75) $65– $85	CB M/F	IP T
Imperial Inn 905 W Broadway Ave nonsmoking rooms, lawn, 1 mile to public park		509-765-8626 pets $5/day	(30) $34– $71	CB K M/F	OP
Inn at Moses Lake　　509-766-7000, 800-576-7500 1741 E Kittleson Rd　　　　www.hiexpress.com completely nonsmoking, laundry, pet walking area			(44) $59– $80	CB M/F	

Interstate Inn 509-765-1777 2801 W Broadway Ave nonsmoking rooms, lawn for walking dogs, 2 miles to public park	(30) $39– $69	C M/F	IP S T
Lakeshore Resort Motel 509-765-9201 3206 W Lakeshore Dr pets $5/day motel rooms and lakefront cabins, laundry, boat launch, large area for walking dogs	(33) $25– $70	K	OP
Motel 6 509-766-0250, 800-466-8355 2822 W Wapato Dr nonsmoking rooms, laundry, open field for walking dogs, 2 blocks to public park	(89) $34– $57	C	OP
Motel Oasis 509-765-8636, 800-456-0708 466 Melva Ln pets $5/day nonsmoking rooms, laundry, large grassy area for walking dogs, BBQ and picnic area, 2 blocks to lake	(36) $35– $75	C (k) M/F	OP T
Sage & Sand Motel 509-765-1755 1011 S Pioneer Way 800-336-0454 nonsmoking rooms, vacant lot for walking dogs, ½ mile to lakeside walking trails	(38) $32– $65	C (k) M/F	OP
Shilo Inn 509-765-9317 1819 E Kittleson Rd 800-222-2244 www.shiloinns.com each pet $7/day pet beds and treats, fitness center, open field for walking dogs	(100) $73– $113	CB M/F	IP S T
Sunland Motor Inn 509-765-1170, 800-220-4403 309 E 3rd Ave nonsmoking rooms, 1 block to public park, guest pass to swimming pool at nearby Sage & Sand Motel	(22) $34– $52	(k) M/F	
Super 8 Motel 509-765-8886 449 Melva Ln 800-800-8000 www.super8.com refundable pet deposit nonsmoking rooms, laundry, open area for walking dogs, across street from walking trail to the lake	(62) $49– $75	C M/F	IP
Travelodge 509-765-8631 316 S Pioneer Way 800-578-7878 www.travelodge.com pets $5/day nonsmoking rooms, city park	(40) $49– $65	CB	OP T

C = coffee
CB = continental
    breakfast
F = refrigerator
FB = full breakfast
	IP = indoor pool
	K = full kitchen
	(k) = kitchenette
	L = lounge
	M = microwave
		OP = outdoor pool
		R = restaurant
		S = sauna or
		    steamroom
		T = spa or hot tub
			(# of units)
			& rates
				food
				& drink
					pool, sauna
					& hot tub

Mossyrock, Washington

Mossyrock Inn 120 E State St nonsmoking rooms, lawn for walking dogs, 1 mile to lake and walking trails	360-983-8641 pets $10/day	(8) $43– $55	M/F	

Mount Vernon, Washington

Best Western College Way Inn 300 W College Way www.bestwestern.com/collegewayinn pets $10/day nonsmoking rooms, small grassy area for walking dogs, ¼ mile to walking trail	360-424-4287 800-793-4024	(66) $54– $130	CB K	OP T
Best Western Cottontree Inn 2300 Market St www.cottontree.net pets $10/stay nonsmoking rooms, laundry, small grassy pet walking areas, 1 block to riverfront trails	360-428-5678 800-662-6886	(120) $59– $89	CB M/F R/L	OP
Days Inn 2009 Riverside Dr www.daysinn.com pets $5/day nonsmoking rooms, open lot for walking dogs	360-424-4141 800-882-4141	(67) $50– $70	CB M/F R/L	OP
Hillside Motel 23002 Bonnieview Rd pets $10/stay nonsmoking rooms, lawn, private road to walk dogs	360-445-3252	(5) $43– $55	C (k)	
West Winds Motel 2020 Riverside Dr pets $5/stay nonsmoking rooms, walking trails, ½ mile to park	360-424-4224	(40) $35– $95	CB M/F	
Whispering Firs B & B 360-428-1990, 800-428-1992 19357 Kanako Ln www.whisperingfirs.com dogs allowed by advance reservation only, dinners available by arrangement, on 250 acres with lake		(4) $65– $95	FB	T

Mountlake Terrace, Washington

Studio 6 North Seattle 425-771-3139 6017 244th St SW 888-897-0202 www.staystudio6.com pets $10/day nonsmoking rooms, laundry, short walking trail	(119) $39– $54	C K	

Mukilteo, Washington

Hogland House B & B 425-742-7639 917 Webster St www.hoglandhouse.com completely nonsmoking rooms and cottage sleep 2, 5 acres for walking dogs, trail to beach	(3) $95– $195	FB CB K	T
TownePlace Suites by Marriott 425-551-5900 8521 Mukilteo Speedway 800-257-3000 www.towneplacesuites.com pets $10/day nonsmoking rooms, wooded area for walking dogs, close to state park	(128) $69– $94	CB K	OP T

Naches, Washington

Cozy Cat B & B 509-658-2953 12604 Hwy 410 20 acres open fields, trail through woods to river	(2) $70– $85	FB	
Natchez Hotel 509-653-1317, 888-282-1317 213 Naches Ave pets $10/day dogs allowed with manager's approval only, 1½ blocks to public park	(6) $63– $119	C M/F R	T

Nahcotta, Washington

Moby Dick Hotel B & B 360-665-4543 25814 Sandridge Rd pets $10/day www.mobydickhotel.com 7 acres for walking dogs, ½ mile to beach and parks	(8) $85– $125	FB	S

Naselle, Washington

Sleepy Hollow Motel 360-484-3232 1032 Hwy 4 wooded area behind building for walking dogs, close to river and small park	(7) $35– $45	C (k) M/F	

C = coffee	IP = indoor pool	OP = outdoor pool	(# of units) & rates	food & drink	pool, sauna & hot tub
CB = continental	K = full kitchen	R = restaurant			
breakfast	(k) = kitchenette	S = sauna or			
F = refrigerator	L = lounge	steamroom			
FB = full breakfast	M = microwave	T = spa or hot tub			

Neah Bay, Washington

Cape Motel & RV Park	360-645-2250		(10)	C	
1510 Bayview Ave S	pets $10/day		$45–	K	
motel rooms, RV sites, tent spaces, laundry, across			$75		
street from beach					

Nespelem, Washington

Reynold's Resort	509-633-1092		(4)		
Buffalo Lake Access Rd			$15–		
rustic fishing cabins at Buffalo Lake, RV and tent			$20		
sites, lots of open area for walking dogs					

Newman Lake, Washington

Sutton Bay Resort	509-226-3660		(9)	(k)	
12016 NW Sutton Bay Rd	pets $5/day		$60		
dogs allowed by advance reservation only, rustic					
cabins sleep 6, RV sites, trails for walking dogs					

Newport, Washington

Golden Spur Motor Inn	509-447-3823		(24)	C	
924 W Hwy 2	pets $10/day		$43–	K	
nonsmoking rooms, walking trail, ¼ mile to park			$63	R/L	
Lakeview Motel	509-447-3664, 888-774-3664		(5)	C	
324051 Hwy 2	pets $5/day		$35–	(k)	
in-room spa, 5 acres with trails			$75		
Marshall Lake Resort	509-447-4158		(10)	K	
1301 Marshall Lake Rd			$25–		
trailers and secluded lakeside cabin, RV sites, 100			$50		
lakeside acres, trails and forestland for walking dogs					
Newport City Inn	509-447-3463		(13)	C	
220 N Washington Ave	pets $5/day		$48–		
open area behind motel for walking dogs, lawn,			$68		
picnic area, 6 blocks to public park and riverfront					

North Bend, Washington

Mt Si Motel 425-888-1621 43200 SE North Bend Way grassy areas for walking dogs, ⅓ mile to walking trail on railroad bed, 2 miles to Mt Si Trail	(4) $35– $50	C F	

Northport, Washington

Clark's Motel 509-732-4495 208 Center Ave 1 block to boat launch with picnic area, 2 blocks to public park	(8) $31– $42	K	

Oak Harbor, Washington

Acorn Motor Inn 360-675-6646, 800-280-6646 31530 Hwy 20 pets $10/day nonsmoking rooms, 1 block to beach park	(32) $64– $118	CB M/F	
Best Western Harbor Plaza 360-679-4567 33175 Hwy 20 800-927-5478 www.bestwestern.com/harborplaza pets $10/day nonsmoking rooms, exercise room, area for walking dogs, 3 miles to beach with trails and playground	(80) $69– $129	CB M/F R	OP T
Jenne Farm Gathering House 360-678-5444 1611 Arnold Rd pets $50/stay http://jennefarm.homestead.com, well-behaved dogs allowed with advance approval only, laundry, nearly 100 year-old 4-bdrm farmhouse sleeps 10, 146 acre working farm, close to beaches	(1) $250	K	
Victorian Rose 360-675-8197 438 E Sea Breeze Way dogs allowed by owner approval and advance reservation only, laundry, fully equipped apartments, on acreage for walking dogs	(3) $600– $675	C K	T

Ocean City, Washington

Blue Pacific Motel & RV Park 360-289-2262 2707 Hwy 109 pets $10/day, 800-453-2262 dogs allowed by manager's approval only, motel units, RV and tent sites, on 9 acres, ¼ mile walk through dunes to the beach	(4) $50– $73	C K	

			# of units) & rates	food & drink	pool, sauna & hot tub
C = coffee CB = continental breakfast F = refrigerator FB = full breakfast	IP = indoor pool K = full kitchen (k) = kitchenette L = lounge M = microwave	OP = outdoor pool R = restaurant S = sauna or steamroom T = spa or hot tub			

Ocean City, Washington (continued)

North Beach Motel 2601 Hwy 109 completely nonsmoking rooms, laundry, 5 minute walk to beach, 2 miles to Ocean City State Park, 5 miles to Ocean Shores	360-289-4116 pets $5/stay	(12) $35– $75	C (k)	
Pacific Sands Resort Motel 2687 Hwy 109 walking area behind building, 10 minutes to beach	360-289-3588 pets $10/day	(9) $40– $60	K	OP
West Winds Resort Motel 2537 Hwy 109 www.wa-accommodations.com/nw/westwinds.htm, creek and 3 acres for walking dogs	360-289-3448 pets $5/day, 800-867-3448	(10) $40– $100	K	

Ocean Park, Washington

Charles Nelson Guest House 26205 Sandridge Rd www.charlesnelsonbandb.com, dogs allowed by advance reservation only, completely nonsmoking, open field, 1 mile to beach, 5 miles to walking trail	360-665-3016 888-862-9756	(3) call for rates	FB	
Coastal Cottages of Ocean Park 1511 264th Pl coastalcottages@webtv.net fireplaces, picnic area, 5 minute walk to beach	360-665-4658 800-200-0424 pets $5/stay	(4) $65– $75	C K	
Harbor View Motel 3204 281st St www.harborviewmotel.net, rooms and 1-bdrm cottage, courtyard setting near bayfront, open field	360-665-4959 pets $3/day	(7) $50– $75	K	
Ocean Park Resort 25904 R St www.opresort.com motel rooms, RV and tent sites, 4 blocks to ocean	360-665-4585 800-835-4634 pets $7/day	(12) $55– $83	C K M/F	OP T

Oceanfront Getaways on Long Beach 360-665-3633 www.willapabay.org/~beachcom refundable deposit completely nonsmoking 2 to 5-bdrm vacation homes sleep 19, laundry, beach access for off-leash walking	(5) $105– $400	K	T
Paulson's Play House 503-861-2288, 800-535-8767 27301 I St pets $5/day epaulson@lektro.com, dogs allowed with owner approval only, completely nonsmoking 2-bdrm 1-bath mobile home, laundry, easy beach access	(1) $95– $125	K	
Shakti Cove Cottages 360-665-4000 25301 Park Ave each pet $5/day www.shakticove.com, on 3 acres with 5 minute walk to beach through the dunes, 8 miles to state park	(10) $70– $85	K	
Sunset View Resort 360-665-4494 25517 Park Ave 800-272-9199 www.washingtoncoast.net pets $15/stay rooms, studios, 2-bdrm suites, fireplaces, laundry, ocean views, on 6½ landscaped acres, 400 ft to beach	(52) $70– $187	C K	S T
Westgate Motor & Trailer Court 360-665-4211 20803 Pacific Hwy 6 fully equipped cabins, RV sites, easy beach access	(46) $55– $65	K	

Ocean Shores, Washington

At the Beach Family Vacation Rentals 360-289-4297 659 Ocean Shores Blvd NW 800-303-4297 www.ricksbeachhouses.com each pet $10/day beachfront vacation homes sleep 2 to 16, laundry, beach access for walking dogs	(14) $125– $349	K	T
Chalet Village 360-289-4297 659 Ocean Shores Blvd NW 800-303-4297 www.ricksbeachhouses.com each pet $10/day beachfront chalets sleep 2 to 6, beach access for walking dogs	(9) $85– $145	K	
Discovery Inn 360-289-3371 1031 Discovery Ave SE 800-882-8821 www.oceanshores.com pets $10/day nonsmoking rooms, laundry, open walking area, close to bay shoreline and Interpretive Center	(22) $48– $93	C K	OP T

		(# of units) & rates	food & drink	pool, sauna & hot tub

C = coffee
CB = continental
   breakfast
F = refrigerator
FB = full breakfast
	IP = indoor pool
	K = full kitchen
	(k) = kitchenette
	L = lounge
	M = microwave
		OP = outdoor pool
		R = restaurant
		S = sauna or
		   steamroom
		T = spa or hot tub		

Ocean Shores, Washington (continued)

Grey Gull Motel 360-289-3381, 800-562-9712 651 Ocean Shores Blvd SW pets $10/stay www.thegreygull.com, nonsmoking rooms, laundry, beachfront units with kitchens and gas fireplaces		(37) $80– $335	C K	OP S T
Linde's Landing Hotel 360-289-3323, 800-448-2433 648 Ocean Shores Blvd NW pets $20/stay www.lindeslanding.com, nonsmoking rooms and suites sleep 8, grassy area, across street to beach		(64) $89– $209	C K	IP S
Nautilus Hotel 360-289-2722, 800-221-4541 835 Ocean Shores Blvd NW pets $20/stay www.nautiluscondos.com, fully equipped 1-bdrm condos, 1 to 2 dogs only, designated pet rest area, trail to beach, pet towels provided		(24) $70– $150	C K	T
Oasis Motel 360-289-2350, 800-290-2899 686 Ocean Shores Blvd NW pets $10/day nonsmoking rooms, next to golf course and beach		(18) $39– $49	K	
Ocean Shores Motel 360-289-3351 681 Ocean Shores Blvd NW 800-464-2526 www.thesandsonline.com pets $10/day nonsmoking rooms, lawn, in-room spa, trail to beach		(40) $49– $130	CB (k) M/F	
Ocean Shores Reservations 360-289-2430 899 Point Brown Ave NW 800-562-8612 www.oceanshoresreservation.com pets $10–20/day nonsmoking rooms, condos, and vacation homes sleep 2 to 16, laundry, easy beach access		(60) $119– $250	C K	IP T
Ocean Shores Resort Homes 360-289-4416 164 Ocean Shores Blvd NW 800-927-6394 www.oceanbeachfronthomes.com pets $10/day rustic cabins to contemporary homes and condos, laundry, easy beach access		(15) $70– $350	K	T

Ocean Shores Vacation Rentals 759 Ocean Shores Blvd NW www.myoceanshores.com condo and house sleep 8, beach access	360-289-3211 877-319-3211 pets $10/day	(2) $89– $200	K	T
Polynesian Oceanfront Resort 615 Ocean Shores Blvd NW www.thepolynesian.com game room, laundry, walking area, close to park	360-289-3361 800-562-4836 pets $15/day	(71) $59– $119	CB (k) R/L	IP S T
Royal Pacific Motel & Sands Resort 801 Ocean Shores Blvd NW www.thesandsonline.com side-by-side beachfront facilities, beach and dunes for walking dogs	360-289-2444 800-841-4001 pets $10/day	(196) $48– $209	CB K	IP OP T
Silver King Motel 1070 Discovery Ave SE nonsmoking rooms, walking trail to bird sanctuary, close to bayfront	360-289-3386, 800-562-6001 pets $10/day	(50) $35– $90	C K	
Silver Waves Inn B & B 982 Point Brown Ave SE www.silverwavesbandb.com dogs allowed in 1-bdrm nonsmoking cottage only, open walking area, 5 minute walk to state park	360-289-2490 888-257-0894 pets $10/stay	(5) $85– $95	FB (k)	
Upper Deck Suites Inn 668 Ocean Shores Blvd NW www.oceanshores.org 1 to 2-bdrm nonsmoking suites, dogs allowed with owner's approval only, in-room spa, laundry, easy beach access for walking dogs	360-289-4555	(6) $95– $185	K	
Westerly Motel 870 Ocean Shores Blvd NW designated pet walking area, 2 blocks to beach	360-289-3711, 800-319-3711 pets $10/stay	(8) $40– $70	K	

Odessa, Washington

Odessa Motel 609 E First St www.deutschesfestmotel.com, rooms to 2-bdrm suites, close to public swimming pool and spa, walking trail along creek	509-982-2412 pets $5/day	(12) $44– $70	C (k) M/F	

C = coffee IP = indoor pool OP = outdoor pool CB = continental K = full kitchen R = restaurant breakfast (k) = kitchenette S = sauna or F = refrigerator L = lounge steamroom FB = full breakfast M = microwave T = spa or hot tub	(# of units) & rates	food & drink	pool, sauna & hot tub

Okanogan, Washington

Cedars Inn 509-422-6431 1 Appleway (Junction Hwy 97 & Hwy 20)pets $5/day www.cedarshotels.com, nonsmoking rooms, open area for walking dogs, ¼ mile to public park	(78) $45– $57	C K R/L	OP
Ponderosa Motor Lodge 509-422-0400, 800-732-6702 1034 2nd Ave S edliz@televar.com nonsmoking rooms, 1½ blocks to park and riverfront	(25) $39– $50	(k) M/F R	OP
U & I Rivers Edge Motel 509-422-2920, 800-422-2920 838 2nd Ave N pacos19@hotmail.com riverfront yard, picnic area, BBQ, 1 block to park	(9) $35– $59	C (k) M/F	

Olalla, Washington

Childs' House B & B 253-857-4252, 800-250-4954 8331 SE Willock Rd www.childshouse.com 5 acres, dogs allowed by advance reservation only	(3) $70– $100	FB	
Still Waters B & B 253-857-5111 13202 Olympic Dr SE pets $10/day www.mystillwaters.com, dogs allowed with owner's approval only, on 3 country acres, next to state land	(3) $65– $75	FB	T

Olympia, Washington

Best Western Aladdin Motor Inn 360-352-7200 900 Capitol Way S 800-367-7771 www.bestwesternwashington.com pets $5/day nonsmoking rooms, laundry, small dogs allowed for 1 night only, 2 blocks to public park, 4 blocks to lake	(99) $64– $200	C M/F R/L	OP T
Lighthouse Bungalow 360-754-0389 1215 East Bay Dr NE www.lighthousebungalow.com nonsmoking 1920s bungalow on Budd Inlet, 4-bdrm 4-bath unit sleeps 10, 1-bdrm 1-bath sleeps 2, dogs allowed by advance reservation only, walking trails	(2) $100– $350	K	

Phoenix Inn 415 Capitol Way N www.phoenixinnsuites.com dogs under 25 lbs allowed in 3 rooms only, 24 hour pool, grassy area and boardwalk for walking dogs	360-570-0555 877-570-0555 pets $25/stay	(102) $89– $109	CB M/F	IP T
Puget View Guesthouse B & B 7924 61st Ave NE www.bbonline.com/wa/pugetview, dogs allowed by advance approval only, 1-bdrm beachfront cottage, next to 100 acre state park	360-413-9474 pets $10/day	(1) $99– $129	CB (k) M/F	
Ramada Inn-Governor House 621 Capitol Way S www.ramada.com nonsmoking rooms, across street from public park	360-352-7700 800-272-6232 pets $50/stay	(123) $58– $140	C M/F R	OP T
Tumwater GuestHouse Int'l Inn 1600 74th Ave SW www.guesthouseintl.com, rooms and 1-bdrm suites, exercise room, in-room spa, quiet road for walking dogs, 5 minute drive to public park	360-943-5040 each pet $15/day	(59) $58– $168	CB K M/F	IP T
WestCoast Hotel 2300 Evergreen Park Dr SW www.westcoasthotels.com laundry, lawn, ½ mile to Capital Lake	360-943-4000 866-896-4000 pets $45/stay	(191) $89– $120	C R/L	OP T

Omak, Washington

Leisure Village Motel 630 Okoma Dr nonsmoking rooms, open area for walking dogs, next to school field and track	509-826-4442 pets $5/stay	(32) $35– $66	C M/F	IP T
Motel Nicholas 527 E Grape St nonsmoking rooms, lawn and open field for walking dogs, 2 blocks to public park	509-826-4611, 800-404-4611 pets $3/day	(21) $30– $46	C M/F	
Omak Inn 912 Koala Ave small dogs only, nonsmoking rooms, laundry, country road for walking dogs	509-826-3822, 800-204-4800 pets $10/stay	(49) $60– $120	CB M/F	IP T

C = coffee CB = continental breakfast F = refrigerator FB = full breakfast	IP = indoor pool K = full kitchen (k) = kitchenette L = lounge M = microwave	OP = outdoor pool R = restaurant S = sauna or steamroom T = spa or hot tub	(# of units) & rates	food & drink	pool, sauna & hot tub

Omak, Washington (continued)

Omak Rodeway Inn & Suites 509-826-0400 122 N Main St pets $5/stay, 888-700-6625 www.choicehotels.com, in-room spa, nonsmoking rooms, laundry, several public parks within 3 blocks	(61) $35– $70	CB (k)	OP
Royal Motel 509-826-5715, 866-504-7155 514 E Riverside Dr refundable pet deposit picnic area, 2 blocks to riverside walking trail, ½ mile to public park	(10) $35– $50	C K M/F	
Stampede Motel 509-826-1161 215 W 4th St 800-639-1161 next to small public park	(14) $30– $45	C (k) M/F	

Oroville, Washington

Camaray Motel 509-476-3684 1320 Main St nonsmoking rooms, open area for walking dogs, ½ block to public park	(26) $33– $60	C M/F	OP
Red Apple Inn 509-476-3694 1815 Main St adult dogs only, nonsmoking rooms, riverfront picnic area, ¼ mile to park with swimming beach	(37) $28– $48	C (k)	

Othello, Washington

Best Western Lincoln Inn 509-488-5671 1020 E Cedar St 800-240-7865 www.bestwesternwashington.com pets $10/day laundry, exercise room, ½ block to public park, bird cleaning station for hunters	(48) $59– $115	CB K	OP S
Cabana Motel 509-488-2605 665 E Windsor St 800-442-4581 dogs allowed by manager's approval only, open field for walking dogs, across street from public park	(56) $32– $90	C (k) M/F	OP T

Pacific Beach, Washington

Beach Avenue B & B 47 Beach Ave www.pacificbeachwa.com (look under Lodging), 1-bdrm nonsmoking cottages sleep 5, fully equipped kitchens, 200 feet to beach, next to state park	360-276-4727 pets $5/day	(4) $95– $115	C K	
Pacific Beach Inn 12 First St S www.pbinn.com, small dogs allowed by manager's approval only, next to beach for walking dogs	360-276-4433 pets $10/day	(12) $75– $95	C K	
Sand Dollar Inn 53 Central Ave nonsmoking rooms and cottages sleep 2 to 6, laundry, across road from public beach	360-276-4525 pets $10/day	(18) $45– $150	C K	T
Sandpiper Beach Resort 4159 Hwy 109 www.mysandpiper.com nonsmoking oceanfront studios to 3-bdrm suites and cottages sleep up to 12, in-room spa, laundry, beach access for walking dogs	360-276-4580 800-567-4737 pets $10/day	(31) $65– $210	(k)	

Packwood, Washington

Hotel Packwood 104 Main St dogs allowed with owner's approval only, completely nonsmoking, lawn, public park across street	360-494-5431	(9) $29– $49	C	
Mountain View Lodge 13163 Hwy 12 www.mtvlodge.com, rustic lodge units sleep up to 9, wooded area for walking dogs, close to hiking trails, 28 miles to Mt St Helens Visitor Center	360-494-5555 each pet $5/day	(21) $37– $100	C K	OP T
Tatoosh Meadows Resort www.tmcproperties.com completely nonsmoking suites and cabins near Mt Rainier and White Pass, pets $25/stay, riverfront trails and meadow for walking dogs	360-494-2311 800-294-2311	(25) $125– $350	C K M/F	T

C = coffee IP = indoor pool OP = outdoor pool CB = continental K = full kitchen R = restaurant breakfast (k) = kitchenette S = sauna or F = refrigerator L = lounge steamroom FB = full breakfast M = microwave T = spa or hot tub	(# of units) & rates	food & drink	pool, sauna & hot tub

Pasco, Washington

Airport Motel 509-545-1460 2532 N 4th Ave pets $5/stay nonsmoking rooms, laundry, rocky area for walking dogs, ½ mile to public park	(42) $30– $44	C K	OP
Budget Inn 509-546-2010 1520 N Oregon Ave 877-800-2010 laundry, open area for walking dogs, 1 mile to park	(104) $37– $50	C M	OP
King City Truck Stop 509-547-3475 2100 E Hillsboro St refundable pet deposit nonsmoking rooms, laundry, picnic area, lawn for walking dogs, 10 minute drive to Columbia Park	(36) $38– $70	C R/L	
Sage 'n' Sun Motel 509-547-2451 1232 S 10th Ave pets $10/day laundry, next to cable bridge and recreational area for walking dogs	(32) $38– $55	C (k)	OP
Sleep Inn 509-545-9554, 800-753-3746 9930 Bedford St pets $15/stay nonsmoking rooms, in-room spa, laundry, open area for walking dogs, 5 minute walk to riverfront park	(62) $55– $100	CB M/F	IP T
Starlite Motel 509-547-7531 2634 N 4th Ave each pet $5/day nonsmoking rooms, open area for walking dogs	(18) $28– $45	K	
WestCoast Hotel 509-547-070 2525 N 20th Ave 800-325-4000 www.westcoasthotels.com, across street from college campus and open area for walking dogs, 24 hour restaurant, fitness center, shuttle to riverside walking/biking path	(279) $79– $135	C R/L	OP T

Pateros, Washington

Lake Pateros Motor Inn 509-923-2203, 866-444-1985 115 S Lake Shore Dr pets $5/day boat rentals, picnic tables, BBQ, RV and tent sites, next to state park	(30) $67– $88	CB M/F	OP

Peshastin, Washington

Alpine Chalets 509-548-5674 3601 Allen Ln A-frame cabins, laundry, walking path to Peshastin River, 1 mile to dog-friendly Ingalls Creek trail	(2) $100– $125	K	OP
Timberline Motel 509-548-7415 8284 Hwy 2 open field and woods for walking dogs	(6) $45– $75	K	

Pomeroy, Washington

Pioneer Motel 509-843-1559 1201 Main St open field for walking dogs, close to trails and public park with swimming pool	(13) $40– $60	C (k) M/F	

Port Angeles, Washington

Chinook Motel 360-452-2336 1414 E 1st St pets $5/day laundry, grassy area, 9 blocks to waterfront	(52) $30– $70	K	
Flagstone Motel 360-457-9494 415 E 1st St 888-304-3465 small dogs only, nonsmoking rooms, small grassy area for walking dogs, 2½ blocks to public park	(45) $63– $84	C M/F	
Indian Valley Motel & RV Park 360-928-3266 235471 Hwy 101 www.grannyscafe.com/motel.html 1 small dog only, completely nonsmoking, open area for walking dogs, 5 minute drive to national park	(8) $41– $46	R	
Lake Crescent Lodge 360-928-3211 416 Lake Crescent Rd pets $13/day dogs allowed in nonsmoking cottages only, area for walking dogs, next to national park	(52) $56– $180	R/L	

C = coffee CB = continental breakfast F = refrigerator FB = full breakfast	IP = indoor pool K = full kitchen (k) = kitchenette L = lounge M = microwave	OP = outdoor pool R = restaurant S = sauna or steamroom T = spa or hot tub	# of units) & rates	food & drink	pool, sauna & hot tub

Port Angeles, Washington (continued)

Log Cabin Resort 360-928-3325 3183 E Beach Rd refundable pet deposit www.logcabinresort.net, laundry, cabins, some with kitchenettes, RV and tent sites, 23 waterfront acres	(28) $60– $150	(k) R/L	
Northwest Manor B & B 360-452-5839 1320 Marie View St pets $10/day, 888-229-7052 completely nonsmoking, private deck, open field for walking dogs, 6 blocks to waterfront trail	(2) $90– $100	FB	
Ocean Crest B & B 360-452-4832, 877-413-2169 402 South M St www.northolympic.com/oceancrest dogs allowed by advance reservation only, fenced yard, public park across street, beach access	(3) $65– $85	FB	
Pond Motel 360-452-8422 1425 W Hwy 101 pets $6/day wooded area for walking dogs	(10) $55	K	
Portside Inn 360-452-4015 1510 E Front St refundable pet deposit www.portsideinn.com, nonsmoking rooms, laundry, open field for walking dogs, 1 mile to walking trail	(109) $49– $129	CB M/F	OP T
Red Lion Hotel 360-452-9215, 800-733-5466 221 N Lincoln St pets $10/day www.redlion.com, nonsmoking rooms, laundry, waterfront walking trail, 1 block from ferry	(186) $65– $155	C M/F R/L	OP T
Riviera Inn 360-417-3955, 877-766-8350 535 E Front St each pet $10/day small dogs allowed by advance approval only, nonsmoking rooms, walking area, 5 blocks to ferry	(38) $49– $90	CB M/F	S
Super 8 Motel 360-452-8401 2104 E 1st St 800-800-8000 www.super8.com refundable pet deposit laundry, lawn, short drive to public parks	(62) $60– $94	C	

Uptown Inn 101 E 2nd St www.uptowninn.com nonsmoking rooms, dogs under 20 lbs only, field for walking dogs, 3 blocks to public swimming pool, 4 blocks to walking trail	360-457-9434 800-858-3812 pets $10/day	(35) $69– $139	CB K	T
Whiskey Creek Beach 1385 Whiskey Creek Beach Rd www.whiskey-creek-beach.com, RV and tent sites, rustic cabins (propane, no electricity), beach access	360-928-3489 pets $3/day	(8) $60– $75	K	

Port Ludlow, Washington

The Resort at Ludlow Bay 1 Heron Rd www.ludlowbayresort.com refundable pet deposit completely nonsmoking, dogs allowed in 4 rooms only, in-room spa, waterfront walking trails	360-437-0411 800-732-1239	(37) $149– $549	CB F R/L	IP S T

Port Orchard, Washington

Days Inn 220 Bravo Ter www.daysinn.com each pet $10/day small dogs only, nonsmoking rooms, laundry, open area across street for walking dogs, 5 miles to park	360-895-7818 800-231-5592	(55) $69– $119	CB M/F	IP T
Vista Motel 1090 Bethel Ave nonsmoking rooms, school field for walking dogs	360-876-8046 pets $10/stay	(28) $50– $62	C	

Port Townsend, Washington

Aladdin Motor Inn 360-385-3747, 800-281-3747 2333 Washington St pets $7/day nonsmoking rooms, laundry, beachfront location for walking dogs		(30) $75– $85	CB M/F	
Annapurna Center for Self-Healing 538 Adams St www.theannapurna.com pets $10/stay B&B, reflexology, massage, cleansing diet and yoga, far infrared detoxifying sauna, near park and beach	360-385-2909 800-868-2662	(6) $95– $165	FB	S T

C = coffee, IP = indoor pool, OP = outdoor pool, CB = continental breakfast, K = full kitchen, R = restaurant, (k) = kitchenette, S = sauna or steamroom, F = refrigerator, L = lounge, FB = full breakfast, M = microwave, T = spa or hot tub	(# of units) & rates	food & drink	pool, sauna & hot tub

Port Townsend, Washington

Big Red Barn 360-385-4837 309 V St pets $30/stay www.bigredbarngetaway.com, 1-bdrm "romantic getaway," jacuzzi tub, breakfast basket, dog treats, fenced yard, pond, 1 block to Fort Worden Park	(1) $135	CB M/F	
Bishop Victorian Hotel 360-385-6122, 800-824-4738 714 Washington St pets $15/day www.rainshadowproperties.com, breakfast basket, lawn, gardens, 1 block to waterfront and trails	(15) $89– $199	CB (k)	
Harborside Inn 360-385-7909, 800-942-5960 330 Benedict St pets $5/day www.ptguide.com, nonsmoking rooms, in-room spa, laundry, grassy walking area, 2 blocks to beach	(63) $60– $150	CB (k) M/F	OP T
James G Swan Hotel 360-385-1718 216 Monroe St 800-776-1718 www.rainshadowproperties.com pets $15/day nonsmoking studio cottages, across street to beach	(9) $85– $475	C M/F	
Palace Hotel 360-385-0773 1004 Water St 800-962-0741 www.olympus.net/palace pets $10/stay in-room spa, ½ block to beach for walking dogs	(17) $59– $159	CB K	
Port Townsend Inn 360-385-2211 2020 Washington St 800-216-4985 www.porttownsendinn.com pets $10/stay single dog under 25 lbs allowed in smoking rooms only, in-room spa, small gravel pet walking area, 7 blocks to small lake and walking path	(36) $53– $178	CB (k)	IP T
Tides Inn 360-385-0595, 800-822-8696 1807 Water St pets $10/stay www.tides-inn.com, dogs allowed in 2 rooms only, beachfront walking area	(45) $85– $125	CB	

Valley View Motel 360-385-1666, 800-280-1666 162 Hwy 20 pets $20/stay nonsmoking rooms, on 75 acres for walking dogs, 1 mile to walking trails along Lake Anderson	(6) $50– $65	C K	

Poulsbo, Washington

Brauer Cove Guest House 360-779-4153 16709 Brauer Rd www.brauercove.com 2-bdrm apartment, kitchen stocked with breakfast provisions, yard and quiet neighborhood for walking dogs	(1) $125	K	
Holiday Inn Express 360-697-2119 19801 7th Ave NE each pet $10/day nonsmoking rooms, in-room spa, picnic tables, grassy area behind building for walking dogs, 7 blocks to marina, 4 blocks to school field and track	(63) $109– $149	CB (k) M/F	T
Poulsbo Inn 360-779-3921 18680 Hwy 305 NE 800-597-5151 www.poulsboinn.com each pet $10/day nonsmoking rooms, laundry, exercise room, grassy walking area, 6 blocks to waterfront park and trails	(71) $90– $113	CB K	OP T

Prosser, Washington

Barn Motor Inn 509-786-2121 490 Wine Country Rd pets $10/stay nonsmoking rooms, small dogs only, in-room spa, laundry, gravel walking area, 2 blocks to trail	(30) $45– $110	F R	OP
Best Western Prosser Inn 509-786-7977 225 Merlot Dr 800-688-2192 www.bestwesternwashington.com pets $10/day nonsmoking rooms, laundry, ½ block to walking path	(49) $79– $89	CB M	OP T
Prosser Motel 509-786-2555 1206 Wine Country Rd pets $3/day nonsmoking rooms, ¼ mile to walking trails	(16) $33– $48	C F	

C = coffee　　IP = indoor pool　　OP = outdoor pool　CB = continental　K = full kitchen　R = restaurant　breakfast　(k) = kitchenette　S = sauna or　F = refrigerator　L = lounge　　steamroom　FB = full breakfast　M = microwave　T = spa or hot tub	(# of units) & rates	food & drink	pool, sauna & hot tub

Pullman, Washington

Carstens B & B　　　　　　　509-332-6162　251 Flat Rd　　completely nonsmoking, laundry,　dog run in yard, quiet country road for walking dogs　www.pullman-wa.com/housing/carstens.htm	(3) $55	FB	T
Country B & B　　　　　　　509-334-4453　2701 Staley Rd　RV sites, country roads and fields for walking dogs	(4) $50–$100	CB M/F	T
Hawthorn Inn & Suites　　　509-332-0928　928 NW Olsen St　　www.hawthorn.com　nonsmoking rooms, laundry, near WSU Veterinary　Hospital (ask about "patient rates"), lawn, field for　walking dogs, 2 blocks to public park, 24 hour pool	(59) $79–$89	FB M/F R/L	IP S T
Holiday Inn Express　　　　509-334-4437　1190 SE Bishop Blvd　nonsmoking rooms, laundry,　¼ mile to walking trail, ½ mile to public park	(130) $84–$114	CB M/F	IP T
Manor Lodge Motel　　　　　509-334-2511　455 SE Paradise St　　pets $5–$10/day　nonsmoking rooms, open lot, 2 blocks to public park	(31) $39–$64	C K M/F	
Nendels Inn　　509-332-2646, 888-619-1202　915 E Main St　　　　pets $15/day　nonsmoking rooms, next to public park for walking　dogs, across street from college campus	(59) $29–$80	CB K R	
Quality Inn　　　　　　　　509-332-0500　1400 SE Bishop Blvd　　800-669-3212　nonsmoking rooms, laundry, paved walking trail	(66) $67–$75	CB	OP S T

Puyallup, Washington

Best Western Park Plaza　253-848-1500, 800-528-1234　620 S Hill Park Dr　　　pets $15/stay　www.bestwesternparkplaza.com, nonsmoking　rooms, pet walking area, 2 miles to public parks	(100) $107–$149	CB M/F	OP T

Holiday Inn Express 253-848-4900, 800-465-4329 812 S Hill Park Dr pets $15/stay www.hiexpress.com, nonsmoking rooms, grassy walking area, 5 minute drive to Bradley Lake Park	(96) $102– $112	CB M/F	IP T
Motel Puyallup 253-845-8825, 800-921-2700 1412 S Meridian St pets $10/day nonsmoking rooms, laundry, gravel area and field for walking dogs, 3 blocks to public park	(63) $44– $87	CB K	
Northwest Motor Inn 253-841-2600, 800-845-9490 1409 S Meridian St pets $5/day undeveloped area for walking dogs, 4 blocks to park	(52) $44– $80	CB K	T

Quilcene, Washington

Maple Grove Motel 360-765-3410 61 Maple Grove Rd pets $10/day nonsmoking rooms, next to national forest and trails for walking dogs, accommodations for horses will be available in Summer 2003 (please call to confirm)	(12) $50– $60	K	

Quinault, Washington

Lake Quinault Lodge 360-288-2900, 800-562-6672 345 S Shore Rd · pets $10/day www.visitlakequinault.com, historic lakeside lodge, dogs allowed in boathouse rooms only, game room, gift shop, national forest and walking trails	(92) $78– $180	C R	IP S

Quincy, Washington

Sundowner Motel 509-787-3587 414 F St SE pets $5/day gravel area for walking dogs, 2 blocks to public park	(24) $33– $71	C K	OP
Traditional Inns 509-787-3525 500 F St SW www.traditionalinns.com nonsmoking rooms, open area for walking dogs, next to paved walking trail	(24) $41– $81	C M/F	
Villager Inn Motel 509-787-3515 711 2nd Ave SW pets $10/stay dogs allowed in smoking rooms only, pet walking area in RV park, 7 blocks to city park	(21) $30– $64	C (k)	OP

C = coffee IP = indoor pool OP = outdoor pool CB = continental K = full kitchen R = restaurant breakfast (k) = kitchenette S = sauna or F = refrigerator L = lounge steamroom FB = full breakfast M = microwave T = spa or hot tub	# of units) & rates	food & drink	pool, sauna & hot tub

Randle, Washington

Mount Adams Motel 360-497-7007 9514 Hwy 12 pets $10/stay laundry, RV and tent sites, rec room, walking trails	(16) $35– $45	(k) M/F	
Randle Motel 360-497-5346 9780 Hwy 12 dogs allowed in tile-floored units only, 36 miles to Mt St Helens Viewpoint	(10) $35– $45	(k)	
Tall Timber Motel 360-497-2991 10023 Hwy 12 pets $10/day next to football field, 5 minute drive to lakes and walking trails	(6) $35– $50	F	
Woodland Motel 360-494-6766 11890 Hwy 12 (11 miles east of Randle) completely nonsmoking rooms, lawn and woods for walking dogs, close to national forest and trails	(6) $40– $60	C K M/F	

Raymond, Washington

Maunu Mountcastle Motel 360-942-5571 524 3rd St 800-400-5571 large yard, 3 blocks to walking trail, pets $5/day	(26) $40– $60	C K M/F	
Willis Motel 360-942-5313 425 3rd St 2 blocks to river and public parks	(3) $35– $40	K R	

Redmond, Washington

Residence Inn 425-497-9226 7575 164th Ave NE 1 to 2 dogs only, each pet $10/day plus $50 cleaning fee, nonsmoking rooms, walking path	(180) $179	K	

Renton, Washington

TownePlace Suites by Marriott 425-917-2000 300 19th St SW pets $15/day www.towneplacesuites.com, nonsmoking rooms, studios and 2-bdrm suites, BBQ and picnic tables, lawn, short drive to public park	(137) $59– $99	CB K	OP
Travelodge 425-251-9591, 800-578-7878 3700 E Valley Rd each pet $10/day www.travelodge.com, nonsmoking rooms, laundry, lawn and field for walking dogs, across street to park	(129) $50– $100	CB K	T

Republic, Washington

Black Beach Resort 509-775-3989 80 Black Beach Rd each pet $8/stay lakeview cabins, duplexes, studio apartments, RV sites, laundry, grassy area for walking dogs, grocery store and gift shop, party boat rentals	(13) $55– $81	K	
Klondike Motel 509-775-3555, 800-213-2812 150 N Clark St refundable pet deposit dogs allowed by advance reservation only, 4 blocks to Wilderness Park trail	(20) $38– $46	C K	T
Northern Inn 509-775-3371 852 S Clark St 888-801-1068 nonsmoking rooms, in-room spa, 2 blocks to park	(23) $43– $53	CB (k) M/F	
Prospector Inn 509-775-3361, 888-844-6480 979 S Clark Ave each pet $7/day nonsmoking rooms, laundry, 2 blocks to public park	(33) $47– $69	CB M/F	S T

Richland, Washington

Bali Hi Motel 509-943-3101 1201 George Washington Way pets $5/day nonsmoking rooms, laundry, across street from creek, 2 blocks to river and park	(44) $46– $78	CB M/F	OP T
Economy Inn 509-946-6117 515 George Washington Way pets $15/day dogs allowed in smoking rooms only, across street to large public park	(40) $39– $49	CB K M/F	OP

C = coffee IP = indoor pool OP = outdoor pool		
CB = continental K = full kitchen R = restaurant		
breakfast (k) = kitchenette S = sauna or		
F = refrigerator L = lounge steamroom		
FB = full breakfast M = microwave T = spa or hot tub	# of units) & rates	food & drink	pool, sauna & hot tub

Richland, Washington (continued)

Motel 6-Richland/Kennewick 509-783-1250 1751 Fowler St 800-466-8356 www.motel6.com, nonsmoking rooms, designated dogwalking area, laundry, 1 block to riverside park	(93) $39– $46	C M/F	OP
Paragon Suites 509-943-0500, 888-632-5511 2550 Duportail St # M176 each pet $10/day www.paragonsuites.com, nonsmoking 1 to 3-bdrm suites and apartments, most have designated pet walking areas and are close to public parks and trails	(100) $55– $90	K	IP S T
Red Lion Hotel 509-946-7611, 800-733-5466 802 George Washington Way refundable pet deposit www.redlion.com, nonsmoking rooms, weight room, laundry, riverside walking trails and public park	(149) $85– $1350	M/F R/L	OP T
Richland Days Inn 509-943-4611 615 Jadwin Ave refundable pet deposit nonsmoking rooms, city park for walking dogs	(95) $52– $72	CB M/F	OP
Royal Hotel 509-946-4121, 800-635-3980 1515 George Washington Way pets $25/stay www.towerinn.net, nonsmoking rooms, laundry, lawn, gravel area, 3 blocks to riverside walking trail	(195) $79– $99	CB M/F	IP T
Shilo Inn 509-946-4661 50 Comstock St 800-222-2244 www.shiloinns.com each pet $10/day nonsmoking rooms, laundry, pet beds and treats, fitness center, steam room, next to riverside park	(151) $68– $115	FB K M/F R/L	IP S T

Rimrock, Washington

Game Ridge Lodge 509-672-2212, 800-301-9354 27350 Hwy 12 pets $10/day www.gameridge.com, RV sites, motel rooms, cabins with private hot tubs, national forest, river, trails	(14) $65– $185	C K	OP T

Ritzville, Washington

Colwell Motor Inn 509-659-1620, 800-341-8000 501 W 1st Ave pets $4/day in-room spa, laundry, small pet walking area, 1 mile to city park	(25) $40– $65	C M/F	OP S
Empire Motel 509-659-1030 101 W 1st Ave laundry, vacant lot for walking dogs, ½ mile to park	(19) $30– $52	C M/F	
La Quinta Inn & Suites 509-659-1007, 800-531-5900 1513 S Smittys Blvd www.laquinta.com nonsmoking rooms, laundry, RV sites, large lawn, across street to public park	(54) $49– $149	CB (k)	OP T
Top Hat Motel 509-659-1100 210 E 1st Ave pets $5/day small to medium dogs allowed with manager's approval only, designated pet walking area	(11) $38– $60	CB F	
Westside Motor Inn 509-659-1164, 800-559-1164 407 W 1st Ave refundable pet deposit walking path across street, 5 minute drive to public park and swimming pool	(11) $26– $46	C M/F	

Rockport, Washington

A Cab in the Woods 360-873-4106 9303 Dandy Pl www.cabinwoods.com cabins sleep 4, riverside walking trails	(5) $75– $85	K	
Clark's Skagit River Resort 360-873-2250 58468 Clark Cabin Rd 800-273-2606 www.northcascades.com pets $10/day 1 to 2 well-behaved dogs only, 1 to 3-bdrm travel trailers and cabins sleep up to 7, also B & B lodge, RV sites, resident rabbits and "bunny-hole" golf, riverside walking trails	(40) $49– $109	C (k) R	
Totem Trail Motel 360-873-4535 57627 Hwy 20 pets $10/stay www.totemtrail.com, dogs allowed at owner's discretion only, completely nonsmoking, BBQ, picnic tables, basketball court, walking trails	(8) $40– $65	C F	

C = coffee IP = indoor pool OP = outdoor pool CB = continental K = full kitchen R = restaurant breakfast (k) = kitchenette S = sauna or F = refrigerator L = lounge steamroom FB = full breakfast M = microwave T = spa or hot tub	# of units) & rates	food & drink	pool, sauna & hot tub

Roslyn, Washington

Harry's Inn 509-649-2551 105½ Pennsylvania Ave theme-decorated studio apartments, 1 block to walking trail on old railroad bed	(4) $65– $75	CB K	
Last Resort 509-649-2222 14254 Salmon La Sac Rd each pet $5/day dogs allowed in smoking rooms only, RV sites, walking trails near lake	(12) $45	F R	
Roslyn Inns 509-649-2936 5th St 3 separate inns sleep 5, 15, or 24 respectively, fully equipped kitchens, picnic tables, BBQ, national forest, walking trails, 3 miles to lake	(3) $130– $290	K	

Salkum, Washington

White Spot Motel 360-985-2737 2527 Hwy 12 RV sites, walking trails	(6) $37– $42	K	

SeaTac, Washington

Mini-Rate Motel 206-824-6930 20620 International Blvd 800-426-5060 nonsmoking rooms, 3 blocks to public park, 5 minute drive to waterfront	(50) $42– $67	C K	
SeaTac Skyway Inn 206-878-3310, 800-872-0202 20045 International Blvd pets $10/stay small dogs only, in-room spa, 2 blocks to public park	(58) $54– $119	CB	

Seattle, Washington

Ace Hotel 206-448-4721 2423 1st Ave www.theacehotel.com nonsmoking rooms, guest pass to athletic club, close to public park	(30) $65– $175	C F	

Airport Plaza Hotel 206-433-0400, 877-433-0400 18601 International Blvd pets $15/day laundry, gravel walking area, 6 blocks to public park	(123) $50– $85	CB	
Alexis Hotel 206-624-4844, 800-945-2240 1007 1st Ave www.alexishotel.com complimentary wine hour, exercise room, in-room spa, pet bowls and treats, dogwalking service, 2 blocks to waterfront, 7 blocks to public park	(109) $195– $395	C K R/L	S T
Aurora Seafair Inn 206-524-3600, 800-445-9297 9100 Aurora Ave N each pet $5/day in-room spa, laundry, gravel area, 10 blocks to lakeside public park	(55) $52– $85	C K	
Best Western Evergreen Inn 206-361-3700 13700 Aurora Ave N 800-213-6308 www.evergreenbestwestern.com, dogs allowed at manager's discretion only, nonsmoking rooms, laundry, exercise room, residential streets for walking dogs, 1½ miles to off-leash park	(71) $72– $150	CB K F	S T
Bridge Motel 206-632-7835 3650 Bridge Way N refundable pet deposit open area for walking dogs, 10 minute walk to park	(13) $40– $65		
Crowne Plaza Hotel 206-464-1980 1113 6th Ave 800-521-2762 www.crowneplazaseattle.com pets $50/stay nonsmoking rooms, laundry, exercise room, next to public park	(415) $109– $280	C R/L	
Days Inn-Town Center 206-448-3434, 800-329-7466 2205 7th Ave www.daysinntowncenter.com nonsmoking rooms, ½ mile to public park	(91) $69– $139	R	
Dibble House B & B 206-783-0320 7301 Dibble Ave NW suvyqgue1@aol.com completely nonsmoking, fenced back yard, close to zoo and public park with off-leash area	(5) $55– $65	FB	
Doubletree Hotel-Seattle Airport 206-246-8600 18740 International Blvd 800-222-8733 www.doubletree.com, nonsmoking rooms, grassy area for walking dogs, 1 block to lakeside park	(850) $79– $159	C F R/L	OP T

C = coffee IP = indoor pool OP = outdoor pool CB = continental K = full kitchen R = restaurant breakfast (k) = kitchenette S = sauna or F = refrigerator L = lounge steamroom FB = full breakfast M = microwave T = spa or hot tub	# of units) & rates	food & drink	pool, sauna & hot tub

Seattle, Washington (continued)

Econo Lodge-SeaTac 206-824-1350, 800-223-4476 19225 International Blvd pets $10/day www.econolodge.com, nonsmoking rooms, across street from lakeside park for walking dogs	(97) $59– $99	CB (k) M/F R/L	
Four Seasons Olympic Hotel 206-621-1700 411 University St 800-223-8772 www.fourseasons.com, dogs under 15 lbs only, nonsmoking rooms, lawn areas for walking dogs, 5 minute walk to public park	(450) $295– $1100	CB M/F R/L	IP S T
Georgian Motel 206-524-1004 8801 Aurora Ave N pets $25/stay thehetlend@aol.com, nonsmoking rooms, residential street for walking dogs, 2 miles to large public park	(19) $40– $50	(k) M	
Gypsy Arms B & B 206-547-8194 3628 Palatine Ave N www.gypsyarms.com small dogs allowed by advance approval only, 1908 Victorian home, patio, BBQ, secluded back yard, covered smoking porch, adult rec room, 2 blocks to walking trail, 1 mile to off-leash park	(2) $100– $135	FB	T
Hillside Motel 206-285-7860 2451 Aurora Ave N small dogs only, grassy area for walking dogs	(11) $37– $50	K	
Hilton-Seattle Airport 206-244-4800 17620 International Blvd pets $50/stay www.hilton.com, nonsmoking rooms, fitness center, laundry, grassy area for walking dogs	(396) $134– $199	C F R/L	OP T
Holiday Inn Express Hotel & Suites 206-824-3200 19621 International Blvd 800-465-4329 www.hiexpress.com pets $10/day laundry, exercise room, across street to lakeside area for walking dogs	(171) $89– $139	CB M/F	

Holiday Inn-SeaTac 17338 International Blvd www.holidayinn.com nonsmoking rooms, laundry, exercise room, 24 hour pool, residential streets to walk dogs, 1 mile to park	206-248-1000 800-465-4329 pets $20/day	(259) $109– $129	C R/L	IP T
Homewood Suites by Hilton 206 Western Ave W www.hilton.com nonsmoking rooms, fitness center, laundry, small grassy walking areas, 5 blocks to waterfront park, 4 blocks to Space Needle	206-281-9393 800-225-5466 pets $20/day	(161) $119– $279	FB K	
Hotel Monaco 1101 4th Ave nonsmoking rooms, evening wine hour, in-room spa, laundry, fitness center, guest pass at health club, dogwalking service available, 3 blocks to public park, 6 blocks to waterfront	206-621-1770, 800-945-2240 www.monaco-seattle.com	(189) $195– $725	C R/L	
Hotel Vintage Park 1100 5th Ave nonsmoking rooms, evening wine reception, guest pass to athletic club, short drive to off-leash dog park	206-624-8000, 800-624-4433 www.hotelvintagepark.com	(126) $175– $285	C R/L	
Howard Johnson 2500 Aurora Ave N small lawn for walking dogs, short drive to park	206-284-1900 nonsmoking rooms,	(94) $69– $110	CB K	OP T
La Quinta Downtown Inn & Suites 2224 8th Ave www.laquinta.com nonsmoking rooms, 2 blocks to Denny Park	206-624-6820 800-531-5900 pets $50/stay	(72) $89– $199	CB (k)	S T
La Quinta Inn-SeaTac 2824 S 188th St area for walking dogs, ¼ mile to public park	206-241-5211, 800-531-5900 laundry, exercise room,	(143) $89– $99	CB	OP T
Marriott Seattle SeaTac 3201 S 176th St nonsmoking rooms, residential street to walk dogs	206-241-2000, 800-228-9290 www.marriott.com	(459) $79– $194	C R/L	IP T
Motel 6-SeaTac North 16500 International Blvd nonsmoking rooms, lawn and walking paths	206-246-4101 800-466-8356	(111) $40– $50	C	

C = coffee IP = indoor pool OP = outdoor pool CB = continental K = full kitchen R = restaurant breakfast (k) = kitchenette S = sauna or F = refrigerator L = lounge steamroom FB = full breakfast M = microwave T = spa or hot tub	(# of units) & rates	food & drink	pool, sauna & hot tub

Seattle, Washington (continued)

Motel 6-SeaTac South 206-241-1648, 800-466-8356 18900 47th Ave S www.motel6.com laundry, 2 blocks to public park	(145) $40– $57	C M/F	OP
Motel 6-Seattle South 206-824-9902, 800-466-8356 20651 Military Rd S www.motel6.com nonsmoking rooms, laundry, lawn for walking dogs	(124) $45– $64	C M/F	OP T
Panama Hotel 206-223-9242 605½ S Main St www.panamahotelseattle.com historic hotel, nonsmoking rooms, shared hall baths, laundry, across street from public park and gardens	(100) $60– $70	M R	
Pensione Nichols B & B 206-441-7125, 800-440-7125 1923 1st Ave #300 www.seattle-bed-breakfast.com completely nonsmoking rooms and suites with full kitchens and sitting rooms, 1 block to public park	(12) $90– $195	CB K	
Ramada Inn-Northgate 206-365-0700 2140 N Northgate Way 800-435-0754 www.ramadainnseattle.com, nonsmoking rooms, laundry	(169) $99– $159	CB K R/L	OP T
Red Lion Hotel-Seattle South 206-762-0300 11244 Pacific Hwy S pets $20/stay www.redlion.com, nonsmoking rooms, open field for walking dogs	(118) $59– $119	CB F R/L	OP
Red Roof Inn SeaTac 206-248-0901, 800-733-7663 16838 International Blvd www.redroof.com nonsmoking rooms, laundry, fitness room, lawn and walking paths across street	(152) $50– $80	CB M/F	
Residence Inn by Marriott-Lake Union 206-624-6000 800 Fairview Ave N 800-331-3131 www.residenceinn.com pets $10/day laundry, exercise room, lakeside walking area	(234) $120– $350	CB K	IP

Residence Inn by Marriott-South Seattle 16201 W Valley Hwy 425-226-5500, 800-331-3131 www.residenceinn.com pets $10/day nonsmoking rooms, laundry, 27-mile walking trail	(144) $109– $199	CB K	OP T
Rodeway Inn-SeaTac 206-246-9300, 800-347-9301 2930 S 176th St pets $10/day www.rodeway.com, nonsmoking rooms, laundry, 24 hour free shuttle to airport, lawn for walking dogs, 5 blocks to public park with lake and beach	(59) $40– $70	CB	
Seal's Motel 206-363-9009 12035 Aurora Ave N pets $10/day dogs allowed in smoking rooms only, ¼ mile to park	(40) $45– $55	K	
Shafer-Baillie Mansion 206-322-4654, 800-922-4654 907 14th Ave E pets $10/day small dogs allowed by advance reservation only, completely nonsmoking, lawn for walking dogs, 2 blocks to public park with off-leash area	(13) $95– $195	CB K	
Sorrento Hotel 206-622-6400, 800-426-1265 900 Madison St pets $50/stay www.hotelsorrento.com, nonsmoking rooms, pets must be kept in travel crate when in room, small grassy pet walking area, 10 blocks to public park	(76) $250– $420	C F R/L	
Sun Hill Motel 206-525-1205 8517 Aurora Ave N small dogs only, 15 blocks to lakeside public park	(28) $45– $60	K	
Super 8 Motel-SeaTac 206-433-8188, 800-800-8000 3100 S 192nd St refundable pet deposit www.super8.com, nonsmoking rooms, lawn area, 3 blocks to Angle Lake Park	(119) $69– $85	C	
The Edgewater Hotel 206-728-7000 2411 Alaskan Way Pier 67 800-624-0670 www.edgewaterhotel.com nonsmoking rooms-suites-penthouse on Elliott Bay, 50 yards to Myrtle Edwards Park	(236) $149– $2500	F R/L	
Travelodge by the Space Needle 206-441-7878 200 6th Ave N 800-578-7878 nonsmoking rooms, close to park pets $10/day	(88) $79– $159	CB M/F	OP T

C = coffee IP = indoor pool OP = outdoor pool CB = continental K = full kitchen R = restaurant breakfast (k) = kitchenette S = sauna or F = refrigerator L = lounge steamroom FB = full breakfast M = microwave T = spa or hot tub	(# of units) & rates	food & drink	pool, sauna & hot tub

Seattle, Washington (continued)

Travelodge-SeaTac Airport South 206-241-9292 2900 S 192nd St 800-393-1856 www.travelodge.com pets $20/day nonsmoking rooms, 1 block to Angle Lake Park	(106) $39– $84	CB F	
Travelodge-West Seattle 206-937-9920, 800-578-7878 3512 SW Alaska St pets $35/stay nonsmoking rooms, in-room spa, laundry, across street from YMCA, parking area and residential streets for walking dogs	(49) $49– $89	CB (k) M/F	
University Inn 206-632-5055 4140 Roosevelt Way NE 800-733-3855 www.universityinnseattle.com pets $10/stay nonsmoking facility, close to public parks	(102) $102– $132	CB	OP T
Vagabond Inn 206-441-0400 325 Aurora Ave N 800-522-1555 www.vagabondinn.com pets $10/day nonsmoking rooms, laundry, 10 blocks to park, 2 blocks to Space Needle	(61) $79– $109	CB M/F	OP T
W Seattle Hotel 206-264-6000 1112 4th Ave nonsmoking rooms, exercise room, pet featherbeds and treats, 2 blocks to public park, dogwalking service available	(426) $199– and up	R	
WestCoast Grand Hotel on Fifth Avenue 1415 5th Ave 206-971-8000 www.westcoasthotels.com 800-325-4000 nonsmoking rooms, exercise room, 4 blocks to public park	(297) $155– $195	C F R/L	
WestCoast SeaTac Hotel 206-246-5535, 800-325-4000 18220 International Blvd www.westcoasthotels.com nonsmoking rooms, small grassy areas for walking dogs, 3 blocks to public park	(146) $85– $99	C F R/L	OP S T

Westin Hotel Seattle 206-728-1000, 800-937-8461 1900 5th Ave www.westin.com nonsmoking rooms, 8 blocks to waterfront, 1 mile to public park	(891) $165– $1500	C M/F K R/L	IP T

Seaview, Washington

Bev's Beach Bungalow 360-642-3544 1101 34th St www.pacifier.com/~bevrolfe 440 sq ft studio sleeps 4+, fenced yard, easy beach access through dunes	(1) $60	(k)	
China Beach B & B 360-642-2442, 800-466-1896 Robert Gray Dr www.chinabeachretreat.com dogs allowed by advance arrangement only, historic building, beachfront access for walking dogs	(3) $179– $219	FB	
Rose Cottage B & B 360-642-3254 4714 L St patti@pacifier.com fully equipped cottage, close to walking trails	(1) $65– $85	FB K	
Seaview Coho Motel 360-642-2531, 800-681-8153 3707 Pacific Hwy pets $10/stay nonsmoking rooms, BBQ, picnic area, grassy area for walking dogs, 2 blocks to beach	(13) $35– $110	C K M/F	
Seaview Motel 360-642-2450 3728 Pacific Way www.beachdog.com RV sites, close to park and trails, no fee for 1 dog, each additional dog $5/day, 3 blocks to ocean	(11) $42– $80	C K	
Shelburne Inn B & B 360-642-2442, 800-466-1896 4415 Pacific Way www.theshelburneinn.com dogs allowed by advance arrangement only, historic building, ground floor rooms with private garden entrances, beachfront access for walking dogs	(15) $119– $189	FB R	
Sou'wester Lodge & Cabins 360-642-2542 Beach Access Rd (38th Place) www.souwesterlodge.com, dogs allowed in cabins and antique (1950s) trailers, RV and tent sites, dunes and beach access, musical and theatrical events, and whimsical fireside discussions—including but not limited to Tea 'n' T'ink Tank and T'ink Tank-U	(24) $42– $149	K	

C = coffee IP = indoor pool OP = outdoor pool CB = continental K = full kitchen R = restaurant breakfast (k) = kitchenette S = sauna or F = refrigerator L = lounge steamroom FB = full breakfast M = microwave T = spa or hot tub	(# of units) & rates	food & drink	pool, sauna & hot tub

Sedro Woolley, Washington

| Skagit Motel   360-856-6001, 800-582-9121
1862 Hwy 20   each pet $5/day
nonsmoking rooms, laundry, wooded area for
walking dogs, 1 mile to public park | (46)
$36–
$65 | C
K | |
| Three Rivers Inn   360-855-2626, 800-221-5122
210 Ball St   pets $10/stay
nonsmoking rooms, some with private patios, lawn
and courtyard, 1 block to walking trail | (40)
$69–
$79 | FB
C
M/F
R | OP
T |

Sekiu, Washington

| Bay Motel   360-963-2444
15562 Hwy 112   pets $5/day
across street from beach, ½ mile to county park | (16)
$46–
$84 | C
K | |
| Herb's Motel & Charters   360-963-2346
411 Front St   pets $10/stay
www.herbsmotel.com, across street from beach | (12)
$40–
$90 | K | |

Sequim, Washington

Brigadoon Vacation Rentals 360-683-2255 62 Balmoral Ct www.sequimrentals.com 1 to 3-bdrm nonsmoking vacation homes sleep 2 to 6, most have yards, short drive to river and beach	(2) $95– $225	K	
Dungeness Bay Motel 360-683-3013 140 Marine Dr 888-683-3013 www.dungenessbay.com, 1 dog allowed by advance reservation only, fully equipped kitchens, completely nonsmoking, private beach access	(6) $80– $125	C K	
Econo Lodge 360-683-7113 801 E Washington St 800-488-7113 www.sequimeconolodge.com pets $10/day laundry, miniature golf, field, 5 minute walk to park	(43) $44– $125	CB M/F	

Groveland Cottage B & B 360-683-3565 4861 Sequim Dungeness Way 800-879-8859 www.sequimvalley.com each pet $10–$25/stay in-room spa, ¼ mile to riverside walking trail, ½ mile to beach, vacation homes also available–call for rates	(5) $85– $115	FB	
Ramada Hotel 360-683-1775 1095 E Washington St 800-683-1775 www.sequimramada.com each pet $10/day nonsmoking rooms, laundry, 5 blocks to public park	(60) $59– $129	CB M/F	IP T
Rancho Llamro B & B 360-683-8133 1734 Woodcock Rd completely nonsmoking, on 2¼ acres, fenced yard for walking dogs, 5 minute drive to beaches and walking trails	(2) $75– $85	CB (k) M/F	
Red Ranch Inn 360-683-4195, 800-777-4195 830 W Washington St pets $8/stay www.redranch.com, nonsmoking rooms, open field for walking dogs, 5 minute drive to public park	(55) $45– $100	CB K R/L	
Sequim Bay Lodge 360-683-0691 268522 Hwy 101 800-622-0691 www.sequimbaylodge.com pets $10/day nonsmoking rooms, 17 acres for walking dogs, ½ mile to state park, 1 mile to marina	(54) $63– $149	C M/F R/L	OP
Sequim West Inn & RV Park 360-683-4144 740 W Washington St 800-528-4527 www.olypen.com/swi pets $7–$10/day small dogs only, RV sites, large grassy pet walking area, 1 mile to park	(37) $52– $109	C M/F	
Sundowner Motel 360-683-5532, 800-325-6966 364 W Washington St each pet $5/day www.sequimsundowner.com, dogs under 30 lbs only, grassy area for walking dogs, 5 minute drive to public park and swim center	(33) $35– $99	CB M/F	
Sunset Marine Resort 360-681-4166 40 Buzzard Ridge Rd pets $10/day www.sunsetmarineresort.com, dogs allowed in 2 fully equipped beachfront cabins that sleep up to 6, beach, canoe and kayak rentals, fresh clams	(6) $130– $165	K	

C = coffee
CB = continental
   breakfast
F = refrigerator
FB = full breakfast
	IP = indoor pool
	K = full kitchen
	(k) = kitchenette
	L = lounge
	M = microwave
		OP = outdoor pool
		R = restaurant
		S = sauna or
		   steamroom
		T = spa or hot tub
			(# of units)
			& rates
				food
				& drink
					pool, sauna
					& hot tub

Shelton, Washington

Canal Side Resort 21660 N Hwy 101 www.canalsideresort.com, rooms and fully furnished cabin and trailer sleep 6, RV sites, waterfront walking area, picnic tables, oyster and clam beds, boat launch		360-877-9422 pets $10/stay	(5) $45– $135	C K M/F	
City Center Best Rates Motel 128 E Alder St www.sheltonchamber.org nonsmoking rooms, large grassy area for walking dogs, 5 minute walk to public park and waterfront		360-426-3397 888-771-2378 pets $5/day	(13) $39– $64	C M/F	
Lake Nahwatzel Resort 12900 W Shelton Matlock Rd cabins, RV and tent sites, 2 blocks to lakeside trail		360-426-8323 pets $5/day	(2) $60	C R/L	
Shelton Inn 628 W Railroad Ave dogs allowed in smoking rooms only, open field for walking dogs, 5 minute walk to public park		360-426-4468 pets $10/day	(30) $58– $73	C K	OP
Super 8 Motel 2943 N View Cir www.super8.com, nonsmoking rooms, open field for walking dogs, 1 mile to walking trail	360-426-1654, 800-800-8000 pets $10/stay		(38) $55– $74	C M	

Shoreline, Washington

Shoreline Motel 16526 Aurora Ave N laundry, lawn and field for walking dogs		206-542-7777 pets $10/stay	(18) $41– $50	C (k) M/F	

Silver Creek, Washington

Lake Mayfield Motel 2911 Hwy 12 ½ mile to lakeside parks and walking trails	360-985-2484, 360-985-2584 6 acres for walking dogs,		(9) $35– $55	R	

Silver Lake, Washington

Silver Lake Motel & Resort 360-274-6141 3201 Spirit Lake Hwy each pet $5/day cabins sleep 2 to 6, RV and tent sites, boat rentals and tackle shop, lakeside area for walking dogs	(11) $65– $95	C K	

Silverdale, Washington

Cimarron Motel 360-692-7777, 800-273-5076 9734 Silverdale Way NW pets $10/stay nonsmoking rooms, laundry, 2 blocks to waterfront walking trail	(63) $59– $85	CB K	
WestCoast Silverdale Hotel 360-698-1000 3073 NW Bucklin Hill Rd 800-544-9799 www.westcoasthotels.com/silverdale, pets $10/day nonsmoking facility, tennis courts, waterfront trail	(150) call for rates	M/F R/L	IP T

Skykomish, Washington

Sky River Inn 360-677-2261, 800-367-8194 333 River Dr E pets $5/day www.skyriverinn.com, riverfront nonsmoking rooms, next to national wilderness and lots of walking area	(18) $75– $100 M/F	C (k)	

Snohomish, Washington

Country Man B & B 360-568-9622, 800-700-9622 119 Cedar Ave Victorian home next to public park, 3 blocks to riverfront walking trails	(3) $85– $95	FB	
Snohomish Grand Valley View B & B 360-668-7096 8816 E Lowell Larimer Rd 866-668-7096 well-behaved dogs only, completely nonsmoking, lunches and dinners by arrangements, private patio or balcony, 3 acres, trails through woods to creek	(2) $75– $125	FB	
Snohomish Inn 360-568-2208, 800-548-9993 323 2nd St www.snohomishinn.com nonsmoking rooms, small dogs allowed at manager's discretion and advance reservation only, in-room spa, espresso stand, across street to pet walking lawn	(22) $65– $95	C M/F	

C = coffee CB = continental breakfast F = refrigerator FB = full breakfast	IP = indoor pool K = full kitchen (k) = kitchenette L = lounge M = microwave	OP = outdoor pool R = restaurant S = sauna or steamroom T = spa or hot tub	(# of units) & rates	food & drink	pool, sauna & hot tub

Snoqualmie, Washington

Honey Farm Inn B & B 9050 384th Ave SE completely nonsmoking, dogs allowed by advance reservation only, 5 acres for walking dogs, close to riverside park, www.myenchantedmoments.com	425-888-9399	(10) $89– $155	FB R	
House in the Trees B & B 35909 SE 96th Way completely nonsmoking, 18 acres of meadow and woods for walking dogs	425-888-2549	(2) $80– $95	FB	

Snoqualmie Pass, Washington

Best Western Summit Inn 603 Hwy 906 www.bwsummitinn.com dogs allowed in smoking rooms only, laundry, vacant lot for walking dogs, ¼ mile to walking trails	425-434-6300 800-557-7829 pets $10/stay	(81) $69– $299	C M/F R/L	OP S T

Soap Lake, Washington

Inn at Soap Lake 226 Main Ave E www.innsoaplake.com nonsmoking lodge rooms and cottages sleep 2 to 6, in-room spa, lawn, walking trails	509-246-1132 800-557-8514 pets $5/day	(29) $55– $110	C M/F	
Lake Motel 322 S Daisy St dogs allowed in smoking rooms only, 1 block to public park, 5 blocks to lake	509-246-1903 pets $10/stay	(28) call for rates	K	
Notaras Lodge 13 Canna N www.notaraslodge.com, nonsmoking rooms, mineral baths in all rooms, massage therapist, close to walking trails, 1 block to lakeside park	509-246-0462 pets $10/stay	(15) $51– $125	C K M/F R/L	

Royal View Motel 509-246-1831 404 4th Ave NE each pet $5/day nonsmoking rooms, lake, field for walking dogs	(17) $39– $70	C K	
Tolo Vista Lodge Cabins by the Lake 509-246-1512 22 Daisy N 888-512-2246 tolovista@hotmail.com pets $10/stay completely nonsmoking cabins sleep 5, mineral water bath in each cabin, lakeside walking trails	(6) $45– $95	C K	
Tumwata Lodge 509-246-1416 340 Main St W studios and 1-bdrm apartments with full kitchens, laundry, RV sites, lakeside area for walking dogs	(12) $45– $65	K	OP

South Bend, Washington

H & H Motel 360-875-5523 101 E Water St RV sites, close to "Rails to Trails" walking trail	(16) $38– $55	K R/L	
Russell House B & B 360-875-6487, 888-484-6907 902 E Water St pets $10/day laundry, RV sites, yard and large open area for walking dogs, 2 blocks to public park	(4) $60– $100	FB	

Spokane, Washington

Airway Express Inn 509-747-7186, 800-772-7186 3809 S Geiger Blvd nonsmoking rooms, laundry, lawn for walking dogs	(83) $29– $50	C K	
Apple Tree Inn 509-466-3020 9508 N Division St 800-323-5796 www.appletreeinnmotel.com, refundable pet deposit, dogs allowed in smoking rooms only, laundry, designated pet walking area, 2 blocks to public park	(71) $50– $80	CB K M/F	OP
Bel-Air Motel 509-535-1677 1303 E Sprague Ave pets $6/day laundry, RV sites, open field for walking dogs	(17) $35– $45	C M/F	
Bell Motel 509-624-0852 9030 W Sunset Hwy pets $5/day nonsmoking rooms, laundry, RV sites, open field	(14) $31– $47	C (k) M/F	

C = coffee IP = indoor pool OP = outdoor pool CB = continental K = full kitchen R = restaurant breakfast (k) = kitchenette S = sauna or F = refrigerator L = lounge steamroom FB = full breakfast M = microwave T = spa or hot tub	(# of units) & rates	food & drink	pool, sauna & hot tub

Spokane, Washington (continued)

	(# of units) & rates	food & drink	pool, sauna & hot tub
Best Western Pheasant Hill 509-926-7432 12415 E Mission Ave refundable pet deposit www.bestwesternwashington.com, nonsmoking rooms, laundry, fitness center, lawn, 3 miles to riverside Centennial Trail, 5 minute drive to park	(105) $69– $189	CB M/F	IP T
Best Western Thunderbird Inn 509-747-2011 120 W 3rd Ave 800-578-2473 www.thunderbirdspokane.com pets $10/day nonsmoking rooms, exercise room, open walking area, 7 blocks to riverside park and Centennial Trail	(89) $65– $88	CB M/F R	OP
Best Western Trade Winds North 509-326-5500 3033 N Division St 800-621-8593 www.bestwesternwashington.com pet deposit nonsmoking rooms, laundry, 2 blocks to public park	(63) $59– $100	CB M/F	IP S T
Broadway Inn & Suites 509-535-7185 6309 E Broadway Ave www.laquinta.com nonsmoking rooms, laundry, exercise room, large pet area, close to fairgrounds	(73) $49– $89	CB K M/F	OP T
Budget Inn 509-838-6101 110 E 4th Ave 800-325-4000 lawn for walking dogs, 8 blocks to riverfront park	(153) $40– $54	C	OP
Budget Saver Motel-Spokane 509-534-0669 1234 E Sprague Ave pets $5/day nonsmoking rooms, pet walking area behind motel, 2 miles to riverfront park	(16) $32– $57	C K	
Cedar Village Motel 509-838-8558 5415 W Sunset Hwy 800-700-8558 www.cedarvillagemotel.com pets $3/day dogs allowed in smoking rooms only, laundry, RV sites, gazebo, picnic tables, BBQ, large yard for walking dogs	(28) $28– $55	C K	

Clinic Center Motel 702 S McClellan St nonsmoking rooms, rock garden area for walking dogs, 2 blocks to public park	509-747-6081 pets $5/day	(31) $38– $50	CB	
Comfort Inn-North 7111 N Division St www.comfortinn.com laundry, designated dog walking area, quiet neighborhood for longer walks	509-467-7111 800-424-6423 pets $5/day	(96) $49– $150	CB	OP S T
Comfort Inn-Valley 905 N Sullivan Rd www.choicehotels.com nonsmoking rooms, lawn, short drive to public park	509-924-3838 800-228-5150 pets $15/stay	(76) $39– $150	CB (k)	OP S T
Days Inn-Spokane Airport 4212 W Sunset Blvd www.daysinn.com laundry, courtyard and open area for walking dogs, 4 miles to riverfront park	509-747-2021 800-329-7466 pets $10/stay	(132) $52– $80	CB M/F R/L	OP
Doubletree Hotel-Spokane City Center N 322 Spokane Falls Ct www.doubletree.com laundry, exercise room, close to riverfront park	509-455-9600 800-222-8733 pets $25/stay	(375) $89– $500	C R/L	IP OP S
Doubletree Hotel-Spokane Valley 1100 N Sullivan Rd nonsmoking rooms, 1½ blocks to riverside trail	509-924-9000 pet deposit, 800-222-8733	(236) $59– $150	CB M/F R/L	OP T
Hampton Inn 2010 S Assembly St dogs under 20 lbs only, nonsmoking rooms, laundry, pet walking area, 5 minute drive to public park	509-747-1100, 800-426-7866 pets $20/stay	(129) $77– $94	CB F R	IP T
Holiday Inn Express-Spokane Valley 9220 E Mission Ave www.hiexpress.com, laundry, lawn and field for walking dogs, short drive to public park	509-927-7100 800-465-4329	(103) $69– $149	CB M/F	IP T
Howard Johnson Inn-Downtown 211 S Division St www.hojo.com, nonsmoking rooms, laundry, grassy pet walking area, 6 blocks to riverfront park	509-838-6630 pets $10/day, 800-446-4656	(79) $75– $80	CB M/F	T

C = coffee
CB = continental
    breakfast
F = refrigerator
FB = full breakfast
	IP = indoor pool
	K = full kitchen
	(k) = kitchenette
	L = lounge
	M = microwave
		OP = outdoor pool
		R = restaurant
		S = sauna or
		    steamroom
		T = spa or hot tub
			(# of units)
			& rates
				food
				& drink
					pool, sauna
					& hot tub

Spokane, Washington (continued)

La Quinta Inn & Suites 509-893-0955, 800-531-5900 3808 N Sullivan Rd #34 www.laquinta.com nonsmoking rooms, laundry, exercise room, lawn, 1½ blocks to Centennial Trail			(59) $59– $129	FB K	IP T
Motel 6-Spokane 509-459-6120, 800-466-8356 1508 S Rustle Rd www.motel6.com nonsmoking rooms, laundry, lawn for walking dogs, 3 miles to riverfront park			(120) $40– $53	C M/F	OP
Motel 6-Spokane Valley 509-926-5399, 800-466-8356 1919 N Hutchinson Rd www.motel6.com nonsmoking rooms, grassy area for walking dogs, 1 mile to public park			(92) $40– $69	C M/F	
Park Lane Motel & RV Park 509-535-1626 4412 E Sprague Ave 800-533-1626 www.parklanemotel.com, in-room spa, laundry, RV sites, fenced grassy play area, ¾ mile to fairgrounds			(28) $47– $95	CB K	
Quality Inn Oakwood-Spokane 509-467-4900 7919 N Division St 888-535-4900 www.northwestinns.com pets $20/stay manager's approval required for dogs over 60 lbs, nonsmoking rooms, 24 hour pool and spa, grassy area for walking dogs, several parks within ½ mile			(131) $63– $250	CB M/F	IP T
Quality Inn Valley Suites 509-928-5218 8923 E Mission Ave 800-777-7355 www.spokanequalityinn.com, refundable pet deposit, laundry, tanning beds, weight room, courtyard for walking dogs, close to riverside Centennial Trail			(128) $78– $250	CB M/F	IP S T
Ramada Inn-Airport 509-838-5211 9000 Airport Rd 800-272-6232 nonsmoking rooms, exercise room, lawn			(165) $70– $105	C M/F R/L	IP T

Ramada Limited Suites 9601 N Newport Hwy www.the.ramada.com/spokane10087 pets $10/day nonsmoking rooms, laundry, walking area, 5 minute drive to park, 15 minute drive to Mt Spokane trails	509-468-4201 800-210-8975	(76) $55– $85	CB M/F	IP S T
Ramada Limited-City Center 123 S Post St www.the.ramada.com/spokane10046 pets $10/day nonsmoking rooms, 5 blocks to riverfront park, 6 blocks to Centennial Trail	509-838-8504 800-210-8465	(46) $45– $70	CB M/F	
Ranch Motel 1609 S Lewis St laundry, lawn and woods for walking dogs, ½ mile to public arboretum and trails	509-456-8919	(10) $29– $35	K	
Red Top Motel 7217 E Trent Ave refundable pet deposit nonsmoking rooms, in-room spa, small area behind building for walking dogs, close to school field	509-926-5728	(35) $40– $125	K	OP
Reid House B & B 2315 W 1st Ave www.thereidhouse.com dogs allowed by advance arrangement only, rooms and fully furnished apartments, nonsmoking facility, fenced yard, 1 block to public park	509-838-9138	(20) $49– $120	FB K	
Rodeway Inn 509-747-1041, 800-228-2000 901 W 1st Ave www.choicehotels.com nonsmoking rooms, exercise room, gravel area for walking dogs, 4 blocks to public park		(36) $39– $59	CB M/F	S
Select Inn 509-838-2026, 800-246-6835 1420 W 2nd Ave nonsmoking rooms, lawn for walking dogs, 6 blocks to public park		(54) $38– $52	C M/F R	OP
Shangri-La Motel 509-747-2066, 800-234-4941 2922 W Government Way nonsmoking rooms, 1 acre lawn, greenbelt area, walking trails to river		(20) $39– $76	CB K	OP
Shilo Inn 509-535-9000, 800-222-2244 923 E 3rd Ave each pet $10/day www.shiloinns.com, nonsmoking rooms, laundry, pet beds and treats, fitness center, steam room, small areas along parking lot for walking dogs		(105) $79– $105	FB M/F R/L	IP S T

C = coffee IP = indoor pool OP = outdoor pool		
CB = continental K = full kitchen R = restaurant		
breakfast (k) = kitchenette S = sauna or		
F = refrigerator L = lounge steamroom		
FB = full breakfast M = microwave T = spa or hot tub		

	(# of units) & rates	food & drink	pool, sauna & hot tub

Spokane, Washington (continued)

Spokane House Travelodge 509-838-1471 4301 W Sunset Blvd 800-550-7635 spokanetravelodge@pwi.net, nonsmoking rooms, laundry, exercise room, next to public arboretum and walking trails	(86) $55– $80	C M/F R/L	OP T
Super 8 Motel 509-928-4888, 800-800-8000 2020 N Argonne Rd refundable pet deposit www.super8.com, laundry, guest pass to fitness club, open field for walking dogs, ½ mile to public park	(181) $56– $70	CB M/F	IP T
Super 8 Motel 509-838-8800 11102 W Westbow Blvd 800-800-8000 www.super8.com pets $10/day nonsmoking rooms, laundry, open field to walk dogs	(80) $45– $75	CB M/F	IP T
TradeWinds Motel 509-838-2091 907 W 3rd Ave 800-586-5397 nonsmoking rooms, laundry, exercise room, 8 blocks to riverfront park, year-round sauna and spa, seasonal pool, pet walking area behind building	(59) $40– $80	CB M/F	OP S T
Travelodge-Spokane 509-623-9727 33 W Spokane Falls Blvd 888-824-0292 www.travelodge.com pets $10/stay nonsmoking rooms, laundry, in-room spa, exercise room, pet walking area, 4 blocks to public park	(80) $50– $70	FB C M/F	
WestCoast Ridpath Hotel 509-838-2711 515 W Sprague Ave 800-325-4000 www.westcoasthotels.com, nonsmoking rooms, laundry, exercise room, 4 blocks to riverfront park	(342) $50– $99	C M/F R/L	OP
WestCoast River Inn 509-326-5577 700 N Division St 800-325-4000 www.westcoasthotels.com, nonsmoking rooms, pet treats, next to riverside Centennial Trail	(245) $69– $240	CB (k) F R/L	OP T

Sprague, Washington

Purple Sage Motel 409 W 1st St www.purplesagemotel.com, nonsmoking rooms, in-room spa, small lawn and fields for walking dogs, 2 miles to Sprague Lake	509-257-2507 877-957-2507	(7) $35– $70	C M/F

St John, Washington

Country Cottage Inn 103 S Main 2-bdrm cottage sleeps 6, laundry, yard and open lot to walk dogs, 2 blocks to park, close to golf course	509-648-3676 pets $10/stay	(1) $50– $70	C K

Stanwood, Washington

Camano Cottages www.camanocottages.com fully equipped secluded cottages sleep 2 to 4, decks, fireplaces, on 10 acres near beach access, short drive to waterfront park, day and overnight pet boarding	360-387-4050 pets $10/stay	(2) $125– $195	CB K	T

Stehekin, Washington

Stehekin Valley Ranch www.courtneycountry.com 1-room rustic cabins, canvas tent cabins, bathhouse, room rates include meals, accessible by boat or float plane, located 9 miles upriver from Lake Stehekin	509-682-4677 800-536-0745	(12) $65– $85	R

Steptoe, Washington

Wheel Inn 21 Scholz Rd lawn and country roads for walking dogs	509-397-3195 refundable pet deposit	(9) $40– $45	R

Stevenson, Washington

Columbia Gorge Riverside Lodge 200 SW Cascade Ave www.cgriversidelodge.com waterfront lodge rooms and log cabins, fireplaces, public park with walking trail around lake	509-427-5650 866-427-5650 each pet $10/day	(12) $69– $149	(k)	T

C = coffee
CB = continental
    breakfast
F = refrigerator
FB = full breakfast
	IP = indoor pool
	K = full kitchen
	(k) = kitchenette
	L = lounge
	M = microwave
		OP = outdoor pool
		R = restaurant
		S = sauna or
		    steamroom
		T = spa or hot tub
			(# of units)
			& rates
				food
				& drink
					pool, sauna
					& hot tub

Sultan, Washington

Dutch Cup Motel 918 Main St www.dutchcup.com nonsmoking rooms, large lawn for walking dogs, 9 blocks to riverfront park	360-793-2215 800-844-0488 pets $8/day	(20) $61– $75	C M/F R/L	

Sumas, Washington

B & B Border Inn 121 Cleveland Ave · vacant lot for walking dogs, 3 blocks to public park	360-988-5800 nonsmoking rooms,	(21) $35– $58		
Sumas Bob's Mountain Village 819 Cherry St in-room spa, small dogs only, 2 blocks to public park	360-988-4483 completely nonsmoking,	(9) $50– $115	C R/L	

Sumner, Washington

Sumner Motor Inn 15506 Main St E nonsmoking rooms, open fields for walking dogs, short drive to parks and lakes	253-863-3250 pets $10/stay	(39) $45– $66	C (k) M/F	

Sunnyside, Washington

Country Inn & Suites 408 Yakima Valley Hwy www.sunnysidecountryinn.com, nonsmoking rooms, in-room spa, laundry, open field for walking dogs, 5 blocks to public park and paved walking path,	509-837-7878 877-896-7878	(73) $38– $63	CB (k) M/F	OP
Rodeway Inn 3209 Picard Pl www.rodeway.com nonsmoking rooms, exercise room, parking lot and open fields for walking dogs, close to walking trail	509-837-5781 800-228-2000 pets $10/day	(46) $79– $89	CB M/F	IP T

Sun Valley Inn 724 Yakima Valley Hwy well-behaved dogs only, nonsmoking rooms, gravel area for walking dogs, 1 mile to public park	509-837-4721	(40) $30– $60	CB K M/F	OP
Town House Motel 509 Yakima Valley Hwy nonsmoking rooms, 1 block to public park	509-837-5500	(21) $30– $60	C (k)	

Tacoma, Washington

Best Western Lakewood Motor Inn 6125 Motor Ave SW www.bestwestern.com nonsmoking rooms, laundry, designated dogwalking area, cleanup scoopers provided	253-584-2212 800-528-1234 each pet $6/day	(78) $71– $82	CB F	OP
Best Western Tacoma Inn 8726 S Hosmer St www.bestwesternwashington.com nonsmoking rooms, laundry, lawn for walking dogs, ¾ mile to lakeside park	253-535-2880 800-305-2880 pets $20/stay	(149) $64– $99	CB K R/L	OP T
Biltmore Motel 12701 Pacific Hwy SW	253-588-3800 pets $5/day	(28) $40– $70	C K M/F	
Blue Spruce Motel 12715 Pacific Ave S dogs under 30 lbs only, nonsmoking rooms, grassy walking area behind building, 5 minute drive to park	253-531-6111 pets $5/day	(27) $35– $60	K M/F	
Comfort Inn 5601 Pacific Hwy E www.choicehotels.com nonsmoking rooms, laundry, open lot for walking dogs, short walk to school field and public park	253-926-2301 800-228-5150 pets $15/stay	(68) $49– $69	CB M/F	
Corporate Suites, Inc. 219 E Division Ct www.corporatesuites.com dogs under 25 lbs only, nonsmoking rooms, small grassy pet walking area, 6 blocks to public park	253-473-4105 800-255-6058 pets $50/stay	(21) $55– $67	K	

	C = coffee IP = indoor pool OP = outdoor pool CB = continental K = full kitchen R = restaurant breakfast (k) = kitchenette S = sauna or F = refrigerator L = lounge steamroom FB = full breakfast M = microwave T = spa or hot tub	(# of units) & rates	food & drink	pool, sauna & hot tub

Tacoma, Washington (continued)

	(# of units) & rates	food & drink	pool
Days Inn 253-475-5900, 800-221-2680 6802 Tacoma Mall Blvd pets $20/day www.daysinn.com, nonsmoking rooms, fitness room, large yard for walking dogs, 10 minute walk to park	(123) $67– $129	CB M/F	OP
Golden Lion Motor Inn 253-588-2171 9021 S Tacoma Way refundable pet deposit nonsmoking rooms, gravel area for walking dogs	(30) $40– $62		
Knights Inn Motel 253-582-7550 9325 S Tacoma Way pets $10-20/day nonsmoking rooms, dogs under 25 lbs only, close to public park	(77) $40– $60	CB M/F	
La Quinta Inn 253-383-0146, 800-531-5900 1425 E 27th St www.laquinta.com, nonsmoking rooms, laundry, exercise room, parking area and side street for walking dogs, short drive to parks	(157) $69– $99	CB M/F R/L	OP T
Motel 6-Tacoma South 253-473-7100, 800-466-8356 1811 S 76th St www.motel6.com, nonsmoking rooms, laundry, open walking area, 1 block to park	(120) $40– $52	C	OP T
Motel 6-Tacoma/Fife 253-922-1270, 800-466-8356 5201 20th St E www.motel6.com, nonsmoking rooms, laundry, lawn, 10 minute drive to public park	(119) $40– $67	C M/F	OP
Ramada Inn-Tacoma Dome 253-572-7272 2611 East E St 800-272-6232 www.ramada.com pets $15/stay nonsmoking rooms, small gravel area to walk dogs, 5 minute drive to park, 10 minutes to waterfront	(160) $72– $250	C R/L	
Ramada Inn-Tacoma/Lakewood 253-588-5241 9920 S Tacoma Way 800-600-9751 www.ramadainntacoma.com pets $25/stay nonsmoking rooms, in-room spa, laundry, exercise room, field for walking dogs, 1½ miles to public park	(103) $66– $119	CB K R/L	

Royal Coachman Inn 253-922-2500, 800-422-3051 5805 Pacific Hwy E refundable pet deposit www.royalcoachmaninn.com, nonsmoking rooms, laundry, large open lot, 10 minute drive to waterfront	(96) $65– $130	CB M/F	T	
Sheraton Tacoma Hotel 253-572-3200 1320 Broadway 800-845-9466 www.sheratontacoma.com refundable pet deposit dogs under 35 lbs only, nonsmoking rooms, exercise room, small courtyard for walking dogs, 3 miles to large waterfront park	(319) $99– $450	C F R/L		
Shilo Inn 253-475-4020 7414 S Hosmer St 800-222-2244 www.shiloinns.com each pet $10/day nonsmoking rooms, laundry, pet beds and treats, fitness center, steam room, designated pet area, 1 block to public park	(132) $89– $139	CB K M/F	IP S T	
Stagecoach Inn 253-922-5421 4221 Pacific Hwy E pets $3/day 15 minute drive to Commencement Bay	(26) $40– $50			
Victory Motel 253-588-9107 10801 Pacific Hwy SW pets $20/day nonsmoking rooms, laundry, gravel pet area	(20) $38– $45	(k) M/F		

Tokeland, Washington

Tokeland Hotel 360-267-7006 2964 Kindred Ave small dogs only, nonsmoking historic 117 year old hotel, hall bathrooms, large lawn, close to beach	(18) $49– $75	R		
Tradewinds-on-the-Bay Motel 360-267-7500 4305 Pomeroy Ln pets $5/day www.westportwa.com/tradewinds, fully equipped kitchens in all rooms, large party room with kitchen and fireplace, RV sites, beach for walking dogs	(18) $55– $85	C K	OP	

Tonasket, Washington

Junction Motel 509-486-4500 23 6th St refundable pet deposit completely nonsmoking, close to park and river	(8) $44– $50	C M		

C = coffee IP = indoor pool OP = outdoor pool CB = continental K = full kitchen R = restaurant breakfast (k) = kitchenette S = sauna or F = refrigerator L = lounge steamroom FB = full breakfast M = microwave T = spa or hot tub	(# of units) & rates	food & drink	pool, sauna & hot tub

Tonasket, Washington (continued)

| Red Apple Inn 509-486-2119
20 S Whitcomb Ave
well-behaved adult dogs only, nonsmoking rooms,
lawn for walking dogs, 2 blocks to public park | (21)
$35–
$76 | C
K | |
| Spectacle Falls Resort 509-223-4141
879 Loomis-Oroville Hwy
fully equipped lakeside mobile homes, dogs allowed
by advance reservation only, lots of walking area | (4)
$50 | K | |

Toppenish, Washington

Best Western Lincoln Inn 509-865-7444 515 S Elm St pets $10/day, 877-509-7444 www.bestwestern.com, dogs under 15 lbs allowed in smoking rooms only, laundry, exercise room, park	(40) $80– $130	CB M/F	IP T
El Corral Motel 509-865-2365 61731 Hwy 97 pets $10/stay lawn for walking dogs, 3 blocks to public park	(17) $39– $49	C M/F	
Oxbow Motor Inn 509-865-5800, 888-865-5855 511 S Elm St pets $10/day nonsmoking rooms, across street to public park	(44) $44– $49	C K	

Trout Lake, Washington

| Kelly's Trout Creek Inn B & B 509-395-2769
25 Mount Adams Rd www.kellysbnb.com
completely nonsmoking, creek and waterfalls, open
fields for walking dogs | (4)
$55–
$65 | FB | |

Tukwila, Washington

| Best Western Southcenter 425-226-1812
15901 W Valley Hwy pets $10/stay, 800-544-9863
www.bestwestern.com, nonsmoking rooms, laundry,
in-room spa, exercise room, walking trail | (146)
$79–
$170 | CB
M/F
R/L | OP
S
T |

Homestead Studio Suites Hotel 15635 W Valley Hwy www.homesteadhotels.com nonsmoking rooms, laundry, across street from walking trail to park	425-235-7160 888-782-9473 pets $75/stay	(94) $46– $95	K	
Homewood Suites 6955 Fort Dent Way www.homewood-suites.com nonsmoking rooms, laundry, next to walking trail, across street Fort Dent Park	206-433-8000 800-225-5466 each pet $20/day	(106) $129– $179	CB K	OP T

Tumwater, Washington

Best Western Tumwater Inn 5188 Capitol Blvd S www.bestwesternwashington.com nonsmoking rooms, laundry, exercise room, large natural area for walking dogs, ½ mile to public park	360-956-1235 800-848-4992 pets $5/day	(90) $58– $90	CB M/F	S T
Motel 6 400 Lee St SW www.motel6.com, nonsmoking rooms, laundry, picnic tables, lawn for walking dogs, 5 minute drive to riverside park and walking trails	360-754-7320 800-466-8356	(119) $38– $49	C M/F	OP

Twisp, Washington

Idle-A-While Motel 505 N Hwy 20 www.methowvalley.com/~idlewile, motel rooms, cottages with fully equipped kitchens sleep up to 6, tennis, picnic area, BBQ, on 5 acres, ½ mile to park	509-997-3222 pets $5/day	(25) $52– $100	CB K	S T

Union, Washington

De Koeyer Hot Tub Cabins 6730 East Hwy 106 www.worldpages.com, dogs allowed by advance authorization only, nonsmoking rooms, cabins, 2-bdrm mobile home, 3-bdrm home, all with private hot tubs, access to beach and public swimming pool, kayak rentals, nature trails for walking dogs	360-898-3434 pets $25/stay	(9) $90– $185	C K M/F	

C = coffee
CB = continental
  breakfast
F = refrigerator
FB = full breakfast
	IP = indoor pool
	K = full kitchen
	(k) = kitchenette
	L = lounge
	M = microwave
		OP = outdoor pool
		R = restaurant
		S = sauna or
		  steamroom
		T = spa or hot tub
			(# of units)
			& rates
				food
				& drink
					pool, sauna
					& hot tub

Union Gap, Washington

Best Western Ahtanun 2408 Rudkin Rd www.bestwestern.com/ahtanun nonsmoking rooms, laundry, in-room spa, lawn for walking dogs, ¼ mile to greenway walking trail	509-248-9700 800-348-9701 pets $10/day		(118) $79– $209	CB K	OP
Pioneer Motel 3107 Main St fenced yard for walking dogs	509-249-1809		(45) $30– $40	(k)	
Quality Inn 12 E Valley Mall Blvd www.qualityinn.com nonsmoking rooms, laundry, 2 miles to greenway walking trail	509-248-6924 800-510-5670 pets $10/day		(86) $59– $79	CB M/F R/L	OP
Super 8 Motel 2605 Rudkin Rd www.super8.com nonsmoking rooms, laundry, open field, 2 blocks to greenway riverside walking trail	509-248-8880 800-800-8000 refundable pet deposit		(95) $39– $78	C	IP

Usk, Washington

Hotel Usk 410 River Rd www.hotelusk.com, field for walking dogs, close to riverfront walking areas	509-445-1526 pets $10/stay		(7) $38– $64	C M	

Valley, Washington

Jump Off Joe Resort 3290 E Jump Off Joe Rd small dogs allowed with advance approval only, RV sites, lakefront cabins with fully equipped kitchens, woods and trails for walking dogs	509-937-2133 pets $5/day		(4) $39– $65	K	

Vancouver, Washington

Best Inn & Suites 360-696-0516, 888-696-0516 7001 NE Hwy 99 pets $10/day completely nonsmoking, laundry, large grasssy area for walking dogs, 4 blocks to public park	(72) $54– $95	CB K	OP T
Comfort Inn 360-574-6000 13207 NE 20th Ave each pet $10/day www.comfortinn.com, nonsmoking rooms, laundry, exercise room, 24 hour pool, lawn for walking dogs, ½ mile to public park	(58) $59– $89	CB M/F	IP
Days Inn 360-256-7044, 800-426-5110 221 NE Chkalov Dr pets $10/day www.daysinn.com, nonsmoking rooms, grassy pet walking area, ½ mile to public park	(116) $49– $95	CB M/F	IP T
Ferryman's Inn 360-574-2151 7901 NE 6th Ave each pet $3/day nonsmoking rooms, laundry, open area behind building for walking dogs, 1 mile to walking trail	(132) $54– $68	C K	OP
Guest House Motel 360-254-4511 11504 NE 2nd St pets $10/stay pateluresh@hotmail.com, nonsmoking rooms, open field for walking dogs, 3 blocks to public park	(47) $40– $65	C M/F	
Homewood Suites 360-750-1100, 800-225-5466 701 SE Columbia Shores Blvd pets $10/day www.homewoodsuites.com plus $25 cleaning fee suites sleep 4, fully equipped kitchens, laundry, Mon–Thur beverages and appetizers, riverside trail	(104) $99– $179	FB K	OP T
Red Lion Hotel at the Quay 360-694-8341 100 Columbia St 800-733-5466 www.redlion.com pets $25/stay nonsmoking rooms, riverside walking trail, 5 blocks to public park	(160) $69– $120	C M/F R/L	OP
Red Lion Inn at Salmon Creek 360-566-1100 1500 NE 134th St pets $25/stay, 877-566-1101 www.redlion.com, nonsmoking rooms, fitness room, laundry, field for walking dogs, close to trails	(89) $69– $79	CB M/F	IP

C = coffee	IP = indoor pool	OP = outdoor pool	(# of units) & rates	food & drink	pool, sauna & hot tub
CB = continental	K = full kitchen	R = restaurant			
breakfast	(k) = kitchenette	S = sauna or			
F = refrigerator	L = lounge	steamroom			
FB = full breakfast	M = microwave	T = spa or hot tub			

Vancouver, Washington (continued)

Residence Inn by Marriott 360-253-4800 8005 NE Parkway Dr pets $15/day, 800-331-3131 nonsmoking rooms, exercise room, laundry, close to walking paths through business park	(120) $79– $139	CB K	OP T
Riverside Motel 360-693-3677 4400 Columbia House Blvd pets $8/day nonsmoking rooms, lawn, ½ mile to public park	(17) $38– $45	K	
Shilo Inn-Hazel Dell 360-573-0511 13206 NE Hwy 99 800-222-2244 www.shiloinns.com each pet $10/day nonsmoking rooms, laundry, pet beds and treats, small walking area, short drive to public park	(66) $60– $110	CB K M/F	IP S T
Shilo Inn-Vancouver 360-696-0411 401 E 13th St 800-222-2244 www.shiloinns.com each pet $10/day nonsmoking rooms, laundry, pet beds and treats, fitness center, grassy pet walking area behind building, 4 blocks to public park	(118) $69– $96	CB M/F	OP S
Staybridge Suites 360-891-8282 7301 NE 41st St 800-238-8000 www.staybridge.com pets $10/day nonsmoking rooms to 2-bdrm suites, light dinner served Tuesday–Thursday, designated pet area	(117) $69– $150	FB K	OP
Value Motel 360-574-2345 708 NE 78th St pets $5/day nonsmoking rooms, in-room spa, laundry, lawn for walking dogs, short drive to public park	(100) $21– $44		OP
Vancouver Lodge 360-693-3668 601 Broadway St pets $8/day nonsmoking rooms, in-room spa, small area behind building for walking dogs, 2 blocks to public park	(45) $39– $81	C M/F	

Vantage, Washington

Vantage Riverstone Resort 509-856-2230 551 Main St pets $5/day laundry, RV sites, convenience store, riverside area for walking dogs	(20) $54– $89		IP

Vashon Island, Washington

Angels of the Sea B & B 206-463-6980 26431 99th Ave SW 800-798-9249 www.angelsofthesea.com, former church building, rooms and 2-bdrm 2-bath home sleeps 6, laundry, fenced yards, short walk to beach and trails	(4) $75– $135	FB	
Castle Hill B & B 206-463-5491 26734 94th Ave SW www.vashonislandlodging.com completely nonsmoking, 5 acres of open field surrounded by woods for walking dogs	(1) $85	FB	
Emerald Isle Guest House 206-567-5133 10520 SW 140th St pets $20/stay cottage sleeps 6, fully equipped kitchen, meadow for walking dogs, close to beaches	(1) $100	C K	
Swallow's Nest Guest Cottages 206-463-2646 6030 SW 248th St 800-269-6378 www.vashonislandcottages.com pets $10/day nonsmoking facility, off-site hot tub available, close to public parks and beaches for walking dogs	(8) $65– $230	C K	T
Van Gelder's Retreat 206-463-3684 18522 Beall Rd SW www.greatrentals.com/wa/4111.html, dogs allowed in 1-bdrm cottage and in campground area only, laundry, large open field for walking dogs	(3) $120– $160	C K	OP T

Waitsburg, Washington

Waitsburg Inn 509-337-8455 731 Preston Ave pets $5/day large parking area and lawn for walking dogs, ¼ mile to public park	(7) $50		

C = coffee IP = indoor pool OP = outdoor pool CB = continental K = full kitchen R = restaurant breakfast (k) = kitchenette S = sauna or F = refrigerator L = lounge steamroom FB = full breakfast M = microwave T = spa or hot tub	# of units) & rates	food & drink	pool, sauna & hot tub

Walla Walla, Washington

Best Western Walla Walla Inn & Suites 7 E Oak St 509-525-4700, 800-937-8376 www.bestwesternwashington.com, pets $5/day nonsmoking rooms, laundry, grassy area for walking dogs, close to walking trail around golf course	(78) $69– $99	CB M/F	IP T
Capri Motel 509-525-1130, 800-451-1139 2003 E Melrose St pets $8/stay nonsmoking rooms, small undeveloped area for walking dogs, ½ mile to public park and ponds	(37) $35– $70	C (k) M/F	OP
City Center Motel 509-529-2660 627 W Main St pets $5/day www.citycentermotelllc.com, rooms and furnished apartments, garden area for walking dogs, 2 blocks to public park	(17) $43– $185	C K	OP
Colonial Motel 509-529-1220 2279 E Isaacs Ave www.colonial-motel.com small dogs only, nonsmoking rooms, large yard for walking dogs, 1 block to park and walking trail	(17) $39– $65	C M/F	
Howard Johnson Express Inn 509-529-4360 325 E Main St 800-446-4656 www.hojo.com, nonsmoking rooms, in-room spa, laundry, weight room, lawn for walking dogs	(85) $78– $159	CB K M/F	OP S T
La Quinta Inn & Suites 509-525-2522 520 N 2nd Ave 800-531-5900 www.laquinta.com, nonsmoking rooms, laundry, exercise room, lawn, 1 mile to public park	(61) $59– $159	CB (k)	IP T
Mill Creek Inn 509-522-1234 2014 Mill Creek Rd pets $15/stay www.millcreekbb.com, dog allowed in 1 cottage by advance arrangement only, completely nonsmoking, creekside walking areas	(4) $145– $205	FB K	

Sicyon Gallery B & B 1283 Star St dogs allowed by owner approval only, lawn for walking dogs, less than 1 mile to public park	509-525-2964 bpiper@bmi.net	(1) $55	FB	
Super 8 Motel 2315 Eastgate St N www.super8.com, nonsmoking rooms, laundry, open lot for walking dogs, ¼ mile to public park	509-525-8800 800-800-8000	(101) $49– $99	CB K M/F	IP T
Travelodge 421 E Main St nonsmoking rooms, microwave available at front desk, 1 block to public park	509-529-4940, 800-578-7878 pets $7/day	(39) $45– $85	CB F	OP T
Vagabond Budget Inn 305 N 2nd Ave laundry, area behind building for walking dogs	509-529-4410, 888-529-4161 pets $5/day	(35) $30– $75	CB K	OP T

Washougal, Washington

Rama Inn 544 6th St nonsmoking rooms, laundry, lawn for walking dogs, 1 mile to riverfront walking area	360-835-8591 pets $3/day	(26) $54– $65	C M/F	
River House B & B 16241 Washougal River Rd www.riverhouseretreat.com, dogs allowed with advance approval only, suite with deck, gazebo, dinners by arrangement, 1½ acres with nature trail, dog run and heated dog house coming soon	360-837-8906	(1) $85	FB	

Wenatchee, Washington

Apple Country B & B 524 Okanogan Ave well-behaved dogs only, completely nonsmoking, open field for walking dogs, ¾ mile to riverfront path	509-664-0400 www.applecountryinn.com	(5) $65– $95	FB	T
Avenue Motel 720 N Wenatchee Ave www.avenuemotel.com, nonsmoking rooms, park- like setting and walking area, 4 blocks to public park	509-663-7161, 800-733-8981 pets $5/day	(38) $50– $80	C K M/F	OP T

C = coffee IP = indoor pool OP = outdoor pool CB = continental K = full kitchen R = restaurant breakfast (k) = kitchenette S = sauna or F = refrigerator L = lounge steamroom FB = full breakfast M = microwave T = spa or hot tub	(# of units) & rates	food & drink	pool, sauna & hot tub

Wenatchee, Washington (continued)

Comfort Inn-Columbia River 509-662-1700 815 N Wenatchee Ave 800-424-6423 nonsmoking rooms, exercise room, pets $10/stay, laundry, ½ mile to public park and walking trail	(81) $62– $78	CB M/F	IP T
Economy Inn 509-663-8133 700 N Wenatchee Ave 800-587-6348 www.economyinn.4mg.com pets $10/day nonsmoking rooms, laundry, 4 blocks to public park	(41) $35– $100	CB K	OP
Hill Crest Motel 509-663-5157 2921 School St nonsmoking rooms, designated pet walking area, ½ mile to public park	(16) $48– $70	C K	OP
Holiday Lodge 509-663-8167 610 N Wenatchee Ave 800-722-0852 www.holidaylodge-wa.com pets $5/day nonsmoking rooms, laundry, lawn for walking dogs, 2 blocks to public park	(59) $32– $65	CB M/F	OP S T
La Quinta Inn & Suites 509-664-6565, 800-531-5900 1905 N Wenatchee Ave www.lq.com nonsmoking rooms, in-room spa, laundry, fitness center, designated pet walking area	(65) $74– $140	CB M/F	IP S T
Lyles Motel 509-663-5155 924 N Wenatchee Ave 800-582-3788 laundry, grassy area for walking dogs	(22) $35– $89	K	OP T
Orchard Inn 509-662-3443 1401 N Miller St 800-368-4571 www.wenatcheeorchardinn.com pets $10/day nonsmoking rooms, riverside walking trail	(103) $49– $78	CB M/F	OP T
Red Lion Hotel 509-663-0711, 800-733-5466 1225 N Wenatchee Ave www.redlion.com nonsmoking rooms, next to walking path and park	(149) $69– $119	C M/F R/L	IP T

Starlite Motel 509-663-8115, 800-668-1862 1640 N Wenatchee Ave laundry, small gravel pet walking area, 2 blocks to public park	(34) $40– $79	C (k) M/F	OP S
Warm Springs Inn B & B 509-662-8365 1611 Love Ln 800-543-3645 www.warmspringsinn.com, small dogs only, nonsmoking ground floor room with private entrance, 10 riverside acres for walking dogs	(5) $95– $120	FB	T
Welcome Inn at Wenatchee Center 509-663-7121 232 N Wenatchee Ave pets $5/day, 800-561-8856 nonsmoking rooms, 3 blocks to riverfront park	(38) $36– $55	C M/F	OP
WestCoast Wenatchee Center Hotel 509-662-1234 201 N Wenatchee Ave 800-325-4000 www.westcoasthotels.com pets $10/stay nonsmoking rooms, fitness center, pet walking area behind building, 2 blocks to riverfront park	(147) $109– $129	C (k) R/L	IP T

West Spokane, Washington

Solar World Estates Motel Alternative 509-244-3535 1832 S Lawson each pet $5/day, 800-650-9484 www.spokanecorporatehousing.com, adult dogs allowed by manager's approval only, in-room spa, laundry, pet walking area, 6 miles to riverfront park	(56) $39– $90	K	

Westport, Washington

Alaskan Motel 360-268-9133, 866-591-4154 708 N 1st St pets $10/stay www.westportwa.com/alaskan, rooms and 2 houses sleep 2 to 13, on 1 acre for walking dogs	(11) $45– $125	C K	
Albatross Motel 360-268-9233 200 E Dock St pets $5–$10/day nonsmoking rooms, dogs under 25 lbs only, grassy area for walking dogs, close to public park	(13) $40	(k) F	
Breakers Motel 360-268-0848, 800-898-4889 971 N Montesano St pets $8/day www.westportwa.com/breakers, nonsmoking rooms and 1 to 5-bdrm suites, go-cart track, public park	(18) $49– $200	C K M/F	

C = coffee	IP = indoor pool	OP = outdoor pool
CB = continental	K = full kitchen	R = restaurant
breakfast	(k) = kitchenette	S = sauna or
F = refrigerator	L = lounge	steamroom
FB = full breakfast	M = microwave	T = spa or hot tub

Westport, Washington (continued)

	(# of units) & rates	food & drink	pool, sauna & hot tub
Coho Charters Motel & RV Park 360-268-0111 2501 N Nyhus 800-572-0177 www.westportwa.com/coho pets $10/day dogs under 10 lbs only, nonsmoking rooms, lawn, trail through dunes to beach	(28) $49– $89	C	
Frank L Motel & Aquatic Gardens 360-268-9200 725 S Montesano St pets $5/day bagwell@olynet.com, nonsmoking rooms sleep 2 to 11, designated pet walking area, 1¼ mile to walking trail and ocean access	(13) $45– $200	C K M/F	
Harbor Resort 360-268-0169 871 E Neddie Rose Dr pets $10/day www.harborresort.com, dogs allowed by advance approval only, nonsmoking motel units and cottages, in-room spa, close to waterfront, paved beach trail	(14) $49– $120	K M/F	
Mariners Cove Inn 360-268-0531, 877-929-9096 303 W Ocean Ave pets $10/day nonsmoking rooms, open lot for walking dogs, 6 blocks to beach, close to 2 state parks	(9) $39– $69	C (k) M/F	
McBee's Silver Sands Motel 360-268-9029 1001 S Montesano St dogs allowed by owner approval only, nonsmoking rooms, pet walking area behind building, 5 minute drive to beach	(19) $42– $56	C	
Ocean Avenue Inn 360-268-9278 275 W Ocean Ave 888-692-5262 www.westportwa.com/oceaninn pets $10/day nonsmoking rooms, lawn, ½ mile to ocean	(12) $49– $135	C K	
Orca Motel 360-268-5010 221 E Dock St pets $10/stay orcamo@techline.com, rooms and 1 to 2-bdrm units, lawn, gravel walking areas, 1½ blocks to waterfront	(8) $30– $80	M/F	

Pacific Motel & RV Park 360-268-9325 330 S Forrest St pets $5/day www.pacificmotelandrv.com, dogs allowed in 2 units only, RV sites, close to walking trails	(12) $64– $69	K	OP
Sands Motel & RV Park 360-268-0091 1416 S Montesano St nonsmoking rooms, RV sites, lawn and designated pet walking area, 6 blocks to state park	(12) $35– $55	C K	
Seagull's Nest Motel 360-268-9711 830 N Montesano St 888-613-9078 seagullsnest@techline.com pets $6/day nonsmoking rooms, open field across street for walking dogs, 1 mile to paved beach trail	(16) $39– $69	C (k)	
Shipwreck Motel 360-268-9151, 888-225-2313 2653 N Nyhus St pets $5/day lounge with live music coming soon, across street from beach	(18) $45– $125	C K M/F	
Surf Spray Motel & RV Park 360-268-9149 949 S Montesano St 888-600-9149 www.surfspraymotel.com pets $10/day fully equipped kitchens, laundry, small lawn for walking dogs, picnic area, BBQ, crab cooker, 1½ miles to beach	(10) $42– $85	K	

White Salmon, Washington

Inn Of the White Salmon 509-493-2335 172 W Jewett Blvd 800-972-5226 www.innofthewhitesalmon.com pets $10/stay completely nonsmoking facility, 1 room has outside entrance, pet walking area behind building, next to public park	(16) $85– $143	FB	
Llama Ranch B & B 509-395-2786 1980 Hwy 141 877-800-5262 www.geocities.com/llamaranch1, completely nonsmoking facility on 100 acres with ponds, creeks, walking trails, resident llamas and "free llama walks" around the property	(7) $69– $99	FB	

C = coffee IP = indoor pool OP = outdoor pool CB = continental K = full kitchen R = restaurant breakfast (k) = kitchenette S = sauna or F = refrigerator L = lounge steamroom FB = full breakfast M = microwave T = spa or hot tub	(# of units) & rates	food & drink	pool, sauna & hot tub

Wilbur, Washington

Eight Bar B Motel 509-647-2400 718 SE Main St each pet $5/stay nonsmoking rooms, undeveloped area for walking dogs, ½ mile to public park, www.wa-accommodations.com/ne/8barb	(16) $30– $75	C (k) M/F	OP

Winthrop, Washington

Best Western Cascade Inn 509-996-3100 960 W Hwy 20 800-468-6754 www.winthropwa.com each pet $10/day nonsmoking rooms, laundry, riverfront picnic and BBQ area, walking trails	(63) $50– $150	CB M/F	OP T
Duck Brand Hotel 509-996-2192 248 Riverside Ave www.methownet.com/duck completely nonsmoking rooms, private decks, lots of open area for walking dogs, ½ mile to public park	(5) $56– $66	R/L	
Methow Valley Central Reservations 509-996-2148 131 Riverside Ave 800-422-3048 www.extrabeds.com pets $5–$10/day hotels-motels-vacation homes, open walking areas, close to pet-friendly ski trail	(10) $65– $200	CB K	OP T
River Run Inn 509-996-2173, 800-757-2709 27 Rader Rd each pet $10/day www.riverrun-inn.com, dogs allowed by advance approval only, completely nonsmoking cabins and houses, patios and decks, 11 riverfront acres	(13) $70– $105	C K	IP T
Virginian Resort 509-996-2535 808 N Cascade Hwy 20 800-854-2834 www.methow.com/~virgnian each pet $5/day nonsmoking rooms and cabins sleep up to 4, walking trails, ¾ mile to city park, 4 miles to state park	(37) $45– $95	C K	OP

Winthrop Inn 960 Hwy 20 www.winthropinn.com completely nonsmoking, close to walking/biking/ cross-country skiing trails	509-996-2217 800-444-1972 pets $7/day	(30) $55– $100	CB M/F	OP T
Wolfridge Resort 412 Wolf Creek Rd #B www.wolfridgeresort.com, pets $10/day plus $25 cleaning fee, nonsmoking log townhouses, close to river and walking/biking trails	509-996-2828 800-237-2388	(17) $79– $184	C K M/F	OP T

Woodinville, Washington

Willows Lodge 14580 NE 145th St www.willowslodge.com refundable pet deposit nonsmoking facility, full service spa, fitness room, special pet treats and toys, courtyards and riverside natural area, 30-mile trail	425-424-3900 877-424-3900	(86) $260– $750	CB R	S T

Woodland, Washington

Econo Lodge 360-225-6548, 800-444-9667 1500 Atlantic Ave pets $10/day nonsmoking rooms, RV sites, undeveloped area for walking dogs, short drive to public park		(61) $40– $60	CB M/F	IP T
Lakeside Motel 360-225-8240 785 Lake Shore Dr pets $5–$7/day nonsmoking rooms, pets MUST be kept off the furniture, on 2½ acres for walking dogs, next to 20 acre public park and lake		(13) $36– $60	M/F	
Lewis River Inn 360-225-6257, 800-543-4344 1100 Lewis River Rd pets $6/day nonsmoking rooms, lawn, 6 blocks to public park		(49) $48– $73	CB M/F	
Scandia Motel 360-225-8006 1123 Hoffman St pets $6/day small yard and open field for walking dogs, 5 minute walk to public park		(13) $36– $44	C (k) M/F	

C = coffee	IP = indoor pool	OP = outdoor pool	(# of units) & rates	food & drink	pool, sauna & hot tub
CB = continental breakfast	K = full kitchen (k) = kitchenette	R = restaurant S = sauna or steamroom			
F = refrigerator FB = full breakfast	L = lounge M = microwave	T = spa or hot tub			

Yakima, Washington

Apple Country B & B 4561 Old Naches Hwy www.applecountryinnbb.com, dogs allowed by advance reservation only, completely nonsmoking, on 40 acres of fruit orchards for walking dogs	509-965-0344 pets $5/day		(3) $75– $90	FB M/F	
Bali Hai Motel 710 N 1st St nonsmoking rooms, open pet walking area behind building, ¾ mile to paved greenway walking path	509-452-7178 800-255-9002		(28) $25– $38	C M/F	OP
Best Western Peppertree Yakima Inn 1614 N 1st St www.bestwesternwashington.com dogs under 10 lbs only, nonsmoking rooms, laundry, open lot for walking dogs, short drive to public park	509-453-88989 800-834-164 pets $10/day		(73) $65– $94	FB M/F	IP T
Birchfield Manor Country Inn 2018 Birchfield Rd www.birchfieldmanor.com, dogs allowed in 2 rooms with private fenced patios, in-room spa, plenty of natural areas for walking dogs	509-452-1960 800-375-3420		(11) $119– $219	FB	
Cedar Inn Suites 1010 E A St guest pass to fitness center-spa-pool across street, quiet neighborhood for walking dogs	509-452-8101 pets $6/stay		(50) $55– $78	M/F	
Comfort Suites 3702 Fruitvale Blvd www.choicehotels.com dogs under 15 lbs only, nonsmoking rooms, laundry, 24 hour fitness center, 2 blocks to greenway trail	509-249-1900 866-423-8960 pets $10/day		(59) $69– $169	CB M/F	IP T

Doubletree Hotel-Yakima Valley	509-248-7850	(208)	C	OP
1507 N 1st St	800-222-8733	$79–	M/F	T
www.doubletree.com	pets $15/stay	$115	R/L	
dogs under 25 lbs only, fitness center, nonsmoking rooms, 5 minute walk to greenway walking trail				
Economy Inn	509-457-6155	(36)	CB	OP
510 N 1st St	888-925-6633	$36–		
www.economyinn-travel.com	pets $10/day	$70		
nonsmoking rooms, short drive to public park				
Holiday Inn Express	509-249-1000	(87)	CB	IP
1001 East A St	800-465-4329	$63–	M/F	T
www.hiexpress.com	pets $6/day	$83		
nonsmoking rooms, laundry, exercise room, 1 mile to greenway paved walking path				
Motel 6	509-454-0080	(95)	C	OP
1104 N 1st St	800-466-8356	$36–		
www.motel6.com, nonsmoking rooms, laundry,		$52		
lawn, 2 miles to paved greenway walking trail				
Nendels Inn	509-453-8981, 800-547-0106	(53)	CB	IP
1405 N 1st St	pets $5/day	$33–	M/F	T
nonsmoking rooms, lawn, 1 mile to greenway trail		$54		
Oxford Inn	509-457-4444	(96)	CB	OP
1603 E Yakima Ave	800-521-3050	$59–	K	T
www.oxfordsuites.com	pets $15/stay	$89	M/F	
nonsmoking rooms, laundry, next to greenway walking trail along the river				
Oxford Suites	509-457-9000	(107)	FB	IP
1701 E Yakima Ave	800-404-7848	$89–	M/F	T
www.oxfordsuites.com	pets $20/stay	$199		
nonsmoking rooms, complimentary hors d'oeuvres, laundry, next to riverside greenway walking trail				
Red Apple Motel	509-248-7150	(60)	CB	OP
416 N 1st St	pets $10/day	$30–	M/F	
nonsmoking rooms, laundry, lawn and gravel pet walking area, short drive to public park		$90		

C = coffee
CB = continental
    breakfast
F = refrigerator
FB = full breakfast
	IP = indoor pool
	K = full kitchen
	(k) = kitchenette
	L = lounge
	M = microwave
		OP = outdoor pool
		R = restaurant
		S = sauna or
		    steamroom
		T = spa or hot tub
			(# of units)
			& rates
				food
				& drink
					pool, sauna
					& hot tub

Yakima, Washington (continued)

Red Carpet Motor Inn 509-457-1131 1608 Fruitvale Blvd pets $10/stay nonsmoking rooms, laundry, small open area for walking dogs, short walk to riverside trail and park	(29) $39– $49	C K	OP S
Red Lion Inn 509-453-0391, 800-547-8010 818 N 1st St pets $10/day nonsmoking rooms, open areas for walking dogs, 3 miles to greenway walking trail	(58) $54– $99	CB	OP
Sun Country Inn 509-248-5650, 800-559-3675 1700 N 1st St pets $5/day laundry, small area for walking dogs, 1 block to greenway walking trail	(70) $52– $66	CB K	OP S
Tourist Motel 509-452-6551 1223 N 1st St pets $5/day nonsmoking rooms, laundry, open field for walking dogs, 6 blocks to greenway walking trail	(70) $29– $60	CB (k) M/F	OP
WestCoast at Yakima Center 509-248-5900 607 E Yakima Ave 800-325-4000 www.westcoasthotels.com pets $5/day nonsmoking rooms, lawn, 10 minute walk to greenway trail along river	(153) $65– $200	C M/F R/L	OP
WestCoast Yakima Gateway Hotel 509-452-6511 9 N 9th St pets $5/day, 800-325-4000 nonsmoking rooms, laundry, 5 minute walk to greenway walking trail along river	(171) $59– $200	C (k) M/F R/L	OP T
Western Motel 509-452-1007 1202 Fruitvale Blvd pets $5/day fenced dog run behind building, 1½ blocks to public park, 4 miles to greenway walking trail	(14) $27– $35	K	

Yelm, Washington

Prairie Hotel 360-458-8300 701 Prairie Park Ln NE each pet $20/day nonsmoking rooms, 7 acres of natural area for walking dogs, 4 blocks to walking trail	(23) $50– $110	C K	

Zillah, Washington

Comfort Inn Zillah 509-829-3399, 800-501-5433 911 Vintage Valley Pkwy pets $5/stay in-room spa	(40) $59– $79	CB	IP T

A: Business Name Index

Just in case you know the name of a particular lodging but aren't sure in exactly which city (or suburb) it is located, here is an alphabetical listing of all the businesses included in the main directory. This time the lodgings are sorted alphabetically by business name (rather than by city) and are cross-referenced to the appropriate page numbers in the main directory on pages 69–347.

Best Western Wallace Inn, Wallace ID 118

Best Western Wesley Inn, Gig Harbor WA 259

Best Western Weston Inn, St Anthony ID 115

Best Western Willamette Inn, Wilsonville OR 221

Best Western Windsor Inn, Ashland OR 123

Bestrest Inn, Boise ID 73

Bev's Beach Bungalow, Seaview WA 313

Bev's Beach Resort, Blaine WA 234

Big K Guest Ranch, Elkton OR 146

Big Red Barn, Port Townsend WA 298

Biggs Motel, Biggs Junction OR 132

Billingsley Creek Lodge & Retreat, Hagerman ID 88

Biltmore Motel, Tacoma WA 327

Birch Bay Vacation Weekly Rental Cottages, Birch Bay WA 233

Birch Leaf B & B, Halfway OR 158

Birch Tree B & B, St Maries ID 115

Birchfield Manor Country Inn, Yakima WA 344

Bird & Hat Inn B & B, Stayton OR 211

Bishop Victorian Hotel, Port Townsend WA 298

Black Beach Resort, Republic WA 303

Black Butte Accommodations, Sisters OR 209

Black Butte Resort Motel, Camp Sherman OR 135

Blackbird Lodge, Leavenworth WA 270

Blackwood Manor English Style B & B, Elk City ID 85

Blair House B & B, Friday Harbor WA 257

Bliss' McKenzie River Inn, Vida OR 218

Blue Cougar Motel, Curlew WA 246

Blue Heron Motel & Restaurant, Bay Center WA 230

Blue Lake Resort, Coulee City WA 245

Blue Mountain Lodge, Mount Vernon OR 178

Blue Mountain Motel, Dayton WA 247

Blue Pacific Motel & RV Park, Ocean City WA 285

Blue Spruce Motel, Tacoma WA 327

Blue Top Motel & RV Park, Coulee City WA 245

Blue Willow by the Sea B & B, Freeland WA 256

Boise Centre Guestlodge, Boise ID 73

Bond Street Motel, Boise ID 73

Bonn Motel, Brookings OR 134

Bonners Ferry Resort, Bonners Ferry ID 76

Bontemps Motel, Burns OR 134

Boon's Red Carpet Motel, Eugene OR 147

Bottle Bay Resort & Marina, Sagle ID 111

M

P

S

Super 8 Motel, Coeur d'Alene
    ID 83
Super 8 Motel, Corvallis OR 142
Super 8 Motel, Ellensburg
    WA 251
Super 8 Motel, Federal Way
    WA 253
Super 8 Motel, Ferndale WA 254
Super 8 Motel, Grangeville ID 88
Super 8 Motel, Grants Pass
    OR 158
Super 8 Motel, Heyburn ID 89
Super 8 Motel, Kellogg ID 94
Super 8 Motel, Kelso WA 265
Super 8 Motel, Kennewick
    WA 265
Super 8 Motel, Klamath Falls
    OR 166
Super 8 Motel, La Grande OR 167
Super 8 Motel, Lacey WA 269
Super 8 Motel, Lewiston ID 98
Super 8 Motel, Long Beach
    WA 274
Super 8 Motel, McCall ID 100
Super 8 Motel, Moscow ID 101
Super 8 Motel, Moses Lake
    WA 281
Super 8 Motel, Nampa ID 103
Super 8 Motel, Pendleton OR 188
Super 8 Motel, Pocatello ID 107
Super 8 Motel, Port Angeles
    WA 296
Super 8 Motel, Portland OR 195
Super 8 Motel, Redmond OR 198
Super 8 Motel, Roseburg OR 203
Super 8 Motel, Salem OR 205
Super 8 Motel, Sandpoint ID 113
Super 8 Motel-SeaTac, Seattle
    WA 311
Super 8 Motel, Shelton WA 316

Super 8 Motel, Spokane WA 324
Super 8 Motel, The Dalles OR 214
Super 8 Motel, Twin Falls ID 117
Super 8 Motel-Yakima, Union Gap
    WA 332
Super 8 Motel, Walla Walla
    WA 337
Super 8 Motel, Wilsonville OR 221
Super 8 Motel, Woodburn OR 223
Surf Motel & Cottages, Grayland
    WA 261
Surf Spray Motel & RV Park,
    Westport WA 341
Surfsand Resort, Cannon Beach
    OR 136
Surfside Oceanfront Resort Motel,
    Rockaway Beach OR 201
Sutherlin Inn, Sutherlin OR 213
Suttle Lake Resort, Sisters OR 209
Sutton Bay Resort, Newman Lake
    WA 284
Swallow Ridge B & B, Bend
    OR 132
Swallow's Nest Guest Cottages,
    Vashon Island WA 335
Sweet Breeze Inn, Grants Pass
    OR 158
Sweet Breeze Inn, Winston
    OR 222
Sweet Home Inn, Sweet Home
    OR 213
Sweetbrier Inn, Tualatin OR 216
Sweetwater Cottage, Clinton
    WA 242
Sweetwater Inn, Lincoln City
    OR 172
Swiftwater Motel & RV Park,
    Avery ID 71
Syringa Lodge B & B, Salmon
    ID 112

T

Table Rock Motel, Bandon
    OR 128
Tall Timber Motel, Randle
    WA 302
Tall Winds Motel, Moro OR 178
Tamarack Inn B & B, Weston
    OR 220
Tapadera Inn, Kennewick WA 266
Tapadera Inn, Pendleton OR 188
Tara Vacation Rentals, Freeland
    WA 257
Tasha's Garden Vacation Rental for
    People with Pets, Cannon
    Beach OR 136
Tatoosh Meadows Resort,
    Packwood WA 293
Terimore Lodging by the Sea,
    Netarts OR 180
Teton Mountain Hideaways, Victor
    ID 118
Teton Mountain View Lodge,
    Tetonia ID 116
Teton Ridge Ranch, Tetonia
    ID 116
Teton Valley Campground &
    Cabins, Victor ID 118
Teton Valley Property
    Management, Driggs
    ID 84
This Olde House B & B, Coos Bay
    OR 141
Three Capes Inn at Netarts,
    Tillamook OR 215
Three Rivers Inn, Sedro Woolley
    WA 314
Three Rivers Motel, Kooskia
    ID 95

Three Rivers Resort, Forks
    WA 256
Thunderbird Motel, Aberdeen
    WA 225
Thunderbird Motel, Ellensburg
    WA 251
Thunderbird Motel, Long Beach
    WA 274
Thunderbird Motel, Pocatello
    ID 107
Thurston House B & B, Maple
    Falls WA 277
Tides Inn, Port Townsend
    WA 298
Tiki Lodge Motel, Salem OR 205
Tillicum Motor Inn, Umatilla
    OR 217
Timber Lodge Inn, Cle Elum
    WA 241
Timber Lodge Motel, Coos Bay
    OR 141
Timbercrest Inn, La Pine OR 168
Timberland Inn & Suites, Castle
    Rock WA 237
Timberline Inn, Hoquiam WA 262
Timberline Motel, Peshastin
    WA 295
Timbers Motel, Ashland OR 124
Timbers Motel, Eugene OR 149
Timberwolf Resort, Palisades
    ID 105
Tokeland Hotel, Tokeland WA 329
Tolo Vista Lodge Cabins by the
    Lake, Soap Lake WA 319
Tolovana Inn, Cannon Beach
    OR 137
Top Hat Motel, Ritzville WA 305
Tops Motel, Heyburn ID 89
Totem Trail Motel, Rockport
    WA 305

W

Y

B: Topics Index

This index contains a cross-referenced list of all the topics related to traveling with your pet, as they appear in the first 68 pages of this book.

We hope you have enjoyed reading this book, and that you have been able to use the information here to travel more often with your dog!

To order additional copies of

Have Dog Will Travel: Northwest Edition

for just $19.95 each (postage included)

please call our tollfree number: **1-888-255-8030**

(We accept VISA and MasterCard)

or mail check or money order for $19.95 per copy to:

Ginger & Spike Publications
PO Box 937
Wilsonville, OR 97070

🐕 If you are ordering books to give as gifts, we can mail them directly to the recipients for you—just include their names and addresses with your order. We will send each book along with a small gift card indicating that it is a gift from you. (And of course, we'll also mail the order receipt to your address, to let you know that the gifts have been sent out.)

🐕 Would you like to have your books autographed by the author, Barbara Whitaker? Simply specify the name of the person that you would like each book personalized to, and Barbara will sign the first page of the book especially to that person.

Thank you, and Happy Travels!